18th Linguistic Annotation Workshop (LAW-XVIII)

St. Julian's, Malta
22 March 2024

ISBN: 978-1-7138-9454-4

Printed from e-media with permission by:

Curran Associates, Inc.
57 Morehouse Lane
Red Hook, NY 12571

Some format issues inherent in the e-media version may also appear in this print version.

Association for Computational Linguistics
209 N. Eighth Street
Stroudsburg, Pennsylvania 18360

Phone: 1-570-476-8006
Fax: 1-570-476-0860

acl@aclweb.org

Additional copies of this publication are available from:

Curran Associates, Inc.
57 Morehouse Lane
Red Hook, NY 12571 USA
Phone: 845-758-0400
Fax: 845-758-2633
Email: curran@proceedings.com
Web: www.proceedings.com

LAW 2024

The 18th Linguistic Annotation Workshop (LAW-XVIII)
Co-located with EACL 2024

Proceedings of the Workshop

March 22, 2024

The LAW organizers gratefully acknowledge the support from the following sponsors.

Order copies of this and other ACL proceedings from:

Association for Computational Linguistics (ACL)
209 N. Eighth Street
Stroudsburg, PA 18360
USA
Tel: +1-570-476-8006
Fax: +1-570-476-0860
acl@aclweb.org

Introduction

Linguistic annotation of natural language corpora is the backbone of supervised methods of statistical natural language processing. The Linguistic Annotation Workshop (LAW) is the annual workshop of the ACL and ELRA Special Interest Group on Annotation (SIGANN), and it provides a forum for the presentation and discussion of innovative research on all aspects of linguistic annotation, including the creation and evaluation of annotation schemes, methods for automatic and manual annotation, use and evaluation of annotation software and frameworks, representation of linguistic data and annotations, semi-supervised "human in the loop" methods of annotation, crowd-sourcing approaches, and more.

As in the past, this year's LAW provides a forum for annotation researchers to work towards standardization, best practices, and interoperability of annotation information and software.

These proceedings include papers that were presented at the 18th Linguistic Annotation Workshop (LAW-XVIII), co-located with EACL 2024 in St. Julian's, Malta, on March 22, 2024.

This edition of the workshop is the eighteenth meeting of the ACL and ELRA Special Interest Group for Annotation. The first workshop took place in 2007 at the ACL in Prague. Since then, the LAW has been held every year, consistently drawing substantial participation (both in terms of paper/poster submissions and participation in the actual workshop) providing evidence that the LAW's overall focus continues to be an important area of interest in the field, a substantial part of which relies on supervised learning from gold standard data sets (despite the advent of LLMs — see below). This year, we received 39 submissions, out of which 20 papers have been accepted to be presented at the workshop, as long or short papers, or as posters.

In addition, LAW-XVIII features an invited talk by Lilja Øvrelid (University of Oslo).

The special theme of LAW-XVIII is *Large Language Models*. In recent years, they have both transformed the field of NLP and alerted the general public to the astonishing powers of new language technologies. Needless to say, they will have an increasing impact also on matters of linguistic annotation; our special session of long papers is meant to stir discussions about prospects and limitations.

Our thanks go to SIGANN, our organizing committee, for their continuing organization of the LAW workshops. Most of all, we would like to thank all the authors for submitting their papers to the workshop and our program committee members for their dedication and their thoughtful reviews.

The LAW-XVIII Program Co-Chairs:
Sophie Henning and Manfred Stede

Organizing Committee

Program Chairs

Sophie Henning, Bosch Center for Artificial Intelligence and LMU Munich
Manfred Stede, University of Potsdam

SIGANN President

Amir Zeldes, Georgetown University

SIGANN Secretary

Ines Rehbein, Mannheim University

SIGANN Officers

Claire Bonial, US Army Research Laboratory
Stefanie Dipper, Ruhr-Universität Bochum
Annemarie Friedrich, University of Augsburg
Chu-Ren Huang, The Hong Kong Polytechnic University
Jena D. Hwang, Allen Institute for AI
Sandra Kübler, Indiana University
Lori Levin, Carnegie Mellon University
Adam Meyers, New York University
Antonio Pareja-Lora, Universidad de Alcalá (UAH) / FITISPos (UAH) / ATLAS (UNED) / DMEG (UdG)
Massimo Poesio, Queen Mary University of London and University of Utrecht
Sameer Pradhan, LDC, Cemantix
Jakob Prange, University of Augsburg
Nancy Ide, Vassar College/Brandeis University
Nathan Schneider, Georgetown University
Manfred Stede, University of Potsdam
Katrin Tomanek, Google
Fei Xia, University of Washington
Nianwen Xue, Brandeis University
Deniz Zeyrek, Middle East Technical University

Program Committee

Chairs

Sophie Henning, Bosch Center for Artificial Intelligence and LMU Munich
Manfred Stede, University of Potsdam

Program Committee

Omri Abend, The Hebrew University of Jerusalem
Berfin Aktaş, University of Potsdam
Claire Bonial, US Army Research Lab
Miriam Butt, University of Konstanz
Marie Candito, LLF (Université Paris Cité / CNRS)
Kathryn Conger, Universitiy of Colorado, Boulder
Daniel Dakota, Indiana University
Stefanie Dipper, Ruhr University Bochum
Lucia Donatelli, Vrije Universiteit Amsterdam
Jonathan Dunn, University of Illinois Urbana-Champaign
Markus Egg, Humboldt-Universität zu Berlin
Annemarie Friedrich, University of Augsburg
Luke Gessler, University of Colorado, Boulder
Nizar Habash, New York University Abu Dhabi
Andrea Horbach, Universität Hildesheim
Nancy Ide, Vassar College/Brandeis University
René Knaebel, University of Potsdam
Sandra Kübler, Indiana University
Ekaterina Lapshinova-Koltunski, University of Hildesheim
Els Lefever, LT3, Ghent University
Adam Meyers, New York University
Alexis Palmer, University of Colorado Boulder
Antonio Pareja-Lora, Universidad de Alcalá (UAH) / FITISPos (UAH) / ATLAS (UNED) / DMEG (UdG)
Siyao Peng, LMU Munich
Massimo Poesio, Queen Mary University of London and University of Utrecht
Jakob Prange, University of Augsburg
Robin Schaefer, University of Potsdam
Nathan Schneider, Georgetown University
Ludovic Tanguy, CLLE: University of Toulouse / CNRS
Joel Tetreault, Dataminr
Lilian Diana Awuor Wanzare, Maseno University
Michael Wiegand, Alpen-Adria-Universität Klagenfurt
Mohammad Yeghaneh Abkenar, Bundesdruckerei Gruppe GmbH Berlin
Amir Zeldes, Georgetown University
Winnie Huiheng Zeng, Hong Kong Shue Yan University
Deniz Zeyrek, Middle East Technical University
Wei Zhou, Bosch Center for Artificial Intelligence
Heike Zinsmeister, Universität Hamburg

Keynote Talk: Who do you love? Fine-grained sentiment annotation, aggregation and data augmentation

Lilja Øvrelid
University of Oslo

Fri, March 22, 2024 – Time: **11:00 - 12:00** – Room: **Radisson Marie Louise Suite 2**

Abstract: In this talk I will discuss insights from several large-scale annotation projects aimed at enriching texts with subjective assessments describing their sentiment. In particular, I will describe a trajectory which is shared by many annotation projects aimed at supplying various Information Extraction systems with data: moving from fine-grained annotation of text spans at the sub-sentence level to aggregation of information within or across documents. I will start out by discussing the task of structured sentiment analysis and in particular, the 2022 SemEval shared task devoted to this task. In follow-up work, we assess the usefulness of these annotations for the aggregation of entity-level sentiment annotation for longer documents and provide a study of remaining challenges for the cross-sentence tracking of sentiment. Finally, I will briefly touch on recent work on data augmentation for sentiment analysis evaluating both masked language models and LLM-based prompting in the context of sentiment annotation.

Bio: Lilja Øvrelid is a Professor of Informatics at the University of Oslo, where she leads the Language Technology Group. She has been involved in a number of large annotation projects devoted to a diverse set of NLP tasks, such as UD syntax, NER, negation, sentiment analysis, coreference resolution and question-answering. She has worked on syntactic and semantic parsing, as well as the application of structured prediction approaches to NLP tasks beyond parsing, such as fine-grained sentiment analysis and event extraction.

Table of Contents

Program

Friday, March 22, 2024

08:50 - 09:00 *Opening Remarks*

09:00 - 10:00 *Long Papers 1*

Automatic Annotation Elaboration as Feedback to Sign Language Learners
Alessia Battisti and Sarah Ebling

Enhancing Text Classification through LLM-Driven Active Learning and Human Annotation
Hamidreza Rouzegar and Masoud Makrehchi

Donkii: Characterizing and Detecting Errors in Instruction-Tuning Datasets
Leon Weber, Robert Litschko, Ekaterina Artemova and Barbara Plank

10:00 - 10:30 *Short Papers 1*

TreeForm: End-to-end Annotation and Evaluation for Form Document Parsing
Ran Zmigrod, Zhiqiang Ma, Armineh Nourbakhsh and Sameena Shah

Annotation Scheme for English Argument Structure Constructions Treebank
Hakyung Sung and Kristopher Kyle

10:30 - 11:00 *Coffee Break*

11:00 - 11:50 *Invited Talk – Lilja Øvrelid: Who do you love? Fine-grained sentiment annotation, aggregation and data augmentation*

11:50 - 12:50 *Long Papers 2*

Surveying the FAIRness of Annotation Tools: Difficult to find, difficult to reuse
Ekaterina Borisova, Raia Abu Ahmad, Leyla Garcia-Castro, Ricardo Usbeck and Georg Rehm

Class Balancing for Efficient Active Learning in Imbalanced Datasets
Yaron Fairstein, Oren Kalinsky, Zohar Karnin, Guy Kushilevitz, Alexander Libov and Sofia Tolmach

Datasets Creation and Empirical Evaluations of Cross-Lingual Learning on Extremely Low-Resource Languages: A Focus on Comorian Dialects
Abdou Mohamed Naira, Benelallam Imade, Bahafid Abdessalam and Erraji Zakarya

12:50 - 14:00 *Lunch Break*

14:00 - 15:00 *In-Person Poster Session*

A Mapping on Current Classifying Categories of Emotions Used in Multimodal Models for Emotion Recognition
Ziwei Gong, Muyin Yao, Xinyi Hu, Xiaoning Zhu and Julia Hirschberg

Using ChatGPT for Annotation of Attitude within the Appraisal Theory: Lessons Learned
Mirela Imamovic, Silvana Deilen, Dylan Glynn and Ekaterina Lapshinova-Koltunski

A GPT among Annotators: LLM-based Entity-Level Sentiment Annotation
Egil Rønningstad, Erik Velldal and Lilja Øvrelid

PropBank goes Public: Incorporation into Wikidata
Elizabeth Spaulding, Kathryn Conger, Anatole Gershman, Mahir Morshed, Susan Windisch Brown, James Pustejovsky, Rosario Uceda-Sosa, Sijia Ge and Martha Palmer

Dependency Annotation of Ottoman Turkish with Multilingual BERT
Şaziye Özateş, Tarık Tıraş, Efe Genç and Esma Bilgin Tasdemir

EEVEE: An Easy Annotation Tool for Natural Language Processing
Axel Sorensen, Siyao Peng, Barbara Plank and Rob Van Der Goot

15:00 - 15:30 *Short Papers 2*

Building a corpus for the anonymization of Romanian jurisprudence
Vasile Păiș, Dan Tufis, Elena Irimia and Verginica Barbu Mititelu

Are You Serious? Handling Disagreement When Annotating Conspiracy Theory Texts
Ashley Hemm, Sandra Kübler, Michelle Seelig, John Funchion, Manohar Murthi, Kamal Premaratne, Daniel Verdear and Stefan Wuchty

Friday, March 22, 2024 (continued)

15:30 - 16:00 *Coffee Break*

16:00 - 17:00 *Long Papers 3*

When is a Metaphor Actually Novel? Annotating Metaphor Novelty in the Context of Automatic Metaphor Detection
Sebastian Reimann and Tatjana Scheffler

Prompting Implicit Discourse Relation Annotation
Frances Yung, Mansoor Ahmad, Merel Scholman and Vera Demberg

Reference and discourse structure annotation of elicited chat continuations in German
Katja Jasinskaja, Yuting Li, Fahime Same and David Uerlings

17:00 - 17:10 *Short Talk*

Towards Better Inclusivity: A Diverse Tweet Corpus of English Varieties
Nhi Pham, Lachlan Pham and Adam Meyers

17:10 - 17:20 *Closing Remarks*

TreeForm: End-to-end Annotation and Evaluation for Form Document Parsing

Ran Zmigrod, Zhiqiang Ma, Armineh Nourbakhsh, Sameena Shah
J.P. Morgan AI Research
{first_name}.{last_name}@jpmchase.com

Abstract

Visually Rich Form Understanding (VRFU) poses a complex research problem due to the documents' highly structured nature and yet highly variable style and content. Current annotation schemes decompose form understanding and omit key hierarchical structure, making development and evaluation of end-to-end models difficult. In this paper, we propose a novel F1 metric to evaluate form parsers and describe a new content-agnostic, tree-based annotation scheme for VRFU: **TreeForm**. We provide methods to convert previous annotation schemes into TreeForm structures and evaluate TreeForm predictions using a modified version of the normalized tree-edit distance. We present initial baselines for our end-to-end performance metric and the TreeForm edit distance, averaged over the FUNSD and XFUND datasets, of 61.5 and 26.4 respectively. We hope that TreeForm encourages deeper research in annotating, modeling, and evaluating the complexities of form-like documents.

1 Introduction

Visually rich document understanding (VRDU) has been a growing field in multimodal AI research. VRDU takes document images as input and applies tasks such as document classification (Gu et al., 2021; Kim et al., 2022; Gu et al., 2022), information extraction (Borchmann et al., 2021; Wang et al., 2022), visual question-answering (VQA) (Mathew et al., 2021; Tito et al., 2021; Li et al., 2022), *inter alia*. Consequently, state-of-the-art VRDU models rely on image-to-text understanding, such as optical character recognition (OCR), as well as multimodal models that can exploit textual, visual, and spatial features of documents.

VRFU is a subset of VRDU that focuses on forms, i.e., documents that contain a collection of hierarchical key-value pairs (in various styles) regarding specific entities. Forms are highly structured documents, and so can be directly parsed into a structured object. Parsing receipts, which share a similar though smaller and simpler structure, have been the focus of much document parsing research (Majumder et al., 2020; Borchmann et al., 2021; Gao et al., 2021). In this work, we focus on the broader field of form parsing.

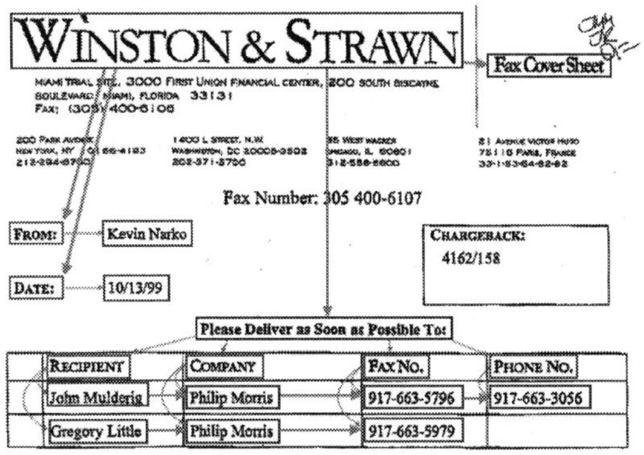

Figure 1: Excerpt of a FUNSD form. Headers are marked in **burgundy**, questions are marked **green**, and answers are marked in **blue**. Entity links provided by the FUNSD annotation schemes are marked in orange. Links in pink were created for TreeForm.

The FUNSD dataset (Jaume et al., 2019), and its multilingual counter-part XFUND (Xu et al., 2022), are standard VRFU datasets used in the literature. These datasets split form parsing into entity labeling and entity linking tasks. Unfortunately, this annotation scheme is unable to fully express the structure of a form. Moreover, to the best of our knowledge, no holistic approach exists for evaluating complete FUNSD-type predictions. Few other form parsing datasets exist, such as FUNSD+ (Zagami and Helm, 2022) and the National Archives Forms (NAF) dataset (Davis et al., 2019). We do not address these directly but many of our contributions can be extended to these annotation schemes.

In this paper, we tackle the problem of complete form parsing through a tree-based approach that

Proceedings of The 18th Linguistic Annotation Workshop (LAW-XVIII), pages 1–11
March 22, 2024 ©2024 Association for Computational Linguistics

successfully captures the hierarchical structure of forms which is often missed in modern annotation schemes. Our contributions are summarized below:

1. We provide novel end-to-end metrics for evaluating FUNSD-type annotations.
2. We present a novel tree-based representation of forms, **TreeForm**, that is conveniently stored as a single JSON object. We also utilize the greedy-aligned tree-edit distance (GAnTED) proposed by Davis et al. (2022) to evaluate TreeForm predictions.
3. We detail a method to transform *any* FUNSD-type annotations into TreeForm. Our method captures additional hierarchical and tabular information, which FUNSD annotations do not contain. The additional information gained from TreeForm is visualized in Figure 1.[1]
4. We evaluate TreeForm and our novel metrics using state-of-the-art models (Kim et al., 2022; Xu et al., 2022) on the FUNSD and XFUND datasets. Our baselines achieve a node-alignment accuracy of 0.22, end-to-end F1 score of 61.5, and TreeForm GAnTED score of 14.5 across all languages.

2 Limitations of Form Parsing Datasets

Most VRFU research employs FUNSD-type annotations (Jaume et al., 2019). This annotation scheme contains two components: First, a list of semantic entities defined by a group of tokens and a semantic label (header, question, or answer).[2] Second, a list of directed links between entities to denote form structure. An example of an FUNSD annotation is given in App. C. While the FUNSD (and XFUND) project was a fundamental step in VRFU, its approach contains underlying issues (Vu and Nguyen, 2020). Other non-FUNSD schematic VRFU datasets exist (Davis et al., 2019; Zagami and Helm, 2022). However, they are not widely used and are not without similar issues. Table 1 provides an overview of form parsing datasets.

Dataset	Lang.	Scheme	|Train|	|Test|
FUNSD	EN	FUNSD	149	50
XFUND	Multi	FUNSD	1043	350
FUNSD+	EN	FUNSD+	1023	116
NAF	EN	NAF	741	63

Table 1: Form Understanding Datasets. XFUND is equally split over seven languages (149 training documents, 50 test documents): DE, ES, FR, IT, JA, PT, ZH.

Task Decomposition. The FUNSD annotation scheme proposes that VRFU should be decomposed into semantic entity labeling and entity linking. This makes a proper end-to-end evaluation of form understanding models difficult as combining the two task metrics does not represent an accurate joint evaluation. Indeed, works that report individual F1 scores do not attempt to combine these (Carbonell et al., 2020; Li et al., 2021b; Gemelli et al., 2022a; Hong et al., 2022) while much research omits the entity linking task (Li et al., 2021a; Appalaraju et al., 2021; Xu et al., 2021b,a; Chen et al., 2022; Luo et al., 2022).

Inconsistent Annotations. The FUNSD annotations contain several inconsistencies in both their entity labeling and entity linking components. Inconsistencies arise in hierarchical forms, handwritten input, and missing entity links. While many of these inconsistencies were improved in (Vu and Nguyen, 2020), some issues still persist

Table Recognition. Tables are a natural component of forms, however, they break the common question-answer structure. The FUNSD annotation scheme handles tables as columns, where a column header is a question and each value in the column is an answer linked to the question. Row headers are sometimes also annotated and linked, but this is a less common pattern in the dataset. Also, as pointed out by Davis et al. (2022), row and column alignment is not present in the annotations, making table parsing or reconstruction not possible in FUNSD.

3 An End-to-end Evaluation of FUNSD

In this section, we propose a new F1 metric to evaluate FUNSD-type predictions on their combined entity labeling and entity linking performance. Our metric, inspired by the labeled attachment score (LAS) (Kübler et al., 2009), is based on constructing a tree of the FUNSD annotations. Each node in the tree represents a semantic FUNSD entity, and each edge in the tree is a link between entities, labeled with the entity label of the child node. Entities with no incoming links have an incoming edge from a dummy root node, labeled with the

[1]Note that for ease of visualization, Figure 1 does not contain boxes for every single annotation. In practice, every piece of information annotated in FUNSD (or the original annotation scheme) will be captured in TreeForm.

[2]The original annotations contain a fourth entity, *other*, for text that does not conform to one of the three aforementioned labels. We follow recent work and ignore these labels (Xu et al., 2021b,a, 2022).

entity's label. An example of this structure is given in Figure 2b. Let T be the set of predicted edges and G be the set of ground truth edges. We can then respectively define the precision and recall as:

$$\mathrm{prec}(T,G) \stackrel{\mathrm{def}}{=} \frac{|T \cap G|}{|T|} \quad \mathrm{rec}(T,G) \stackrel{\mathrm{def}}{=} \frac{|T \cap G|}{|G|}$$

These can be combined as normal to yield an F1 metric that examines both entity labels and links. Note that this metric equally punishes incorrect edges regardless of where they lie in the nested tree. For example, mis-predicting a top level node (i.e., one connected to the dummy root node) is punished equally to mis-predicting the edge connecting an answer to a question.

The above F1 metric does not consider node-alignment (i.e., word grouping) in its evaluation. Indeed, it assumes that the nodes of the predicted and ground truth trees are aligned. Node alignment can be done through a greedy algorithm. For each predicted entity, we compute the normalized Levenshtein distance (Mathew et al., 2021) to each true entity.[3] We then greedily select alignments that meet a certain threshold (edit distance less than 0.4), until no possible alignments remain. We define the node-alignment accuracy (NAA) metric as the mean normalized Levenshtein distance between each pair of aligned nodes.[4]

4 A Tree-based Annotation Scheme

In this section we present a novel tree-based form annotation scheme, **TreeForm**. Unlike our F1 and NAA metrics, TreeForm does not assume the FUNSD task decomposition. Instead, TreeForm provides a fully structured object that enables complete representation of a form.

A TreeForm node is represented by a JSON object (i.e., a dictionary) whose key and value respectively contain the node's (textual) value and a dictionary where each key is either another node or an edge label that leads to a group of child nodes. Therefore, a TreeForm tree is represented using a single JSON object which efficiently contains all form information necessary for any down-stream VRFU task. Davis et al. (2022) also parses complete forms into JSON objects, however, their approach requires multiple objects per form and so annotations are less readable. TreeForm considers forms to be comprised of three key structures: headers, question-answer pairs, and tables; each of these structures is represented in a tree structure which is detailed in App. B. An example of a TreeForm annotation is given in Figure 2c.

4.1 Evaluating TreeForm

We assess TreeForm predictions using a variant of the normalized tree-edit distance (nTED) (Hwang et al., 2021b), a distance metric that informs us how much work is needed to convert the predicted tree into the ground-truth tree (and so a lower nTED is better). Specifically, we follow the greedy-aligned nTED (GAnTED) metric proposed by Davis et al. (2022). This is a more holistic metric than those proposed in Section 3 as it does not assume any task decomposition.

4.2 Converting FUNSD into TreeForm

We propose a set of transformations and heuristics to convert FUNSD-type annotations into TreeForm structures. We first apply simple conversions for straight-forward cases such as single-answer questions and hierarchical headers which fit directly into the TreeForm annotation scheme. Next, we elaborate on the more complex heuristics we have chosen to create the most accurate and complete TreeForm structure. Note an important caveat to our transformations, TreeForm cannot attain information that was not annotated in FUNSD (or the original annotation scheme).

Discarding Incomplete Information. TreeForm does not include free-form text, unanswered questions, or unprompted answers. Any such annotations in the dataset are discarded here.

Choosing the Form Title. If headers exist in the form, we aim to assign a form title to each TreeForm structure. Since FUNSD does not necessary nest headers correctly (as seen in Figure 1), we consider the form title to be the non-nested header that is spatially highest on the page. This seems like a sensible heuristic as we typically expect titles to be at the top of documents.[5]

Constructing Tables. Table structure is not directly recoverable from FUNSD annotations (as

[3]We choose the Levenshtein distance to follow related work and to enable measuring the edit distance in a more meaningful way as we can assign context-specific penalties to additions, deletions, and alterations.

[4]For unaligned nodes, we use the normalized Levenshtein distance between a node and the empty string, i.e., 1.

[5]This heuristic is not perfect, as for example, the form title in Figure 1 could be "Fax Cover Sheet" rather than "WINSTON & STRAWN"; this also raises an inconsistency issue as it is unclear whether the latter header is indeed a header entity.

```
[{"id": 0, "text": "WINSTON & STRAWN",
  "label": "header", "linking": []},
 {"id": 1, "text": "FROM",
  "label": "question", "linking": [[1,
     2]]},
 {"id": 2, "text": "Kevin Narko",
  "label": "answer", "linking": [[1,2]
     ]},
 ...
 {"id": 7, "text": "RECIPIENT",
  "label": "question", "linking": [[7,
     8], [7,9]]},
 {"id": 8, "text": "John Mulderig",
  "label": "answer", "linking": [[7,8]
     ]},
 {"id": 9, "text": "Gregory Little",
  "label": "answer", "linking": [[7,9]
     ]},
 ...]
```

(a) FUNSD Annotation

```
{"nodes": [
   "WINSTON & STRAWN", "FROM",
   "Kevin Narko", ...,
   "RECIPIENT", "John Mulderig",
   "Gregory Little", ...],
 "edges": [
   [-1, 0, "header"], [-1, 1, "
       question"],
   [2, 1, "answer"], ...,
   [6, 7, "question"], [7, 8, "answer
       "],
   [7, 9, "answer"], ...]}
```

(b) Aggregated FUNSD Annotation

```
{"header": {
  "value": "WINSTON & STRAWN",
  "question": [
   {"value": "FROM",
    "answer": "Kevin Narko"}, ...],
  "header": [
   {"value": "Please Deliver...",
    "entry": [
     {"question": [
      {"value": "RECIPIENT",
       "answer": "John Mulderig"},
           ...
     ], ...}
    ]}, ...]}}
```

(c) TreeForm Annotation

```
{"WINSTON & STRAWN": {
   "FROM": "Kevin Narko",
   ...
     "entry": {
       "RECIPIENT": "John Mulderig",
       "COMPANY": "Phillip Morris",
       ...
     }, ...
   }
}}
```

(d) Concise TreeForm Annotation

Figure 2: Different annotation schemes for excerpt of FUNSD form given in Figure 1.

discussed in Section 2). We utilize bounding box details to align columns and rows such that we can approximate the full table. Similar heuristics were also used in (Davis et al., 2022). Some questions with multiple answers in FUNSD may indicate a multi-line answer rather than a table column (or row). Therefore, we require multiple answers to start roughly in the same horizontal (or vertical) position to be considered a table entry.

5 Experiments

To evaluate TreeForm as well as our end-to-end FUNSD metrics, we fine-tune LayoutXLM (Xu et al., 2022) and Donut (Kim et al., 2022) on each of the FUNSD and XFUND datasets.[6] We chose these two models as they represent the two current approaches to form parsing: Pipelined[7] (LayoutXLM) and end-to-end (Donut). We describe pre- and post-processing steps required for applying the FUNSD and TreeForm evaluations to each model in App. D. Importantly, we performed post-processing steps to the output of LayoutXLM to enable evaluation using our metrics. The results are given in Table 2.

For all languages, our end-to-end F1 metric is lower than one or both of the standard labeling and linking F1 scores. This indicates that while past work may have high labeling (or linking) F1 scores, they may not have full form understanding capabilities. This is further exacerbated as our F1 metric requires the NAA score to provide a holistic overview. As expected, LayoutXLM outperforms Donut with respect to NAA as it has access to OCR tokens. However, Donut still outperforms Lay-

[6] We fine-tune one variant of each model on FUNSD annotations and another on TreeForm. Details are given in App. D.

[7] The pipelined approach first predicts the entity labels and uses said predictions to perform the entity linking task.

Metric	Model	FUNSD EN	XFUND DE	ES	FR	IT	JA	PT	ZH
Labeling F1 ↑	LayoutXLM	77.6	79.5	74.1	78.9	77.3	79.1	79.4	88.9
Linking F1 ↑	LayoutXLM	48.8	57.3	63.8	61.4	53.5	64.4	53.0	67.8
NAA ↓	LayoutXLM	**0.21**	**0.24**	**0.28**	**0.23**	**0.23**	**0.24**	**0.23**	**0.12**
	Donut	0.69	0.58	0.69	0.61	0.64	0.75	0.75	0.74
Tree F1 ↑	LayoutXLM	62.6	57.0	**60.6**	**65.7**	59.6	**59.3**	**59.9**	**66.9**
	Donut	**64.8**	**61.5**	53.0	62.4	**62.9**	51.7	46.8	55.6
GAnTED ↓	LayoutXLM	18.0	27.7	20.7	22.3	20.6	7.2	25.1	**7.3**
	Donut	**15.1**	**21.0**	**15.8**	**13.6**	**17.5**	**6.7**	**17.3**	8.9

Table 2: Standard and end-to-end evaluation metrics for FUNSD and TreeForm annotations.

outXLM on F1 for some languages, suggesting it is better at understanding hierarchical structure.

We consider the median GAnTED score for evaluating TreeForm predictions. Donut outperformed LayoutXLM in all languages except for Chinese. This is expected as Donut was designed with document parsing in mind and so could be directly fine-tuned on TreeForm data whereas LayoutXLM was pipelined using the FUNSD annotation scheme (see App. D). As GAnTED has not yet been widely used in the literature, it is difficult to assess the effectiveness of these systems. Nevertheless, Dessurt (Davis et al., 2022) reported a GAnTED score of 23.4 on the FUNSD dataset which aligns with the scores in Table 2.[8] Additionally, the GAnTED scores seem to be similar across languages which attests to the generalizability of TreeForm.

6 Conclusion

In this paper, we described the challenges of current form understanding and the limitations of the current datasets and their annotation schemes. We introduced a novel F1 metric that can be applied to current annotation schemes and further proposed a new tree-based annotation scheme, TreeForm, that enables complete form parsing. We applied state-of-the-art models (LayoutXLM and Donut) to provide the first TreeForm baselines. We envision future work to create a new TreeForm dataset, that contains correct and consistent annotations.

Disclaimer

[8] In the experimental set-up of Davis et al. (2022), a flatter tree representation (with some other key differences) is used and so the results are not directly comparable.

References

Milan Aggarwal, Hiresh Gupta, Mausoom Sarkar, and Balaji Krishnamurthy. 2020a. Form2Seq : A framework for higher-order form structure extraction. In *Proceedings of the 2020 Conference on Empirical Methods in Natural Language Processing (EMNLP)*, pages 3830–3840, Online. Association for Computational Linguistics.

Milan Aggarwal, Mausoom Sarkar, Hiresh Gupta, and Balaji Krishnamurthy. 2020b. Multi-modal association based grouping for form structure extraction. In *The IEEE Winter Conference on Applications of Computer Vision*, pages 2075–2084.

Srikar Appalaraju, Bhavan Jasani, Bhargava Urala Kota, Yusheng Xie, and R. Manmatha. 2021. Docformer: End-to-end transformer for document understanding. In *2021 IEEE/CVF International Conference on Computer Vision, ICCV 2021, Montreal, QC, Canada, October 10-17, 2021*, pages 973–983. IEEE.

Lukasz Borchmann, Michal Pietruszka, Tomasz Stanislawek, Dawid Jurkiewicz, Michal Turski, Karolina Szyndler, and Filip Gralinski. 2021. DUE: End-to-end document understanding benchmark. In *Proceedings of the Neural Information Processing Systems Track on Datasets and Benchmarks 1, NeurIPS Datasets and Benchmarks 2021, December 2021, virtual*.

Manuel Carbonell, Pau Riba, Mauricio Villegas, Alicia Fornés, and Josep Lladós. 2020. Named entity recognition and relation extraction with graph neural networks in semi structured documents. In *25th International Conference on Pattern Recognition, ICPR 2020, Virtual Event / Milan, Italy, January 10-15, 2021*, pages 9622–9627. IEEE.

Jingye Chen, Tengchao Lv, Lei Cui, Cha Zhang, and Furu Wei. 2022. XDoc: Unified pre-training for cross-format document understanding. *CoRR*, abs/2210.02849.

Brian L. Davis, Bryan S. Morse, Scott Cohen, Brian L. Price, and Chris Tensmeyer. 2019. Deep visual template-free form parsing. In *2019 International Conference on Document Analysis and Recognition, ICDAR 2019, Sydney, Australia, September 20-25, 2019*, pages 134–141. IEEE.

Brian L. Davis, Bryan S. Morse, Brian L. Price, Chris Tensmeyer, and Curtis Wigington. 2021. Visual FUDGE: form understanding via dynamic graph editing. In *16th International Conference on Document Analysis and Recognition, ICDAR 2021, Lausanne, Switzerland, September 5-10, 2021, Proceedings, Part I*, volume 12821 of *Lecture Notes in Computer Science*, pages 416–431. Springer.

Brian L. Davis, Bryan S. Morse, Bryan Price, Chris Tensmeyer, Curtis Wigington, and Vlad I. Morariu. 2022. End-to-end document recognition and understanding with dessurt. *CoRR*, abs/2203.16618.

Mingfei Gao, Zeyuan Chen, Nikhil Naik, Kazuma Hashimoto, Caiming Xiong, and Ran Xu. 2021. Field extraction from forms with unlabeled data. *CoRR*, abs/2110.04282.

Andrea Gemelli, Sanket Biswas, Enrico Civitelli, Josep Lladós, and Simone Marinai. 2022a. Doc2Graph: A task agnostic document understanding framework based on graph neural networks. *CoRR*, abs/2208.11168.

Andrea Gemelli, Emanuele Vivoli, and Simone Marinai. 2022b. Graph neural networks and representation embedding for table extraction in PDF documents. In *26th International Conference on Pattern Recognition, ICPR 2022, Montreal, QC, Canada, August 21-25, 2022*, pages 1719–1726. IEEE.

Jiuxiang Gu, Jason Kuen, Vlad I. Morariu, Handong Zhao, Nikolaos Barmpalios, Rajiv Jain, Ani Nenkova, and Tong Sun. 2022. Unified pretraining framework for document understanding. *CoRR*, abs/2204.10939.

Jiuxiang Gu, Jason Kuen, Vlad I. Morariu, Handong Zhao, Rajiv Jain, Nikolaos Barmpalios, Ani Nenkova, and Tong Sun. 2021. UniDoc: Unified pretraining framework for document understanding. In *Advances in Neural Information Processing Systems 34: Annual Conference on Neural Information Processing Systems 2021, NeurIPS 2021, December 6-14, 2021, virtual*, pages 39–50.

Jonathan Herzig, Pawel Krzysztof Nowak, Thomas Müller, Francesco Piccinno, and Julian Martin Eisenschlos. 2020. Tapas: Weakly supervised table parsing via pre-training. In *Proceedings of the 58th Annual Meeting of the Association for Computational Linguistics, ACL 2020, Online, July 5-10, 2020*, pages 4320–4333. Association for Computational Linguistics.

Teakgyu Hong, Donghyun Kim, Mingi Ji, Wonseok Hwang, Daehyun Nam, and Sungrae Park. 2022. BROS: A pre-trained language model focusing on text and layout for better key information extraction from documents. In *Thirty-Sixth AAAI Conference on Artificial Intelligence, AAAI 2022, Thirty-Fourth Conference on Innovative Applications of Artificial Intelligence, IAAI 2022, The Twelveth Symposium on Educational Advances in Artificial Intelligence, EAAI 2022 Virtual Event, February 22 - March 1, 2022*, pages 10767–10775. AAAI Press.

Zheng Huang, Kai Chen, Jianhua He, Xiang Bai, Dimosthenis Karatzas, Shijian Lu, and C. V. Jawahar. 2019. ICDAR2019 competition on scanned receipt OCR and information extraction. In *2019 International Conference on Document Analysis and Recognition, ICDAR 2019, Sydney, Australia, September 20-25, 2019*, pages 1516–1520. IEEE.

Wonseok Hwang, Seonghyeon Kim, Minjoon Seo, Jinyeong Yim, Seunghyun Park, Sungrae Park, Junyeop Lee, Bado Lee, and Hwalsuk Lee. 2019. Post-OCR parsing: Building simple and robust parser via BIO tagging. In *Workshop on Document Intelligence at NeurIPS 2019*.

Wonseok Hwang, Hyunji Lee, Jinyeong Yim, Geewook Kim, and Minjoon Seo. 2021a. Cost-effective end-to-end information extraction for semi-structured document images. In *Proceedings of the 2021 Conference on Empirical Methods in Natural Language Processing, EMNLP 2021, Virtual Event / Punta Cana, Dominican Republic, 7-11 November, 2021*, pages 3375–3383. Association for Computational Linguistics.

Wonseok Hwang, Jinyeong Yim, Seunghyun Park, Sohee Yang, and Minjoon Seo. 2021b. Spatial dependency parsing for semi-structured document information extraction. In *Findings of the Association for Computational Linguistics: ACL/IJCNLP 2021, Online Event, August 1-6, 2021*, volume ACL/IJCNLP 2021 of *Findings of ACL*, pages 330–343. Association for Computational Linguistics.

Guillaume Jaume, Hazim Kemal Ekenel, and Jean-Philippe Thiran. 2019. FUNSD: A dataset for form understanding in noisy scanned documents. In *2nd International Workshop on Open Services and Tools for Document Analysis, OST@ICDAR 2019, Sydney, Australia, September 22-25, 2019*, pages 1–6. IEEE.

Geewook Kim, Teakgyu Hong, Moonbin Yim, JeongYeon Nam, Jinyoung Park, Jinyeong Yim, Wonseok Hwang, Sangdoo Yun, Dongyoon Han, and Seunghyun Park. 2022. OCR-free document understanding transformer. In *Computer Vision - ECCV*

2022 - 17th European Conference, Tel Aviv, Israel, October 23-27, 2022, Proceedings, Part XXVIII, volume 13688 of *Lecture Notes in Computer Science*, pages 498–517. Springer.

Sandra Kübler, Ryan T. McDonald, and Joakim Nivre. 2009. *Dependency Parsing*. Synthesis Lectures on Human Language Technologies. Morgan & Claypool Publishers.

Kenton Lee, Mandar Joshi, Iulia Raluca Turc, Hexiang Hu, Fangyu Liu, Julian Martin Eisenschlos, Urvashi Khandelwal, Peter Shaw, Ming-Wei Chang, and Kristina Toutanova. 2023. Pix2Struct: Screenshot parsing as pretraining for visual language understanding. In *International Conference on Machine Learning, ICML 2023, 23-29 July 2023, Honolulu, Hawaii, USA*, volume 202 of *Proceedings of Machine Learning Research*, pages 18893–18912. PMLR.

Chenliang Li, Bin Bi, Ming Yan, Wei Wang, Songfang Huang, Fei Huang, and Luo Si. 2021a. Structurallm: Structural pre-training for form understanding. In *Proceedings of the 59th Annual Meeting of the Association for Computational Linguistics and the 11th International Joint Conference on Natural Language Processing, ACL/IJCNLP 2021, (Volume 1: Long Papers), Virtual Event, August 1-6, 2021*, pages 6309–6318. Association for Computational Linguistics.

Xiangpeng Li, Bo Wu, Jingkuan Song, Lianli Gao, Pengpeng Zeng, and Chuang Gan. 2022. Text-instance graph: Exploring the relational semantics for text-based visual question answering. *Pattern Recognit.*, 124:108455.

Yulin Li, Yuxi Qian, Yuechen Yu, Xiameng Qin, Chengquan Zhang, Yan Liu, Kun Yao, Junyu Han, Jingtuo Liu, and Errui Ding. 2021b. Structext: Structured text understanding with multi-modal transformers. In *MM '21: ACM Multimedia Conference, Virtual Event, China, October 20 - 24, 2021*, pages 1912–1920. ACM.

Chuwei Luo, Guozhi Tang, Qi Zheng, Cong Yao, Lianwen Jin, Chenliang Li, Yang Xue, and Luo Si. 2022. Bi-VLDoc: Bidirectional vision-language modeling for visually-rich document understanding. *CoRR*, abs/2206.13155.

Bodhisattwa Prasad Majumder, Navneet Potti, Sandeep Tata, James Bradley Wendt, Qi Zhao, and Marc Najork. 2020. Representation learning for information extraction from form-like documents. In *Proceedings of the 58th Annual Meeting of the Association for Computational Linguistics, ACL 2020, Online, July 5-10, 2020*, pages 6495–6504. Association for Computational Linguistics.

Minesh Mathew, Dimosthenis Karatzas, and C. V. Jawahar. 2021. DocVQA: A dataset for VQA on document images. In *IEEE Winter Conference on Applications of Computer Vision, WACV 2021, Waikoloa, HI, USA, January 3-8, 2021*, pages 2199–2208. IEEE.

Puneet Mathur, Rajiv Jain, Ashutosh Mehra, Jiuxiang Gu, Franck Dernoncourt, Quan Tran, Verena Kaynig-Fittkau, Ani Nenkova, Dinesh Manocha, Vlad I. Morariu, et al. 2023. LayerDoc: Layer-wise extraction of spatial hierarchical structure in visually-rich documents. In *Proceedings of the IEEE/CVF Winter Conference on Applications of Computer Vision*, pages 3610–3620.

Seunghyun Park, Seung Shin, Bado Lee, Junyeop Lee, Jaeheung Surh, Minjoon Seo, and Hwalsuk Lee. 2019. CORD: A consolidated receipt dataset for post-OCR parsing. In *Workshop on Document Intelligence at NeurIPS 2019*.

Shah Rukh Qasim, Hassan Mahmood, and Faisal Shafait. 2019. Rethinking table recognition using graph neural networks. In *2019 International Conference on Document Analysis and Recognition, ICDAR 2019, Sydney, Australia, September 20-25, 2019*, pages 142–147. IEEE.

Pau Riba, Anjan Dutta, Lutz Goldmann, Alicia Fornés, Oriol Ramos Terrades, and Josep Lladós. 2019. Table detection in invoice documents by graph neural networks. In *2019 International Conference on Document Analysis and Recognition, ICDAR 2019, Sydney, Australia, September 20-25, 2019*, pages 122–127. IEEE.

Mausoom Sarkar, Milan Aggarwal, Arneh Jain, Hiresh Gupta, and Balaji Krishnamurthy. 2020. Document structure extraction using prior based high resolution hierarchical semantic segmentation. In *European Conference on Computer Vision*, pages 649–666. Springer.

Sebastian Schreiber, Stefan Agne, Ivo Wolf, Andreas Dengel, and Sheraz Ahmed. 2017. Deepdesrt: Deep learning for detection and structure recognition of tables in document images. In *14th IAPR International Conference on Document Analysis and Recognition, ICDAR 2017, Kyoto, Japan, November 9-15, 2017*, pages 1162–1167. IEEE.

Štěpán Šimsa, Milan Šulc, Michal Uřičář, Yash Patel, Ahmed Hamdi, Matěj Kocián, Matyáš Skalickỳ, Jiří Matas, Antoine Doucet, Mickaël Coustaty, and Dimosthenis Karatzas. 2023. DocILE benchmark for document information localization and extraction.

Rubèn Tito, Minesh Mathew, C. V. Jawahar, Ernest Valveny, and Dimosthenis Karatzas. 2021. ICDAR 2021 competition on document visual question answering. In *16th International Conference on Document Analysis and Recognition, ICDAR 2021, Lausanne, Switzerland, September 5-10, 2021, Proceedings, Part IV*, volume 12824 of *Lecture Notes in Computer Science*, pages 635–649. Springer.

Hieu M. Vu and Diep . Nguyen. 2020. Revising FUNSD dataset for key-value detection in document images. *CoRR*, abs/2010.05322.

Wenjin Wang, Zhengjie Huang, Bin Luo, Qianglong Chen, Qiming Peng, Yinxu Pan, Weichong Yin, Shikun Feng, Yu Sun, Dianhai Yu, and Yin Zhang. 2022. mmLayout: Multi-grained multimodal transformer for document understanding. In *MM '22: The 30th ACM International Conference on Multimedia, Lisboa, Portugal, October 10 - 14, 2022*, pages 4877–4886. ACM.

Yang Xu, Yiheng Xu, Tengchao Lv, Lei Cui, Furu Wei, Guoxin Wang, Yijuan Lu, Dinei A. F. Florêncio, Cha Zhang, Wanxiang Che, Min Zhang, and Lidong Zhou. 2021a. LayoutLMv2: Multi-modal pre-training for visually-rich document understanding. In *Proceedings of the 59th Annual Meeting of the Association for Computational Linguistics and the 11th International Joint Conference on Natural Language Processing, ACL/IJCNLP 2021, (Volume 1: Long Papers), Virtual Event, August 1-6, 2021*, pages 2579–2591. Association for Computational Linguistics.

Yiheng Xu, Tengchao Lv, Lei Cui, Guoxin Wang, Yijuan Lu, Dinei Florêncio, Cha Zhang, and Furu Wei. 2021b. LayoutXLM: Multimodal pre-training for multilingual visually-rich document understanding. *CoRR*, abs/2104.08836.

Yiheng Xu, Tengchao Lv, Lei Cui, Guoxin Wang, Yijuan Lu, Dinei Florencio, Cha Zhang, and Furu Wei. 2022. XFUND: A benchmark dataset for multilingual visually rich form understanding. In *Findings of the Association for Computational Linguistics: ACL 2022*, pages 3214–3224, Dublin, Ireland. Association for Computational Linguistics.

Davide Zagami and Christopher Helm. 2022. FUNSD+: A larger and revised funsd dataset.

Richard Zanibbi, Dorothea Blostein, and James R. Cordy. 2004. A survey of table recognition: Models, observations, transformations, and inferences. *Document Analysis and Recognition*, 7:1–16.

Xu Zhong, Elaheh ShafieiBavani, and Antonio Jimeno-Yepes. 2020. Image-based table recognition: Data, model, and evaluation. In *Computer Vision - ECCV 2020 - 16th European Conference, Glasgow, UK, August 23-28, 2020, Proceedings, Part XXI*, volume 12366 of *Lecture Notes in Computer Science*, pages 564–580. Springer.

Xu Zhong, Jianbin Tang, and Antonio Jimeno-Yepes. 2019. PubLayNet: Largest dataset ever for document layout analysis. In *2019 International Conference on Document Analysis and Recognition, ICDAR 2019, Sydney, Australia, September 20-25, 2019*, pages 1015–1022. IEEE.

A Related Work

We discuss work regarding form information extraction (i.e., entity labeling and entity linking) in the main paper. Here, we briefly describe other relevant VRFU tasks as well as other domains for document parsing.

Form Structure Extraction. Complete form parsing is related to form structure extraction, a task which aims to learn the structure and type of field values in forms such as a text field or a checkbox (Aggarwal et al., 2020b,a; Sarkar et al., 2020; Gao et al., 2021; Mathur et al., 2023). The tasks differ in that structure extraction does not aim to extract the answers of a form (indeed the input forms do not need to be filled in), nor does it aim to necessarily learn hierarchical structure. As such, its datasets do not need to be filled in forms, and can just be form templates. We note that structure extraction is a possible approach to form parsing.

Table Detection. Tables are a natural occurrence in semi-structured documents and so have merited much study in the literature (Riba et al., 2019; Qasim et al., 2019; Zhong et al., 2019). There has been a plethora of work on table understanding that dates back several decades; (Zanibbi et al., 2004) provides a through analysis of initial methods for table detection. More recent work has leveraged image, text, and spatial features to train neural networks to achieve F1 scores of over 80 for cell and table header detection (Schreiber et al., 2017; Herzig et al., 2020; Zhong et al., 2020; Gemelli et al., 2022b).

Receipt and Invoice Parsing. Document parsing is the task of assigning structure to a document image. While work exists for a variety of document types such as namecards (Hwang et al., 2019, 2021a) and even forms (Davis et al., 2022), receipts and invoices have been the most prominent domain for document parsing (Huang et al., 2019; Majumder et al., 2020; Borchmann et al., 2021; Gao et al., 2021; Šimsa et al., 2023). This is largely due to shared characteristics among receipts (e.g., item names and prices) and their structured layout. Indeed, the end-to-end model used in this work, Donut (Kim et al., 2022), was chosen due to its effectiveness in invoice parsing.

B Detailed TreeForm Annotation Scheme

In this section, we describe the TreeForm construction in more detail. Specifically we discuss two versions of TreeForm: Concise and non-concise. We view forms as being comprised of four components: headers, question-answer pairs, tables, and free-form text.[9] In the non-concise TreeForm, we use tree leaves to capture all textual information of a form. Non-leaf nodes are then used to describe the type of textual information (e.g., question, answer) as well as structural information (e.g., question-answer pairs, table entries). A similar structure is suggested in the supplementary materials of (Davis et al., 2022). TreeForm differs in that leaves of the tree always correspond to the textual content of the form.[10] We present the non-concise version of TreeForm to show the underlying structure of the form; an example of this annotation scheme is given in Figure 2c. We hope that future annotations of TreeForm will not need this more verbose version and will immediately use the structure described in App. B.1.

Headers. Headers are represented by an intermediate header node with a connected leaf node containing the header value (if a value is given). A header node contains the sub-tree of all information that falls under that header (and associated section). Therefore, the header node associated with the form title (if one exists) is the root of the tree.

Question-answer Pairs. Question-answer pairs are represented by a chained question node and answer node. The question node has two children: a leaf node containing the question text, and an answer node that has its own leaf node containing the answer text. In this work, we have opted to omit answer-less questions and question-less answers, however, TreeForm can be extended to included these.

Tables. Tables can be viewed as a collection of entries where each entry has a potential header, and the same set of question-answer pairs. We thus represent tables through nested trees. Each entry to the table forms its own node, and contains a leaf node with the entry header or table header if either exist. We then connect each question-answer pair of the entry as described above. TreeForm considers ta-

[9] Question-answer pairs cover any single question response, including checkboxes or similar structures.

[10] We may also want to include bounding box information in TreeForm annotations, this can be done by attaching a child to each text value that contains the node's bounding box. Note that (Davis et al., 2022) did not offer bounding box information in their proposed tree scheme.

bles to be read in row-major order, i.e., we consider each row to be an entry to the table with a potential entry header (row name), and each column to be a specific question that an entry answers.

Free-form Text. Much like recent work that ignores the *other* entity of FUNSD, we believe that free-form text does not capture the important structural information of a form, and so we do not include such components in TreeForm. Nevertheless, they can be included as leaf nodes connected to non-leaf nodes (e.g., headers) that they relate to.

B.1 Concise TreeForm

The above structure contains additional information to enable structured prediction and evaluation. However, it is possible to push textual information up the tree to construct a much denser structure. We can replace intermediate header and answer nodes by their textual information to reduce both the depth and breadth of the tree. This can also be done for table entry names (if they exist). Similarly, we can condense question-answer pairs into a question node whose value is the question text with a child answer node whose value is the answer text. This concise TreeForm structure removes any unnecessary labeling; for a well structured and well annotated form, this would likely mean all node values will contain the content of the form. We provide an example of the concise TreeForm structure in Figure 2d.

C Representation of Different Annotation Schemes

Figure 2 provides examples of JSON annotations for FUNSD, aggregated FUNSD (used for NAA and tree F1 metric), non-concise TreeForm, and concise TreeForm annotations.

D Experimental Set-up

In this section, we discuss the necessary pre- and post-processing steps we took to fine-tune evaluate LayoutXLM and Donut for TreeForm.

D.1 LayoutXLM

LayoutXLM (Xu et al., 2022) is a multilingual layout language model for document understanding. It is an extension of the popular LayoutLM models (Xu et al., 2021b,a) that were pre-trained for English documents only. The model takes as input the document image as well tokenized OCR output such that it knows the ground-truth text values in the form. The fine-tuned model first predicts the entities which are then used to predict the entity links such that it provides FUNSD-like predictions.[11] We can then evaluate the model's NAA and F1 performance as described in Section 3. We can further apply the same transformations to the predictions described in Section 4.2 to get the TreeForm predictions. Since bounding boxes are already known for each token, they can be used to apply the TreeForm transformations previously described.

D.2 Donut

Donut (Kim et al., 2022) is an end-to-end (document) image-to-JSON model. It is pre-trained for a variety of VRDU tasks such as document classification, VQA, and document parsing. Specifically, Donut was shown to do well in complete document parsing for receipts and invoices, and so applying it to forms is a natural progression. We note that Donut was developed concurrently with a similar end-to-end model, Dessurt (Davis et al., 2022). While Dessurt builds on work more closely related to VRFU (Davis et al., 2019, 2021), we chose to run experiments using Donut as the model is more accessible for custom training purposes. Furthermore, Donut was pre-trained with additional synthetic data in Chinese, English, Korean, and Japanese while Dessurt was pre-trained purely on English data. Therefore, Donut is more suited to be fine-tuned for multiple languages than Dessurt. More recently, Pix2Struct (Lee et al., 2023) has been introduced and generally achieves better performance than Donut. However, much like Dessurt, it was only trained on English data and so we use Donut in this work.

In order to fine-tune the model[12] to predict FUNSD-like annotations, we create JSON objects that represent the trees constructed in Section 3. This does mean that if a node has multiple parents, its text is repeated several times in the JSON representation. To fine-tune Donut for TreeForm annotations, we use the non-concise TreeForm representation as the model expects all textual components to be leaves in the JSON tree. For both annotation

[11]We fine-tuned the model using the recommended commands and configurations given by (Xu et al., 2022) at `https://github.com/microsoft/unilm/tree/master/layoutxlm`. Due to resource availability, we use the base version of the model and only trained LayoutXLM with a single GPU. Consequently, our models did not reproduce the results of (Xu et al., 2022).

[12]Donut is available at `https://github.com/clovaai/donut`.

schemes, we follow the training configuration of (Kim et al., 2022) for the Consolidated Receipt Dataset (CORD) dataset (Park et al., 2019), which predicts a full parse tree for receipts. We make two minor changes to the training-set up. Firstly, we use a maximum sequence length of 1024 rather than 768 due to forms naturally containing more information than receipts. Secondly, we fine-tune on the transformed FUNSD dataset for 50 epochs rather than the 30 epochs used for CORD as our training set of 149 documents (per dataset) is much smaller than the 800 of CORD.

Donut is a generative model, and as such its input is not always formatted in line with the tree structure of the ground truth. Consequently, we applied a few greedy post-processing transformations that either created valid annotations, or discarded non-viable structures.[13] Furthermore, we observed that the model seemed to sometimes suffer from duplicating text and tree components.[14] As such, we applied a further greedy transformation that removed similar looking leaves and their paths if their normalized Levenshtein distance was greater than 0.6. When discarding a path, we always kept the path containing the longest text. We used a similar heuristic to remove repeated long entities (greater than 20 characters) for the FUNSD-type prediction. We only applied the heuristic for long entities as we expect more repetition as previously described.

[13]E.g., unanswered questions, empty trees, *inter alia*.

[14]We suspected this may be due to the increased maximum sequence length, but also saw similar issues when using 768 as in (Kim et al., 2022).

Annotation Scheme for English Argument Structure Constructions Treebank

Hakyung Sung and **Kristopher Kyle**
Learner Corpus Research and Applied Data Science Lab
Department of Linguistics
University of Oregon
hsung,kkyle2@uoregon.edu

Abstract

We introduce a detailed annotation scheme for argument structure constructions (ASCs) along with a manually annotated ASC treebank. This treebank encompasses 10,204 sentences from both first (5,936) and second language English datasets (1,948 for written; 2,320 for spoken). We detail the annotation process and evaluate inter-annotation agreement for overall and each ASC category.

1 Introduction

The usage-based constructionist approach posits that language evolves from form-meaning pairings within linguistic structures. As language learners are exposed to a variety of inputs and outputs, they develop constructions of varying complexities (Goldberg, 2013). Among these, argument structure constructions (ASCs) represent core sentence meanings and are essential communication tools (Goldberg, 1995, 2003, 2009, 2013; Rappaport Hovav and Levin, 1998; O'Connor and Kay, 2003).

In cognitive linguistics, ASCs have played a central role in shaping cognition and language learning. Language learners categorize experience into structured frames. During this process, ASCs provide a conceptual framework, especially during the initial period of interaction with their surroundings. For example, with a transitive ASC, language learners can articulate a "conceptual archetype" related to situations in which a subject affects an object (e.g., *I kick the ball*) (Langacker, 1987). The significance of ASCs has been further underscored by research for both first (L1; Cameron-Faulkner et al., 2003; Goldberg, 2013, 2019; Ninio, 1999) and second language (L2; Ellis, 2002; Ellis and Larsen-Freeman, 2009; Ellis and Ferreira-Junior, 2009; Kyle and Crossley, 2017) learning. Recently, computational linguists have also been interested in investigating how well constructional information is learned and induced by large language models (Dunn, 2017; Li et al., 2022; Madabushi et al., 2020, 2023; Weissweiler et al., 2023).

In this paper, we introduce an ASC annotation procedure, its accompanying treebank (22,069 ASC tokens), and a supplementary annotation manual (32 pages). Our work includes both L1 and L2 English datasets, which serves two purposes: to augment the first version of the ASC treebank (Kyle and Sung, 2023), and to enable a comprehensive analysis across different linguistic contexts. The inclusion of L2 data is particularly helpful for researchers in the field of L2 acquisition (e.g., Kyle et al., 2021) and for developers of automatic writing evaluation systems used in language proficiency assessments (e.g., Yancey et al., 2023). Previous findings have suggested that the accuracy of part-of-speech and dependency tagging models on L2 datasets improves when these models improves on L2 datasets when L1 training data is supplemented with even relatively small amounts of L2 data (e.g., Kyle et al., 2022; Sung and Shin, 2023).

This dataset is expected to be instrumental in the evaluation and enhancement of tools for linguistic feature analysis, particularly for ASC-related statistical measures, such as the association strength between verbs and ASCs (Gries and Ellis, 2015; Kyle, 2016). Additionally, the dataset would offer opportunities for investigating how large language models process ASCs within both L1 and L2 contexts.

2 Related Work

Research into ASC annotation has been limited. Some pioneering efforts have focused on specific ASC types, such as a caused-motion ASC (Hwang, 2014) or ASCs with light verbs (e.g., *take, make*) (Bonial, 2014). Recently, Kyle and Sung (2023) developed a publicly available silver-annotated treebank of ASCs based on previous related projects such as PropBank (Palmer et al., 2005), FrameNet (Fillmore et al., 2003), VerbNet (Schuler, 2005)

Proceedings of The 18th Linguistic Annotation Workshop (LAW-XVIII), pages 12–18

and Universal PropBank (UP) for multilingual semantic role labeling (Akbik et al., 2015). Using a semi-automatic approach, they extracted large-grained semantic role frames from PropBank (e.g., *ARG0-Verbsense-ARG1*) then refined them (e.g., *agent-Verbsense-theme*) using PropBank mapping protocols with FrameNet and VerbNet databases. They then manually assigned each semantic role frame to an ASC (e.g., *agent-Verbsense-theme* → Transitive simple ASC). After resolving ambiguities and conducting spot-checks for errors, they categorized 94.1% of the ASCs (*n* = 26,437)[1] in the English Web treebank (EWT) (Bies et al., 2012; Silveira et al., 2014). The reliability of the semi-automatic annotation was preliminarily evaluated using a small sample of manually annotated sentences (*n* = 100) from the treebank. The results suggested that the semi-automatic approach was reasonable, but far from perfect (simple agreement rate = 92.1%, *kappa* = .884). While this approach presents an initial effort in building the silver-standard ASC treebank, the accuracy of their semi-automatic approach is still unclear.

Beyond annotations, researchers have explored the relationship between ASCs and language learning or understanding (recently processed by large language models) in various ways. These include psycholinguistic experiments (Bencini and Goldberg, 2000; Li et al., 2022), manual extractions based on researchers' judgments (Ellis and Ferreira-Junior, 2009), automatic extractions that leverage the syntactic forms of the ASCs (using automatic dependency annotations) (Kyle and Crossley, 2017; Hwang and Kim, 2023). Furthermore, some studies delved into broader linguistic constructions, identifying them through unsupervised approach that leverage statistical association measures (Dunn, 2017; Madabushi et al., 2020).

3 Annotation Scheme

In the development of the annotation scheme, we first address two important levels of linguistic annotation (Nivre et al., 2004). The first level is selecting the annotation unit, and the second level is choosing the ASC categories to be employed during the annotation process.

[1]For a detailed representation of ASCs in the treebank, including the frequencies and the most frequent verbs of each ASC, see Kyle and Sung, 2023, p. 54, Table 1).

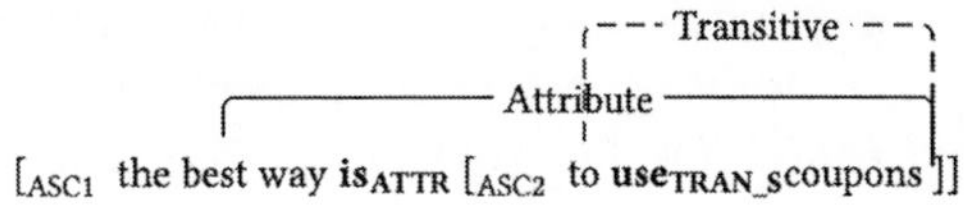

Figure 1: Example of annotation unit. In visual representations, a solid line denotes an ASC span in a finite clause form, while a dashed line indicates an ASC span in a non-finite form.

3.1 Analysis unit and basic principles

The unit of analysis is centered on the ASCs, which built upon arguments interpreted by specific semantic roles, specifying *Who did What to Whom* (e.g., agent, beneficiary, goal, theme)[2] in the given context (Goldberg, 1995).

Verbs serve as annotation targets due to their interactions with adjacent arguments (Fillmore, 1968; Goldberg, 1995). While early studies on ASCs (e.g., Goldberg, 1995) predominantly discussed finite clauses as ASCs, we encompassed both finite clauses and/or non-finite clauses. This comprehensive approach ensures every meaning constrained by an ASC is captured. As a result, some sentences are parsed into multiple layers which include both finite and non-finite clauses, with each layer presenting a distinct ASC (Figure 1).

Word order is considered a separate construction layer. This means we treated different word orders for the same ASC type (due to pragmatic reasons like framing a question) as identical[3]. This approach aligns with the understanding that ASCs do not dictate specific word orders (Goldberg, 2019, p. 39).

3.2 ASC categories

We adopted nine ASC categories. Meanwhile, we recognize the flexibility in ASC selection (Kyle and Sung, 2023) and the varying complexity levels in ASC representation (e.g., focusing solely on light verb constructions; Bonial, 2014).

Initially, our focus was on seven primary ASCs, predominantly characterized by active voice as often outlined in earlier studies (Bencini and Goldberg, 2000; Ellis and Ferreira-Junior, 2009; Goldberg, 1995; Hwang and Kim, 2023): (1) intransitive simple (e.g., ***worked** a lot*); (2) intransitive motion

[2]For a comprehensive set of recognized semantic role labels, we refer to Palmer et al., 2011, p. 4.

[3]For example, we may tag two expressions with different syntactic frames *they **wanted** the thing* and *the thing which they **wanted***, as TRAN_S, even though the latter has an inverted object (*the thing*) due to its relative clause structure.

(e.g., ***went** out the door*); (3) intransitive resultative (e.g., ***got** healthier*); (4) transitive simple (e.g., ***met** my friends*); (5) ditransitive (e.g., ***told** them my plan*); (6) caused-motion (e.g., ***put** the date on the calendar*); (7) transitive resultative (e.g., ***made** me happy*).

In our analysis, we choose to expand our category beyond the active voice to comprehensively account for the ASC types appearing in the data. As a result, we augmented our category with two additional constructions: (8) attributive (e.g., ***be** the first*) and (9) passive. Furthermore, we classified the sentences with middle voice (e.g., *the pot **broke** on the floor*) under our (1) intransitive simple category because of its syntactic resemblance. While our categorization aligns with the goal of this study, future research may adopt finer-grained approaches to sub-categorize each voice tag. Different voices such as active, middle, passive have the potential to be considered distinct layers (Goldberg, 2013, p. 455). These voices may play an important role in shaping syntactic/semantic frames, altering dynamics of agency and focus within sentences[4].

Table 1 illustrates the nine ASC types included in this study, with the most prototypical syntactic[5] and semantic frame representations. Note that these frames were not utilized as strict criteria for annotating ASCs. Instead, they represent typical or frequently encountered patterns observed during our annotation process and in comparisons with the silver ASC treebank. We have compiled a more comprehensive set of syntactic and semantic frames in our annotation manual, which served as a detailed reference for the annotators.

4 Datasets

We utilized L1 and L2 English datasets that were publicly and freely available and are part of Universal Dependency (UD) projects. Both datasets use the CoNLL-U format, which presents sentences vertically with columns detailing morphological and syntactic attributes. We annotated ASC tags into the 10th MISC column. Due to limited annotation capacity, we randomly selected a subset of sentences from L1 and L2 written datasets.

4.1 L1 dataset

Following the related work (Kyle and Sung, 2023), we continued to use the English portion of the UP project, which combined the UD version of the EWT with semantic role labels based on the PropBank annotation scheme. The original EWT corpus contains sentences sampled from five web registers: blogs, newsgroups, emails, reviews, and Yahoo Answers. Within the EWT's total of 16,621 sentences, we manually tagged 5,936 sentences (104,640 word tokens).

4.2 L2 dataset

We used both L2 written (ESL-WR) and spoken (ESL-SP) corpora to cover a broader range of L2 English registers.

4.2.1 L2 written

The ESL-WR dataset (Berzak et al., 2016) is sourced from the CLC FCE dataset (Yannakoudakis et al., 2011), containing written answers from the Cambridge English exams across five registers (letter, report, article, composition, and short story). Extracts in the ESL dataset came from upper-intermediate English learners representing 10 different native languages. Of the 5,124 sentences in the original corpus, we manually tagged 1,948 sentences (37,055 word tokens).

4.2.2 L2 spoken

The ESL-SP dataset (Kyle et al., 2022) is derived from sentences randomly sampled from the NICT JLE (Izumi et al., 2004) corpus. This corpus features transcriptions from oral proficiency interviews that contained utterances produced by Japanese English learners. We manually tagged all 2,320 sentences (21,312 word tokens) that have annotations with syntactic dependency relation tags in the corpus.

5 Annotation

The annotation project spanned about 8 months, from April 2023 to November 2023.

[4]For example, when a sentence *a car **hit** the man* is transformed into *the man was **hit** by a car*, the arguments and their semantic roles remain consistent (*car*-agent; *man*-theme), but only the focus within the statement is shifted. This allows for ASCs from active voice categories, which have *agent* and *theme* arguments (i.e., transitive simple, ditransitive, cause-motion, transitive resultative), may have respective passive counterparts and could potentially be grouped into separate passive categories. However, in our current categorization, we have grouped them all under the PASSIVE tag. We acknowledge that this is a methodological decision and that exploring distinct passive categories for different ASC types could be a valuable direction for future research.

[5]Syntactic frames are described by syntactic dependency tags, drawing upon the tags from the UD project: `https://universaldependencies.org/u/dep/index.html`.

ASC (tag)	Syntactic Frame	Semantic Frame
Intransitive simple (INTRAN_S)	*nsubj*-root	*agent*-V
Intransitive motion (INTRAN_MOT)	*nsubj*-root-*obl*	*theme*-V-*goal*
Intransitive resultative (INTRAN_RES)	*nsubj*-root-*advmod*	*patient*-V-*goal*
Transitive simple (TRAN_S)	*nsubj*-root-*obj*	*agent*-V-*theme*
Ditransitive (DITRAN)	*nsubj*-root-*iobj-obj*	*agent*-V-*recipient-theme*
Caused-motion (CAUS_MOT)	*nsubj*-root-*obj-obl*	*agent*-V-*theme-destination*
Transitive resultative (TRAN_RES)	*nsubj*-root-*obj-xcomp*	*agent*-V-*result-result*
Attributive (ATTR)	*nsubj-cop*-root	*theme*-V-*attribute*
Passive (PASSIVE)	*nsubj:pass-aux:pass*-root	*theme-aux*-V_{passive}

Table 1: ASCs representation in treebank

5.1 Annotator training

We enlisted and trained six undergraduate Linguistics majors, all of whom were native English speakers and had previously undertaken advanced courses in functional English syntax. These annotators participated in three structured 1-hour training sessions.

During the initial training session, the annotators were introduced to the overarching theoretical background and objectives, as well as their expected roles. They were also familiarized with the data format, tagging schemes, and the procedures for accessing and storing data within a shared folder. For the annotation process, we utilized standard text editors (e.g., *BBEdit*) and/or spreadsheet software (e.g., *Microsoft Excel*), which provided a straightforward interface for manual tagging. In the subsequent two sessions, they engaged in hands-on practice with sample sentences, individually tagging items and discussed any challenges they encountered. Feedback was provided after each exercise.

5.2 Annotation process and review

After training, the annotators began remote work, uploading files to a monitored shared folder. They also had access to a thoroughly documented webpage, which was updated regularly by the researchers, and a Discord server for discussing challenges. Based on these discussions, the tagging guidelines were frequently updated and eventually formed the basis of the annotation manual.

While the original L1/L2 datasets, sourced from the UD project, provided some syntactic cues (e.g., *nsubj, root*) our annotators were not strictly bound to these existing annotations. In other words, annotators had flexibility to rely on the matching patterns between UD tags and ASC categories when they deemed these reliable. They were also encouraged to ignore the UD tags in cases in which the UD syntactic frame did not align with the ASC's semantic arguments.

Each ASC token was primarily tagged by two randomly assigned annotators through a blind review process. If there was disagreement between the two annotators, a third annotation was done, either by one of the undergraduate annotators or one of the researchers. If disagreement persisted, a fourth annotator, typically one of the researchers, tagged the case.

5.3 Annotation summary and evaluation

Inter-annotator agreement during the first round of annotation was reasonable[6] (exact agreement = 85.7%; *kappa* = .801; Landis and Koch, 1977). Table 2 provides the number of annotated ASCs in each dataset. For a visual representation of annotator agreement on each ASC tag, refer to the confusion matrix depicted in Figure 2.

Tag	EWT	ESL_WR	ESL_SP
INTRAN_S	1,395	662	525
INTRAN_MOT	607	250	240
INTRAN_RES	213	44	23
TRAN_S	6,094	2,488	1,385
DITRAN	285	160	37
CAUS_MOT	766	87	53
TRAN_RES	763	76	16
ATTR	2,539	1,289	760
PASSIVE	1,058	224	50
Total	**13,720**	**5,260**	**3,089**

Table 2: ASCs distribution in treebank

[6]These figures are slightly lower when misspelled and missed tags are included (exact agreement = 82.5%, *kappa* = .759). These are not represented in the confusion matrix in Figure 2.

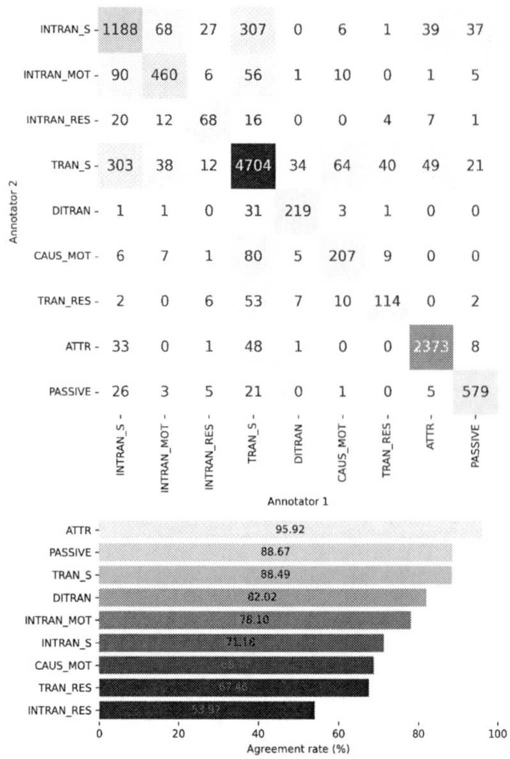

Figure 2: Evaluation of inter-annotator agreement

Semi-automatic annotations from the silver ASC treebank (11,245 ASCs) were also evaluated against the gold standard. By-tag evaluation scores are outlined in Table 3.

Tag	Count	P	R	F1
INTRAN_S	1,014	.895	.787	.837
INTRAN_MOT	353	.758	.691	.723
INTRAN_RES	124	.861	.649	.740
TRAN_S	5,195	.919	.909	.914
DITRAN	206	.851	.789	.819
CAUS_MOT	517	.807	.776	.791
TRAN_RES	673	.707	.917	.798
ATTR	2,445	.982	.972	.977
PASSIVE	718	.924	.948	.936

Table 3: Evaluation of semi-automatic annotations

5.4 Annotation manual overview

In categorizing ASCs, making informed choices is important, as often seen in other annotation projects (Gerdes and Kahane, 2016). Our annotation manual details the "what" and "why" behind the annotators' choices, providing various exemplar sentences from the ASC treebank. These highlight various verb usages in each ASC, associated with syntactic frames (based on dependency tags) and, for L1 data, semantic frames (based on semantic role labels). The manual also addresses challenges in annotating ASC tags, such as ambiguous cases and complexities arise from verb-ASC combinations. Through the manual, we seek to ensure transparency and consistency in both current and future endeavors.

6 Conclusion

In this study, we introduced a manually annotated ASC treebank, complemented by a detailed annotation procedure. Access to the ASC treebank and the accompanying annotation manual is available here: `https://osf.io/v75qu/?view_only=410a39910fd1438bbf1ef0368ce51c3b`.

Limitations

The study has limitations that should be addressed in future work. First, the current ASC treebank is confined to English, limiting the applicability of findings to other languages. Second, the tagging scheme could be refined to capture subtle language nuances (e.g., PASSIVE tag). Third, expanding the dataset to include a broader range of genres and registers would improve the understanding of ASC patterns.

Ethics Statement

The annotated dataset presented in this work utilized publicly available datasets from previous studies, including the silver-standard ASC treebank (Kyle and Sung, 2023), ESL-WR (Berzak et al., 2016), ESL-SP (Kyle et al., 2022), and Universal PropBank (Akbik et al., 2015).

Acknowledgements

The authors would like to express their gratitude to the annotators—Hana Dussan, Bella Graham, Marianne Hatley, Augustus Paddock, Holly Renshaw, and Ryan Walker (listed in alphabetical order)—for their contributions to the manual annotations and the valuable discussions that have improved the ASC tagging guidelines.

References

Alan Akbik, Laura Chiticariu, Marina Danilevsky, Yunyao Li, Shivakumar Vaithyanathan, and Huaiyu Zhu. 2015. Generating high quality proposition banks for multilingual semantic role labeling. In *Proceedings of the 53rd Annual Meeting of the Association for Computational Linguistics and the 7th International Joint Conference on Natural Language Processing (Volume 1: Long Papers)*, pages 397–407.

Giulia ML Bencini and Adele E Goldberg. 2000. The contribution of argument structure constructions to sentence meaning. *Journal of Memory and Language*, 43(4):640–651.

Yevgeni Berzak, Jessica Kenney, Carolyn Spadine, Jing Xian Wang, Lucia Lam, Keiko Sophie Mori, Sebastian Garza, and Boris Katz. 2016. Universal dependencies for learner english. *arXiv preprint arXiv:1605.04278*.

Ann Bies, Justin Mott, Colin Warner, and Seth Kulick. 2012. English web treebank. *Linguistic Data Consortium, Philadelphia, PA*.

Claire Nicole Bonial. 2014. *Take a look at this! Form, function and productivity of English light verb constructions*. Ph.D. thesis, University of Colorado at Boulder.

Thea Cameron-Faulkner, Elena Lieven, and Michael Tomasello. 2003. A construction based analysis of child directed speech. *Cognitive science*, 27(6):843–873.

Jonathan Dunn. 2017. Computational learning of construction grammars. *Language and cognition*, 9(2):254–292.

Nick C Ellis. 2002. Frequency effects in language processing: A review with implications for theories of implicit and explicit language acquisition. *Studies in second language acquisition*, 24(2):143–188.

Nick C Ellis and Fernando Ferreira-Junior. 2009. Construction learning as a function of frequency, frequency distribution, and function. *The Modern language journal*, 93(3):370–385.

Nick C Ellis and Diane Larsen-Freeman. 2009. Constructing a second language: Analyses and computational simulations of the emergence of linguistic constructions from usage. *Language Learning*, 59:90–125.

Charles J Fillmore. 1968. Lexical entries for verbs. *Foundations of language*, pages 373–393.

Charles J Fillmore, Christopher R Johnson, and Miriam RL Petruck. 2003. Background to framenet. *International journal of lexicography*, 16(3):235–250.

Kim Gerdes and Sylvain Kahane. 2016. Dependency annotation choices: Assessing theoretical and practical issues of universal dependencies. In *LAW X (2016) The 10th Linguistic Annotation Workshop: 131*.

Adele E Goldberg. 1995. *Constructions: A construction grammar approach to argument structure*. University of Chicago Press.

Adele E Goldberg. 2003. Constructions: A new theoretical approach to language. *Trends in cognitive sciences*, 7(5):219–224.

Adele E. Goldberg. 2009. Constructions work. *Cognitive Linguistics*, 20(1):201–224.

Adele E Goldberg. 2013. The emergence of the semantics of argument structure constructions. In *The emergence of language*, pages 215–230. Psychology Press.

Adele E Goldberg. 2019. *Explain me this: Creativity, competition, and the partial productivity of constructions*. Princeton University Press.

Stefan Th Gries and Nick C Ellis. 2015. Statistical measures for usage-based linguistics. *Language Learning*, 65(S1):228–255.

Haerim Hwang and Hyunwoo Kim. 2023. Automatic analysis of constructional diversity as a predictor of efl students' writing proficiency. *Applied Linguistics*, 44(1):127–147.

Jena D Hwang. 2014. *Identification and representation of caused motion constructions*. Ph.D. thesis, University of Colorado at Boulder.

Emi Izumi, Kiyotaka Uchimoto, and Hitoshi Isahara. 2004. The nict jle corpus: Exploiting the language learners' speech database for research and education. *International Journal of the Computer, the Internet and Management*, 12(2):119–125.

K. Kyle. 2016. *Measuring syntactic development in L2 writing: Fine grained indices of syntactic complexity and usage-based indices of syntactic sophistication*. Ph.D. thesis, Georgia State University, Atlanta, GA.

K. Kyle and S. Crossley. 2017. Assessing syntactic sophistication in l2 writing: A usage-based approach. *Language Testing*, 34(4):513–535.

Kristopher Kyle, Scott Crossley, and Marjolijn Verspoor. 2021. Measuring longitudinal writing development using indices of syntactic complexity and sophistication. *Studies in Second Language Acquisition*, 43(4):781–812.

Kristopher Kyle, Masaki Eguchi, Aaron Miller, and Theodore Sither. 2022. A dependency treebank of spoken second language english. In *Proceedings of the 17th Workshop on Innovative Use of NLP for Building Educational Applications (BEA 2022)*, pages 39–45.

Kristopher Kyle and Hakyung Sung. 2023. An argument structure construction treebank. In *Proceedings of the First International Workshop on Construction Grammars and NLP (CxGs+ NLP, GURT/SyntaxFest 2023)*, pages 51–62.

J Richard Landis and Gary G Koch. 1977. An application of hierarchical kappa-type statistics in the assessment of majority agreement among multiple observers. *Biometrics*, pages 363–374.

Ronald W Langacker. 1987. Nouns and verbs. *Language*, pages 53–94.

Bai Li, Zining Zhu, Guillaume Thomas, Frank Rudzicz, and Yang Xu. 2022. Neural reality of argument structure constructions. *arXiv preprint arXiv:2202.12246*.

Harish Tayyar Madabushi, Laurence Romain, Dagmar Divjak, and Petar Milin. 2020. Cxgbert: Bert meets construction grammar. *arXiv preprint arXiv:2011.04134*.

Harish Tayyar Madabushi, Laurence Romain, Petar Milin, and Dagmar Divjak. 2023. Construction grammar and language models. *arXiv preprint arXiv:2308.13315*.

Anat Ninio. 1999. Pathbreaking verbs in syntactic development and the question of prototypical transitivity. *Journal of child language*, 26(3):619–653.

Joakim Nivre, Koenraad De Smedt, and Martin Volk. 2004. Treebanking in northern europe: A white paper. *Nordisk Sprogteknologi*, pages 2000–2004.

Mary Catherine O'Connor and Paul Kay. 2003. Regularity and idiomaticity in grammatical constructions: The case of let alone. In *The new psychology of language*, pages 243–270. Psychology Press.

Martha Palmer, Daniel Gildea, and Paul Kingsbury. 2005. The proposition bank: An annotated corpus of semantic roles. *Computational linguistics*, 31(1):71–106.

Martha Palmer, Daniel Gildea, and Nianwen Xue. 2011. *Semantic role labeling*. Morgan & Claypool Publishers.

Malka Rappaport Hovav and Beth Levin. 1998. Building verb meanings. *The projection of arguments: Lexical and compositional factors*, pages 97–134.

Karin Kipper Schuler. 2005. *VerbNet: A broad-coverage, comprehensive verb lexicon*. Ph.D. thesis, University of Pennsylvania.

Natalia Silveira, Timothy Dozat, Marie-Catherine De Marneffe, Samuel R Bowman, Miriam Connor, John Bauer, and Christopher D Manning. 2014. A gold standard dependency corpus for english. In *LREC*, pages 2897–2904. Citeseer.

Hakyung Sung and Gyu-Ho Shin. 2023. Diversifying language models for lesser-studied languages and language-usage contexts: A case of second language Korean. In *Findings of the Association for Computational Linguistics: EMNLP 2023*, pages 11461–11473, Singapore. Association for Computational Linguistics.

Leonie Weissweiler, Taiqi He, Naoki Otani, David R Mortensen, Lori Levin, and Hinrich Schütze. 2023. Construction grammar provides unique insight into neural language models. *arXiv preprint arXiv:2302.02178*.

Kevin P Yancey, Geoffrey Laflair, Anthony Verardi, and Jill Burstein. 2023. Rating short l2 essays on the cefr scale with gpt-4. In *Proceedings of the 18th Workshop on Innovative Use of NLP for Building Educational Applications (BEA 2023)*, pages 576–584.

Helen Yannakoudakis, Ted Briscoe, and Ben Medlock. 2011. A new dataset and method for automatically grading esol texts. In *Proceedings of the 49th annual meeting of the association for computational linguistics: human language technologies*, pages 180–189.

A Mapping on Current Classifying Categories of Emotions Used in Multimodal Models for Emotion Recognition

Ziwei Gong
Columbia University
zg2272@columbia.edu

Xinyi Hu
Boston University
xhu07@bu.edu

Muyin Yao
Tufts University
yaomuyin@gmail.com

Xiaoning Zhu
JYLlink Co., Ltd.
zhuxiaoning@jylink.com

Julia Hirschberg
Columbia University
julia@cs.columbia.edu

Abstract

In Emotion Detection within Natural Language Processing and related multimodal research, the growth of datasets and models has led to a challenge: disparities in emotion classification methods. The lack of commonly agreed upon conventions on the classification of emotions creates boundaries for model comparisons and dataset adaptation. In this paper, we compare the current classification methods in recent models and datasets and propose a valid method to combine different emotion categories. Our proposal arises from experiments across models, psychological theories, and human evaluations, and we examined the effect of proposed mapping on models.

1 Introduction

Emotion recognition, as an essential ability for good interpersonal relations (Mancini et al., 2018), has long been a major subject in psychology, and for the last two decades has received increasing attention from the field of computer science, especially artificial intelligence (De Silva et al., 1997; Gong et al., 2023). Yet in this process a divergence has emerged from newly published datasets and models — the misalignment between different categories of emotions. To resolve such disparity between emotion datasets, we propose a psychology-based solution for computer scientists to solve the problem of misalignment in emotion classification datasets, which is caused by the independent nature of emotion classification theories.

In the field of psychology, there are many different theories on how to classify emotions focusing on different aspects. Various theories classify emotions based on different factors: Ekman's theory focuses on universal facial expressions (Ekman, 1992), comparing the facial expressions of westerners and Aboriginal residents of New Guinea; Plutchik's evolutionary perspective categorizes emotions into 8 primary emotions with 3 levels of intensity (Plutchik, 2001) based on the communication function of emotions; Barrett's (Wilson-Mendenhall et al., 2011) biological approach studies brain responses to emotions through intepreting EEGs and physiological changes (Hess, 2017); and emphasizing cultural influence, the constructionist theory adds social and linguistic elements to emotion understanding (Wilson-Mendenhall et al., 2011). These theories are independent but sometimes interconnected, providing a foundation for potential integration. Different theories are mostly considered to be independent theories of emotion, yet these classification approaches are often interconnected and sometimes built upon each other, providing a basis to connect them. However, few studies explore ways to connect or combine these different categorizations.

In computer science, researchers face the challenge of choosing an emotion theory when building datasets for emotion detection. Recent work in emotion classification has shifted towards using multimodal data sources like audio, video, and text (Poria et al., 2019; Shen et al., 2020), and some even explore incorporating additional factors like personality and social connections to leverage more information for deep learning models (Kahou et al., 2015). Due to varying annotation methods and mismatch in the set of labels, a model typically selects a single dataset for experiments, although more data could improve its performance. A significant issue arises from the lack of alignment in labeling schemas across datasets, making it challenging for models to leverage multiple datasets in supervised learning (Bostan and Klinger, 2018). This disparity results in a lack of cohesion in the literature, hinders direct performance comparisons, and complicates dataset combination and training. Since annotating such datasets is costly and time-consuming, a mapping method that can unify existing datasets could benefit the community. Currently, little research in both psychology and com-

Proceedings of The 18th Linguistic Annotation Workshop (LAW-XVIII), pages 19–28
March 22, 2024

puter science explores the relationship between different emotion categories. While there are studies mapping categorical emotions onto dimensional models (Hoffmann et al., 2012) and recent work inproviding more grounded emotion categories in Dutch (De Bruyne et al., 2020), the mapping between multiple categorical emotions, which creates misalignment in emotion datasets for machine learning, remains unstudied.

This paper aims to establish a valid mapping of emotion categories based on psychological theories and validated through machine learning models. We select the five most commonly used emotion classification methods in large emotion datasets, propose a valid mapping method rooted in psychological theory, verify it through human evaluation, and assess its impact on emotion recognition models. Our mapping method is an initial effort to create a continuous mapping approach connecting these discrete emotion classification methods.

2 Methods

2.1 Datasets

We choose 4 diverse datasets, each employing distinct modalities and emotion classification methods. We include both datasets that reflect real-life scenarios such as MEmoR (Shen et al., 2020) and MELD (Poria et al., 2019), and those focusing on facial features like IEMOCAP (Busso et al., 2008). Additionally, we include the FER-2013 (Goodfellow et al., 2013) computer vision dataset to investigate our mapping method's impact on a single-modality dataset. These datasets span various classification methods: MEmoR employs Plutchik's Wheel of Emotion (14 emotions), MELD and IEMOCAP adopt Ekman's basic 6 emotions, and FER-2013 features 7 common emotions as labels.

2.2 Mapping Method

Our approach to developing a mapping theory between emotion classification methods follows the following procedure.

Common Emotions: Emotions shared by both categories remain unaltered. Although these emotions might have different definitions across theories, our sample annotation process suggests annotators seldom find them non-transferable. Considering the annotation process of large datasets, it is common that their annotators are asked to choose an emotion that best describes the current scene or utterance rather than strictly following the definition of that emotion. So it it possible that in the annotation process annotators sometimes use common sense understanding of emotions to annotate and only use the definitions provided as references. Given these considerations and results, we decide not to modify emotions common to both categories.

Higher-Level Emotions: Emotions exclusive to higher-level categories, such as anticipation and surprise, are mapped based on past literature, often considering valence and arousal of various emotions. Valence measures the positiveness or negativity of an emotional stimulus (De Silva et al., 1997), and emotions with similar valence are presumed to be more closely related. Arousal level, measuring the intensity of emotion, is also a cue to the similarity of emotions. Emotions with comparable arousal and valence levels are more likely to be paired, contrasting with emotions that differ in these aspects.

Human Evaluations: When faced with tied choices, we conduct human evaluations on each theory to determine the best mapping choice in the situation of a tie. Detailed evaluations are carried out for each theory. We illustrate our mapping choice for the emotion "surprise" as an example of our decision-making process.

2.3 The Classification for Surprise as Example

Surprise characterizes the feeling of shock due to perceiving things or experience out of expectation. To map surprise onto a 6-emotion classification (neutral, sadness, joy, disgust, anger, and fear), we employed a bipolar model integrating valence and arousal dimensions. Russell introduced this model in 1977 (Russell and Mehrabian, 1977), with motivation as an initial component. Surprise may be considered a negative emotion, since previous studies associate surprise with a negative valence (Noordewier and Breugelmans, 2013) and high arousal levels (Russell and Mehrabian, 1977). Based on Liu et al.'s research, high-arousal, low-valence emotions are akin to anger (Liu et al., 2010). However, the potential for positive valence-associated surprise introduces ambiguity in conversion, possibly favoring mapping to neutral.

We leverage biological distinctions between emotions as a reference. A recent study utilizing biomarkers to analyze EEG profiles across brain regions offers valuable findings. Among surprise-combined emotions, the spectral biomarker's mean differences (0.114) and the temporal biomarker's

<table>
<tr><th>14 fine-grained</th><th>9 primary</th><th>7 basic</th><th>6 emotions</th><th>3 sentiments</th></tr>
<tr><td>anticipation</td><td rowspan="2">anticipation</td><td rowspan="3">neutral</td><td rowspan="3">neutral</td><td rowspan="3">neutral</td></tr>
<tr><td>interest</td></tr>
<tr><td>neutral</td><td>neutral</td></tr>
<tr><td>fear</td><td>fear</td><td>fear</td><td>fear</td><td rowspan="9">negative</td></tr>
<tr><td>disgust</td><td rowspan="2">disgust</td><td rowspan="2">disgust</td><td rowspan="2">disgust</td></tr>
<tr><td>boredom</td></tr>
<tr><td>sadness</td><td>sadness</td><td>sadness</td><td>sadness</td></tr>
<tr><td>anger</td><td rowspan="2">anger</td><td rowspan="2">anger</td><td rowspan="4">anger</td></tr>
<tr><td>annoyance</td></tr>
<tr><td>surprise</td><td rowspan="2">surprise</td><td rowspan="2">surprise</td></tr>
<tr><td>distraction</td></tr>
<tr><td>joy</td><td rowspan="2">joy</td><td rowspan="3">joy</td><td rowspan="3">joy</td><td rowspan="3">positive</td></tr>
<tr><td>serenity</td></tr>
<tr><td>trust</td><td>trust</td></tr>
</table>

Table 1: Mapping results. This table demonstrates how 14 fine-grained emotions, listed on the leftmost column, are mapped onto 9 primary emotions, Ekman's basic emotions, 6 emotions, and the 3 sentiments.

mean differences (0.058) are lowest for the neutral-surprise pairing (Mancini et al., 2018). Hence, both anger and neutral are considered possible mappings for surprise. To test this hypothesis, we implemented a program to convert surprise into anger and neutral. These converted emotions were mixed with randomly selected samples of other emotions. Annotators, at least two per data point, participated in the evaluation. All annotators were English-speaking college students, with half of them familiar with the TV show "The Big Bang Theory." Annotation materials included clips, scripts, and emotion definitions per category. Evaluation results favored the surprise-to-anger conversion, as it achieved higher accuracy. Hence, we chose to map surprise to anger based on annotation outcomes.

2.4 The Annotation Process

At least two annotators are asked to annotate one data point. All annotators are college students studying in a university where English is the first language, since the datasets are all in English. The students age between 18 to 22. The annotators are provided with clips and scripts during the annotation, and half of the annotators are familiar with the TV show, the Big Bang Theory. The emotions and definitions of each emotion in each category are also provided to the annotators to help interpretation.

3 Mapping Between Different Emotion Categories

3.1 Mapping Results

Table 1 shows the resulting unique mapping table between the 5 most popular emotion classification methods, ranging from 14 categories to 3 categories. To validate our mapping, a re-annotation of randomly sampled emotions mapped to their categories achieves an accuracy of 0.96 (Annotator 1) and 0.917 (Annotator 2), with a fair inter-annotator agreement of 0.318 (Cohen's Kappa). Thus, this mapping method has proved to have fairly high accuracy when used to reconstruct datasets. We conclude that it is possible to map emotion categories onto each other with relatively high accuracy. The proposed mapping method is one directional, from more categories to fewer categories. Mapping data from fewer categories to more categories is possible but requires additional annotation to determine the resulting co-domain labels. Additionally, this mapping method can be used by future researchers with more fine grained labeling methods when creating datasets, since mapping from more fine grained labeling to less fine grained labeling requires no additional information.

3.2 Map analysis

The main contribution of our work is that we are the first to propose a mapping method for numerous emotion categorization methods from psychological theories and have validated it with human evaluation and experiments. Analyzing the final mapping produced, we found that across all categorization methods, the categories in negative emotions are more fine-grained than either positive or neutral emotions, given the number of emotions that are mapped into negative emotions. For example, from the 14-categories, there are 8 emotions that were mapped into "negative", 3 mapped into "positive" and 3 mapped into "neutral". This imbalance could be caused by both biases in the dataset and underlying psychological mechanisms. Since the data for the datasets are collected from TV shows or other commercialized media, it could be that a dataset may not necessarily contain emotion proportions that are reflective of actual human emotional expressions. The underlying psychological mechanisms would also be an aspect to discuss for other researchers.

Moreover, while several emotions seem more difficult to be mapped into other categories, such as surprise and trust, in the experiment we found it still has an acceptable evaluation score. For example, it is difficult to determine whether 'surprise' is a good surprise or a bad surprise in real life, but in our mapping, 'surprise' is mapped into anger with a high agreement in human evaluation. One possible reason for this is that the current categories make humans, the annotators, more likely to choose negative surprise as "surprise" and consider taking positive surprise as "joy" or "hopeful". We attribute this alignment to the disparity among emotion classification theories and their unique aspects in understanding human emotions. Nevertheless, our mapping method establishes a consistent standard grounded in existing datasets.

Although the same emotion categories may have different definitions for different classification methods, each of the emotions are still mapped into the corresponding emotion with the same name in our mapping. Although we acknowledge the slight difference in meaning, for the purpose of mapping, emotions still prove to be more similar to corresponding emotion with the same name despite the different interpretations. Our current mapping method sucessfully proposes a uniform standard, yet its accuracy is limited in datasets that are largely different from the existing datasets in terms of domain, conversation style, etc. Furthermore, since we are the first to propose a mapping for different emotion classification theories from a psychological perspective, there are a limited number of existing studies that we could compare to. We hope our proposal, as a first attempt to solve this disparity, could also serve as a start point for others who seek to solve the problem.

4 Mapping effects on ML Models

To analysis the effect of the proposed mapping on machine learning models, we set up an experiment to check the accuracy of emotion re-categorization after applying the mapping method in Table 1 to both the MEmoR and the CNN dataset. We selected two models to study the effect of the mapping methods on emotion detection models.

4.1 Models

Vision CNN is commonly used in recognition and classification tasks (Albawi et al., 2017; Suryani et al., 2016). We reconstructed the FER-2013 Dataset (7 basic emotions) based on our mapping in Table 1 to recreated the dataset with 6 emotions and 3 sentiments respectively.

Emotion Category	3	6	7	9	14
MEmoR Accuracy	**0.924**	0.867	0.884	0.869	0.864
CNN Accuracy	**81.78**	65.39	65.28	-	-

Table 2: Experimental results from the MEmoR model and the CNN model. This table shows the overall accuracy of the models trained and tested on datasets reconstructed based on each 3 classification method. The highest achieved is bolded. The MEmoR model uses visual, audio, textual features. In the CNN model, only visual information is used.

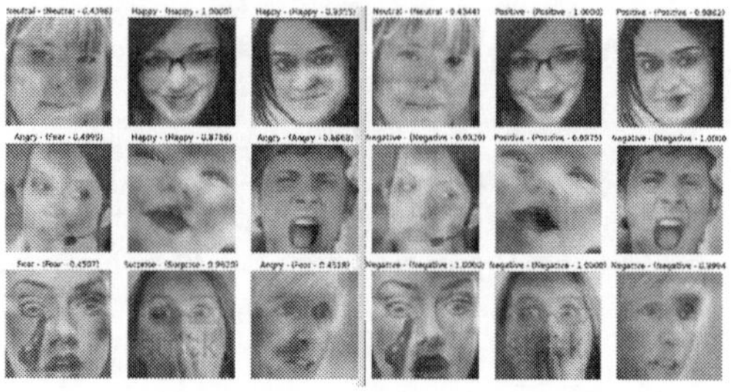

Figure 1: Contrast in attention heat maps across 9 random images: a CNN model trained on a 7-category dataset (left) vs. the same dataset categorized into 3 groups (right). Regions of high attention are shown in red.

Multimodality MEmoR Model (Shen et al., 2020) is a fusion multi-modal model is provided by (Shen et al., 2020). The model extracts representative multimodal features, including audio features, video features, and text features, personality features, and uses an attention-based multimodal reasoning method. In the experiment we use the MEmoR dataset reconstructed based on our mapping, which has 5 groups of labels. Each model will be trained tested on each classification method.

4.2 Results

Results of the experiments on the MEmoR model and CNN model are shown in Table 2. From these experiments, we have found that models generally perform better when there are fewer emotion categories, meaning that more fine-grained emotions are more difficult for models to differentiate, regardless of which modality or which combination of modalities is used. This finding validates that our mapping is accurate, as it is the general understanding in the machine learning community that using fewer classification categories, when correctly applied, leads to higher accuracy since the complexity of the task is reduced. However, the experimental results for the MEmoR model show that training and testing on 7 categories does achieve

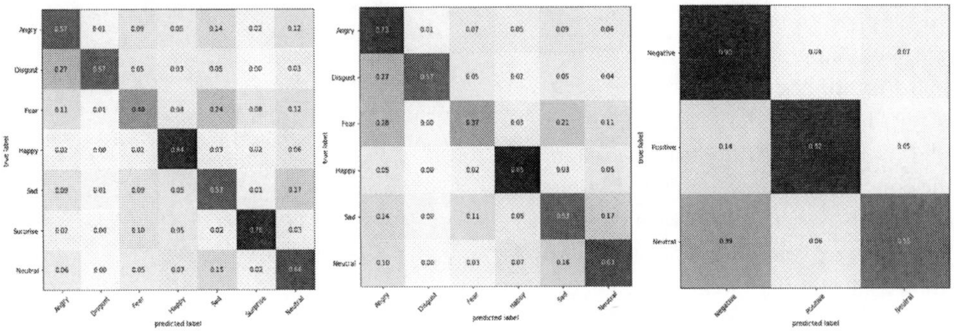

Figure 2: Confusion matrices generated by three CNN models trained on a dataset, all learning from the same set of pictures but with labels categorized into 7 (left), 6 (middle) and 3 categories (left). Columns represent the predicted label and rows represent the true label.

higher accuracy than 6 categories, while still lower than results on 3 categories. However, on the CNN model, we see a higher accuracy on 6 categories compared to the 7 categories. By looking closely at the confusion matrices (Figure 2) of CNN models, we see that the improvement was mainly on the adjusted category, and the accuracy of the categories that remain untouched from the transition remains in the same range. A possible reason for this is that classifying emotion into 7 categories is derived from Ekman's basic emotion theory, which is based on facial expression. Thus it is possible that such a categorization method is easier for models to learn through facial expression recognition. However, to determine the cause, there should be more research on separated models and modalities. We encourage future researchers to look into this question.

Visualization of the CNN model's attention is shown in Table 1. We observe that the attention of the model trained with more fine-grained emotions is more spread out through the face, with some stress around the eye and mouth area. In comparison, the attention of the model trained on sentiments is more focused on specific areas and created red dots on the heat map. The difference indicates that there are more subtle cues to distinguish fine-grained emotion on the face, requiring the model to learn to predict based on more information from different areas, compared to sentiments that are simpler and distinguishable through some key area like the mouth (smiling or not, for example).

5 Conclusion

In this paper, we propose the first complete mapping that connects different emotion categories for multimodal emotion recognition studies, and provide a study of the effect of using different emotion classification methods when training models. We are the first group of researchers attempting to bridge the different psychological emotion theories and lend them consistency in the computer science world. Moreover, using our mapping allows researchers to obtain a larger and more flexible dataset for training and testing and to analyze the model's ability to differentiate emotions using different emotion categories, as well as identify the best model across all datasets.

Acknowledgements

We thank Dr.Robert Brotherton, Bingpu Zhao, and Jingyi Song for their support and valuable feedback. This research is supported in part by the Defense Advanced Research Projects Agency (DARPA), via the The Computational Cultural Understanding (CCU) program contract HR001122C0034. The views, opinions and/or findings expressed are those of the author and should not be interpreted as representing the official views or policies of the Department of Defense or the U.S. Government.

Limitations

A limitation of our mapping is that it proposes a unified standard within a set range of 3 to 14 categories. Yet for some particular tasks, creating a recognizer that is sensitive to a particular facial expression or emotion that is not included in our proposed method may be necessary. We encourage future researchers to expand on top of our classification method using similar methods. However, we hope that providing a unified standard would benefit the community by decreasing deviance and making it easier for scholars who wish to adopt an existing dataset for a particular task.

Moreover, while several emotions seem harder to be mapped into other categories, we found acceptable evaluation score for the mapping, but there are limitations. Similarly to the mapping of "surprise", whether the emotion “trust” was a neutral emotion or a positive emotion is hard to decide. In our classification, we followed the steps described in our “Methods” section to determine which classification gives better accuracy and thus determines the mapping. Although our current mapping method proposes a uniform standard, its accuracy is limited in datasets that are largely different from the existing datasets in terms of domain, conversation style, etc. we also acknowledge potential difficulties in mapping certain emotions, and we anticipate revisions and improvements to our current mapping method after the construction of larger datasets in the future to better bridge the differences between various data sets.

Furthermore, since we are the first to propose a mapping for different emotion classification theories from a psychological perspective, there is a limited number of existing studies that we could compare to. We hope our proposal, as a first attempt to solve this disparity, could also serve as a start point for others who seek to solve the problem.

References

Saad Albawi, Tareq Abed Mohammed, and Saad Al-Zawi. 2017. Understanding of a convolutional neural network. In *2017 International Conference on Engineering and Technology (ICET)*, pages 1–6.

Laura-Ana-Maria Bostan and Roman Klinger. 2018. An analysis of annotated corpora for emotion classification in text. In *Proceedings of the 27th International Conference on Computational Linguistics*, pages 2104–2119, Santa Fe, New Mexico, USA. Association for Computational Linguistics.

Carlos Busso, Murtaza Bulut, Chi-Chun Lee, Abe Kazemzadeh, Emily Mower Provost, Samuel Kim, Jeannette Chang, Sungbok Lee, and Shrikanth Narayanan. 2008. Iemocap: Interactive emotional dyadic motion capture database. *Language Resources and Evaluation*, 42:335–359.

Luna De Bruyne, Orphee De Clercq, and Veronique Hoste. 2020. An emotional mess! deciding on a framework for building a Dutch emotion-annotated corpus. In *Proceedings of the Twelfth Language Resources and Evaluation Conference*, pages 1643–1651, Marseille, France. European Language Resources Association.

L.C. De Silva, T. Miyasato, and R. Nakatsu. 1997. Facial emotion recognition using multi-modal information. In *Proceedings of ICICS, 1997 International Conference on Information, Communications and Signal Processing. Theme: Trends in Information Systems Engineering and Wireless Multimedia Communications (Cat.*, volume 1, pages 397–401 vol.1.

Paul Ekman. 1992. Are there basic emotions? *Psychological review*, 99 (3).

Ziwei Gong, Qingkai Min, and Yue Zhang. 2023. Eliciting rich positive emotions in dialogue generation. In *Proceedings of the First Workshop on Social Influence in Conversations (SICon 2023)*, pages 1–8, Toronto, Canada. Association for Computational Linguistics.

Ian J. Goodfellow, Dumitru Erhan, Pierre Luc Carrier, Aaron Courville, Mehdi Mirza, Ben Hamner, Will Cukierski, Yichuan Tang, David Thaler, Dong-Hyun Lee, Yingbo Zhou, Chetan Ramaiah, Fangxiang Feng, Ruifan Li, Xiaojie Wang, Dimitris Athanasakis, John Shawe-Taylor, Maxim Milakov, John Park, Radu Ionescu, Marius Popescu, Cristian Grozea, James Bergstra, Jingjing Xie, Lukasz Romaszko, Bing Xu, Zhang Chuang, and Yoshua Bengio. 2013. Challenges in representation learning: A report on three machine learning contests.

Ursula Hess. 2017. Chapter 5 - emotion categorization. In Henri Cohen and Claire Lefebvre, editors, *Handbook of Categorization in Cognitive Science (Second Edition)*, second edition edition, pages 107–126. Elsevier, San Diego.

Holger Hoffmann, Andreas Scheck, Timo Schuster, Steffen Walter, Kerstin Limbrecht, Harald C. Traue, and Henrik Kessler. 2012. Mapping discrete emotions into the dimensional space: An empirical approach. In *2012 IEEE International Conference on Systems, Man, and Cybernetics (SMC)*, pages 3316–3320.

Samira Ebrahimi Kahou, Xavier Bouthillier, Pascal Lamblin, Caglar Gulcehre, Vincent Michalski, Kishore Konda, Sébastien Jean, Pierre Froumenty, Yann Dauphin, Nicolas Boulanger-Lewandowski, Raul Chandias Ferrari, Mehdi Mirza, David Warde-Farley, Aaron Courville, Pascal Vincent, Roland Memisevic, Christopher Pal, and Yoshua Bengio. 2015. Emonets: Multimodal deep learning approaches for emotion recognition in video.

Yisi Liu, Olga Sourina, and Minh Khoa Nguyen. 2010. Real-time eeg-based human emotion recognition and visualization. In *2010 International Conference on Cyberworlds*, pages 262–269.

Giacomo Mancini, Roberta Biolcati, Sergio Agnoli, Federica Andrei, and Elena Trombini. 2018. Recognition of facial emotional expressions among italian preadolescents, and their affective reactions. *Frontiers in psychology*, 9:1303.

Marret K. Noordewier and Seger M. Breugelmans. 2013. On the valence of surprise. *Cognition and Emotion*, 27(7):1326–1334. PMID: 23560688.

Robert Plutchik. 2001. The nature of emotions: Human emotions have deep evolutionary roots, a fact that may explain their complexity and provide tools for clinical practice. *American Scientist*, 89(4):344–350.

Soujanya Poria, Devamanyu Hazarika, Navonil Majumder, Gautam Naik, Erik Cambria, and Rada Mihalcea. 2019. MELD: A multimodal multi-party dataset for emotion recognition in conversations. In *Proceedings of the 57th Annual Meeting of the Association for Computational Linguistics*, pages 527–536, Florence, Italy. Association for Computational Linguistics.

James A Russell and Albert Mehrabian. 1977. Evidence for a three-factor theory of emotions. *Journal of Research in Personality*, 11(3):273–294.

Guangyao Shen, Xin Wang, Xuguang Duan, Hongzhi Li, and Wenwu Zhu. 2020. Memor: A dataset for multimodal emotion reasoning in videos. In *Proceedings of the 28th ACM International Conference on Multimedia*, MM '20, page 493–502, New York, NY, USA. Association for Computing Machinery.

Dewi Suryani, Patrick Doetsch, and Hermann Ney. 2016. On the benefits of convolutional neural network combinations in offline handwriting recognition. In *2016 15th International Conference on Frontiers in Handwriting Recognition (ICFHR)*, pages 193–198.

Christine D. Wilson-Mendenhall, Lisa Feldman Barrett, W. Kyle Simmons, and Lawrence W. Barsalou. 2011. Grounding emotion in situated conceptualization. *Neuropsychologia*, 49(5):1105–1127.

A Appendix

A.1 Experiment Design for CNN Model

To explore the effects of our mapping method on CNN models, we built a simple CNN model with three convolutional layers, feeds into a fully connected layer, and outputs from a softmax layer. The model is trained on unimodal (visual) information on the FER-2013 (Goodfellow et al., 2013) dataset for emotion classification. The CNN model is selected to study the effect of the mapping methods on unimodal models.The model was trained using batch size=256 for 60 epoches on single GPU. We reconstructed the FER-2013 (Goodfellow et al., 2013) Dataset based on our mapping. Since the dataset is originally classified labeled with 7 basic emotions, we recreated the dataset with 6 emotions and 3 sentiments classification methods respectively (Table 3 (Appendix)). The mapping method is shown in Figure 3 (Appendix). Each CNN model will be tested on all 3 classification methods using the same hyper-parameter and trained for 60 epochs in two stages on the same hardware. All three models are trained to convergence before stopping at epochs 60.

A.2 Experiment Design for MEmoR Model

MEmoR Model (Shen et al., 2020) is a fusion multi-modal model is provided by (Shen et al., 2020). The model extracts representative multimodal features, including audio features, video features, and text features, personality features, and uses an attention-based multimodal reasoning method. The experiment use the MEmoR (Shen et al., 2020) dataset reconstructed based on our mapping. The reconstructed dataset has 5 groups of labels, following the 5 most popular emotion classification theories. Each model will be tested on all 5 classification methods and each modality (visual, textual, audio) in order to explore the effect of our mapping on models. For simplicity, we choose the default parameters and model structure given in the MEmoR model, except to revise the model to fit the change in the size of the label. All 5 classification methods experimented with are listed in Table 3 (Appendix). The mapping method is shown in Figure 3 (Appendix).

14 fine-grained emotions	9 primary emotions	7 basic emotions	6 emotions	3 sentiments
joy, anger, disgust, sadness, surprise, fear, anticipation, trust, serenity, interest, annoyance, boredom, distraction, neutral	joy, anger, disgust, sadness, surprise, fear, anticipation, trust, neutral	joy, anger, disgust, sadness, fear, surprise, neutral	joy, anger, disgust, sadness, fear, neutral	positive, negative neutral

Table 3: Emotion Categories

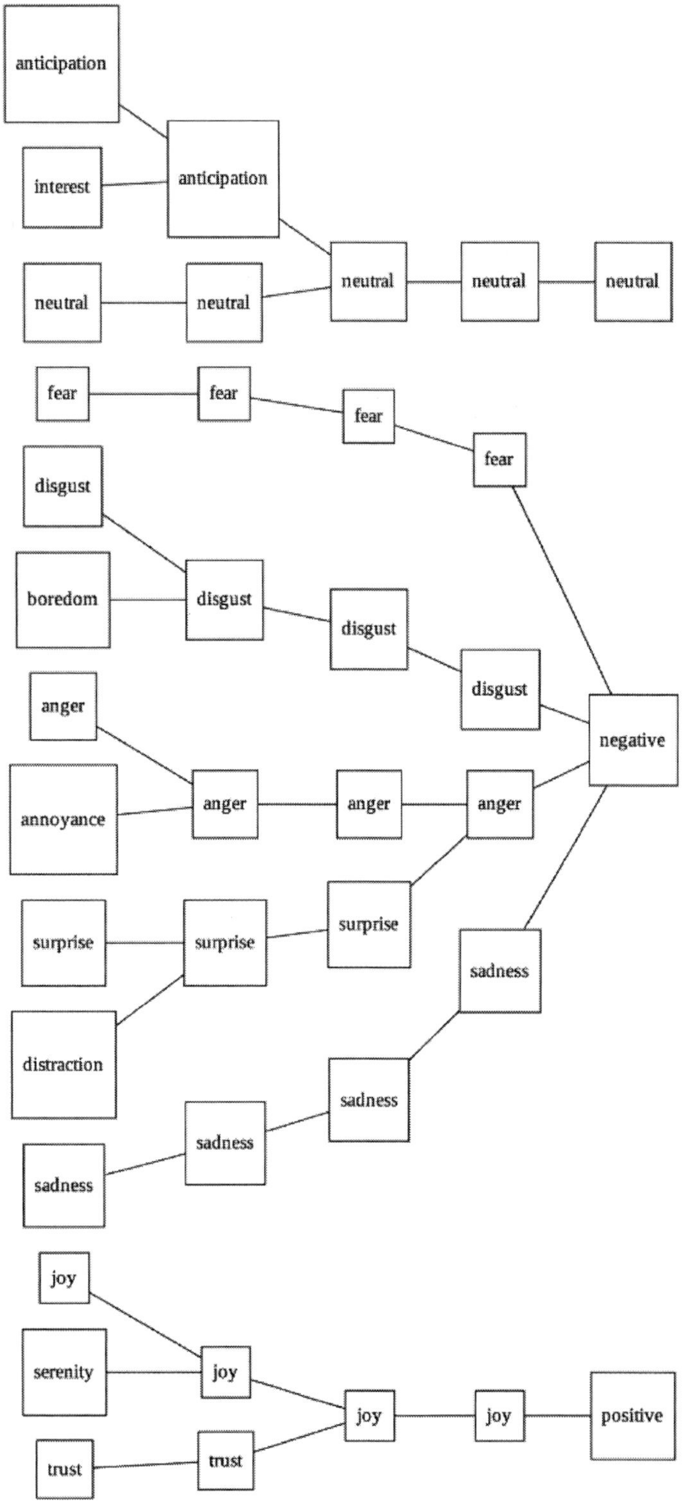

Figure 3: Mapping method in graph. This graph demonstrates how 14 fine-grained emotions, listed on the leftmost column, are mapped onto 9 primary emotions, Ekman's basic emotions, 6 emotions, and the 3 sentiments.

Surveying the FAIRness of Annotation Tools: Difficult to find, difficult to reuse

Ekaterina Borisova[1], **Raia Abu Ahmad**[1], **Leyla Jael Garcia-Castro**[2], **Ricardo Usbeck**[3], **Georg Rehm**[1]

[1]Deutsches Forschungszentrum für Künstliche Intelligenz GmbH (DFKI), Germany,
[2]ZB MED Information Centre for Life Sciences, Germany,
[3]Leuphana Universität Lüneburg, Germany
[1]ekaterina.borisova@dfki.de, raia.abu_ahmad@dfki.de, georg.rehm@dfki.de,
[2]ljgarcia@zbmed.de, [3]ricardo.usbeck@leuphana.de

Abstract

In the realm of Machine Learning and Deep Learning, there is a need for high-quality annotated data to train and evaluate supervised models. An extensive number of annotation tools have been developed to facilitate the data labelling process. However, finding the right tool is a demanding task involving thorough searching and testing. Hence, to effectively navigate the multitude of tools, it becomes essential to ensure their *findability*, *accessibility*, *interoperability*, and *reusability* (FAIR). This survey addresses the FAIRness of existing annotation software by evaluating 50 different tools against the FAIR principles for research software (FAIR4RS). The study indicates that while being accessible and interoperable, annotation tools are difficult to find and reuse. In addition, there is a need to establish community standards for annotation software development, documentation, and distribution.

1 Introduction

Coinciding with the rise of Machine Learning (ML), annotation projects started being conducted to create labelled datasets for the training and testing of models, especially those based on supervised approaches (Ide and Pustejovsky, 2017). A wide range of software has been developed to address data labelling. Existing annotation tools vary in terms of supported modality (i. e., text, image, video, audio), access type (e. g., desktop, web-based, etc.), license (commercial vs. open-source), and annotation task(s) they are designed for (Neves and Ševa, 2019). This sheer abundance of different annotation tools hinders the search, access, and choice of an appropriate tool. Researchers often spend a lot of time downloading and installing tools that turn out to be irrelevant to their projects (Neves and Ševa, 2019).

To improve the *findability*, *accessibility*, *interoperability*, and *reusability* (FAIR) of research artifacts such as annotation tools, the FAIR (Wilkinson et al., 2016) and FAIR for Research Software (FAIR4RS, Chue Hong et al., 2022; Barker et al., 2022) principles have been proposed. Although previous surveys of annotation tools exist (Dasiopoulou et al., 2011; Neves and Leser, 2012; Nixon and Troncy, 2014; Neves and Ševa, 2019; Oliveira and Rocha, 2013; Aljabri et al., 2022), none of them evaluated their FAIRness. However, the development of FAIR annotation tools is essential to facilitate knowledge discovery and to ensure transparent research. This paper addresses this gap by assessing a range of 50 different annotation tools according to the FAIR4RS principles.

Our contributions can be summarised as follows:

- We offer interpretations of the FAIR4RS principles tailored to the specific use-case of annotation tools. These can be a valuable resource for developers and researchers while designing and reusing annotation software.
- We perform a thorough FAIRness assessment of 50 different annotation tools, providing insights into the current documentation and sharing strategies. These findings can serve as a basis for defining best practices for annotation tool management.
- Through our assessment, we provide a comparison of annotation tools, addressing their different features and adherence to community standards. This can be used by researchers as a reference while searching for appropriate tools for a specific task.
- We define ten essential functionalities that ideally should be incorporated into an annotation tool for an easier user experience.

Proceedings of The 18th Linguistic Annotation Workshop (LAW-XVIII), pages 29–45

The rest of the paper is structured as follows: Section 2 discusses the annotation lifecycle, FAIR and FAIR4RS principles in more detail. Section 3 describes the annotation tools selection process and introduces our interpretation of the FAIR4RS principles. Section 4 and Section 5 present the evaluation results and main findings, respectively. Section 6 discusses the limitations of our study. Concluding remarks are provided in Section 7.

2 Background

2.1 Annotation Lifecycle

Annotated data is fundamental for training, evaluating and validating ML models. In particular, supervised and semi-supervised algorithms directly rely on labelled data and their performance is highly dependent on the annotation quality (Hao et al., 2020; Alhazmi et al., 2021). Furthermore, in the context of transfer learning and fine-tuning, annotated data is essential for fostering the adaptation of models to specific tasks and domains (Pan and Yang, 2010).

Annotation can be performed for diverse modalities of data, i.e., text, image, audio, and video as well as at various levels depending on the data type and task at hand (Ide and Pustejovsky, 2017). For instance, in the case of text annotation, labels can be assigned to an entire document, paragraph, sentence, phrase, word or character. Annotation approaches range from manual (e. g., crowdsourcing, Vander Schee, 2009), semi-automatic (e. g., active learning, Settles, 2009) to fully automatic, relying on ML and Natural Language Processing (NLP) techniques. Each method has its advantages and drawbacks, and the choice usually depends on specific project goals, data, and resources.

Annotation is a complex process which usually involves a wide range of activities such as collecting the data, preparing an annotation schema and guidelines, recruiting and training annotators, curating the assigned labels, and computing inter-annotator agreement (IAA) scores (Ide and Pustejovsky, 2017). To facilitate the annotation lifecycle (Rehm, 2016), various tools have been developed which deal with the data labelling stage. These tools vary in complexity and functionality, ranging from simple *desktop* interfaces, such as TagEditor[1] and ELAN (Wittenburg et al., 2006), to advanced *web-based* applications, such as INCEpTION (Klie et al., 2018) and Doccano (Nakayama et al., 2018), supporting teams, user roles, automatic IAA calculation, ML models, etc. Annotation tools also come in various types ranging from those tailored towards *specific domains*, e. g., MedTag (Giachelle et al., 2021) and BioQRator (Kwon et al., 2013), *modalities*, e. g., ELAN and Annotation Web (Smistad et al., 2021), and *tasks*, e. g., PDF sentence annotator[2] and Praat (Boersma and Weenink, 2023), to *general-purpose* applications, e. g., prodigy[3] and Label Studio (Tkachenko et al., 2020-2022), also see Rehm (2020).

2.2 FAIR and FAIR4RS

Sharing research data is essential for accelerating scientific progress as it encourages collaborative research and decision-making. However, research data management techniques vary greatly across disciplines leading to inconsistencies in documentation and sharing of scientific artifacts (Akers and Doty, 2013). Such heterogeneous and disjoint data management practices hinder the validation, replication, and improvement of previous solutions. Given the rapid progress in ML and Artificial Intelligence coupled with the ever increasing number of new datasets, models, and software, it has become crucial to define common data sharing policies to ensure transparency and reproducibility.

In order to promote the *findability*, *accessibility*, *interoperability*, and *reuse* of scholarly data from both human and machine perspectives, the FAIR guiding principles (Wilkinson et al., 2016) were proposed. This set of principles is meant to be directly applied to all digital objects such as datasets, algorithms, software, and toolkits. However, several studies (Patel et al., 2023; Katz et al., 2016) demonstrated that the FAIR principles are not fully applicable to research software (RS). As was highlighted by Katz et al. (2016), even though data and software share certain characteristics, e. g., potential for having a license or a Digital Object Identifier (DOI), these two digital objects possess several significant differences. In contrast to data, software is an inherently executable and continuously evolving object characterised by a composite structure as it is frequently developed based on other components. Unlike data, software requires maintenance due to its dependency on other packages, tools, and software which are subject to constant change. Software also tends to have a shorter lifespan than

[1]http://tinyurl.com/TagEditor

[2]https://orkg.org/pdf-text-annotation

[3]https://prodi.gy

data due to technological progress.

In response to the need for software-specific principles, the original FAIR principles have been revised several times (Lamprecht et al., 2020; Katz et al., 2021). As a result of those efforts, the FAIR4RS principles geared towards ensuring a FAIR lifecycle of RS were developed (Barker et al., 2022; Chue Hong et al., 2022). According to these principles, software should be thoroughly described through metadata, it should be possible to execute, replicate, combine, reinterpret, reimplement, and expand upon it as well as to utilise it in diverse settings (Chue Hong et al., 2022).

The FAIR and FAIR4RS principles gave rise to a range of tools for the FAIRness evaluation of digital objects. Those include manual questionnaires and checklists (Do I-PASS for FAIR de Bruin et al., 2020, FAIR Data Self Assessment Tool[4], FAIR Aware[5]) as well as automated tests (FAIR Evaluation Services Wilkinson et al., 2019, howfairis Spaaks et al., 2022, FAIR Enough[6], FAIR-Checker Gaignard et al., 2023). However, since both FAIR and FAIR4RS are open to interpretation, the assessment results can vary depending on the tool.

3 Methods

In this study, we performed a *manual* assessment of annotation tools against the FAIR4RS principles. We refrained from using automatic solutions primarily due to the variability in results mentioned in Section 2.2. Furthermore, *howfairis* is the only tool based on FAIR4RS, designed specifically for analysing the compliance of GitHub/GitLab repositories with the principles. Consequently, its applicability is limited to tools hosted on those platforms.

Due to the huge amount of existing tools (Neves and Ševa, 2019) and time constraints, we limited the evaluation to 50 annotation tools. As a first step, we randomly selected annotation tools surveyed by Neves and Ševa (2019). However, those are specifically developed for text data annotation. To make the set of tools more diverse in terms of covered modalities, we conducted a search on Google Scholar to find publications related to annotation and corpus creation that mention or cite annotation software. In addition, we looked for tools on platforms such as European Language Grid (ELG, Rehm, 2023), Zenodo[7], SourceForge[8] and Software Heritage[9]. We did not consider tools that were archived or have become part of another project (e. g., WebAnno, Eckart de Castilho et al., 2016), were not found (e. g., a publication exists but the link to the home page or source code does not work) or are for crowd-sourcing purposes (Amazon Mechanical Turk[10]).

Since the FAIR4RS principles do not serve as a set of strict rules but rather as a guideline, they are not rigidly defined, sometimes allowing for a broad range of interpretations. Therefore, below we introduce our interpretations and the evaluation strategies defined and followed in this study[11].

F1. Software is assigned a globally unique and persistent identifier. An annotation tool should have a globally unique and persistent identifier (PID), such as DOI, which assures longevity and consistently points to the software despite changes in its location, content or other attributes. Thus, we investigated whether a tool is available on platforms that provide PIDs, i. e., Software Heritage and Zenodo. Other widely utilised software publishing services, such as GitHub, GitLab, or SourceForge, are not suitable as the URLs they offer cannot be considered persistent.

F1.1. Components of the software representing levels of granularity are assigned distinct identifiers. In addition to the annotation tool itself, distinct PIDs should be assigned to all its components. Thus, following the software granularity levels schema offered by Chue Hong et al. (2022), we researched whether files, directories, commits, releases, and other tool attributes possess PIDs. In contrast to F1, we considered only Software Heritage since it assigns distinct PIDs to every digital object component compared to Zenodo, which provides individual DOIs only for various versions.

F1.2. Different versions of the software are assigned distinct identifiers. Each release of an annotation tool should be assigned a distinct PID allowing users to track its development and refer to a specific version they utilised. Similar to F1, we checked the presence of tools on both Software Heritage and Zenodo.

F2. Software is described with rich metadata.

[4] https://ardc.edu.au/resource/fair-data-self-assessment-tool/

[5] https://fairaware.dans.knaw.nl

[6] https://fair-enough.semanticscience.org

[7] https://zenodo.org

[8] https://sourceforge.net

[9] https://www.softwareheritage.org

[10] https://www.mturk.com

[11] The interpretations of the FAIR4RS principles are also summarised in Appendix A.

Metadata should be semantically structured, i. e., being both human and machine-readable. It should contain a thorough description of an annotation tool allowing users to understand how to utilise and replicate it without looking into its source code. Metadata is considered to be rich when it goes beyond basic information. To define the minimum metadata we followed the Bioschemas ComputationalTool[12]. Bioschemas is an effort to improve findability in Life Sciences by relying on the widely used Schema.org[13] vocabulary. Although Bioschemas is domain-specific, it includes general types and properties to describe research artifacts such as datasets and software. Unlike other vocabularies, Bioschemas offers minimum, recommended, and optional property types, making it easier to define rich metadata. Accordingly, the minimum metadata of an annotation tool should include *name*, *URL*, and *description*. The metadata is considered to be rich if at least one additional property from any marginality level is provided[14].

F3. Metadata clearly and explicitly include the identifier of the software they describe. If an annotation tool is assigned a PID, it should be referenced by it in the respective structured metadata. Thus, in case F1 is not fulfilled, F3 fails as well.

F4. Metadata are FAIR, searchable and indexable. Metadata is FAIR when it is semantically structured. Therefore, if an annotation tool fails F2 due to the lack of structured metadata, it automatically fails F4. Any metadata exposed via web pages in a format understood by search engines or deposited in a repository/registry with search functionality is indexable.

A1. Software is retrievable by its identifier using a standardised communications protocol. An annotation tool should be accessed through a commonly used communication protocol such as Hypertext Transfer Protocol (HTTP), Hypertext Transfer Protocol Secure (HTTPS) or File Transfer Protocol (FTP).

A1.1. The protocol is open, free, and universally implementable. There should be no restrictions and fees to implement the communication protocol.

A1.2. The protocol allows for an authentication and authorisation procedure, where necessary. The protocol should include mechanisms to verify the identity of users and to determine their access rights where necessary. Authentication and authorisation are supported by HTTP/HTTPS and FTP protocols, therefore if a tool is retrievable via those, it automatically fulfills A1.2.

A2. Metadata are accessible, even when the software is no longer available. As software tend to be deprecated over time, ideally structured metadata should be published separately with its own PID. In practice, it is often embedded into the source code of software. Therefore, this principle is satisfied when metadata is assigned a distinct PID and published either separately from a tool or along with it on an archive which ensures longevity.

I1. Software reads, writes and exchanges data in a way that meets domain-relevant community standards. While file conversion is possible, RS support for standard formats is more user-friendly (Ide and Pustejovsky, 2017). In the context of annotation, this allows the reuse of labelled data across the tools, e. g., for error corrections, active learning or automatic predictions (Neves and Ševa, 2019). Currently, there do not seem to be well-defined standards for annotation tools' input/output formats. The formats vary depending on the input modality, domain, and specific task at hand. For instance, *CoNLL* is widely used in linguistic annotation projects (Ide and Pustejovsky, 2017), while *Dicom* is commonly utilised in medical imaging (Larobina and Murino, 2014; Aljabri et al., 2022). Therefore, to evaluate I1, we relied on formats mentioned in previous surveys on annotation tools (Neves and Ševa, 2019; Oliveira and Rocha, 2013; Dasiopoulou et al., 2011; Aljabri et al., 2022) and by Ide and Pustejovsky (2017)[15]. We searched for input/output format information in both structured and unstructured (e. g., README) metadata. The principle is considered to be fully fulfilled if an annotation tool supports at least one of the standard formats for both input and output.

I2. Software includes qualified references to other objects. This principle calls for references to any objects other than software such as datasets, hardware, programming language, operating system or browser. Qualified references include identifiers (URLs, PIDs, etc.) and controlled vocabularies. We investigated whether such references are provided in structured or unstructured metadata.

R1. Software is described with a plurality of

[12]`https://bioschemas.org/profiles/ComputationalTool/1.0-RELEASE`

[13]`https://schema.org`

[14]For the full list of structured and unstructured metadata sources per annotation tool, please see Appendix B.

[15]For the full list of formats, please see Appendix C.

accurate and relevant attributes.

An annotation tool should be described in terms of metadata categories (F2), license (R1.1), and provenance (R1.2). The relevance of attributes is usually determined by repositories and/or communities that create and use a tool. Whenever feasible, multiple terms for the same, similar or overlapping concepts should be provided to allow reuse. However, to the best of our knowledge, there are no community-agreed standards for the metadata vocabulary of annotation tools. Therefore, R1 is considered to be fulfilled if a tool fully adheres to F2, R1.1 and R1.2 and partially fulfilled if one of the principles is partially met.

R1.1. Software is given a clear and accessible license. The annotation tool's license should be clearly stated in either structured or unstructured metadata.

R1.2. Software is associated with detailed provenance. This principle calls for an explanation of the annotation tool's origins and development history. To this end, we evaluated whether structured or unstructured metadata provides answers to the following questions: *Why and how a tool came to be? Who contributed what, when, and where? How to cite a tool?* The principle is fully satisfied when all questions receive complete answers. However, in case some questions are only partially addressed, the principle is considered partially met.

R2. Software includes qualified references to other software. As with any other software, annotation tools usually have dependencies. Thus, in contrast to I2, we researched whether qualified references to other software (e. g., libraries, packages) are provided in either structured or unstructured metadata.

R3. Software meets domain-relevant community standards. Currently, there do not seem to be well-established community standards for annotation tools. The desired capabilities of software are influenced by the annotation project scope and goals. According to Ide and Pustejovsky (2017), there are two main requirements affecting the choice of a tool: Support for *custom schemas* and *multiple languages*. We defined eight additional criteria that could ease the annotation workflow, thus being potentially important for any project (Ide and Pustejovsky, 2017; Neves and Ševa, 2019). First, since annotation usually involves a team of experts, a tool should be *web-based* supporting *teams and roles* to enable remote collaboration and user rights settings (Ide and Pustejovsky, 2017). Second, following I1, it is essential that an annotation software reads and writes using *standard file formats*. Furthermore, a tool should support *importing/exporting multiple file formats* to allow integrating annotations with existing datasets or directly importing/exporting of data in a desired format. An application should also offer *document-level annotation* as document classification is one of the core NLP tasks. Additionally, given that the same object or entity can belong to various categories, support for *multi-label annotation* should be available. Built-in automatic *IAA score calculation* should be provided as well since it is fundamental for any annotation project. Finally, data under annotation can be sensitive (e. g., patient data) requiring certain privacy measures. Therefore, a tool should guarantee *data privacy* by possessing authentication and authorisation features along with the local installation option.

To test whether a tool complies with R3, we searched for information on the described features in both structured and unstructured metadata. The principle is fully fulfilled when all 10 community standards are met. Partial fulfilment is considered when a tool meets an established threshold based on the average number of fulfilled standards across the tools[16]. The threshold is equal to 6, thus a tool that meets less than 6 of the defined community standards fails R3.

4 Results

We present an assessment of 50 annotation tools based on the 17 FAIR4RS principles. The complete list of tools and the results are provided in Table 1. The annotation tools vary in terms of their complexity, license, supported features, and modalities (see Table 2).

According to our results, none of the tools fully adhere to all of the 17 principles. The maximum number of fulfilled principles across the tools is 13, while the minimum is 3. Out of 50 tools, 6 have reached the maximum of 13 and only one fulfills 3 principles. On average, tools comply with approximately 9 principles.

When it comes to *findability*, our analysis reveals that 29 annotation tools satisfy the requirements for F1, while the rest fall short as they are hosted on

[16]Note that a community standard is satisfied only when a tool fully supports a feature.

Tools	F1	F1.1	F1.2	F2	F3	F4	A1	A1.1	A1.2	A2	I1	I2	R1	R1.1	R1.2	R2	R3
INCEpTION (Klie et al., 2018)	✔	✔	✔	✔	✖	✔	✔	✔	✔	✔	✔	✔	★	✔	★	✔	★
brat (Stenetorp et al., 2012)	✔	✔	✖	✖	✖	✖	✔	✔	✔	✖	✔	✔	✖	✔	★	✔	★
Doccano (Nakayama et al., 2018)	✔	✔	✖	✔	✖	✔	✔	✔	✔	✔	✔	✔	★	✔	★	✔	★
BioQRator (Kwon et al., 2013)	✔	✔	✖	✖	✖	✖	✔	✔	✔	✖	✔	✔	✖	✔	✖	✔	✖
Catma (Gius et al., 2023)	✔	✔	✔	✖	✖	✔	✔	✔	✔	✔	✔	✔	✖	✔	★	✔	★
Djangology (Apostolova et al., 2010)	✖	✖	✖	✖	✖	✖	✔	✔	✔	✖	✔	✔	✖	✖	✖	✔	★
ezTag (Kwon et al., 2018)	✔	✔	✖	✖	✖	✖	✔	✔	✔	✖	✔	✔	✖	✖	✖	✔	✖
FLAT	✔	✔	✔	✔	✖	✔	✔	✔	✔	✔	✔	✔	✖	✔	✖	✔	★
LightTag (Perry, 2021)	✖	✖	✖	✖	✖	✖	✔	✔	✔	✖	★	✖	✖	✖	✖	✖	★
MAT	✖	✖	✖	✖	✖	✖	✔	✔	✔	✖	✔	✔	✖	✔	✖	✔	★
PDFAnno (Shindo et al., 2018)	✔	✔	✖	✔	✖	✔	✔	✔	✔	✔	✔	✔	✖	✔	✖	✔	✖
prodigy	✖	✖	✖	✖	✖	✖	✔	✔	✔	✖	✔	✔	✖	✖	✖	✔	★
TextAE	✔	✔	✔	✔	✖	✔	✔	✔	✔	✔	✔	✔	✖	✔	✖	✔	✖
WAT-SL (Kiesel et al., 2017)	✔	✔	✖	✖	✖	✔	✔	✔	✔	✔	✔	✔	✖	✔	✖	✔	✖
Hypothesis	✔	✔	✔	✔	✖	✔	✔	✔	✔	✔	★	✔	✖	✔	✖	✔	✖
Haystack	✔	✔	✔	✔	✖	✔	✔	✔	✔	✔	✔	✔	✖	✔	✖	✔	★
PDF sentence annotator	✖	✖	✖	✖	✖	✖	✔	✔	✔	✖	✔	✔	✖	✔	✖	✔	✖
PAWLS (Neumann et al., 2021)	✖	✖	✖	✖	✖	✔	✔	✔	✔	✖	✔	✔	✖	✔	✖	✔	✖
TeamTat (Islamaj et al., 2020)	✔	✔	✖	✖	✖	✔	✔	✔	✔	✔	✔	✔	✖	✔	✖	✔	★
TagEditor	✔	✔	✖	✖	✖	✖	✔	✔	✔	✖	✔	✔	✖	✔	✖	✔	★
TS-ANNO (Stodden and Kallmeyer, 2022)	✖	✖	✖	✖	✖	✖	✔	✔	✔	✖	✔	✔	✖	✔	✖	✔	✖
MedTator (He et al., 2022)	✖	✖	✖	✖	✖	✖	✔	✔	✔	✖	✔	✔	✖	✔	✖	✔	✖
DocTAG (Giachelle et al., 2022)	✔	✔	✔	✖	✖	✖	✔	✔	✔	✖	✔	✔	✖	✔	★	✔	✔
PubTator (Wei et al., 2013)	✖	✖	✖	✖	✖	✖	✔	✔	✔	✖	✔	✔	✖	✖	✖	✔	✖
Ellogon (Ntogramatzis et al., 2022)	✖	✖	✖	✖	✖	✖	✔	✔	✔	✖	✔	✔	✖	✔	✖	✔	★
Markup	✖	✖	✖	✖	✖	✔	✔	✔	✔	✖	★	✔	✖	✖	✖	✔	✖
Label Studio	✖	✖	✖	✔	✖	✔	✔	✔	✔	✖	✔	✔	✖	✔	✖	✔	★
MedTag (Giachelle et al., 2021)	✔	✔	✔	✖	✖	✖	✔	✔	✔	✖	✔	✔	✖	✔	★	✔	★
BAT (Meléndez-Catalán et al., 2017)	✔	✔	✖	✖	✖	✖	✔	✔	✔	✖	★	✔	✖	✔	✖	✔	✖
Seshat (Titeux et al., 2020)	✔	✔	✖	✖	✖	✖	✔	✔	✔	✖	★	✔	✖	✔	✖	✔	✖
VIA (Dutta and Zisserman, 2019)	✔	✔	✔	✖	✖	✖	✔	✔	✔	✖	✔	✔	✖	✔	✔	✔	✖
Potato (Pei et al., 2023)	✖	✖	✖	✔	✖	✔	✔	✔	✔	✖	✔	✔	✖	✔	✖	✔	★
Annotation Web (Smistad et al., 2021)	✖	✖	✖	✖	✖	✖	✔	✔	✔	✖	★	✔	✖	✔	✖	✔	✖
audino (Grover et al., 2020)	✔	✔	✖	✖	✖	✖	✔	✔	✔	✖	★	✔	✖	✔	✖	✔	✖
MATILDA	✖	✖	✖	✖	✖	✖	✔	✔	✔	✖	★	✔	✖	✔	✖	✔	★
ELAN (Wittenburg et al., 2006)	✖	✖	✖	✖	✖	✖	✔	✔	✔	✖	✔	✔	✖	✔	★	✔	✖
Praat (Boersma and Weenink, 2023)	✖	✖	✖	✖	✖	✖	✔	✔	✔	✖	✔	✔	✖	✔	✖	✔	✖
Pundit	✖	✖	✖	✖	✖	✔	✔	✔	✔	✖	★	✔	✖	✔	✖	✔	✖
UAM CorpusTool (O'Donnell, 2008)	✖	✖	✖	✖	✖	✖	✔	✔	✔	✖	✔	✔	✖	✖	✖	✔	✖
TIARA (Putra et al., 2020)	✔	✔	✖	✖	✖	✖	✔	✔	✔	✖	✔	✔	✖	✔	✖	✔	✖
COCO Annotator (Brooks, 2019)	✔	✔	✖	✖	✖	✖	✔	✔	✔	✖	★	✔	✖	✔	★	✔	✖
Gate Teamware (Karmakharm et al., 2023)	✔	✖	✔	✔	✖	✔	✔	✔	✔	✖	✔	✔	✖	✔	✖	✔	✔
ActiveAnno (Wiechmann et al., 2021)	✔	✔	✖	✖	✖	✔	✔	✔	✔	✔	✔	✔	✖	✔	✖	✔	★
YEDDA (Yang et al., 2018)	✔	✔	✔	✖	✖	✖	✔	✔	✔	✖	✔	✔	✖	✔	★	✔	✖
Textinator (Kalpakchi and Boye, 2022)	✔	✔	✖	✔	✖	✔	✔	✔	✔	✔	✔	✔	★	✔	★	✔	★
Argilla (Vila-Suero and Aranda, 2023)	✔	✔	✔	✔	✖	✔	✔	✔	✔	✔	✔	✔	★	✔	★	✔	★
Orbis Annotator (Süsstrunk et al., 2023)	✖	✖	✖	✖	✖	✔	✔	✔	✔	✖	✔	✔	✖	✔	✖	✔	✖
CVAT (Corporation, 2023)	✔	✔	✔	✔	✖	✔	✔	✔	✔	✔	✔	✔	✖	✔	✖	✔	★
DataGym.ai	✖	✖	✖	✖	✖	✔	✔	✔	✔	✖	✔	✔	✖	✔	✖	✔	✖
DeepLabel (Veitch-Michaelis, 2021)	✔	✔	✔	✖	✖	✖	✔	✔	✔	✖	✔	✔	✖	✔	✖	✔	✖

Table 1: **Annotation tools assessment results according to FAIR4RS principles.**
Symbols: ✔ = fulfills principle, ✖ = does not fulfill principle, ★ = partially fulfills principle.

platforms such as GitHub, GitLab[17], SourceForge, ELG, Hugging Face[18] or the official project website. The same set of tools except one adheres to F1.1. However, the number of applications meeting the criteria for F1.2 is considerably less and is equal to 14. This is due to cases where one version of a tool is published on Software Heritage/Zenodo but other releases are available on different platforms like GitHub. Only 13 tools adhere to F2, and the most frequently provided additional metadata for those is *dependencies*, *license*, *author*, and *version*. Several tools (8) fail the principle as they lack some of the required metadata, most commonly description and/or URL. Other software, with the exception of DataGym.ai, do not have structured metadata at all. None of the annotation tools comply with F3 due to one of the following reasons: 1. no semantically structured metadata is available, 2. the tool fails to meet F1, 3. PID exists but is not referenced in the metadata. Finally, less than half of the tools (22) have semantically structured metadata, and thus satisfy F4.

In terms of *accessibility*, all annotation tools fulfill A1-1.2 as they are retrievable without any restrictions via HTTP/HTTPs. However, only 14 tools comply with the A2 principle as they are available on Software Heritage. It is worth noting that only INCEpTION comes with structured metadata, published separately from the software on ELG.

Most tools fully support *interoperability* as they

[17]https://about.gitlab.com

[18]https://huggingface.co

Tools	Modality	License	Web-based	Custom schemas	Multiple languages	Users and roles	Standard file formats	Multiple file formats	Document-level annotation	Overlapping labels	IAA	Data privacy
INCEpTION	🗎	Apache-2.0	✔	✔	✔	✔	✔	✔	✖	✔	✔	✔
brat	🗎	MIT	✔	✔	✔	★	✔	✖	✖	✔	✖	✔
Doccano	🗎	MIT	✔	✔	✔	✔	✔	★	✔	✔	✖	✔
BioQRator	🗎	Apache-2.0	✔	✔	✖	★	✔	✔	✖	✖	✖	✖
Catma	🗎	GNU GPL-3.0	✔	✔	✔	✔	✔	✔	★	✔	✖	✖
Djangology	🗎	–	✔	✔	✖	✔	✔	✖	✖	✔	✔	✔
ezTag	🗎	–	✔	✔	✖	★	✔	✖	✖	✔	✖	✔
FLAT	🗎	GNU GPL-3.0	✔	✔	✔	✔	✔	✖	✖	✔	✖	✔
LightTag	🗎	–	✔	✔	✔	✔	★	★	✔	✔	✔	✔
MAT	🗎	BSD	✔	✔	✔	✖	✔	★	✔	✔	✖	✖
PDFAnno	🗎	MIT	✔	✖	✔	★	✔	✖	✖	✖	✖	✔
prodigy	🗎 📹 🎙 🖼	–	✔	✔	✔	★	✔	★	✔	✔	✔	✔
TextAE	🗎	MIT	✔	✔	✔	✖	✔	✖	✖	✖	✖	✔
WAT-SL	🗎	MIT	✔	✔	✖	★	✔	✖	✖	✖	✖	✔
Hypothesis	🗎	BSD-2-Clause	✔	✖	✖	★	★	★	✖	✖	✖	✖
Haystack	🗎	Apache-2.0	✔	✔	✔	✔	✔	★	✖	✔	✖	✔
PDF sentence annotator	🗎	Apache-2.0	✔	✖	✔	✖	✔	✖	✔	✔	✖	✖
PAWLS	🗎	Apache-2.0	✔	✖	✖	✖	✔	✖	✖	✔	★	✖
TeamTat	🗎	MIT	✔	✔	✔	✔	✔	★	✖	✔	✔	✖
TagEditor	🗎	MIT	✖	✖	✔	✖	✔	✔	✔	✔	✖	✔
TS-ANNO	🗎	GNU GPL-3.0	✔	✖	✔	✔	✔	★	✖	✖	✔	✔
MedTator	🗎	Apache-2.0	✔	✔	✖	✖	✔	✔	✔	✖	✔	✖
DocTAG	🗎	MIT	✔	✔	✔	✔	✔	✔	✔	✔	✔	✔
PubTator	🗎	–	✔	✖	✖	✖	✔	★	✖	✖	✖	✖
Ellogon	🗎	GNU LGPL-3.0	✔	✔	✖	✔	✔	✔	✔	✖	✔	✔
Markup	🗎	–	✔	✔	✖	★	★	✖	✖	✔	✖	✔
Label Studio	🗎 📹 🎙 🖼	Apache-2.0	✔	✔	✖	✔	✔	✔	✔	✔	✔	✔
MedTag	🗎	MIT	✔	✔	✔	✔	✔	★	✔	✔	✔	✔
BAT	🎙	GNU AGPL-3.0	✔	✔	✖	✔	★	✖	✖	★	✖	✔
Seshat	🎙	EUPL-1.2	✔	✔	✖	✔	★	★	✖	✖	✔	✔
VIA	📹 🎙 🖼	BSD-2-Clause	✔	✖	✖	✖	✔	★	✖	✖	✖	✔
Potato	🗎 📹 🖼	Polyform Shield	✔	✔	✔	★	✔	✔	✔	✖	✖	✔
Annotation Web	🖼	MIT	✔	✖	✖	✔	★	✖	✔	✖	✖	✔
audino	🎙	MIT	✔	✔	✔	✔	★	✖	✖	✖	✖	✔
MATILDA	🗎	GNU GPL-2.0	✔	✔	✔	✔	★	✖	✔	✖	✖	✔
ELAN	📹 🎙	GPL-3.0	✖	✔	✔	✖	✔	★	✖	✖	✖	✔
Praat	🎙	GNU GPL	✖	✔	✔	✖	✔	★	✖	✖	✖	✔
Pundit	🗎	GNU AGPL-3.0	✔	✖	✖	★	★	★	✖	✖	✖	✖
UAM CorpusTool	🗎	–	✖	✔	✖	✖	✔	✖	✔	✔	✖	✔
TIARA	🗎	MIT	✔	✔	✖	✖	✔	★	✖	✖	✖	✔
COCO Annotator	🖼	MIT	✔	✔	✖	✔	★	★	✖	✔	✖	✔
Gate Teamware	🗎	GNU AGPL-3.0	✔	✔	✔	✔	✔	✔	✔	✔	✔	✔
ActiveAnno	🗎	MIT	✔	✖	✔	✔	✔	✖	✔	✖	✔	✔
YEDDA	🗎	Apache-2.0	✖	✖	✔	★	✔	✖	✖	✖	✖	✔
Textinator	🗎	GNU AGPL-3.0	✔	✔	✔	✔	✔	★	✔	✖	✖	✔
Argilla	🗎	Apache-2.0	✔	✔	✔	✔	✔	★	✔	✔	✖	✔
Orbis Annotator	🗎	Apache-2.0	✔	✖	✖	★	✔	✔	✖	✖	✖	✔
CVAT	📹 🖼	MIT	✔	✔	✖	✔	✔	✔	✖	✖	✖	✔
DataGym.ai	📹 🖼	MIT	✔	✔	✖	✔	✔	✖	✖	✖	✖	✔
DeepLabel	📹 🖼	MIT	✖	✔	✖	✖	✔	✔	✖	✔	✖	✔

Table 2: **Evaluation criteria for FAIR4RS principle R3 along with details on modality and license.** Symbols: 🗎 = text, 📹 = video, 🎙 = audio, 🖼 = image, ✔ = fulfills criterion, ✖ = does not fulfill criterion, ★ = partially fulfills criterion.

fulfill both I1 and I2. In particular, 40 annotation tools support standard data formats for both input and output. Only 10 tools partially adhere to I1, most of which (9 tools) do not provide details on either input or output formats, and one application (Pundit) writes data into notebooks that are not considered standard. All but one annotation software (LightTag) fulfill I2 by offering qualified reference to other objects in either structured JSON/XML metadata files or in unstructured documentation using standard naming conventions. Commonly referenced objects are programming languages, compatible browsers, and datasets.

Assessing *reusability*, we note that none of the tools fully comply with R1 as they fail F2 or R1.2. There are 11 tools that achieve partial fulfillment. The majority of tools (43) provide a clear description of the license in either semantically structured or unstructured metadata, thereby adhering to R1.1. However, only 12 tools offer license information in both metadata types. Most annotation tools (31) specify license in unstructured README/LICENSE files or on the project webpage. Doccano, Textinator, and Gate Teamware do not update license information in a structured metadata file. In terms of provenance, only VIA fully complies with R1.2. There are 11 tools that partially adhere to the principle since they provide citation information and details on origin, development history, and/or contributors/authors. The remaining software either have minimal provenance, limited to release history or authors/contributors or lack it entirely. Similar to the I2 principle, only LighTag fails to satisfy the criteria for R2.

Finally, when it comes to R3, results indicate that only DocTAG and Gate Teamware fully fulfil it. Among the rest of the tools, 21 have partial compliance and 27 fail the principle. Table 2 presents an overview of the results per application and community standard. As can be seen, most of the tools (44) are web-based. However, only 25 of those support users and roles, while 12 allow collaborative work but do not offer user rights functionality. For the remaining 13 tools, either no information on this feature was available or it was clear from the software architecture that there is no support for teams and roles (e. g., ELAN, PDF sentence annotator). A vast majority of the tools (37) allow custom ontologies/schemas and about half of them (27) are compatible with several languages. A limited number of annotation tools (13) offer data import and export in multiple file formats, while 19 applications partially fulfill the criteria as details on either only input or output were found. As was already discussed above, 40 tools support standard file formats. Table 2 also demonstrates that 19 tools allow document-level annotation. Only Catma partially supports this feature since a user has to manually highlight the whole text. Overlapping labels functionality is available for almost half of the tools (24). BAT is a single tool that partially meets the criteria as the overlaps have to be resolved before finishing annotating. Less than half of tools (14) include built-in IAA calculation. In the case of PAWLS, IAA is available but not integrated into the tool (the score can be computed separately through the command line interface). Hence, we categorise it as a partial fulfillment. Finally, 40 tools ensure data privacy since they either allow local installation and/or require a user to log into the system.

5 Discussion

The FAIRness assessment indicates that while annotation tools are accessible and interoperable, there is a strong need for improving their findability and reusability. In particular, a large number of tools lack PIDs on various levels (files, releases, etc.). Even in cases when an annotation software possesses a PID, there is no reference to it in the respective metadata. These factors hinder the accurate and unambiguous citation of a tool as well as tracking its developmental changes over time.

The results also show that the vast majority of annotation software suffers from the absence of semantically structured metadata. As was noted in Section 4, even if there is one, some details such as license or input/output data formats tend to be provided in unstructured formats. Furthermore, such tools do not have structured metadata published separately either. Consequently, tools are less discoverable and linkable to other related systems. It becomes difficult to reuse and replicate these annotation applications without delving into the implementation details or testing them. The situation is even worse when it comes to provenance descriptions. Most tools do not have fine-grained documentation of their origin and development history. The lack of sufficient provenance information contributes to low reproducibility and makes it difficult to build upon existing annotation tools.

Additionally, there is a clear need for agreed-upon community standards and best practices regarding annotation tools functionalities, metadata vocabulary and import/export file formats. The absence of those influenced the assessment results.

6 Limitations

While our analysis is rather comprehensive, it is not without limitations. First, the manual approach to evaluation is error prone. It would be beneficial to align our findings with the results from automatic FAIRness assessment solutions, namely using howfairis (at least for tools hosted on GitHub/GitLab). Second, tools were not tested with respect to their executability. Thus, there is no guarantee that all surveyed tools can actually be installed and run properly. This also means that a tool could possibly have a specific feature but it is not stated in its metadata. Third, when it comes to annotation tools, not only the software itself should be FAIR but the labelled data it produces should be FAIR, too. However, the FAIRness evaluation of annotated data produced by or with annotation tools is out of scope with regard to this study and we leave it for future work. Finally, as previously noted, the FAIR4RS principles are aspirational in nature. Thus, the interpretations defined in this paper should be treated as initial suggestions rather than rigid definitions.

7 Conclusion

In this paper, we investigated how annotation tools comply with the FAIR4RS principles. We performed a manual evaluation of 50 tools following interpretations of the FAIR4RS principles adapted specifically to annotation software. The findings reveal that the findability and reusability of annotation tools require improvement. Specifically, the lack of PIDs, semantically structured metadata and detailed provenance are the most problematic aspects. Additionally, the study shows that there is a demand for agreed-upon community standards for annotation software management.

Ethics Statement

No private or sensitive data was used, stored or shared during this study.

Acknowledgements

The research presented in this article was supported by the consortium NFDI for Data Science and Artificial Intelligence (NFDI4DS)[19] as part of the non-profit association National Research Data Infrastructure (NFDI e. V.). The NFDI is funded by the Federal Republic of Germany and its states. The paper received funding through the German Research Foundation (DFG) project NFDI4DS (no. 460234259). The authors wish to thank both for funding and support. A special thanks goes to all institutions and actors engaging for the association and its goals.

References

Katherine Akers and Jennifer Doty. 2013. Disciplinary differences in faculty research data management practices and perspectives. *International Journal of Digital Curation*, 8(2):5–26.

Khaled Alhazmi, Walaa Alsumari, Indrek Seppo, Lara Podkuiko, and Martin Simon. 2021. Effects of annotation quality on model performance. In *2021 International Conference on Artificial Intelligence in Information and Communication (ICAIIC)*, pages 063–067.

Manar Aljabri, Manal AlAmir, Manal AlGhamdi, Mohamed Abdel-Mottaleb, and Fernando Collado-Mesa. 2022. Towards a better understanding of annotation tools for medical imaging: A survey. *Multimedia Tools and Applications*, 81(18):25877–25911.

Emilia Apostolova, Sean Neilan, Gary An, Noriko Tomuro, and Steven Lytinen. 2010. Djangology: A light-weight web-based tool for distributed collaborative text annotation. In *Proceedings of the Seventh International Conference on Language Resources and Evaluation (LREC'10)*, Valletta, Malta. European Language Resources Association (ELRA).

[19] `https://www.nfdi4datascience.de`

Michelle Barker, Neil P. Chue Hong, Daniel S. Katz, Anna-Lena Lamprecht, Carlos Martinez-Ortiz, Fotis Psomopoulos, Jennifer Harrow, Leyla Jael Castro, Morane Gruenpeter, Paula Andrea Martinez, and Tom Honeyman. 2022. Introducing the FAIR principles for research software. *Scientific Data*, 9(622).

Paul Boersma and David Weenink. 2023. Praat: Doing phonetics by computer [computer program].

Justin Brooks. 2019. COCO annotator.

Neil P. Chue Hong, Daniel S. Katz, Michelle Barker, Anna-Lena Lamprecht, Carlos Martinez, Fotis E. Psomopoulos, Jen Harrow, Leyla Jael Castro, Morane Gruenpeter, Paula Andrea Martinez, Tom Honeyman, Alexander Struck, Allen Lee, Axel Loewe, Ben van Werkhoven, Catherine Jones, Daniel Garijo, Esther Plomp, Francoise Genova, Hugh Shanahan, Joanna Leng, Maggie Hellström, Malin Sandström, Manodeep Sinha, Mateusz Kuzak, Patricia Herterich, Qian Zhang, Sharif Islam, Susanna-Assunta Sansone, Tom Pollard, Udayanto Dwi Atmojo, Alan Williams, Andreas Czerniak, Anna Niehues, Anne Claire Fouilloux, Bala Desinghu, Carole Goble, Céline Richard, Charles Gray, Chris Erdmann, Daniel Nüst, Daniele Tartarini, Elena Ranguelova, Hartwig Anzt, Ilian Todorov, James McNally, Javier Moldon, Jessica Burnett, Julián Garrido-Sánchez, Khalid Belhajjame, Laurents Sesink, Lorraine Hwang, Marcos Roberto Tovani-Palone, Mark D. Wilkinson, Mathieu Servillat, Matthias Liffers, Merc Fox, Nadica Miljković, Nick Lynch, Paula Martinez Lavanchy, Sandra Gesing, Sarah Stevens, Sergio Martinez Cuesta, Silvio Peroni, Stian Soiland-Reyes, Tom Bakker, Tovo Rabemanantsoa, Vanessa Sochat, Yo Yehudi, and RDA FAIR4RS WG. 2022. FAIR principles for research software (FAIR4RS principles). Zenodo.

CVAT.ai Corporation. 2023. Computer vision annotation tool (CVAT). Zenodo.

Stamatia Dasiopoulou, Eirini Giannakidou, Georgios Litos, Polyxeni Malasioti, and Yiannis Kompatsiaris. 2011. A survey of semantic image and video annotation tools. In Georgios Paliouras, Constantine D. Spyropoulos, and George Tsatsaronis, editors, *Knowledge-Driven Multimedia Information Extraction and Ontology Evolution: Bridging the Semantic Gap*, pages 196–239. Springer Berlin Heidelberg, Berlin, Heidelberg.

Taco de Bruin, Sarah Coombs, Jutta de Jong, Irene Haslinger, Henk van den Hoogen, Frans Huigen, Mijke Jetten, Jacko Koster, Margriet Miedema, Sjef Öllers, Inge Slouwerhof, Ingeborg Verheul, and Jacquelijn Ringersma. 2020. Do I-PASS for FAIR. A self assessment tool to measure the FAIR-ness of an organization. Zenodo.

Abhishek Dutta and Andrew Zisserman. 2019. The VIA annotation software for images, audio and video. In *Proceedings of the 27th ACM International Conference on Multimedia*. ACM.

Richard Eckart de Castilho, Éva Mújdricza-Maydt, Seid Muhie Yimam, Silvana Hartmann, Iryna Gurevych, Anette Frank, and Chris Biemann. 2016. A web-based tool for the integrated annotation of semantic and syntactic structures. In *Proceedings of the Workshop on Language Technology Resources and Tools for Digital Humanities (LT4DH)*, pages 76–84, Osaka, Japan. The COLING 2016 Organizing Committee.

Alban Gaignard, Thomas Rosnet, Frédéric De Lamotte, Vincent Lefort, and Marie-Dominique Devignes. 2023. FAIR-Checker: Supporting digital resource findability and reuse with knowledge graphs and semantic web standards. *Journal of Biomedical Semantics*, 14(7).

Fabio Giachelle, Ornella Irrera, and Gianmaria Silvello. 2021. Medtag: A portable and customizable annotation tool for biomedical documents. *BMC Medical Informatics and Decision Making*, 21.

Fabio Giachelle, Ornella Irrera, and Gianmaria Silvello. 2022. Doctag: A customizable annotation tool for ground truth creation. In *Advances in Information Retrieval: 44th European Conference on IR Research, ECIR 2022, Stavanger, Norway, April 10–14, 2022, Proceedings, Part II*, volume 13186 of *Lecture Notes in Computer Science*, pages 288–293. Springer.

Evelyn Gius, Jan Christoph Meister, Malte Meister, Marco Petris, Mareike Schumacher, and Dominik Gerstorfer. 2023. Catma. Zenodo.

Manraj Singh Grover, Pakhi Bamdev, Yaman Kumar Singla, Mika Hama, and Rajiv Ratn Shah. 2020. audino: A modern annotation tool for audio and speech. *arXiv*, abs/2006.05236.

Degan Hao, Lei Zhang, Jules Sumkin, Aly Mohamed, and Shandong Wu. 2020. Inaccurate labels in weakly-supervised deep learning: Automatic identification and correction and their impact on classification performance. *IEEE Journal of Biomedical and Health Informatics*, 24(9):2701–2710.

Huan He, Sunyang Fu, Liwei Wang, Sijia Liu, Andrew Wen, and Hongfang Liu. 2022. Medtator: A serverless annotation tool for corpus development. *Bioinformatics*, 38(6):1776–1778.

Nancy Ide and James Pustejovsky. 2017. *Handbook of Linguistic Annotation*. Heidelberg: Springer.

Rezarta Islamaj, Dongseop Kwon, Sun Kim, and Zhiyong Lu. 2020. Teamtat: A collaborative text annotation tool. *Nucleic Acids Research*, 48(W1):W5–W11.

Dmytro Kalpakchi and Johan Boye. 2022. Textinator: An internationalized tool for annotation and human evaluation in natural language processing and generation. In *Proceedings of the Thirteenth Language Resources and Evaluation Conference*, pages 856–866, Marseille, France. European Language Resources Association.

Twin Karmakharm, David Wilby, Ian Roberts, and Kalina Bontcheva. 2023. GATE teamware 2. Zenodo.

Daniel S. Katz, Morane Gruenpeter, and Tom Honeyman. 2021. Taking a fresh look at FAIR for research software. *Patterns*, 2(3):100222.

Daniel S. Katz, Kyle E. Niemeyer, Arfon M. Smith, William L. Anderson, Carl Boettiger, Konrad Hinsen, Rob Hooft, Michael Hucka, Allen Lee, Frank Löffler, Tom Pollard, and Fernando Rios. 2016. Software vs. data in the context of citation. *PeerJ Preprints*, 4(e2630v1).

Johannes Kiesel, Henning Wachsmuth, Khalid Al-Khatib, and Benno Stein. 2017. WAT-SL: A customizable web annotation tool for segment labeling. In *Proceedings of the Software Demonstrations of the 15th Conference of the European Chapter of the Association for Computational Linguistics*, pages 13–16, Valencia, Spain. Association for Computational Linguistics.

Jan-Christoph Klie, Michael Bugert, Beto Boullosa, Richard Eckart de Castilho, and Iryna Gurevych. 2018. The inception platform: Machine-assisted and knowledge-oriented interactive annotation. In *Proceedings of the 27th International Conference on Computational Linguistics: System Demonstrations*, pages 5–9.

Dongseop Kwon, Sun Kim, Soo Yong Shin, and John Wilbur. 2013. Bioqrator: A web-based interactive biomedical literature curating system.

Dongseop Kwon, Sun Kim, Chih-Hsuan Wei, Robert Leaman, and Zhiyong Lu. 2018. eztag: Tagging biomedical concepts via interactive learning. *Nucleic Acids Research*, 46(W1):W523–W529.

Anna-Lena Lamprecht, Leyla Garcia, Mateusz Kuzak, Carlos Martinez, Ricardo Arcila, Eva Martin Del Pico, Victoria Dominguez Del Angel, Stephanie van de Sandt, Jon Ison, Paula Andrea Martinez, Peter McQuilton, Alfonso Valencia, Jennifer Harrow, Fotis Psomopoulos, Josep Ll. Gelpi, Neil Chue Hong, Carole Goble, and Salvador Capella-Gutierrez. 2020. Towards FAIR principles for research software. *Data Science*, 3(1):37–59.

Michele Larobina and Loredana Murino. 2014. Medical image file formats. *Journal of Digital Imaging*, 27:200–206.

Blai Meléndez-Catalán, Emilio Molina, and Emilia Gómez. 2017. Bat: An open-source, web-based audio events annotation tool. In *Proceedings of the 3rd Web Audio Conference*.

Hiroki Nakayama, Takahiro Kubo, Junya Kamura, Yasufumi Taniguchi, and Xu Liang. 2018. doccano: Text annotation tool for human. Software available from `https://github.com/doccano/doccano`.

Mark Neumann, Zejiang Shen, and Sam Skjonsberg. 2021. PAWLS: PDF annotation with labels and structure. *arXiv*.

Mariana Neves and Ulf Leser. 2012. A survey on annotation tools for the biomedical literature. *Briefings in Bioinformatics*, 15(2):327–340.

Mariana Neves and Jurica Ševa. 2019. An extensive review of tools for manual annotation of documents. *Briefings in Bioinformatics*, 22(1):146–163.

Lyndon Nixon and Raphaël Troncy. 2014. Survey of semantic media annotation tools for the web: Towards new media applications with linked media. In *The Semantic Web: ESWC 2014 Satellite Events*, pages 100–114, Cham. Springer International Publishing.

Alexandros Fotios Ntogramatzis, Anna Gradou, Georgios Petasis, and Marko Kokol. 2022. The ellogon web annotation tool: Annotating moral values and arguments. In *Proceedings of the Thirteenth Language Resources and Evaluation Conference*, pages 3442–3450, Marseille, France. European Language Resources Association.

Michael O'Donnell. 2008. The UAM CorpusTool: Software for corpus annotation and exploration. In Carmen M. Bretones Callejas, José Francisco Fernández Sánchez, José Ramón Ibáñez Ibáñez, María Elena García Sánchez, Ma Enriqueta Cortés de los Ríos, Sagrario Salaberri Ramiro, Ma Soledad Cruz Martínez, Nobel Perdú Honeyman, and Blasina Cantizano Márquez, editors, *Applied Linguistics Now: Understanding Language and Mind / La Lingüística Aplicada Hoy: Comprendiendo el Lenguaje y la Mente*, pages 1433–1447. Universidad de Almería.

Pedro Oliveira and João Rocha. 2013. Semantic annotation tools survey. In *2013 IEEE Symposium on Computational Intelligence and Data Mining (CIDM)*, pages 301–307.

Sinno Jialin Pan and Qiang Yang. 2010. A survey on transfer learning. *IEEE Transactions on Knowledge and Data Engineering*, 22(10):1345–1359.

Bhavesh Patel, Sanjay Soundarajan, Hervé Ménager, and Zicheng Hu. 2023. Making biomedical research software FAIR: Actionable step-by-step guidelines with a user-support tool. *Scientific Data*, 10(557).

Jiaxin Pei, Aparna Ananthasubramaniam, Xingyao Wang, Naitian Zhou, Jackson Sargent, Apostolos Dedeloudis, and David Jurgens. 2023. Potato: The portable text annotation tool. *arXiv*.

Tal Perry. 2021. Lighttag: Text annotation platform. *arXiv*.

Jan Wira Gotama Putra, Simone Teufel, Kana Matsumura, and Takenobu Tokunaga. 2020. TIARA: A tool for annotating discourse relations and sentence reordering. In *Proceedings of the Twelfth Language Resources and Evaluation Conference*, pages 6912–6920, Marseille, France. European Language Resources Association.

Georg Rehm. 2016. The language resource life cycle: Towards a generic model for creating, maintaining, using and distributing language resources. In *Proceedings of the Tenth International Conference on Language Resources and Evaluation (LREC'16)*, pages 2450–2454, Portorož, Slovenia. European Language Resources Association (ELRA).

Georg Rehm. 2020. Observations on annotations. In Julia Nantke and Frederik Schlupkothen, editors, *Annotations in Scholarly Edition and Research. Functions, Differentiation, Systematization*, pages 299–324. De Gruyter, Berlin, Boston.

Georg Rehm, editor. 2023. *European Language Grid: A language technology platform for multilingual europe*. Cognitive Technologies. Springer, Cham, Switzerland.

Burr Settles. 2009. Active learning literature survey. *University of Wisconsin-Madison Department of Computer Sciences*.

Hiroyuki Shindo, Yohei Munesada, and Yuji Matsumoto. 2018. PDFAnno: A web-based linguistic annotation tool for PDF documents. In *Proceedings of the Eleventh International Conference on Language Resources and Evaluation (LREC 2018)*, Miyazaki, Japan. European Language Resources Association (ELRA).

Erik Smistad, Andreas Østvik, and Lasse Løvstakken. 2021. Annotation web - an open-source web-based annotation tool for ultrasound images. In *2021 IEEE International Ultrasonics Symposium (IUS)*, pages 1–4.

Jurriaan H. Spaaks, Stefan Verhoeven, Erik Tjong Kim Sang, Faruk Diblen, Carlos Martinez-Ortiz, Edidiong Etuk, Mateusz Kuzak, Ben Werkhoven, Abel Soares Siqueira, Shyam Saladi, and Andrew Holding. 2022. howfairis.

Pontus Stenetorp, Sampo Pyysalo, Goran Topić, Tomoko Ohta, Sophia Ananiadou, and Jun'ichi Tsujii. 2012. brat: a web-based tool for NLP-assisted text annotation. In *Proceedings of the Demonstrations at the 13th Conference of the European Chapter of the Association for Computational Linguistics*, pages 102–107, Avignon, France. Association for Computational Linguistics.

Regina Stodden and Laura Kallmeyer. 2022. TS-ANNO: An annotation tool to build, annotate and evaluate text simplification corpora. In *Proceedings of the 60th Annual Meeting of the Association for Computational Linguistics: System Demonstrations*, pages 145–155, Dublin, Ireland. Association for Computational Linguistics.

Norman Süsstrunk, Andreas Fraefel, Albert Weichselbraun, and Adrian M. P. Brasoveanu. 2023. Orbis annotator: An open source toolkit for the efficient annotation and refinement of text. In *Proceedings of the 4th Conference on Language, Data and Knowledge*, pages 294–305, Vienna, Austria. NOVA CLUNL, Portugal.

Hadrien Titeux, Rachid Riad, Xuan-Nga Cao, Nicolas Hamilakis, Kris Madden, Alejandrina Cristia, Anne-Catherine Bachoud-Lévi, and Emmanuel Dupoux. 2020. Seshat: A tool for managing and verifying annotation campaigns of audio data. In *Proceedings of the Twelfth Language Resources and Evaluation Conference*, pages 6976–6982, Marseille, France. European Language Resources Association.

Maxim Tkachenko, Mikhail Malyuk, Andrey Holmanyuk, and Nikolai Liubimov. 2020-2022. Label Studio: Data labeling software. Open source software available from `https://github.com/heartexlabs/label-studio`.

Brian Vander Schee. 2009. Crowdsourcing: Why the power of the crowd is driving the future of business. *Journal of Consumer Marketing*, 26:305–306.

Josh Veitch-Michaelis. 2021. jveitch-michaelis/deeplabel: v0.16.1. Zenodo.

Daniel Vila-Suero and Francisco Aranda. 2023. Argilla - open-source framework for data-centric NLP.

Chih-Hsuan Wei, Hung-Yu kao, and Zhiyong Lu. 2013. Pubtator: A web-based text mining tool for assisting biocuration. *Nucleic Acids Research*, 41:W518–W522.

Max Wiechmann, Seid Muhie Yimam, and Chris Biemann. 2021. ActiveAnno: General-purpose document-level annotation tool with active learning integration. In *Proceedings of the 2021 Conference of the North American Chapter of the Association for Computational Linguistics: Human Language Technologies: Demonstrations*, pages 99–105, Online. Association for Computational Linguistics.

Mark D. Wilkinson, Michel Dumontier, I. Jsbrand Jan Aalbersberg, Gabrielle Appleton, Myles Axton, Arie Baak, Niklas Blomberg, Jan-Willem Boiten, Luiz Bonino da Silva Santos, Philip E. Bourne, Jildau Bouwman, Anthony J. Brookes, Tim Clark, Mercè Crosas, Ingrid Dillo, Olivier Dumon, Scott Edmunds, Chris T. Evelo, Richard Finkers, Alejandra Gonzalez-Beltran, Alasdair J. G. Gray, Paul Groth, Carole Goble, Jeffrey S. Grethe, Jaap Heringa, Peter A. C 't Hoen, Rob Hooft, Tobias Kuhn, Ruben Kok, Joost Kok, Scott J. Lusher, Maryann E. Martone, Albert Mons, Abel L. Packer, Bengt Persson, Philippe Rocca-Serra, Marco Roos, Rene van Schaik, Susanna-Assunta Sansone, Erik Schultes, Thierry Sengstag, Ted Slater, George Strawn, Morris A. Swertz, Mark Thompson, Johan van der Lei, Erik van Mulligen, Jan Velterop, Andra Waagmeester, Peter Wittenburg, Katherine Wolstencroft, Jun Zhao, and Barend Mons. 2016. The FAIR guiding principles for scientific data management and stewardship. *Scientific Data*, 3(160018).

Mark D. Wilkinson, Michel Dumontier, Susanna-Assunta Sansone, Luiz Olavo Bonino da Silva Santos, Mario Prieto, Dominique Batista, Peter McQuilton, Tobias Kuhn, Philippe Rocca-Serra, Mercè Crosas, and Erik Schultes. 2019. Evaluating FAIR maturity through a scalable, automated, community-governed framework. *Scientific Data*, 6:2052–4463.

Peter Wittenburg, Hennie Brugman, Albert Russel, Alex Klassmann, and Han Sloetjes. 2006. ELAN: A professional framework for multimodality research. In *Proceedings of the Fifth International Conference on Language Resources and Evaluation (LREC'06)*, Genoa, Italy. European Language Resources Association (ELRA).

Jie Yang, Yue Zhang, Linwei Li, and Xingxuan Li. 2018. Yedda: A lightweight collaborative text span annotation tool. In *Proceedings of the 56th Annual Meeting of the Association for Computational Linguistics*.

A FAIR4RS Principles Interpretations

F: Software, and its associated metadata, is easy for both humans and machines to find.

Principle	Interpretation
F1. Software is assigned a globally unique and persistent identifier.	An annotation tool should have a globally unique and persistent identifier (PID), such as Digital Object Identifier (DOI), which assures longevity and consistently points to the software despite changes in its location, content or other attributes.
F1.1. Components of the software representing levels of granularity are assigned distinct identifiers.	In addition to the annotation tool itself, distinct PIDs should be assigned to all its components (files, directories, commits, releases, and other attributes).
F1.2. Different versions of the software are assigned distinct identifiers.	Each release of an annotation tool should be assigned a distinct PID allowing users to track its development and refer to a specific version they utilised.
F2. Software is described with rich metadata.	Metadata should be semantically structured, i. e., being both human and machine-readable. It should contain a thorough description of an annotation tool allowing users to understand how to utilise and replicate it without looking into its source code. Metadata is considered to be rich when it goes beyond basic information. Following Bioschemas ComputationalTool, the minimum metadata of an annotation tool should include *name*, *URL*, and *description*. The metadata is considered to be rich if at least one additional property from any marginality level is provided.
F3. Metadata clearly and explicitly include the identifier of the software they describe.	If an annotation tool is assigned a PID, it should be referenced by it in the respective structured metadata. Thus, in case F1 is not fulfilled, F3 fails as well.
F4. Metadata are FAIR, searchable and indexable.	Metadata is FAIR when it is semantically structured. Therefore, if an annotation tool fails F2 due to the lack of structured metadata, it automatically fails F4. Any metadata exposed via web pages in a format understood by search engines or deposited in a repository/registry with search functionality is indexable.

A: Software, and its metadata, is retrievable via standardized protocols.

Principle	Interpretation
A1. Software is retrievable by its identifier using a standardised communications protocol.	An annotation tool should be accessed through a commonly used communication protocol such as Hypertext Transfer Protocol (HTTP), Hypertext Transfer Protocol Secure (HTTPS) or File Transfer Protocol (FTP).
A1.1. The protocol is open, free, and universally implementable.	There should be no restrictions and fees to implement the communication protocol.
A1.2. The protocol allows for an authentication and authorisation procedure, where necessary.	The protocol should include mechanisms to verify the identity of users and to determine their access rights where necessary. Authentication and authorisation are supported by HTTP/HTTPS and FTP protocols, therefore if an annotation tool is retrievable via those, it automatically fulfills A1.2.
A2. Metadata are accessible, even when the software is no longer available.	As software tend to be deprecated over time, ideally structured metadata should be published separately with its own PID. In practice, it is often embedded into the source code of software. Therefore, this principle is satisfied when metadata is assigned a distinct PID and published either separately from a tool or along with it on an archive which ensures longevity.

I: Software interoperates with other software by exchanging data and/or metadata, and/or through interaction via application programming interfaces (APIs), described through standards.

I1. Software reads, writes and exchanges data in a way that meets domain-relevant community standards.	Currently, there do not seem to be well-defined standards for annotation tools' input/output formats. The formats vary depending on the input modality, domain, and specific task at hand. Thus, input formats for text documents include *DOC*, *PDF*, *TXT*, *RTF*, *CSV*, *TSV*, *XML*, and *JSON*. Audio inputs are commonly available in *WAV*, *MP3*, *OGG*, *AIF*, and *FLAC*. Image inputs tend to be *PNG*, *JPEG*, and *JPG*, while video data typically comes as *MPEG*, *DIVX*, *AVI*, and *MOV*. Semantic annotation outputs are usually in *XML* (or *XMI*), *RDF*, *RDFa*, *RDFS*, *OWL*, *CSV*, *TXT*, *JSON*, *TEI*, *EAF*, *CMML*, *IRI*, *SMIL*, and *TFRecord* formats. The principle is considered to be fully fulfilled if an annotation tool supports at least one of the standard formats for both input and output.
I2. Software includes qualified references to other objects.	This principle calls for references to any objects other than software such as datasets, hardware, programming language, operating system or browser. Qualified references include identifiers (URLs, PIDs, etc.) and controlled vocabularies.
R: Software is both usable (can be executed) and reusable (can be understood, modified, built upon, or incorporated into other software).	
R1. Software is described with a plurality of accurate and relevant attributes.	An annotation tool should be described in terms of metadata categories (F2), license (R1.1), and provenance (R1.2). The relevance of attributes is usually determined by repositories and/or communities that create and use a tool. Whenever feasible, multiple terms for the same, similar or overlapping concepts should be provided to allow reuse. However, to the best of our knowledge, there are no community-agreed standards for the metadata vocabulary of annotation tools. Therefore, R1 is considered to be fulfilled if a tool fully adheres to F2, R1.1 and R1.2.
R1.1. Software is given a clear and accessible license.	The annotation tool's license should be clearly stated in either structured or unstructured metadata.
R1.2. Software is associated with detailed provenance.	This principle calls for an explanation of the annotation tool's origins and development history. To this end, structured or unstructured metadata should provide answers to the following questions: *Why and how a tool came to be? Who contributed what, when, and where? How to cite a tool?*
R2. Software includes qualified references to other software.	As with any other software, annotation tools usually have dependencies. Thus, qualified references to other software (e. g., libraries, packages) should be provided in either structured or unstructured metadata.
R3. Software meets domain-relevant community standards.	Currently, there do not seem to be well-established community standards for annotation tools. The desired capabilities of software are influenced by the annotation project scope and goals. However, there are ten essential functionalities that ideally should be incorporated into an annotation tool for an easier user experience: 1. custom schemas support, 2. multilingual support, 3. web-based access, 4. support for teams and roles, 5. support for standard input/output file formats, 6. allowance for import/export of multiple file formats, 7. allowance for document-level annotation, 8. support for multi-label annotation, 9. allowance for automatic IAA score calculation, 10. data privacy support.

Table 3: Interpretations of the FAIR4RS principles (Chue Hong et al., 2022) tailored to the specific use-case of annotation tools.

B Metadata Sources

Annotation tool	Unstructured metadata	Structured metadata
INCEpTION (Klie et al., 2018)	README, Documentation	GitHub, ELG
brat	README, Documentation	–
Doccano	README	GitHub
BioQRator (Kwon et al., 2013)	README, Documentation	–
Catma (Gius et al., 2023)	README, Documentation	GitHub
Djangology (Apostolova et al., 2010)	SourceForge	–
ezTag (Kwon et al., 2018)	README, Documentation	–
FLAT	README, Documentation	GitHub
LightTag (Perry, 2021)	Documentation	–
MAT	Documentation	–
PDFAnno (Shindo et al., 2018)	README	GitHub
prodigy	–	–
TextAE	Documentation	GitHub
WAT-SL	README	GitHub
Hypothesis	GitHub, Homepage	GitHub
Haystack	README, Documentation	GitHub
PDF sentence annotator	README	–
PAWLS (Neumann et al., 2021)	README	GitHub
TeamTat (Islamaj et al., 2020)	README, Documentation	GitHub
TagEditor	README	–
TS-ANNO (Stodden and Kallmeyer, 2022)	README	–
MedTator (He et al., 2022)	README	–
DocTAG (Giachelle et al., 2022)	README	–
PubTator	–	–
Ellogon (Ntogramatzis et al., 2022)	ELG, Documentation	–
Markup	README	GitHub
Label Studio	README, Documentation	GitHub
MedTag (Giachelle et al., 2021)	README	–
BAT (Meléndez-Catalán et al., 2017)	README	–
Seshat (Titeux et al., 2020)	README, Documentation	–
VIA (Dutta and Zisserman, 2019)	README, Homepage	–
Potato (Pei et al., 2023)	README, Documentation	GitHub
Annotation Web (Smistad et al., 2021)	README	–
audino (Grover et al., 2020)	README	–
MATILDA	README	–
ELAN (Wittenburg et al., 2006)	Homepage, Documentation	–
Praat (Boersma and Weenink, 2023)	README, Documentation	–
Pundit	README	GitHub
UAM CorpusTool (O'Donnell, 2008)	Homepage	–
TIARA (Putra et al., 2020)	README, Documentation	–
COCO Annotator (Brooks, 2019)	README	–
Gate Teamware (Karmakharm et al., 2023)	README, Homepage, Documentation	GitHub
ActiveAnno (Wiechmann et al., 2021)	README	GitHub
YEDDA (Yang et al., 2018)	README	–
Textinator (Kalpakchi and Boye, 2022)	README, Documentation	GitHub
Argilla (Vila-Suero and Aranda, 2023)	README, Documentation	GitHub
Orbis Annotator (Süsstrunk et al., 2023)	README	GitHub
CVAT (Corporation, 2023)	README	GitHub
DataGym.ai	README, Documentation	GitHub
DeepLabel (Veitch-Michaelis, 2021)	README	–

Table 4: Sources for structured and unstructured metadata for each annotation tool.

C Input and Output Formats

The input and output formats of annotation tools vary depending on the data modality at hand. However, output annotations should ideally be semantically structured using formats such as XML or RDF. We surveyed the literature in order to identify the most commonly used input/output formats per modality and to refer to those while evaluating the principle I1. The results are as follows: Input formats for text documents include *DOC, PDF, TXT, RTF, CSV, TSV, XML*, and *JSON* (Dasiopoulou et al., 2011; Oliveira and Rocha, 2013; Ide and Pustejovsky, 2017). Audio input formats are commonly available in terms of *WAV, MP3, OGG, AIF*, and *FLAC* formats (Dasiopoulou et al., 2011). Image inputs tend to be *PNG, JPEG*, and *JPG*, while video data is typically supported in the form of *MPEG, DIVX, AVI*, and *MOV* (Dasiopoulou et al., 2011). Semantic annotation outputs are usually in *XML* (or *XMI*), *RDF, RDFa, RDFS, OWL, CSV, TXT, JSON, TEI, EAF, CMML, IRI, SMIL*, and *TFRecord* formats (Dasiopoulou et al., 2011; Oliveira and Rocha, 2013; Ide and Pustejovsky, 2017; Aljabri et al., 2022). Table 5 summarises the input and output formats available in the 50 surveyed tools according to the information found in their metadata.

Annotation tool	Input formats	Output formats
INCEpTION	BioC (experimental), CoNLL 2000, CoNLL 2002, CoNLL 2003, CoNLL 2006, CoNLL 2009, CoNLL 2012, CoreNLP CoNLL-like format, CoNLL-U, HTML (legacy), HTML, IMS CWB (aka VRT), NLP Interchange Format (NIF), PDF Format, PDF Format (legacy), Perseus Ancient Greek and Latin Dependency Treebank 2.1 XML, WebLicht TCF, TEI P5 XML, Plain Text, Plain Text (one sentence per line), Plain Text (pretokenized), UIMA Binary CAS, UIMA Inline XML, UIMA CAS JSON (experimental), UIMA CAS JSON (legacy), UIMA CAS XMI, WebAnno TSV 1 (legacy), WebAnno TSV 2 (legacy), WebAnno TSV 3.x, XML (generic)	BioC (experimental), CoNLL 2000, CoNLL 2002, CoNLL 2003, CoNLL 2006, CoNLL 2009, CoNLL 2012, CoreNLP CoNLL-like format, CoNLL-U, HTML (legacy), HTML, IMS CWB (aka VRT), NIF, PDF Format, PDF Format (legacy), Perseus Ancient Greek and Latin Dependency Treebank 2.1 XML, WebLicht TCF, TEI P5 XML, Plain Text, Plain Text (one sentence per line), Plain Text (pretokenized), UIMA Binary CAS, UIMA Inline XML, UIMA CAS JSON (experimental), UIMA CAS JSON (legacy), UIMA CAS XMI, WebAnno TSV 1 (legacy), WebAnno TSV 2 (legacy), WebAnno TSV 3.x, XML (generic)
brat	Plain Text	.ann
Doccano	JSON, Plain Text, CoNLL	XML
BioQRator	PubMed, BioC	CSV, BioC
Catma	HTML, Plain Text	CSV, Plain Text, TEI XML
Djangology	Plain Text	Plain Text
ezTag	BioC	BioC
FLAT	FoLiA	FoLiA
LightTag	Plain Text, JSON, WebAnno TSV, TSV, CSV	–
MAT	XML	XML, JSON
PDFAnno	PDF	TOML
prodigy	JSONL, JSON, CSV, Plain Text, JPG, JPEG, PNG, GIF, SVG, MP3, M4A, WAV, MPEG, MPG, MP4	JSON
TextAE	JSON	JSON
WAT-SL	Plain Text	Plain Text
Hypothesis	HTML, PDF	–
Haystack	Plain Text	SQuAD JSON, XLSX, CSV
PDF sentence annotator	PDF	RDF
PAWLS	PDF	JSON
TeamTat	BioC, PDF, Plain Text	BioC
TagEditor	Plain Text, JSON, .spacy	JSON, .spacy
TS-ANNO	HTML, Plain Text	CSV
MedTator	Plain Text, XML	WebAnno TSV, TSV, JSONL
DocTAG	CSV, JSON, Plain Text	JSON, Plain Text
PubTator	Plain Text	BioC, JSON, POST, PubTator
Ellogon	Plain Text, TEI XML	JSON, CSV, XLSX, image formats(for the case of the charts)
Markup	Plain Text	ZIP
Label Studio	HTML, HTM, XML, BMP, GIF, JPG, PNG, SVG, WebP, JSON, Plain Text, TSV, CSV, FLAC, M4A, MP3, OGG, WAV, MP4, WebM, AVI	ASR MANIFEST (JSON manifest), NumPy, PNG, COCO, CoNLL 2023, CSV, JSON, JSON MIN, Pascal VOC XML, spacy, TSV, YOLO
MedTag	CSV	XML, JSON, CSV, BioC
BAT	WAV	–
Seshat	WAV, FLAC, MP3	ZIP
VIA	JPEG, PNG, URL of a webpage	CSV, JSON, COCO
Potato	JSON, TSV, CSV	JSON, TSV, CSV, JSONL
Annotation Web	PNG, MHD, RAW	–
audino	WAV, MP3, OGG	–
MATILDA	JSON	–

ELAN	MPG, MP4, WAV, etc.	HTML, Plain Text, XML, JSON, CSV, FLEx, CHAT, SMIL3-compliant clips, EAF, etc.
Praat	able to read most standard types of sound files, e.g. WAV files	UIMA Binary CAS/Binary
Pundit	URL of a webpage, PDF, Plain Text	Notebooks
UAM CorpusTool	Plain Text	HTML
TIARA	Plain Text	HTML, TSV
COCO Annotator	–	JSON, COCO
Gate Teamware	CSV, JSON	CSV, JSON
ActiveAnno	JSON	JSON
YEDDA	Plain Text	.ann
Textinator	Plain Text, JSON	JSON
Argilla	JSON	JSON, CSV, Parquet, XLSX, PKL (Python pickle file)
Orbis Annotator	NIF turtle, CareerCoach JSON	CareerCoach 2022, NIF turtle
CVAT	CVAT for images, CVAT for videos, Datumaro, PASCAL VOC, Segmentation masks from PASCAL VOC, YOLO, MS COCO Object Detection, MS COCO Keypoints Detection, TFrecord, MOT, MOTS PNG, LabelMe 3.0, ImageNet, CamVid, WIDER Face, VGGFace2, Market-1501, ICDAR13/15, Open Images V6, Cityscapes, KITTI, Kitti Raw Format, LFW, Supervisely Point Cloud Format	CVAT for images, CVAT for videos, Datumaro, PASCAL VOC, Segmentation masks from PASCAL VOC, YOLO, MS COCO Object Detection, MS COCO Keypoints Detection, TFrecord, MOT, MOTS PNG, LabelMe 3.0, ImageNet, CamVid, WIDER Face, VGGFace2, Market-1501, ICDAR13/15, Open Images V6, Cityscapes, KITTI, Kitti Raw Format, LFW, Supervisely Point Cloud Format
DataGym.ai	JPEG, PNG	JSON
DeepLabel	Darknet (provide image list and names), COCO (provide an annotation JSON file and image folder), MOT, TFRecord (parsing works, but full import is not possible yet) Pascal VOC	KITTI, Darknet for YOLO Pascal VOC, COCO (experimental), Google Cloud Platform, TFRecord, Video (experimental, command line only)

Table 5: Available input and output formats for each of the 50 surveyed tools.

Automatic Annotation Elaboration as Feedback to Sign Language Learners

Alessia Battisti and **Sarah Ebling**
Department of Computational Linguistics
University of Zurich, Switzerland
{battis,ebling}@cl.uzh.ch

Abstract

Beyond enabling linguistic analyses, linguistic annotations may serve as training material for developing automatic language assessment models as well as for providing textual feedback to language learners. Yet these linguistic annotations in their original form are often not easily comprehensible for learners. In this paper, we explore the utilization of GPT-4, as an example of a large language model (LLM), to process linguistic annotations into clear and understandable feedback on their productions for language learners, specifically sign language learners.

1 Introduction

Annotating linguistic data is a complex task, presenting ongoing challenges such as interpreting ambiguities and accounting for annotators' perceptions (Basile et al., 2021). In the context of sign languages, this complexity is increased by the absence of common writing systems and codified grammars (Baker et al., 2016), along with the challenge posed by the simultaneous production of manual and non-manual components[1] in expressing information.

Annotating sign language data is still a human-based and extremely time-consuming process. As evidenced by the ongoing German Sign Language (*Deutsche Gebärdensprache*, DGS) Corpus project, the annotation task proves to be highly labor-intensive, demanding approximately up to 600 minutes to transcribe and annotate a single minute of signing (Hanke, 2017).

These challenges slow down advancements in (semi-)automatic annotation of sign language data. No computational tools at a production stage are currently capable of supporting the process of generating (high-quality) annotations as part of a semi-automatic setting.

Recent years have seen the rise of Large Language Models (LLMs), enabling the annotation of large textual datasets. LLMs have proven effective in reliably annotating data by supporting human annotators (Gilardi et al., 2023). This concept of LLM-based annotation has extended to language teaching and assessment (Kasneci et al., 2023; Mahlow, 2023). In this area, efforts have been made to provide language learners with formative feedback by processing data annotations, although only tested with written learner data (Caines et al., 2023).

In this paper, we align with this latter research area and explain our idea of using linguistic annotations for providing feedback to sign language learners with the assistance of a large language model. First, we introduce in Section 2 the process of annotating sign language (learner) data as well as the first approaches to using LLMs for providing feedback to learners based on previous written annotation. In Section 3, we outline the annotation process and the annotation scheme. We provide a brief explanation of how our annotation process works, to make it accessible to a non-expert audience. Our goal is to illustrate the steps necessary to generate formative feedback.

Then, in Section 4, we present an experiment by employing GPT-4 (OpenAI, 2023) to process the linguistic annotations from data of our corpus of continuous sign language learner productions. Leveraging GPT-4 as an instance of LLMs, our goal is to transform the linguistic annotations into clear and understandable feedback to sign language learners. An evaluation of the feedback with sign language learners is also presented. The findings suggest that our initial approach holds promise in aiding sign language learning.

[1] Manual and non-manual components represent the phonological linguistic units that differentiate signs. The manual components comprise four main parameters: hand shape, orientation, position, and movement. Non-manual components consist of the movement of eyebrows, mouth, nose, gaze, and position and movement of the head and upper body.

Proceedings of The 18th Linguistic Annotation Workshop (LAW-XVIII), pages 46–60

2 Related Work

2.1 Annotating Sign Language (Learner) Data

Sign language annotation is a human-based process that consists of two steps: transcription, where a written version of the signed production is created, and annotation, which enriches video data with additional information, such as linguistic features (Konrad, 2011). For this task, in the context of sign languages, expert annotators employ annotation software such as ELAN (Crasborn and Sloetjes, 2008), iLex (Hanke and Storz, 2008), or SignStream (Neidle et al., 2001). These tools do not offer automatic annotation, that is, they do not automatically segment and label the video stream.

Glosses are commonly used as semantic labels of signs, written in capital letters and corresponding to the base form of a word in the surrounding spoken language[2] (Johnston, 2010). They find extensive use in (automatic) Sign Language Processing (SLP), particularly in the domain of Sign Language Translation (SLT) (Müller et al., 2023). The Hamburg Notation System (HamNoSys; Prillwitz, 1989) is a transcription system designed for representing the form of signs, employing approximately 200 symbols to depict the phonetic parameters of signs.

While recent years have witnessed various efforts in SLP introducing methods for automatic data annotation, these approaches are often language-dependent or target only one specific aspect of annotation (e.g., De Sisto et al., 2021; Mukushev et al., 2022, for sign segmentation; Bull et al., 2020 for sentence segmentation; Varol et al., 2021, for sentence alignment; Östling et al., 2015, for part-of-speech tagging; Chaaban et al., 2021 for non-manual segmentation and sign segmentation). Nevertheless, these tools currently either remain unavailable or are not well-suited for automated data annotation without extensive human post-editing.[3]

None of these studies specifically address the processing of sign language data originating from language learners. In recent years, research into second language acquisition of sign languages (SSLA) has increased, proposing various datasets from non-native signers (L2) (Schönström, 2021). The L2 data undergoes an initial annotation comparable to the process applied to native signer (L1) data, including the addition of glosses and HamNoSys information (see above), for example. Following this, error annotation is applied to highlight deviations from canonical forms or disfluencies, a common practice also used in the study of spoken language learning (Gilquin and De Cock, 2011).

On the one hand, deviations are annotated and analyzed at a single sign level, focusing on individual glosses and manual errors (Rosen, 2004; Ortega and Morgan, 2015; Ebling et al., 2021). On the other, deviations are labeled and analyzed at a sentence level, highlighting the need for annotating non-manual components (Mesch and Schönström, 2020; Gulamani et al., 2020).

2.2 LLMs Applied to L2 Data

LLMs have demonstrated their effectiveness in reliably supporting human annotators (Gilardi et al., 2023). This capability of LLMs for annotation has been extended to the domain of language teaching and assessment, demonstrating the potential to enhance the teaching and learning experience across various education levels (Kasneci et al., 2023; Mahlow, 2023).

For example, LLMs can automatically annotate and evaluate learners' written work by assigning scores. As highlighted in previous studies, they play a crucial role in providing immediate feedback and explanations of errors (Nagata et al., 2021; Caines et al., 2023). This immediacy has been proven to be more effective for student learning (Steiss et al., 2023). However, it is important to note that the focus of all these studies is limited to writings and automated essay scoring.

Focusing on the use of corpora in language classes, teachers commonly extract insights into both correct and incorrect usage of terms and linguistic constructs from annotated corpora to provide formative feedback to learners. Nagata et al. (2020) present an approach which leverages annotation in existing feedback comments to automatically generate new feedback comments.

The idea of offering sign language learners automatic and immediate feedback during sign language learning assignments is a recent topic that has not been explored to a great extent (Huenerfauth et al., 2015; Hassan et al., 2022).

Research suggests that sign language learners prefer feedback that not only identifies the precise

[2]In this study, the term "spoken language" refers to any language that is not signed, whether expressed in written or oral form.

[3]For a general introduction to sign language processing, refer to Bragg et al. (2019). To explore existing sign language corpora, consult Kopf et al. (2021) (where, albeit, sign language learner corpora are not included). Additionally, for an overview of the various annotation formats employed in signed corpora, refer to Kopf et al. (2022).

moment of an error in a video but also includes detailed written feedback alongside visual cues (Huenerfauth et al., 2017; Hassan et al., 2022).

Existing systems, limited in number, utilize annotations to analyze learner inputs but typically offer binary correct/incorrect feedback or, at most, assign a numerical score (Tarigopula et al., 2022).

In contrast to the research presented above, our work explores the use of GPT-4 for elaborating existing annotations created for sign language linguistics research, reframing them as feedback for sign language learners. The motivation behind this is that individuals not used to linguistic annotations may find them challenging to understand without additional explanation.

3 Annotating the Corpus Data

In this section, we offer an overview of our annotation process, outlining the annotation scheme. This scheme encompasses the features extracted from the annotated data, which are then used to input into the GPT-4 model for our experiments (Section 4).

For our experiment, we utilized data from a Swiss German Sign Language (*Deutschschweizerische Gebärdensprache*, DSGS) corpus including a longitudinal sign language learner sub-corpus and a corresponding sub-corpus of native signers. The L2 data was gathered from the same learners at four collection points separated by six-month intervals between March 2022 and November 2023. Both L1 and L2 videos underwent post-processing and were imported into iLex (Section 2.1).

3.1 Annotators

In the case of low-resourced languages such as sign languages, human expert annotators are not widely available (Mehta and Srikumar, 2023). Our team of annotators comprises two deaf expert annotators, bringing years of experience in teaching and researching sign language to the task, along with two annotators in training. All of them, including the annotators in training, are project team members.

To ensure data integrity, we performed continuous validation and cross-checking of annotated data. Annotations adhere to a four-eyes principle, subject to cross-checks by the two expert annotators. Difficult and divergent cases are discussed in the presence of a sign language linguist. Annotations by annotators in training undergo a double-check and corrections if necessary.

Since the annotations by annotators in training are still under review, we have decided to consider only the sentences annotated by the experts for the experiment introduced in Section 4.

3.2 Transcription and Annotation Scheme

Table 1 presents the features included in the full transcription and annotation scheme underlying the creation of our DSGS corpus. Each feature corresponds to a tier within an iLex transcript. Tiers, in this context, are distinct layers used to encode the simultaneous usage of various information channels or features, such as hands, eyebrows, and mouthing. Figure 3 in Appendix C shows an example of a sentence produced by a DSGS learner, annotated in iLex.

The scheme was designed so as to include annotation at both a segmental and suprasegmental[4] level, including the non-manual components. The scheme aims at capturing the complexity and nature of the co-occurrence of features, including information at higher levels, as indicated in the "Additional information" column (cf. Table 1).

Item refers to an exercise used as elicitation task for the creation of our corpus, such as picture or video retelling, along with exercise boundaries and name. Information in this tier was automatically annotated based on the starting and ending times registered by the video recording software.

Each *Item* contains one to n sentences marked in the *Sentence* tier. Specifically, this tier contains a segmentation of the video into sentence-like units.

Each sentence is then segmented into manual and non-manual components. Annotation of the manual components involves inserting *glosses* and describing the sign form with the four parameters of hand shape, orientation, position, and movement using *HamNoSys* (Ebling et al., 2018).

For non-manual components, annotation consists of labeling linguistic facial or upper body form and movement. The labels assigned to each non-manual feature were based on schemes employed in previous sign language studies (Gabarró-López and Meurant, 2014; Lackner, 2019). These labels were adapted to suit DSGS and the objectives of the corpus. In sum, we defined 81 labels for mouth gestures, comprising 57 labels for lip form and movement, twelve for identifying cheek movement and shape, and 22 for tongue movement (e.g., *upper lip left raised*). Concerning the nose, we defined

[4]The term "suprasegmental" is employed as these components constitute a layer atop the segmental layer (Pfau, 2017).

Levels	Manual components	Non-manual components (nmc)	Additional information	Error annotations
Item	Gloss: right hand (rh)	Mouthing	Topic/focus	Parameter(s) different (rh) + acceptability
Sentence	Gloss: left hand (lh)	Mouth gesture	Function	Parameter(s) different (lh) + acceptability
	Gloss: both hands (bh)	Nose	Prosody	Parameter(s) different (bh) + acceptability
	HamNoSys: rh	Shoulders + Upper body	Role	Parameter(s) different (nmc) + acceptability
	HamNoSys: lh	Head	*Comment*	Sentence Problem + acceptability sentence
	HamNoSys: bh	Gaze		*Comment*
	HamNoSys: variance rh	Eye lids		
	HamNoSys: variance lh	Eyebrows		

Table 1: Tiers in the transcription and annotation scheme of our DSGS corpus. Each column corresponds to a main annotation block. Each block contains a list of tiers or features.

seven labels (e.g., *wrinkled nose*). We identified 19 labels for upper body and shoulder movement, and 20 labels for head movements (e.g., *nodding head*). Additionally, we established 30 labels for eye gaze, ten for eyelids, and eight for the eyebrow movements (e.g., *raised eyebrows*).[5]

For L2 data, the annotation scheme was expanded to incorporate the tiers outlined in the *Error annotations* column in Table 1. These tiers provide information about deviations from the canonical form for manual and non-manual components, as well as any deviation occurring at the sentence level. For each deviation, annotators assigned a degree of (non-)acceptability (*not acceptable, acceptable, fully acceptable*). This value indicating whether the deviating feature remained comprehensible and to what extent it affected the overall comprehensibility of the sentence. Appendix A presents two versions of a sample signed sentence, one judged as acceptable and the other deemed not acceptable.

4 Using GPT-4 for Sign Language Annotation Elaboration

The primary aim of this experiment was to leverage the ability of GPT-4[6] to produce coherent textual feedback from keywords representing linguistic annotations, intended to be presented to sign language learners. Our final scenario is to incorporate the feedback generated through this process into a prototype sign language assessment system, providing additional feedback alongside visual hints. Figure 1 shows a predecessor prototype system giving feedback on lexical items, i.e., on individual signs. Note that our aim is to provide feedback on the production of continuous sign sentences, thereby naturally also touching on the correctness of production of non-manual components of signing.

4.1 Data

We retrieved the error annotations from iLex, randomly selecting 100 annotated sentences, and structured the input prompt in a JSON format suitable for the GPT-4 model. Each sentence contains between 0 and 12 errors (μ 4.7, σ 2.1).

We chose a direct prompting approach, that is, we provided the model with a single prompt that included comprehensive task details. This contained the task definition, purpose, and the intended target user, simulating how a person would instruct another person to explain a list of errors to a learner. Since the annotations are in German and the generated feedback needs to be in German, we formulated the prompt in the same language. The prompt specifically instructed the model to elaborate on annotations, categorizing them into three types: annotations regarding manual components, non-manual components, and annotations at the sentence level.

We requested the exclusion of any information about the language or input sentence. This was motivated by our observation that GPT-4 had previously consistently provided explanations about sign languages in general. We established precise terminology for the term "sign" to address semantic ambiguity. This ensured that the model used the German word "Gebärde" instead of "Zeichen", as both are homonyms for "sign" in English. Likewise, we specified the use of the term "Komponenten" instead of "Signale" to refer to non-manual components. The final prompt template is provided in Table 2.

To restrict inappropriate inferences for our purpose, we set the temperature parameter to 0.2. This value allows for prompt rephrasing without becoming repetitive or excessively creative. We kept the other parameters unchanged and set the seed to 42 to guarantee consistent generations.

Tables in Appendix D report examples of prompts and generated outputs.

[5] For further details on the annotation scheme and labels, please contact the first author.

[6] https://openai.com/gpt-4

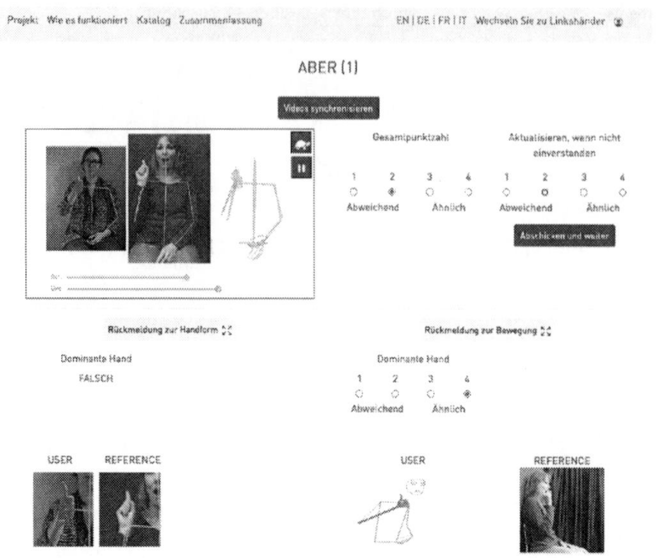

Figure 1: Screenshot displaying the earlier prototype system offering feedback on hand shape (*Handform*) and movement (*Bewegung*) at sign level.

DE: *Analysiere Fehler in einem in Deutschschweizerischer Gebärdensprache (DSGS) produzierten Satz ohne Sprach- oder Satzdetails. Verfasse eine klare, ganz kurze Erklärung wie für einen DSGS-Lernenden. Nutze ‚Gebärde' statt ‚Zeichen', ‚Komponente' statt ‚Signale'. Bitte duzen, auf Förmlichkeiten verzichten. Verzichte auf zusätzliche Informationen. Hier sind die Annotationen: %. Manuelle Fehler: %. Nicht-manuelle Fehler: %. Problem auf Satzebene: %. Akzeptabilität ganzer Satz: %.*
EN: 'Analyze errors in a sentence produced in Swiss German Sign Language (DSGS) without language or sentence details. Write a clear, very short explanation as for a DSGS learner. Use 'sign' instead of 'sign', 'component' instead of 'signals'. Please use first names, avoid formalities. Do without additional information. Here are the annotations: %. Manual errors: %. Non-manual errors: %. Problem at sentence level: %. Whole sentence acceptability: %.'

Table 2: Basic prompt template, where % is a placeholder for annotations. German version is on top, English translation done using DeepL on bottom. Note the wrongly translated sentence 'Use sign instead of sign' due to the semantic ambiguity explained in the section.

4.2 Accuracy Evaluation

To assess the performance, we conducted two distinct evaluations. The first analysis aimed at identifying the primary challenges for the model. In this evaluation, we manually examined the generated text for each prompt, checking the included error information to count the number of *true positives*, i.e., instances in which the model correctly included the error information from the prompt in its output; *false positives*, i.e., cases in which the model incorrectly included information in the output that was not present in the original prompt; and *false negatives*, where the model failed to include the error information from the prompt in the formulated output.

We counted individual error instances, not the overall generated text, since we wanted to observe how the model treated and explained each single error. We then computed precision, recall, and F1-score.

4.3 Learner Evaluation

The second evaluation aimed at assessing the quality of the generated feedback texts from the perspective of the target users, namely sign language learners. Specifically, the goal was to determine the comprehensibility of the generated texts for sign language learners and evaluate their subjective usefulness, with the expectation that our approach will be integrated into the sign language assessment prototype. To achieve this, we invited sign language learners to read and judge the generated texts. We enrolled five volunteers, each with beginner to intermediate level of DSGS.

For every generated text, evaluators were tasked with comparing the output to the errors included in the prompts. They were asked to respond to three questions (translated into English in the following): *Q1.* Is the generated output correct and does it include the expected information? *Q2.* Is the generated output readable? *Q3.* Is the generated output understandable?

Each question was designed to assess a specific aspect of the generated text. The first question focused on investigating the accuracy and completeness of the text. Especially, it considered an output as accurate only when it encompassed all the anticipated information. The second question targeted its fluency, and the third evaluated its clarity in the error presentation. The evaluators had the possibility to add a comment about the text if they deemed it necessary.

All evaluators were instructed to select a value on a 5-point Likert scale, where 1 represented a poor rating (*strongly disagree*) and 5 indicated a very good rating (*strongly agree*). The decision to use an odd scale was taken to allow respondents to choose the midpoint in cases of neutral understanding, without being compelled to extreme evaluations. The anonymized input information and generated outputs, including the number of errors, as well as the evaluations of the outputs are published on Zenodo.[7]

Annotator agreement was measured on the 100 items annotated by all evaluators separately. We calculated the pairwise raw percentage as well as Gwet *AC2*[8] for ordinal data. We decided to use Gwet *AC2* as measure of inter-rater reliability for ordinal and interval measurement because it addresses the limitation of label's distribution of the Krippendorff's α (Feng, 2014; Gwet, 2014). In our data, for each question, evaluators agreed to the extent of 72% to 90% on a single label, that is the label of value 5 (Figure 2). This imbalanced distribution can result in meaningless α coefficients; hence our choice of Gwet *AC2*.

4.4 Results

Accuracy Results By manually analyzing the generated output text, we noticed that in general the texts were correct, fluent and readable, but the model sometimes failed to generate informative elaborations suitable to the given task.

As reported in the Table 3, out of all of the error information, 99% was correctly inserted in the generated output, showing a high level of accuracy.

The model achieved a recall of 93%. While this is a high number, it still indicates that the model missed to insert or wrongly inserted some information on errors. We investigated this value and identified that the system incorrectly provided information about non-manual errors for 32 instances: In general, it stated that the non-manual components were produced correctly instead of acknowledging an error (Example 57 in Table 9). The errors made by GPT-4 in generating the explanations and the non-manual error annotation show a positive correlation that is statistically significant (ρ = 0.16, p-value < 0.001). This implies the existence of a certain ambiguity either in the prompt or in the error annotation, which proves challenging for the LLM to manage.

In cases where the prompt did not contain any error, the model generated irrelevant texts by explaining the range of possible errors in sign language learning (Example 35 in Table 10). This might be due to the limited context of the prompt. In two cases, for example, the model included a description of a manual error that was not originally present in the prompt (Example 44 in Table 8).

Overall, GPT-4 achieved an F1-score of 0.96, suggesting a good trade-off between precision and recall in elaborating on the error annotations to produce a textual feedback for learners.

Precision	0.99
Recall	0.93
F1	0.96

Table 3: Evaluation scores of the GPT-4-generated outputs calculated on the single error instances.

Learner Evaluation Results To better understand the perceived fluency and the clarity of the texts on the part of the sign language learners, we calculated the percentage of the Likert values assigned by the learner evaluators to each question.

As shown in Figure 2, the three aspects obtained high percentages for the highest values for all three aspects of correctness, fluency, and clarity. In particular, 90.3% of the answers to the second aspect obtained a value of 5. Consistent with these percentages, the Pearson correlations between the investigated aspects were highly significant. This suggests that the texts with the correct representations of the content were also evaluated as being more readable and comprehensible by the learners (*Q1-Q2*: ρ = 0.32, p-value < 0.001; *Q1-Q3*: ρ = 0.60, p-value < 0.001; *Q2-Q3*: ρ = 0.34, p-value < 0.001).

Overall reliability was 0.88 (Gwet's *AC2*), calculated as the mean of the values for the individual

[7] https://zenodo.org/doi/10.5281/zenodo.10567377

[8] https://irrcac.readthedocs.io/en/latest/index.html

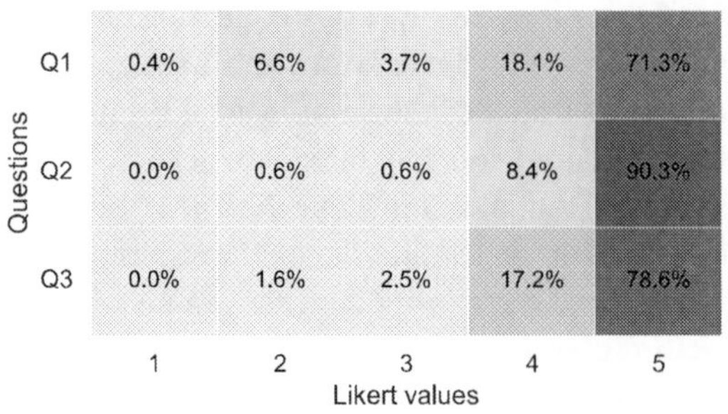

Figure 2: Percentage values of the answers given by the evaluators. Q1: accuracy and completeness of the text; Q2: fluency of the text; Q3: clarity in error presentation.

aspects: 0.83, 0.95, and 0.87 for *Q1*, *Q2*, and *Q3*, respectively. The average pairwise raw percentage estimated on the evaluated items was 58.6% for *Q1*, 79.7% for *Q2*, and 64% for *Q3*. The lowest label, i.e., 1, was never assigned to *Q2* and *Q3*. This label was assigned only by one evaluator to *Q1*. Most discrepancies in the evaluations were observed between labels 4 and 5, indicating that the nuances between a value of 4 and 5 were poorly defined. Specific scores between each pair of evaluators can be found in Tables 4, 5, and 6 in Appendix B.

A qualitative analysis of the comments revealed common patterns in the positive reception of supportive statements such as *Keep up the good work!* present in the output generated by the model (Example 4 in Table 9). Even though we did not specifically ask for such comments in the initial prompt, the model produced them. This observation led us to reflect on the importance of incorporating a more personal touch in the feedback generated for learners.

Less appreciated by the evaluators were phrases that asked learners to pay attention to the correct repetition of a hand movement or shape of the sign as shown in an (invented) example video. Similarly, they criticized the lack of specificity in the description of errors concerning non-manual components. Besides, the evaluators negatively commented on the length of the outputs (length in sentences: μ 7.9, σ 3.2; length in tokens: μ 105.4, σ 43.8). During the creation of the prompt and the experimentation to find suitable parameters for our experiment, we had attempted to limit the number of output tokens; however, the model tended to cut off the feedback, especially when there were numerous errors to explain within the prompt.

5 Conclusion and Outlook

In this paper, we have presented the multifaceted challenges associated with annotating sign language data. We have covered the steps included in the annotation process and summarized the main features in a sign language annotation scheme.

We have also reported on an experiment using GPT-4 to elaborate on linguistic error annotations from the scheme to provide more comprehensible feedback to sign language learners (cf. Example 2 in Table 7). The rationale behind this experiment was that the annotation reprocessing offers an opportunity to offer immediate feedback to sign language learners, enhancing their learning experience.

The evaluation results demonstrated the successful application of GPT-4 in this task. They also obviated a need for more concision, evidence, and specificity in the generated error elaborations. The level of details of our annotation scheme may have constrained the quality of the generated feedback, leading to inconsistencies in GPT-4's treatment of non-manual errors, as shown in Examples 4 and 57 in Table 9. A preliminary cleaning step and paraphrasing of the linguistic annotations could potentially address these issues.

In a practical scenario, GPT-4 can be guided to provide additional explanations or customized support by using clear prompts that incorporated human-written explications. Within the linguistic annotations of the corpus, we offer insights into errors tied to specific grammatical constructs. A future enhancement could involve instructing GPT-4 to generate feedback comments explaining linguistic concepts and grammatical structure, moving beyond solely error-focused elaborations. This shift could contribute to a more comprehensive and educational feedback system, aiding sign language learners in grasping the underlying linguistic principles. This aspect could be evaluated by performing a study comparing feedback generated by sign language experts with that produced by GPT-4.

In future research, we also aim to explore few-shot methods to improve the model's capability of elaboration. We tried different promptings and adjusted settings. Even though we aimed for a clear prompt, the choice of the 0.2 temperature parameter was somewhat arbitrary. Future work could explore different parameter settings.

Lastly, in this paper, the numbers related to annotators, the amount of annotated data and evaluators may seem small compared to the data commonly used in Natural Language Processing (NLP) tasks employing deep learning methods. Yet this paper aims at enhancing knowledge and awareness of annotation efforts in sign languages, presently recognized as under-resourced languages (Joshi et al., 2020). It sheds light on how the community addresses the demands for large, high-quality, and annotated datasets required for technological progress.

Ethics Statement

Ensuring fair and respectful collaboration is a fundamental aspect of our ethical commitment to this research initiative. Within this project, expert annotators are members of the team and receive fair compensation for their valuable contributions. The evaluators who assessed the GPT-4 outputs participated voluntarily, retaining the option to withdraw at any point and the freedom to reconsider their involvement in the evaluation work.

Acknowledgments

This work was funded through the Swiss National Science Foundation (SNSF) Sinergia project "Scalable Multimodal Sign Language Technology for Sign Language Learning and Assessment II" (SMILE II) (grant agreement no. CRSII5_193686) and the Swiss Innovation Agency (Innosuisse) flagship IICT (PFFS-21-47). The authors would like to thank the learners for their assistance in evaluating the GPT-4-generated texts and the reviewers for providing valuable feedback.

References

A. Baker, B. van den Bogaerde, and R. Pfau. 2016. *The Linguistics of Sign Languages: An Introduction*. John Benjamins Publishing Company.

Valerio Basile, Federico Cabitza, Andrea Campagner, and Michael Fell. 2021. Toward a perspectivist turn in ground truthing for predictive computing. *CoRR*, abs/2109.04270.

Danielle Bragg, Oscar Koller, Mary Bellard, Larwan Berke, Patrick Boudreault, Annelies Braffort, Naomi Caselli, Matt Huenerfauth, Hernisa Kacorri, Tessa Verhoef, Christian Vogler, and Meredith Ringel Morris. 2019. Sign language recognition, generation, and translation: An interdisciplinary perspective. In *Proceedings of the 21st International ACM SIGACCESS Conference on Computers and Accessibility*, ASSETS '19, page 16–31, New York, NY, USA. Association for Computing Machinery.

Hannah Bull, Michèle Gouiffès, and Annelies Braffort. 2020. Automatic Segmentation of Sign Language into Subtitle-Units. In *Computer Vision – ECCV 2020 Workshops*, Lecture Notes in Computer Science, pages 186–198, Cham. Springer International Publishing.

Andrew Caines, Luca Benedetto, Shiva Taslimipoor, Christopher Davis, Yuan Gao, Oeistein Andersen, Zheng Yuan, Mark Elliott, Russell Moore, Christopher Bryant, Marek Rei, Helen Yannakoudakis, Andrew Mullooly, Diane Nicholls, and Paula Buttery. 2023. On the application of large language models for language teaching and assessment technology.

Hussein Chaaban, Michèle Gouiffès, and Annelies Braffort. 2021. Automatic annotation and segmentation of sign language videos: Base-level features and lexical signs classification. In *Proceedings of the 16th International Joint Conference on Computer Vision, Imaging and Computer Graphics Theory and Applications, VISIGRAPP 2021, Volume 5: VISAPP, Online Streaming, February 8-10, 2021*, pages 484–491. SCITEPRESS.

Onno Crasborn and Han Sloetjes. 2008. Enhanced ELAN functionality for sign language corpora. In *Proceedings of LREC 2008, Sixth International Conference on Language Resources and Evaluation.*

Mirella De Sisto, Dimitar Shterionov, Irene Murtagh, Myriam Vermeerbergen, and Lorraine Leeson. 2021. Defining meaningful units. Challenges in sign segmentation and segment-meaning mapping (short paper). In *Proceedings of the 1st International Workshop on Automatic Translation for Signed and Spoken Languages (AT4SSL)*, pages 98–103, Virtual. Association for Machine Translation in the Americas.

Sarah Ebling, Necati Cihan Camgoz, Penny Boyes Braem, Katja Tissi, Sandra Sidler-Miserez, Stephanie Stoll, Simon Hadfield, Tobias Haug, Richard Bowden, Sandrine Tornay, Marzieh Razavi, and Mathew Magimai-Doss. 2018. SMILE Swiss German sign language dataset. In *Proceedings of the Eleventh International Conference on Language Resources and Evaluation (LREC 2018)*, pages 4221–4229, Miyazaki, Japan. European Language Resources Association (ELRA).

Sarah Ebling, Katja Tissi, Sandra Sidler-Miserez, Cheryl Schlumpf, and Penny Boyes Braem. 2021. Single-parameter and parameter combination errors in L2 productions of Swiss German Sign Language. *Sign Language & Linguistics*, 24(2):143–181.

Charles Feng. 2014. Mistakes and how to avoid mistakes in using intercoder reliability indices. *Methodology: European Journal of Research Methods for the Behavioral and Social Sciences*, 1:1–10.

Sílvia Gabarró-López and Laurence Meurant. 2014. When nonmanuals meet semantics and syntax: a practical guide for the segmentation of sign language discourse. In *6th Workshop on the Representation and*

Processing of Sign Languages: Beyond the Manual Channel, Reykjavik, Iceland.

Fabrizio Gilardi, Meysam Alizadeh, and Maël Kubli. 2023. Chatgpt outperforms crowd workers for text-annotation tasks. *Proceedings of the National Academy of Sciences*, 120(30):e2305016120.

Gaëtanelle Gilquin and Sylvie De Cock. 2011. Errors and disfluencies in spoken corpora: Setting the scene. *International Journal of Corpus Linguistics*, 16(2):141–172. Publisher: John Benjamins Type: Journal Article.

Sannah Gulamani, Chloë Marshall, and Gary Morgan. 2020. The challenges of viewpoint-taking when learning a sign language: Data from the 'frog story' in British Sign Language. *Second Language Research*, 38(1):55–87.

Kilem Li Gwet. 2014. *Handbook of inter-rater reliability: the definitive guide to measuring the extent of agreement among raters*, fourth edition edition. Advances Analytics, LLC, Gaithersburg, Md.

Thomas Hanke. 2017. Wörterbuch ohne Wörter? Zum Entstehen eines Wörterbuches der Deutschen Gebärdensprache. In *Jahrbuch der Heidelberger Akademie der Wissenschaften für 2016*, pages 84–88. Universitätsverlag Winter, Heidelberg, Germany.

Thomas Hanke and Jakob Storz. 2008. iLex – A Database Tool for Integrating Sign Language Corpus Linguistics and Sign Language Lexicography. In *Proceedings of the 6th Language Resources and Evaluation Conference (LREC)*, pages 64–67, Marrakesh, Marocco. ELRA.

Saad Hassan, Sooyeon Lee, Dimitris Metaxas, Carol Neidle, and Matt Huenerfauth. 2022. Understanding ASL Learners' Preferences for a Sign Language Recording and Automatic Feedback System to Support Self-Study. In *The 24th International ACM SIGACCESS Conference on Computers and Accessibility*, pages 1–5, Athens Greece. ACM.

Matt Huenerfauth, Elaine Gale, Brian Penly, Sree Pillutla, Mackenzie Willard, and Dhananjai Hariharan. 2017. Evaluation of Language Feedback Methods for Student Videos of American Sign Language. *ACM Transactions on Accessible Computing*, 10(1):2:1–2:30.

Matt Huenerfauth, Elaine Gale, Brian Penly, Mackenzie Willard, and Dhananjai Hariharan. 2015. Comparing methods of displaying language feedback for student videos of american sign language. In *Proceedings of the 17th International ACM SIGACCESS Conference on Computers & Accessibility*, ASSETS '15, page 139–146, New York, NY, USA. Association for Computing Machinery.

Trevor Johnston. 2010. From archive to corpus: Transcription and annotation in the creation of signed language corpora:. *International Journal of Corpus Linguistics*, 15(1):106–131. Publisher: John Benjamins Publishing Company.

Pratik Joshi, Sebastin Santy, Amar Budhiraja, Kalika Bali, and Monojit Choudhury. 2020. The State and Fate of Linguistic Diversity and Inclusion in the NLP World. In *Proceedings of the 58th Annual Meeting of the Association for Computational Linguistics*, pages 6282–6293, Online. Association for Computational Linguistics.

Enkelejda Kasneci, Kathrin Sessler, Stefan Küchemann, Maria Bannert, Daryna Dementieva, Frank Fischer, Urs Gasser, Georg Groh, Stephan Günnemann, Eyke Hüllermeier, Stephan Krusche, Gitta Kutyniok, Tilman Michaeli, Claudia Nerdel, Jürgen Pfeffer, Oleksandra Poquet, Michael Sailer, Albrecht Schmidt, Tina Seidel, Matthias Stadler, Jochen Weller, Jochen Kuhn, and Gjergji Kasneci. 2023. ChatGPT for good? On opportunities and challenges of large language models for education. *Learning and Individual Differences*, 103:102274.

Reiner Konrad. 2011. *Die lexikalische Struktur der Deutschen Gebärdensprache im Spiegel empirischer Fachgebärdenlexikographie*. Ph.D. thesis.

Maria Kopf, Marc Schulder, and Thomas Hanke. 2021. Overview of Datasets for the Sign Languages of Europe.

Maria Kopf, Marc Schulder, Thomas Hanke, and Sam Bigeard. 2022. Specification for the Harmonization of Sign Language Annotations.

Andrea Lackner. 2019. Describing Nonmanuals in Sign Language. In Andrea Lackner, editor, *Grazer Linguistische Studien*, volume 91, pages 45–103. University of Graz, Graz, Austria.

Cerstin Mahlow. 2023. Large Language Models and Artificial Intelligence as Tools for Teaching and Learning Writing. *Osnabrücker Beiträge zur Sprachtheorie*, 101:175–196.

Maitrey Mehta and Vivek Srikumar. 2023. Verifying annotation agreement without multiple experts: A case study with Gujarati SNACS. In *Findings of the Association for Computational Linguistics: ACL 2023*, pages 10941–10958, Toronto, Canada. Association for Computational Linguistics.

Johanna Mesch and Krister Schönström. 2020. Use and acquisition of mouth actions in L2 sign language learners: A corpus-based approach. *Sign Language & Linguistics*, 24(1):36–62. Publisher: John Benjamins Publishing Company.

Medet Mukushev, Aigerim Kydyrbekova, Vadim Kimmelman, and Anara Sandygulova. 2022. Towards large vocabulary Kazakh-Russian Sign Language dataset: KRSL-OnlineSchool. In *Proceedings of the LREC2022 10th Workshop on the Representation and Processing of Sign Languages: Multilingual Sign Language Resources*, pages 154–158, Marseille, France. European Language Resources Association.

Mathias Müller, Zifan Jiang, Amit Moryossef, Annette Rios, and Sarah Ebling. 2023. Considerations for meaningful sign language machine translation based on glosses. In *Proceedings of the 61st Annual Meeting of the Association for Computational Linguistics (Volume 2: Short Papers)*, pages 682–693, Toronto, Canada. Association for Computational Linguistics.

Ryo Nagata, Masato Hagiwara, Kazuaki Hanawa, Masato Mita, Artem Chernodub, and Olena Nahorna. 2021. Shared task on feedback comment generation for language learners. In *Proceedings of the 14th International Conference on Natural Language Generation*, pages 320–324, Aberdeen, Scotland, UK. Association for Computational Linguistics.

Ryo Nagata, Kentaro Inui, and Shin'ichiro Ishikawa. 2020. Creating corpora for research in feedback comment generation. In *Proceedings of the Twelfth Language Resources and Evaluation Conference*, pages 340–345, Marseille, France. European Language Resources Association.

Carol Neidle, Stan Sclaroff, and Vassilis Athitsos. 2001. SignStream: A tool for linguistic and computer vision research on visual-gestural language data. *Behavior Research Methods, Instruments, & Computers*, 33(3):311–320.

OpenAI. 2023. Gpt-4 technical report.

Gerardo Ortega and Gary Morgan. 2015. Phonological Development in Hearing Learners of a Sign Language: The Influence of Phonological Parameters, Sign Complexity, and Iconicity: Phonological Development in Sign L2 Learners. *Language Learning*, 65(3):660–688.

Robert Östling, Carl Börstell, and Lars Wallin. 2015. Enriching the Swedish Sign Language corpus with part of speech tags using joint Bayesian word alignment and annotation transfer. In *Proceedings of the 20th Nordic Conference of Computational Linguistics (NODALIDA 2015)*, pages 263–268, Vilnius, Lithuania. Linköping University Electronic Press, Sweden.

Roland Pfau. 2017. Non-manuals and tones : a comparative perspective on suprasegmentals and spreading. *Linguística : Revista de Estudos Linguísticos da Universidade do Porto*, 11:19–58.

S. Prillwitz. 1989. *HamNoSys Version 2.0. Hamburg Notation System for Sign Languages: An Introductory Guide*. Intern. Arb. z. Gebärdensprache u. Kommunik. Signum Press.

Russel S. Rosen. 2004. Beginning L2 production errors in ASL lexical phonology: A cognitive phonology model. *Sign Language & Linguistics*, 7(1):31–61.

Krister Schönström. 2021. Sign languages and second language acquisition research: An introduction. *Journal of the European Second Language Association*.

Jacob Steiss, Tamara P Tate, Steve Graham, Jazmin Cruz, Michael Hebert, Jiali Wang, Youngsun Moon, Waverly Tseng, and mark w uci. 2023. Comparing the quality of human and chatgpt feedback on students' writing.

Neha Tarigopula, Sandrine Tornay, Skanda Muralidhar, and Mathew Magimai-Doss. 2022. Towards accessible sign language assessment and learning. In *International Conference on Multimodal Interaction, ICMI 2022, Bengaluru, India, November 7-11, 2022*, pages 626–631. ACM.

Gul Varol, Liliane Momeni, Samuel Albanie, Triantafyllos Afouras, and Andrew Zisserman. 2021. Read and Attend: Temporal Localisation in Sign Language Videos. In *2021 IEEE/CVF Conference on Computer Vision and Pattern Recognition (CVPR)*, pages 16852–16861, Nashville, TN, USA. IEEE.

A Annotation Example

Below, we provide an sample sentence, "I am not hard-of-hearing", produced by two DSGS learners. In the first version, the sentence was deemed acceptable because both head and eyebrow movements were executed correctly. In the second version, non-manual components are either missing or used incorrectly (e.g., the head is moved in correspondence with the adjective, not with manual negation), rendering the sentence incorrect.

```
Version 1:
      shaking head    shaking head
                   (furrowed eyebrows) ||
IX-1  NICHT ++  |   SCHWERHOERIG     ||
I      not          hard-of-hearing

Version 2:
                     shaking head
                                     ||
IX-1  NICHT ++  |   SCHWERHOERIG     ||
I      not          hard-of-hearing

DE: Ich bin nicht schwerhörig
EN: I   am  not   hard-of-hearing
```

B Percentage Agreement

	A_0	A_1	A_2	A_3	A_4
A_0	-				
A_1	**68.7**	-			
A_2	60.7	73.9	-		
A_3	54.0	62.6	59.6	-	
A_4	51.5	49.0	44.3	46.5	-

Table 4: Raw percentage agreement across evaluators on *Q1*, the question about accuracy and completeness aspect.

	A_0	A_1	A_2	A_3	A_4
A_0	-				
A_1	97.0	-			
A_2	84.3	85.2	-		
A_3	96.0	**99.0**	86.5	-	
A_4	66.7	69.4	67.0	70.7	-

Table 5: Raw percentage agreement across evaluators on *Q2*, the fluency aspect.

	A_0	A_1	A_2	A_3	A_4
A_0	-				
A_1	**81.8**	-			
A_2	71.9	76.1	-		
A_3	54.0	52.5	53.9	-	
A_4	74.7	78.6	67.0	53.5	-

Table 6: Raw percentage agreement across evaluators on *Q3*, the question about the clarity aspect.

C iLex Example

In the Figure, we show an example of a DSGS sentence produced by a learner, annotated in iLex. The columns represents the tiers, namely the features of Table 1.

D Output Examples

In the following tables, we will display some prompts and their corresponding generated outputs. The German versions are presented at the top. The English translations of the prompts and the generated outputs were automatically done using DeepL[9] (at the bottom).

[9] https://www.deepl.com/translator

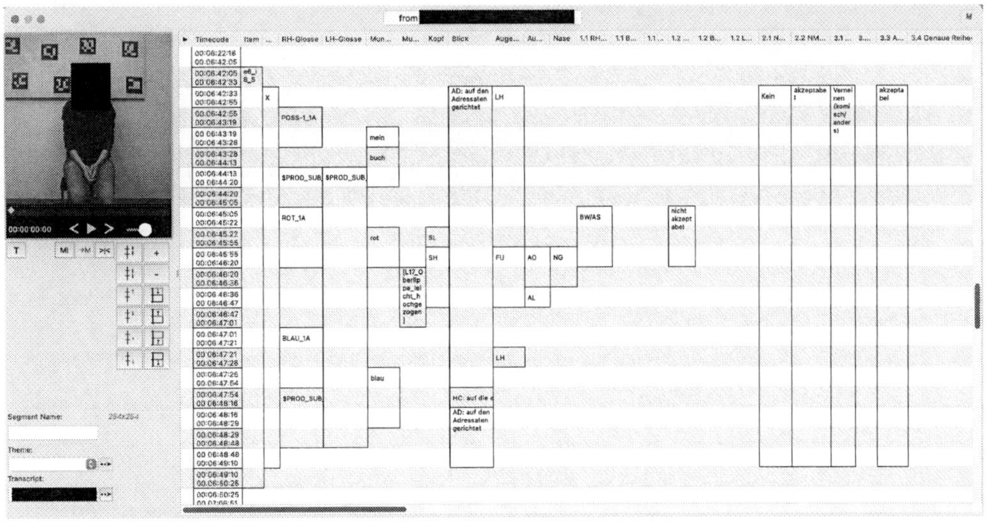

Figure 3: Example of a sentence annotation in iLex, with the transcript name and participant's face anonymized.

	Prompt	Output
2	*Analysiere Fehler in einem in Deutschschweizerischer Gebärdensprache (DSGS) produzierten Satz ohne Sprach- oder Satzdetails. Verfasse eine klare, ganz kurze Erklärung wie für einen DSGS-Lernenden. Nutze ‚Gebärde' statt ‚Zeichen', ‚Komponente' statt ‚Signale'. Bitte duzen, Förmlichkeiten verzichten. Verzichte auf zusätzliche Informationen. Hier sind die Annotationen: Manuelle Fehler: 1. Glosse SALAT_1A ist akzeptabel, Fehler in der Handbewegung. Nicht-manuelle Fehler: Fehler in Augenbrauenbewegung, Mundbild, Mundform, Kopfbewegung ist nicht akzeptabel. Problem auf Satzebene: Kein. Akzeptabilität ganzer Satz: akzeptabel.*	*Beim Gebärden des Satzes mit der Gebärde SALAT_1A ist die Handbewegung nicht ganz richtig. Achte auch auf deine Augenbrauen, Mundbild, Mundform und Kopfbewegung – diese sind nicht korrekt und sollten verbessert werden. Der gesamte Satz ist trotzdem verständlich.*
	'Analyze errors in a sentence produced in Swiss German Sign Language (DSGS) without language or sentence details. Write a clear, very short explanation as for a DSGS learner. Use 'sign' instead of 'sign', 'component' instead of 'signals'. Please use first names, avoid formalities. Do without additional information. Here are the annotations: Manual errors: 1st gloss SALAT_1A is acceptable, error in hand gesture. Non-manual errors: Errors in eyebrow movement, mouth image, mouth shape, head movement is not acceptable. Problem at sentence level: None. Acceptability of whole sentence: acceptable.'	'When signing the sentence with the SALAT_1A gesture, the hand movement is not quite correct. Also pay attention to your eyebrows, mouth image, mouth shape and head movement - these are not correct and should be improved. The whole sentence is still understandable.'

Table 7: Example of generated elaborations judged as good explanation by the learner annotators.

	Prompt	Output
44	*Analysiere Fehler in einem in Deutschschweizerischer Gebärdensprache (DSGS) produzierten Satz ohne Sprach- oder Satzdetails. Verfasse eine klare, ganz kurze Erklärung wie für einen DSGS-Lernenden. Nutze ‚Gebärde' statt ‚Zeichen', ‚Komponente' statt ‚Signale'. Bitte duzen, Förmlichkeiten verzichten. Verzichte auf zusätzliche Informationen. Hier sind die Annotationen:* ***Manuelle Fehler: Kein****. Nicht-manuelle Fehler: Fehler in Augenbrauenbewegung, Kopfbewegung ist nicht akzeptabel. Problem auf Satzebene: Geschwindigkeit oder Fluss des produzierten Satzes. Akzeptabilität ganzer Satz: akzeptabel.*	*In deinem Satz in DSGS gibt es ein paar Fehler:* ***1. Manuelle Fehler: Achte darauf, dass jede Gebärde korrekt geformt und ausgeführt wird.*** *2. Nicht-manuelle Fehler: Deine Augenbrauenbewegung und Kopfbewegung passen nicht zum Inhalt des Satzes. Diese Komponenten sind wichtig, um den Satz richtig zu betonen und zu strukturieren. 3. Problem auf Satzebene: Die Geschwindigkeit oder der Fluss deiner Gebärden ist nicht gleichmässig. Versuche, einen natürlichen Rhythmus zu finden, damit der Satz flüssig wirkt. Obwohl es diese Fehler gibt, ist der Satz insgesamt akzeptabel. Übe weiter, um die Genauigkeit zu verbessern!*
	'Analyze errors in a sentence produced in Swiss German Sign Language (DSGS) without language or sentence details. Write a clear, very short explanation as for a DSGS learner. Use 'sign' instead of 'sign', 'component' instead of 'signals'. Please use first names, avoid formalities. Do without additional information. Here are the annotations: **Manual errors: None**, non-manual errors: error in 1st eyebrow movement, head movement is not acceptable. Sentence level problem: speed or flow of sentence produced. Acceptability of whole sentence: acceptable.'	'There are a few errors in your sentence in DSGS: **1. Manual errors: Make sure that each gesture is formed and executed correctly.** 2. non-manual errors: Your eyebrow movement and head movement do not match the content of the sentence. These components are important to emphasize and structure the sentence correctly. 3. problem at sentence level: the speed or flow of your gestures is not even. Try to find a natural rhythm to make the sentence flow. Although there are these mistakes, the sentence is acceptable overall. Keep practicing to improve accuracy!'

Table 8: Example a of generated hallucination. It includes a manual error (in bold), even though it was not in the original prompt.

	Prompt	Output
4	*Analysiere Fehler in einem in Deutschschweizerischer Gebärdensprache (DSGS) produzierten Satz ohne Sprach- oder Satzdetails. Verfasse eine klare, ganz kurze Erklärung wie für einen DSGS-Lernenden. Nutze ‚Gebärde' statt ‚Zeichen', ‚Komponente' statt ‚Signale'. Bitte duzen, Förmlichkeiten verzichten. Verzichte auf zusätzliche Informationen. Hier sind die Annotationen: Manuelle Fehler:* ***Nicht-manuelle Fehler: Fehler in Augenbrauenbewegung, ist akzeptabel.*** *Problem auf Satzebene: Kein. Akzeptabilität ganzer Satz: voll akzeptabel.*	*Da keine spezifischen Fehler in den manuellen oder nicht-manuellen Komponenten angegeben sind und der Satz als "voll akzeptabel" bewertet wurde, gibt es nichts zu korrigieren. Deine Gebärden sind korrekt, und die Augenbrauenbewegung ist auch akzeptabel. Mach weiter so!*
	'Analyze errors in a sentence produced in Swiss German Sign Language (DSGS) without language or sentence details. Write a clear, very short explanation as for a DSGS learner. Use 'sign' instead of 'sign', 'component' instead of 'signals'. Please use the first name, avoid formalities. Do without additional information. Here are the annotations: Manual errors: **non-manual errors: error in eyebrow movement, is acceptable.** Sentence-level problem: None. Whole sentence acceptability: fully acceptable.'	'Since there are no specific errors indicated in the manual or non-manual components and the sentence was rated as "fully acceptable", there is nothing to correct. Your gestures are correct, and the eyebrow movement is also acceptable. Keep up the good work!'
57	*Analysiere Fehler in einem in Deutschschweizerischer Gebärdensprache (DSGS) produzierten Satz ohne Sprach- oder Satzdetails. Verfasse eine klare, ganz kurze Erklärung wie für einen DSGS-Lernenden. Nutze ‚Gebärde statt ‚Zeichen', ‚Komponente' statt ‚Signale'. Bitte duzen, Förmlichkeiten verzichten. Verzichte auf zusätzliche Informationen. Hier sind die Annotationen: Manuelle Fehler: 1. Glosse GESTERN_1A ist akzeptabel, Fehler in der Aufführungsstelle.2. Glosse ESSEN_1A ist nicht akzeptabel, Fehler in der Handbewegung.3. Glosse SCHLECHT_1A ist nicht akzeptabel, Fehler in der Handbewegung und Aufführungsstelle.4. Glosse IX_1A ist akzeptabel, Fehler in der Handbewegung.* ***Nicht-manuelle Fehler: Fehler in Augenbrauenbewegung, Mundform, ist akzeptabel.*** *Problem auf Satzebene: Kombination der Probleme. Akzeptabilität ganzer Satz: nicht akzeptabel.*	*In deinem Satz gibt es einige Fehler: 1. Bei der Gebärde für "GESTERN" ist die Position, wo du die Gebärde machst, nicht richtig. 2. Die Gebärde für "ESSEN" ist nicht korrekt, weil du die Handbewegung falsch machst. 3. Bei "SCHLECHT" machst du sowohl die Handbewegung als auch die Position falsch. 4. Die Gebärde, die auf etwas zeigt (IX), ist okay, aber die Bewegung deiner Hand ist nicht richtig.* ***Ausserdem hast du einen Fehler bei der Bewegung deiner Augenbrauen, aber deine Mundform ist in Ordnung.*** *Weil diese Fehler zusammenkommen, ist der ganze Satz leider nicht akzeptabel. Achte darauf, die einzelnen Komponenten der Gebärden und ihre Kombination im Satz zu verbessern.*
	'Analyze errors in a sentence produced in Swiss German Sign Language (DSGS) without language or sentence details. Write a clear, very short explanation as for a DSGS learner. Use 'sign' instead of 'sign', 'component' instead of 'signals'. Please use first names, avoid formalities. Do without additional information. Here are the annotations: Manual errors: 1. gloss GESTERN_1A is acceptable, error in performance part.2. gloss ESSEN_1A is not acceptable, error in hand movement.3. gloss SCHLECHT_1A is not acceptable, error in hand movement and performance part.4. gloss IX_1A is acceptable, error in hand movement. **Non-manual errors: error in 1st eyebrow movement, mouth shape, is acceptable.** Problem at sentence level: combination of problems. Acceptability of whole sentence: not acceptable.'	'There are a few mistakes in your sentence: 1. in the gesture for "GESTERN", the position where you make the gesture is not correct. 2. the gesture for "ESSEN" is not correct because you are making the hand movement incorrectly. 3. for "SCHLECHT" you are making both the hand movement and the position incorrectly. 4. the gesture pointing to something (IX) is okay, but the movement of your hand is not correct. You also have a mistake in the movement of your eyebrows, but your mouth shape is fine. Unfortunately, because these errors come together, the whole sentence is not acceptable. Make sure to improve the individual components of the gestures and their combination in the sentence.'

Table 9: Examples of generated elaborations wrongly formulating the errors in the non-manual components.

	Prompt	Output
35	*Analysiere Fehler in einem in Deutschschweizerischer Gebärdensprache (DSGS) produzierten Satz ohne Sprach- oder Satzdetails. Verfasse eine klare, ganz kurze Erklärung wie für einen DSGS-Lernenden. Nutze ‚Gebärde' statt ‚Zeichen', ‚Komponente' statt ‚Signale'. Bitte duzen, Förmlichkeiten verzichten. Verzichte auf zusätzliche Informationen. Hier sind die Annotationen: Manuelle Fehler: Kein. Nicht-manuelle Fehler: Kein. Problem auf Satzebene: Kein. Akzeptabilität ganzer Satz: Kein.*	*Ohne konkrete Details zum Satz oder den spezifischen Fehlern kann ich keine spezifische Analyse durchführen. Allgemein gesagt, wenn in einem Satz in der Deutschschweizerischen Gebärdensprache (DSGS) Fehler auftreten, können diese in verschiedenen Bereichen liegen: 1. Manuelle Fehler: Diese betreffen die Ausführung der Gebärden mit den Händen. Zum Beispiel könnte die Handform, die Orientierung, die Bewegung oder die Position im Raum falsch sein. 2. Nicht-manuelle Fehler: Diese beziehen sich auf Ausdrücke, die nicht mit den Händen gemacht werden, wie Mimik, Kopfbewegungen oder Körperhaltung, die für die Bedeutung eines Satzes wichtig sein können. 3. Problem auf Satzebene: Hier geht es um die Struktur des Satzes, also wie die Gebärden zusammengesetzt sind. Es könnte ein Problem mit der Reihenfolge der Gebärden geben oder mit der Grammatik der DSGS. 4. Akzeptabilität ganzer Satz: Dies bezieht sich darauf, wie gut der gesamte Satz verstanden wird. Selbst wenn einzelne Gebärden korrekt sind, kann der Satz als Ganzes unklar oder missverständlich sein. Um Fehler zu vermeiden, achte darauf, dass jede Komponente der Gebärde korrekt ist, die nicht-manuellen Signale passend sind, die Satzstruktur der DSGS entspricht und der Gesamtsatz klar und verständlich ist.*
	'Analyze errors in a sentence produced in Swiss German Sign Language (DSGS) without language or sentence details. Write a clear, very short explanation as for a DSGS learner. Use 'sign' instead of 'sign', 'component' instead of 'signals'. Please use the first name, avoid formalities. Do without additional information. Here are the annotations: Manual errors: None. Non-manual errors: None. Sentence-level problem: None. Whole sentence acceptability: None.'	'Without concrete details about the sentence or the specific errors, I cannot carry out a specific analysis. Generally speaking, when errors occur in a sentence in Swiss German Sign Language (DSGS), these can be in different areas: 1. Manual errors: These concern the execution of the gestures with the hands. For example, the hand shape, orientation, movement or position in space may be incorrect. 2. non-manual errors: These relate to expressions that are not made with the hands, such as facial expressions, head movements or body posture, which can be important for the meaning of a sentence. 3rd problem at sentence level: This concerns the structure of the sentence, i.e. how the gestures are put together. There could be a problem with the order of the signs or with the grammar of the DSGS. 4. acceptability of the whole sentence: This refers to how well the whole sentence is understood. Even if individual signs are correct, the sentence as a whole may be unclear or misunderstood. To avoid errors, make sure that each component of the gesture is correct, the non-manual signals are appropriate, the sentence structure conforms to DSGS, and the overall sentence is clear and understandable.'

Table 10: Example of a generated hallucination. This is a completely invented text due to the absence of errors in the prompt.

Towards Better Inclusivity: A Diverse Tweet Corpus of English Varieties

Nhi Pham*
New York University
nhi.pham@nyu.edu

Lachlan Pham*
New York University
lp2233@nyu.edu

Adam Meyers
New York University
meyers@cs.nyu.edu

Abstract

The prevalence of social media presents a growing opportunity to collect and analyse examples of English varieties. Whilst usage of these varieties is often used only in spoken contexts or hard-to-access private messages, social media sites like Twitter provide a platform for users to communicate informally in a scrapeable format. Notably, Indian English (Hinglish), Singaporean English (Singlish), and African-American English (AAE) can be commonly found online. These varieties pose a challenge to existing natural language processing (NLP) tools as they often differ orthographically and syntactically from standard English for which the majority of these tools are built. NLP models trained on standard English texts produced biased outcomes for users of underrepresented varieties (Blodgett and O'Connor, 2017). Some research has aimed to overcome the inherent biases caused by unrepresentative data through techniques like data augmentation or adjusting training models. We aim to address the issue of bias at its root - the data itself. We curate a dataset of tweets from countries with high proportions of underserved English variety speakers, and propose an annotation framework of six categorical classifications along a pseudo-spectrum that measures the degree of standard English and that thereby indirectly aims to surface the manifestations of English varieties in these tweets. The code and dataset are available on phamleyennhi/diverse_english_corpus.

1 Introduction

In many respects, there is a lack of linguistic and geographic diversity in NLP research. Whether that be in authorship identity, conference location, or target language (Faisal et al., 2022), it can be seen that wealthy, English-speaking nations are overrepresented. Even within these overrepresented nationalities, there exist subgroups, usually correlated with socioeconomic factors, who are not fairly represented (Blodgett et al., 2020). A natural consequence is that the international proliferation and rapid advancement of language technologies serve the interests of the privileged.

One major influence on the fairness of modern NLP systems is data availability. Our research targets the geographic diversity of NLP datasets and specifically seeks to introduce a new corpus that captures a range of English varieties. English's status as a global lingua franca - as a consequence of historical colonialism and the current social influence of the western world - has meant that it has been adopted as an official language or, at least, it has become widely spoken in many countries across the world (Jenkins, 2009). In each culture, English takes on a different flavor to match the identities and needs of its speakers. In some cases, English is blended with other regional languages, forming pidgins and creoles.[1] In others, English takes over as a dominant language and phonetic indicators like accents or remnantal discourse markers become the main differentiators for that variety of English. Sometimes, English becomes a complementary language, children learning it alongside one or more other distinct languages, regularly code-switching according to contextual circumstances or to take advantage of nuances in connotation of different languages (Kortmann et al., 2008); each manifestation evinces a unique narrative about a speaker's cultural and socio-economic background. With such a range of Englishes spoken, it seems a missed opportunity that widely-used English data sets significantly overrepresent samples from America and Great Britain relative to their respective proportional constitution of global English speakers (Faisal et al., 2022).

*These authors contributed equally to this work

[1]This assumes a model of pigeons and creoles in which there is a shared dominant lexifier (e.g., English) and a diverse linguistic community that develops a shared language using modified words from the lexifier and other syntactic and phonological features from other languages, e.g., Caribbean languages (Kouwenberg and Singler, 2008)

Proceedings of The 18th Linguistic Annotation Workshop (LAW-XVIII), pages 61–70
March 22, 2024 ©2024 Association for Computational Linguistics

As a direct consequence, language technologies are predominantly trained with western varieties of standard English and make algorithmic assumptions based on standard English grammar. Since the usage of English varieties are coupled tightly with geography and demography, there are numerous social and ethical implications of unrepresentative data. Cámbara et al. (2021) demonstrates there are accuracy biases in state-of-the-art speech recognition tools favoring accents and dialects most prevalent in training corpora. This reduces the effectiveness of, e.g., auto-captioning tools reducing the accessibility of global spoken media. Blodgett and O'Connor (2017) shows that language identification performs worse on AAE than white-aligned English. This is notable because language identification is often an early filtration step in online text processing pipelines. For example, sentiment analysis research may discard anything labeled non-English including the higher proportion of false negatives for tweets of English varieties.

This research aims to address this need to diversify data by producing a corpus of tweets posted from English-speaking countries across Asia and Africa, as well as English tweets from the United States and the United Kingdom. Our work leverages the availability of geo-tagged and informal written texts provided by Twitter to create a dataset permeated by conversational dialectal features - features which were historically limited to the spoken medium. Furthermore, the recruited annotators come from the international student body of New York University which consists of multilingual individuals. Thus, these annotators are capable of extracting insights drawn from their experience in communities where a select English variety is commonplace. We propose a new annotation system that caters to social media tweets of English varieties, and assess the linguistic diversity of our corpus by examining its distribution across 6 categories and frequently-used words or phrases in each location. We apply common language identifiers such as langid.py, spaCy, and Google Translate API to highlight their performance disparities compared to tweets of non-western English varieties.

In section 2, we examine related NLP work on underserved English varieties, and outline some other attempts at addressing unrepresentative corpora. Section 3 elaborates on the choice of Twitter as a data source, explains the data collection approach and provides a brief linguistic variation analysis on our data. Section 4 describes the annotation process including: a summarised set of annotation guidelines and its justification (section 4.1), inter-annotator agreement benchmarks (section 4.2) and the recruitment and training of annotators (section 4.3). Section 4.5 evaluates the resulting corpus. In Section 5, we investigate biases in several off-the-shelf language identification tools towards non-western English varieties. Section 6 discusses potential applications and the continuation of this research. We also acknowledge several limitations of our corpus.

2 Related Work

The need to address the underrepresentation of English varieties in corpora has been recognised and approached in a number of ways ranging from manual collection to automatic generation. Dacon et al. (2022) develops a rule-based method to translate standard American English (SAE) sentences to African-American English (AAE). This tool - CodeSwitch - relies on a list of 20 deterministic substitutions that aim to preserve "textual accuracy i.e., the original structure, intent, semantic equivalence and quality of a text." These are derived from the translations and annotations of 3 AAE speaking workers. An independent set of AAE speakers generally believed that the machine generated output of the tool resembled human translations. The researchers note that a deterministic substitution method lacks contextual awareness and, consequently, some of the machine generated text were indeed identified as most likely machine generated. Such a tool simultaneously overgeneralises and undergeneralises the use of AAE. Not only would the rules be reflective of the patterns of the 3 AAE-speaking workers, it assumes that every instance of a 'translatable' sequence would be converted into an AAE form. Similarly, the substitutions lack the inclusion of more complex varietal features such as idiomatic phrases or regional-specific lingo. Nevertheless, CodeSwitch is a highly scalable and rapid way to augment current SAE datasets with an English variety, leveraging most of the existing labels since substitutions preserve the overall syntactic qualities of the text and thereby reducing the labor-demanding need to create and label new datasets.

The International Corpus of English (ICE) project (Greenbaum and Nelson, 1996) relies on the efforts of global linguistic research teams to produce English corpora for regions and countries where English is an official first or additional language. They curate and annotate various spoken and written texts like press editorials, news broadcasts and classroom lessons. This process is significantly labour-intensive and requires specialised local researchers. These corpora are much more suited towards qualitative sociolinguistic investigations due to the limited sample sizes. Furthermore, each corpus is composed predominantly of formal texts so most comparative observations would be made on the standard national varieties of English as opposed to the more dialectal and informal varieties that our investigation is targeting.

Cook and Brinton (2017) create national web corpora which are also largely composed of formal texts. They scrape websites which have national-top level domains (e.g. .au, .ca) corresponding to the countries. The authors conduct some frequency comparisons between each national corpus and are able to surface some terms unique to a country (e.g. Canadianisms like "heritage language" or "pot light"). This process is more automated but the resultant corpora similarly lack the informal variations we are studying.

Finally, the Twitter AAE corpus by Blodgett and O'Connor (2017) most closely resembles the ones we are developing. It is a corpus of African American-aligned English tweets categorised based on probabilistic assumptions about tweet authorship. A tweet was placed in the African American-aligned corpus if it contained terms that were more frequently observed in tweets posted from areas with high concentrations of African-Americans. We make a comparable, albeit less statistically complex, geographic assumption in the creation of our corpus that tweets from a particular country are more likely to exhibit features of a given variety.

3 Data

We use Twitter as a source for our data for two primary reasons. First, its international popularity and accessible API allows for simple data collection, due to the large volume of data which can be filtered based on location.[2] Secondly, despite its written mode, the informal social media context means that some samples will be able to capture the differences between English varieties that would usually be found in casual spoken conversations. These differences include: code-switching, non-standard spellings to reflect phonetic variation and regional lexical markers.

3.1 Data Collection

To minimize topical influence, our approach involves randomly selecting 100 tweets per day posted between January 1, 2022, and September 1, 2022. We explicitly consider 5 non-western cities: Accra, Islamabad, Manila, New Delhi, and Singapore. Our early observations show that tweets from the capital city capture linguistic variations better than tweets from smaller cities in the same country. We also collect tweets from New York and London as representatives of western English varieties. This results in a total of 170,800 tweets, with 24,400 tweets collected for each city [3].

An attempt to filter tweets with less than 60% English words shows that roughly 71.2% tweets of our corpus satisfied the threshold. Upon our investigation, most filtered tweets are non-English. To ensure the quality of our corpus, we decide to retain only tweets that have at least 60% English words. This will help us maintain a diverse range of code-switching and non-standard English terms in our corpus. This does not guarantee that non-English tweets are completely removed, as some non-English words may have the same spelling as English words.

3.2 Linguistic Variation Analysis

In our initial corpus evaluation, we identify orthographic variations, regional lexical markers, and syntactic differences in English varieties. Our analysis reveals differentiating features of these varieties, which in turn help us develop a comprehensive system of labeling for our annotation process.

3.2.1 Orthographic Variation

We find various instances of English phrases or words that are abbreviated, shortened, or altered. For example, "tbh" for "to be honest," "smh" for "shake my head," and "omg" for "oh my God" are frequently encountered abbreviations. Within Twitter's 280-character limit, such acronyms serve as linguistic shortcuts that enable users to convey their message efficiently. Similarly, English contractions like "gimme" (give me), "damit" (damn it), "needa" (need to), and "lemme" (let me) reflect the informal and conversational tone of tweets. Another important orthographic variation includes unconventional

[2]The Twitter API was only publicly-available until February 9, 2023.

[3]Retweets were not omitted

spellings and slang words like "bruh," "yey," "wassup," "lmao," and "hella." Some words are modified by adding repeated characters at the end, such as "hmmm," "omggg," and "plsss." These examples are used to express a specific tone, emphasis, or emotion, and have become increasingly prevalent among younger generations on social media. While such orthographic variations exist in both western and non-western tweets, tweets from New York and London tend to adhere more closely to formal language conventions. In fact, the percentage of formally-aligned English tweets in these cities is roughly 29% higher than in other English-speaking communities we studied.

3.2.2 Lexical Variation

To confirm the existence of lexical variation in our dataset, we calculate the percentage of non-English words present in the collected data. We first create a list of English words using several existing Natural Language Toolkit corpora, including wordnet2021, masc_tagged, English stopwords, and Word Lists (Loper and Bird, 2002). For the tweets collected from all locations, we pre-process the data by removing digits, hashtags, mentions, links, punctuation, and non-alphanumeric characters (such as emojis). Our analysis shows that tweets from Accra, Islamabad, Manila, New Delhi, and Singapore had a higher percentage (67.9%) of non-English words compared to tweets from London and New York (48.5%). This is expected as tweets from London and New York are more likely to adhere to standard English. However, it is worth noting that some words were classified as non-English due to misspellings or named entities.

Some written varieties such as Singlish and Ghanaian English can be identified by the inclusion of additional non-English words. In Singlish tweets, discourse particle "lah" is often added in the end of the sentence. It has a range of pragmatic functions and serves a similar function to "了" (le) in Mandarin – an aspect marker, roughly translating to "already". The latter example is reflective of the significant Chinese influences on the language. In multiple tweets from Accra, the word "paa" is frequently used to add emphasis to a sentence, often appearing at the end.

3.2.3 Syntactic Variation

Code-switching is commonly observed in multilingual locations like Accra, Islamabad, Manila, New Delhi, and Singapore. It involves the use, in English, of syntax structures and grammar rules from another language. This leads to significant syntactic differences between (standard) American/British English and other English varieties. This phenomenon is particularly ubiquitous in informal social media settings, where speakers of multiple languages switch between them resulting in a high frequency of code-switched tweets. For example, Singapore has four official languages: English, Malay, Mandarin, and Tamil; the Philippines has two official languages: Filipino and English; Ghana's official language is English, but local languages are widely spoken (including Twi, Fante, and Ewe).

Another syntactic difference between English varieties and standard American and British English is reflected in verb conjugation. For example, consider the following tweet from Accra:

> *"Bro! We be too relaxed for this side! We make am small then we relax"*

The use of "be" instead of "are" or "are being" to indicate ongoing or habitual action is an example of non-standard English verb conjugation. Additionally, the use of "am" instead of "it" is another example of a non-standard usage.

4 Annotation

The priority in designing annotation guidelines is ensuring that the classifications are (a) meaningful so annotators are able to confidently differentiate between labels whilst also coming to independent agreement about the classification of a text and (b) useful so the tweets in different categories contain extractable and informative features. The two primary researchers iteratively refine the annotation criteria, alternating between collaborative and independent labeling. They regularly apply inter-annotator agreement metrics to measure incremental improvements. The goal is to use class labels to isolate English varieties, by first distinguishing broadly between English and non-English words or sentences, and then distinguishing standard written English from English varieties. The following list has been taken directly from Blake (2018) and reflects the guidelines we sought to follow in the creation of the annotation guidelines and throughout the annotation process:

1. Annotate using tags at one level more finely than the research question requires.

2. Provide clear rules and examples in which boundary cases are discussed in an annotation booklet.

3. Develop, trial and require all annotators to complete a training course or session.

4. Require annotators to reach a benchmarked standard.

5. Mentor and provide constructive actionable feedback to annotators.

6. Report inter-annotator agreement in sufficient detail to convince skeptical readers.

4.1 Annotation Guidelines

Below is a summarised version of annotation guidelines used by the primary researchers and the annotators. The labels do not correspond to their formal linguistic denotations. Rather, the labels succinctly conveyed the intended definition.

4.1.1 Rules

- Treat existing standard named entities (person names, geopolitical entities, etc) as English when calculating the proportion of English
- Ignore tags, hashtags and emojis
- If a tweet meets the criteria for multiple labels in the list below, select the label that appears later in the list

4.1.2 Labels

1. **Syntactic English** includes sentences which follow standard syntactic rules and are composed of standard English words.

2. **Non-syntactic English** includes sentences of standard English words where at least one grammar rule is not followed (conjugation, word order, capitalisation, etc.)

3. **Informal English** includes sentences with at least one word or term is misspelled (e.g. gnite) or is an informal or non-standard term, such as slang (e.g. yeet) or acronym (e.g. YOLO)

4. **Code-switched** includes sentences with at least one region- or language-specific word such that someone from a different country and who speaks only English would not understand it. At least 40% of the words are in English.

5. **Incidental English** includes sentences where less than 40% of the words are in English and there is at least one English word.

6. **No English** includes sentences with exclusively non-English words.

Some of the rules aim to indirectly isolate the various features of English varieties; for example, an analysis on the tweets composing rules 2 and 3, could highlight the morpho-syntactic and lexical differences of an English variety while rule 4 targets tweets which incorporate use of other languages.

Annotators are provided a simple interface consisting of the raw original tweet and a cleaned version consisting of the uncapitalised tweet with hashtags, user tags, hyperlinks and punctuation removed. The raw tweet is necessary when assessing the syntactic correctness of the tweet while the cleaned tweet allows for a simpler way to identify and count any non-English words.

4.2 Inter-annotator agreement benchmarks

After the final iteration of the annotation guidelines, the primary researchers independently annotated 500 novel tweets from Singapore.

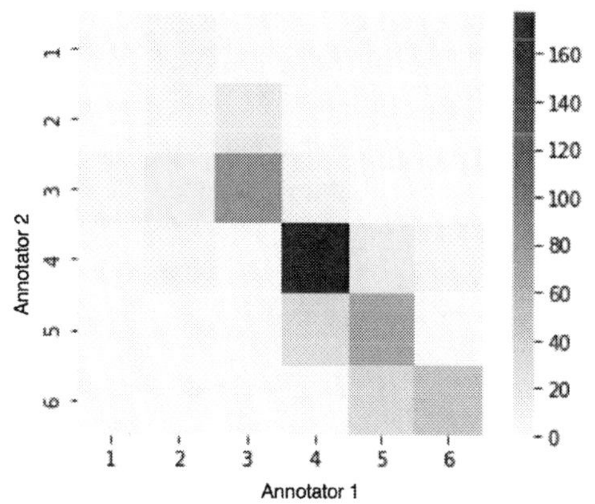

Figure 1: Confusion matrix – 500 Singapore tweets

Using metrics for independent, nominal categories, the percent agreement between the researchers is 77% and the Cohen's Kappa coefficient - a commonly used statistical measure of inter-rater reliability that accounts for the possibility of agreement by chance (Gisev et al., 2013) - is 0.69 which is considered 'substantial' (Landis and Koch, 1977). Given the large number of categories and their relative complexity, these scores can be seen as strong indicators that the definitions allow for meaningful differentiation.

One important observation in the confusion matrix (Figure 1) is that the disagreement is concentrated around the diagonal. This suggests that adjacent categories resemble each other much more closely than distant ones. This makes sense for categories 4-6 because there are quantitative boundaries (i.e. proportion of English). The relationship between categories 1-4 is less obvious except for the fact that later categories are chosen if criteria is met for multiple categories, meaning that there are stricter requirements for lower-ranked categories. As soon as an annotator detects the presence of one category's defining characteristics, they could not classify the tweet into an earlier category. This trend is confirmed by the decreasing number of tweets classified from *Code-switched* to *Syntactic English*. The relationship between adjacent categories points to an implicit ordinality, which reflects our intention to create labels that indirectly measures distance from formal standard English.

For ordinal categories, inter-annotator agreement can be additionally and appropriately measured by correlation coefficients that weigh the similar categories as an indication of partial agreement (Gisev et al., 2013). Applying the quadratically-weighted Cohen's Kappa (0.87) and the Kendall coefficient of concordance (0.86), we observe very strong agreement between annotators. As a benchmark for annotators, we required a quadratically-weighted Cohen's Kappa exceeding 0.8 before allowing them to independently annotate.

4.3 Annotation training

We recruited 5 students who are nationals of the countries we aimed to study. A brief summary of their profiles can be seen in Table 1. All students are completing their tertiary education in English and are thus fluent in English. They are also speakers of dominant local languages from their respective countries. While it was not strictly necessary for annotators to understand the content of each tweet, this annotation process was an opportunity to gather informed insights about tweet topics and linguistic nuances that individuals of diverging backgrounds could identify.

Each annotator was guided through a training session in which they were briefed about the research goals and provided with a comprehensive explanation of the annotation guidelines. They were guided through a tutorial and given 25 examples of Singaporean tweets for each category and instructions for handling edge cases. We then provided them with 100 pre-labelled tweets from Singapore that served as a qualification task for which they needed to achieve a quadratically-weighted Cohen's Kappa exceeding 0.8. While we had prepared a further 200 pre-labelled tweets for an additional two rounds of iterative feedback before disqualification, all 5 annotators met our benchmark on their first attempt (Table 1), which is further evidence of the distinctiveness of each category.

We asked the annotators to list any ambiguities they faced in this process and we provided individualised feedback to further improve the quality of their annotations before allowing them to move on to annotating their assigned tweets. Subsequently, we sampled the collected and filtered tweets into batches of 100 and distributed the sets corresponding to their country. The number of batches completed varied for each annotator depending on their availability. By their last batches, annotators were able to label around 200 tweets per hour on average. In future, each tweet should be classified by independent annotators to further ensure reliability.

4.4 Annotator observations

We asked each participant to do a short voice note recording of any observations they made through the process of annotation. Many highlighted demographic and topical trends. For example, all indicated that local politics was a common subject; annotator 4 frequently noticed expressions of patriotism or praise for the Indian Prime Minister. They also repeatedly saw tweets about religion and cricket which are in line with the common national interests. Annotator 1 noticed that the political tweets in the Philippines tended to be critical of the ruling party and that users more frequently discussed daily activities with their followers. These reports verify that Twitter serves differing social functions in different countries (Poblete et al., 2011), which means that subject matter could be used as an indicator for tweet origin.

The annotators were also asked about their experience with the annotation guidelines. Some expressed confusion about what constitutes a syntactic English sentence when deciding whether a tweet constitutes *Syntactic* or *Non-syntactic* English. Annotators are not expected to know formal morpho-syntactic rules, especially when most

Country of Origin (Languages Spoken)	Datasets labelled	Weighted Cohen's Kappa
The Philippines (Tagalog and dialect)	Philippines	0.86
Pakistan (Urdu)	Pakistan	0.87
Pakistan (Urdu)	Pakistan and India	0.82
India (Hindi and Urdu)	India	0.85
Ghana (English, Twi, Hausa, Pidgin)	Ghana	0.84

Table 1: Results of annotation qualification task in annotation training

language users can rarely articulate the reason a sentence is well-formed. Given that there were proportionally few examples of tweets labeled *Syntactic English*, it seems appropriate to merge these categories in future.

In contrast, two annotators indicated that the *Code-switched* category lacked granularity and felt like they were 'lumping' linguistically dissimilar tweets into the same bucket. For example, annotator 5 said they used the *Code-switched* label for tweets in which users switched between English and a local language and for tweets which used Ghanaian Pidgin English (Broken English). Similarly, annotator 1 distinguished between (i) tweets where only one language (English or Tagalog) was used in each of multiple composing sentences and (ii) tweets where Tagalog words were interwoven in predominantly English sentences. Both types were labeled *Code-switched* according to the criteria. This suggests that the *Code-switched* category could be broken up into even more descriptive categories, especially given that it constituted the plurality of labeled tweets. However, since each annotator identified different distinguishing linguistic features - e.g. lexicon for Ghanaian tweets and sentence composition for Filipino tweets - appropriate new categories may have to be specific and contextually-appropriate for each country.

4.5 Corpus Statistics

Our manually labeled subset of 3564 tweets constitutes approximately 7.2% of the total corpus. From these, we selected 350 labeled tweets with at least 70% English from each location to examine the category distribution. Figure 2 shows that *Code-switched* and *Informal English* are the dominant categories in tweets from Accra, Islamabad, and Singapore, while *Code-switched* is clearly the most significant category for Manila and New Delhi tweets. The variations in category distributions across these locations are evidence for linguistic diversity among English varieties in our corpus.

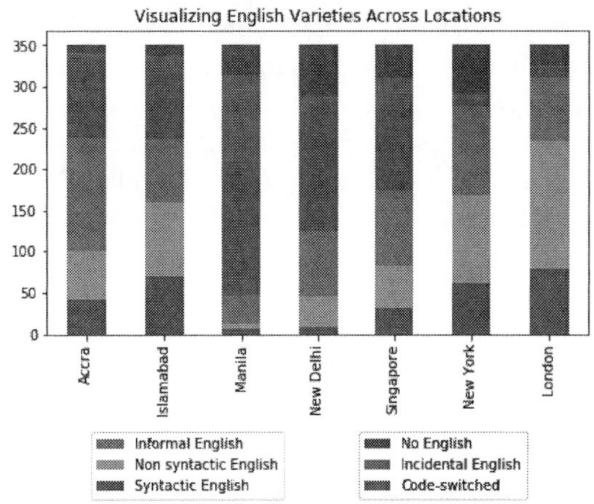

Figure 2: Overall label distribution of 350 tweets in each of the locations: Accra, Islamabad, Manila, New Delhi, Singapore, New York and London

Specifically, the presence of code-switching in tweets from these locations highlights the blending of English with local languages, resulting in a more diverse and unique dataset that cannot be captured in standard formal English texts. Furthermore, the dominance of *Code-switched* tweets in Manila and New Delhi further emphasizes the prevalence and importance of multilingualism in these regions.

While it is expected that tweets from New York and London are more likely to resemble standard English, we still observe a higher percentage of *Non-syntactic English* and *Informal English* tweets. This may be attributed to the informal nature of social media platforms such as Twitter, where users tend to communicate in a more casual and less structured manner. The *Code-switched* category was rarest in these two locations. This is not surprising since code-switching typically occurs in multilingual contexts, and thus the predominance of monolingual English speakers in New York and London may account for the lower incidence of code-switching.

5 NLP Tools on English Varieties

We evaluate three language identifiers - *langid.py*, *spaCy-langdetect*, and *Google Translate API* - for detecting English vs. non-English tweets in our corpus. In our annotation framework, tweets in categories 1-3 should be classified as English without question. For category 4, code-switching, we randomly sampled 100 tweets from Accra, Islamabad, Manila, New Delhi, and Singapore, and manually determined the proportion of English words, including both standard and informal language. Our analysis reveals that 82% of the *Code-switched* tweets had at least half of their content in English. Thus, we consider *Code-switched* tweets as English.

When evaluating these tools on 350 tweets from each city, we find that their accuracies are much higher for American and British English than for other English varieties. Our results are tallied up in Table 2 and 3. The differences are 21.82%, 19.77%, and 32.58% for *langid.py*, *spaCy-langdetect*, and *Google Translate API*. Even when we use a more conservative approach and do not consider tweets in *Code-switched* category as English, the tools demonstrate higher accuracy for western English than non-western English. The differences in accuracy scores between western and non-western English are 12.43%, 7.33%, and 8.93% respectively. These gaps in accuracy between English varieties highlight ethical implications. Such NLP tools are built and trained on large datasets of American and British English, which leads to bias and inaccuracies when applied to other English varieties. This can result in discrimination against individuals who speak non-standard varieties of English, e.g., in automated hiring processes (Köchling and Wehner, 2020).

6 Future Work

While the initial annotation process was labor-intensive, it was essential for us to develop a thorough annotation framework. This serves as a potentially valuable resource in the continuing labeling process, ensuring that the labeled data is consistent and of high quality. Nevertheless, the limited amount of labeled data in our corpus poses a significant challenge to achieve sufficient coverage and accuracy in many NLP tasks. To address this issue, we plan to explore active learning techniques or large language models (LLMs) such as GPT-3 to expand our corpus. The labeled portion of our corpus will serve either as seeds to train a machine learning model that can then identify similar, yet unlabeled, data points in the remaining corpus, or as a baseline to evaluate annotations produced by LLMs. Moreover, our corpus experiments focus on a fundamental NLP task: language identification, specifically identifying English vs. non-English tweets. We demonstrate the biases in pre-trained language models towards non-western English varieties. However, we recognize the need to broaden the scope of our investigation to other NLP tasks, with the goal of developing more robust, inclusive and accurate NLP models. For example, our corpus could be useful in training sentiment analysis models to analyze the sentiments of writers from different linguistic backgrounds. Finally, we are committed to expand our corpus to include a wider range of global English-speaking communities. While our current corpus covers several countries in Asia and Africa, we recognize that there are many more English varieties around the world with linguistic characteristics different from those in our corpus. We believe that this continued expansion of our corpus will benefit researchers studying subfields of linguistics like sociolinguistics and corpus linguistics and enable the development of robust NLP models that are better suited to the needs of diverse linguistic communities.

7 Conclusion

We have presented a diverse tweet corpus of English varieties and an annotation framework to label tweets. We analyse linguistic indicators of these English varieties and demonstrate that, despite a superficially independent relationship between some 'adjacent' labels, the classifications exist along a spectrum which intuitively measures distance from formal, standard English. We train several linguistically-diverse and geographically-appropriate individuals to annotate a collective 3564 tweets. Our experiments also show that there exists bias towards English varieties in off-the-shelf language identification tools when evaluated on our diverse corpus.

Limitations

We acknowledge some limitations of Twitter, notably that its usage is concentrated among wealthy, white and western individuals and even within non-western countries, the majority of active users is typically younger and more educated (Blank and Lutz, 2017). This means that our corpus may be

Language Identifier	Accra	Islamabad	Manila	New Delhi	Singapore	New York	London
langid.py	72.32	69.62	60.19	62.45	71.32	87.32	90.68
spaCy	77.38	85.76	55.45	73.98	77.57	92.25	95.34
Google Translate API	80.95	81.86	33.65	58.74	61.03	95.42	96.27

Table 2: Percentage of the 350 tweets in each English variety classified as English

Language Identifier	American & British English	Other English varieties	Difference
langid.py	89.00	67.18	**21.82**
spaCy	93.80	74.03	**19.77**
Google Translate API	95.85	63.27	**32.58**

Table 3: Average accuracy of western English and non-western English varieties

skewed towards more privileged populations of certain demographics and thus not accurately represent the linguistic diversity of English-speaking communities, especially those that are underserved. Nevertheless, we believe that our corpus is still a valuable contribution towards inclusivity in NLP as we increase the representation of English varieties beyond American and British English. Moreover, we point out the issue of existing bias in off-the-shelf language identification models, but we do not directly address it. This is because such a task would require a much more substantial amount of annotated training data than we currently have. As outlined in Section 6, we plan to scale our labeled data in a more efficient and automated manner, which will enable us to better address this limitation.

References

John Blake. 2018. Inter-annotator agreement: By hook or by crook.

Grant Blank and Christoph Lutz. 2017. Representativeness of social media in great britain: investigating facebook, linkedin, twitter, pinterest, google+, and instagram. *American Behavioral Scientist*, 61(7):741–756.

Su Lin Blodgett, Solon Barocas, Hal Daumé III, and Hanna Wallach. 2020. Language (technology) is power: A critical survey of "bias" in NLP. In *Proceedings of the 58th Annual Meeting of the Association for Computational Linguistics*, pages 5454–5476, Online. Association for Computational Linguistics.

Su Lin Blodgett and Brendan O'Connor. 2017. Racial disparity in natural language processing: A case study of social media african-american english. *CoRR*, abs/1707.00061.

Paul Cook and Laurel J Brinton. 2017. Building and evaluating web corpora representing national varieties of english. *Language Resources and Evaluation*, 51(3):643–662.

Guillermo Cámbara, Alex Peiró-Lilja, Mireia Farrús, and Jordi Luque. 2021. English accent accuracy analysis in a state-of-the-art automatic speech recognition system.

Jamell Dacon, Haochen Liu, and Jiliang Tang. 2022. Evaluating and mitigating inherent linguistic bias of African American English through inference. In *Proceedings of the 29th International Conference on Computational Linguistics*, pages 1442–1454, Gyeongju, Republic of Korea. International Committee on Computational Linguistics.

Fahim Faisal, Yinkai Wang, and Antonios Anastasopoulos. 2022. Dataset geography: Mapping language data to language users. In *Proceedings of the 60th Annual Meeting of the Association for Computational Linguistics (Volume 1: Long Papers)*, pages 3381–3411, Dublin, Ireland. Association for Computational Linguistics.

Natasa Gisev, J. Simon Bell, and Timothy F. Chen. 2013. Interrater agreement and interrater reliability: Key concepts, approaches, and applications. *Research in Social and Administrative Pharmacy*, 9(3):330–338.

Sidney Greenbaum and Gerald Nelson. 1996. The international corpus of english (ice) project.

Jennifer Jenkins. 2009. English as a lingua franca: interpretations and attitudes. *World Englishes*, 28(2):200–207.

Alina Köchling and Marius Claus Wehner. 2020. Discriminated by an algorithm: a systematic review of discrimination and fairness by algorithmic decision-making in the context of hr recruitment and hr development. *Business Research*, 13(3):795–848.

Bernd Kortmann, Clive Upton, Edgar Werner Schneider, Kate Burridge, and Rajend Mesthrie. 2008. *Varieties of English*, volume 1. Mouton de Gruyter Berlin.

Editors: Silvia Kouwenberg and John Victor Singler. 2008. *The Handbook of Pidgin and Creole Studies*. Wiley-Blackwell, Chichester, West Sussex, and Malden, MA.

J. Richard Landis and Gary G. Koch. 1977. The measurement of observer agreement for categorical data. *Biometrics*, 33(1):159–174.

Edward Loper and Steven Bird. 2002. Nltk: The natural language toolkit.

Barbara Poblete, Ruth Garcia, Marcelo Mendoza, and Alejandro Jaimes. 2011. Do all birds tweet the same? characterizing twitter around the world. In *Proceedings of the 20th ACM international conference on Information and knowledge management*, pages 1025–1030.

Building a corpus for the anonymization of Romanian jurisprudence

Vasile Păiș and **Dan Tufiș** and **Elena Irimia**
and **Verginica Barbu Mititelu**
Research Institute for Artificial Intelligence "Mihai Drăgănescu", Romanian Academy
Bucharest, Romania
vasile@racai.ro

Abstract

Access to jurisprudence is of paramount importance both for law professionals (judges, lawyers, law students) and for the larger public. In Romania, the Superior Council of Magistracy holds a large database of jurisprudence from different courts in the country, which is updated daily. However, granting public access to it requires its anonymization. This paper presents the efforts behind building a corpus for the anonymization process. We present the annotation scheme, the manual annotation methods, and the platform used.

1 Introduction

The astonishing advancement of Machine Learning (ML) and Artificial Intelligence (AI) during the last decade has generated a global rush for collecting more and diverse data, as clean as possible, with an eye to the General Data Protection Regulation (GDPR)[1] compliance. Large language models (LLMs), fueling the most successful AI applications, are built from data collected from various sources, the web being the most frequent one, but not the only one. When access to the data is open to the public, according to global GDPR requirements, any personal/private information must be hidden.

The procedure of hiding/obscuring/obfuscating personal data in documents released to the public is known as documents anonymization. It has to be performed so that the remaining context could not unveil the purposely hidden information. This is, generally speaking, a hard task, but, for specialized texts/language, it gains in accuracy.

The judicial systems all over the world are under the scrutiny of people, who naturally claim the right to have access to information on the decisions affecting their lives. Transparency of judicial decisions, as well as consistency of national courts decisions among themselves and with the international practices and recommendations are highly sensitive topics.

To tackle these issues, the Council of Europe is implementing the project "Fostering transparency of judicial decisions and enhancing the national implementation of the European Court on Human Rights" (TJENI)[2], which aims to improve the transparency and consistency of national judicial decisions, to strengthen the quality of their judicial decision-making and to streamline information on human rights jurisprudence to national judiciaries. The protection of human rights and the rule of law are strengthened by transparency of the judicial process, increasing the consistency of national courts decisions with European human rights and rule of law standards. These objectives can be supported through the publication of court decisions, which requires their prior anonymization. This can be done by applying specific technical solutions meant to automate the preparation of the documents for publication.

Romania is the only TJENI beneficiary that publishes decisions of all courts in Romania through the portal specifically developed by the Superior Council of Magistracy (SCM), with the exception of the High Court of Casation and Justice, which maintains its own case law database. The case law database of the SCM, the official beneficiary of our project, contains all court decisions from criminal, civil, commercial and administrative case types. The only exceptions from publication are documents marked in ECRIS (the case management system) as confidential, such as the judgements or other decisions related to minors, sexual harassment, divorces/family matters, decisions acknowledging mediation settlements, verdicts on offences as treason, espionage, rape and child pornography

[1] https://eur-lex.europa.eu/legal-content/EN/TXT/HTML/?uri=CELEX:32016R0679

[2] https://www.coe.int/en/web/national-implementation/tjeni

Proceedings of The 18th Linguistic Annotation Workshop (LAW-XVIII), pages 71–76
March 22, 2024

and upon a request of a party in the proceeding. So far, more than 40 million decisions have been published since 2011 in the Romanian case law database and the database is updated daily. Initially, decisions were anonymized before publication by means of regular expressions. A new anonymizer, developed based on this work, more accurate and much faster, will replace the previous one.

The new tool is being built with out-of-the-box scalability, by means of parallelism and containerization mechanisms, allowing for high-performance processing of an increasing number of documents. Furthermore, the new system employs state-of-the-art LLMs, such as Romanian language BERT (Devlin et al., 2019) models, for detecting named entities (NEs) that need to be anonymized, thus increasing the recognition performance. The corpus described in this work will be used for training the tool. The system still employs dictionaries and regular expression lists for certain types of NEs, that are particularly suited for such recognition processes (like personal identification codes, vehicle registration, email addresses).

The rest of this paper is structured as follows: Section 2 presents related work, Section 3 describes the annotation scheme, Section 4 presents the manual annotation process in the RELATE platform, Section 5 introduces preliminary statistics on the corpus, and we conclude in Section 6.

2 Related work

The anonymization process implies named entity recognition (NER). However, not all NEs require anonymization (as detailed in Section 3). Given this link between anonymization and NER, this section will cover corpora built either for NER or for anonymization in the legal domain. Plamondon et al. (2004) admit that anonymization of court decisions presupposes proper identification of more than just person names, while too much anonymization reduces the text readability and usability.

Trias et al. (2021) are concerned with the identification of lawyer names in historical legal text. They acknowledge problems arising from using nicknames or initials instead of complete names. Leitner et al. (2019) perform fine-grained NER on a corpus (Leitner et al., 2020) of German legal documents. The corpus was constructed from already anonymized court decisions, thus affecting the NEs belonging to personal data. Their specification contains 19 fine-grained NE classes. Au et al. (2022) constructed the E-NER dataset, based on legal company filings available from the US Securities and Exchange Commission's EDGAR data set, containing 7 NE classes.

Legal-ES (Samy et al., 2020) is a large Spanish corpus covering different types of legislative, administrative and jurisprudential texts. Kalamkar et al. (2022) describe a NER corpus for Indian court judgements, covering 14 NE classes.

Considering the Romanian language, Păiș et al. (2021a) constructed the LegalNERo corpus, covering persons, locations, organizations, time expressions, and legal references (5 NE classes). The corpus consists of a manually annotated subset of the larger MARCELL-Ro corpus (Tufiș et al., 2020; Váradi et al., 2020), containing legal domain texts, primarily legislation. This corpus, without the legal reference annotations (which do not have a corresponding class for the current project), could be used to augment the jurisprudence corpus described in the rest of this paper.

All these papers admit the necessity to annotate more types of entities in corpora from the legal domain. As detailed in Section 3, we also considered the annotation of more types of entities, as well as the necessity of their annotation (see Table 1 and the discussion about the data it shows).

3 Annotation scheme

Our annotation scheme is based on NE labels commonly used in the NER field (like LOC, ORG, PER and DATE) and is extended to accommodate entities specific to the legal domain, especially the jurisprudence context of our project (with labels like ECLI, CASE, DECISION, etc.). The scheme contains 17 entity types (see Table 2 for the complete list of labels), in accordance with the anonymization requirements defined in the Decision of the Section for Judges of the Superior Council of the Magistracy no. 998/17.03.2022 [3].

The guidelines for using the annotation scheme were adapted to the anonymization task, which is different from NER in the sense that not all NEs need being anonymized.

The anonymization task particularities resulted in a classification of the entity types according to their consistency of annotation: all occurrences of certain entity types (e.g., ECLI, EMAIL, CUI, IBAN, etc.) in the target documents are annotated,

[3] http://old.csm1909.ro/csm/linkuri/02_05_2022__105390_ro.pdf

while for other types (such as PER, DATE, LOC, ORG, etc.), the decision to annotate is based on the type of reference those entities have (see below). To have a sense of the degree of distinction between the anonymization and the NER task in our framework, we randomly selected 20 documents from the set already manually annotated for anonymization and supplemented the annotation to include all the NE occurrences corresponding to our entity types of interest. Table 1 shows the number of annotated entities in the anonymization task and the number of those annotated in the NER task. It is easily visible that the total number of entities is almost double (794 vs. 1,479) in the NER task as compared to the anonymization one.

	Anonymization Task	NER Task
PER	312	318
DATE	26	359
LOC	70	147
ORG	113	376
TOTAL	794	1,479

Table 1: The number of annotated entities for NER task vs. Anonymization task in the same documents. Entity types whose number of annotated occurrences is identical in the two tasks are not detailed in the table, but the total includes them.

PER entities, which include human names, surnames and nicknames, are to be annotated in the vast majority of situations, regardless of the person's role in the trial (petitioner, respondent, convict, witness, judge, clerk, etc.); yet, there is one exception to this rule: when the person's name is cited in connection with a European Court of Human Rights case, which is, by its nature, public, and does not need to be anonymized (examples from our corpus: "cauza Salabiaku c. Franței" ("the case of Salabiaku v. France"), "cauza Västberga Taxi Aktiebolag și Vulic c. Suediei" ("the case of Västberga Taxi Aktiebolag and Vulic v. Sweden"). Person names also occur preceded by some phrases indicating a legal entity: e.g. "birou de avocatură" ("law office"), "cabinet medical" ("medical office"); in this case they are annotated as ORG.

DATE entities (used to annotate time expressions) are in the opposite situation, i.e. they must be annotated on a few specific occasions, namely when they refer to the date of birth of a person; the jurisprudence documents are rich in occurrences of DATE NEs which are not to be anonymized: dates when the trial takes place, when a decision is made, a document is issued, etc.

LOC entities are anonymized only if otherwise they could disclose the identity of persons or organizations. Therefore, they are always anonymised when referring to residence, place of birth, headquarters and buildings/land in possession. Locations where accidents and events take place are not normally annotated, but there are exceptions to this rule: e.g., when the event takes place in a small town/village or a specific geographical location that is very close to the individual residence and whereabouts information could endanger the anonymity of the parties. The decision to annotate such occurrences is made for each case separately.

ORG entities include all groups defined by a formal organisational structure, whether public or private. While private organizations are always anonymized, public organisations are annotated only when they are parts in the trial. By their nature, the jurisprudence documents abound in ORG named entities, with many of them representing law institutions that do not require anonymization. This is reflected in the tripling of ORG entities in our evaluation trial (see Table 1).

All remaining NE types (see Table 2 for a complete list of labels) are always annotated. INITIALS only refer to occurrences of initials instead of signatures (of the judge and clerk) at the end of the documents. Other types of abbreviations occurring in documents are annotated as the NE type they abbreviate: e.g., companies initials are annotated as ORG, person initials are annotated as PER. Court decisions, CNP, ID, EMAIL, ECLI, CUI, IBAN, NCAD and AUTO are annotated without any exception. Some of them have a homogeneous format (for example, EMAIL is easily recognized by the presence of @ and of a dot), while others can take different forms. AUTO is such an example: it is used to annotate both Romanian plate numbers and foreign ones, which can have a different format; even in Romania, plate numbers belonging to official institutions cars or provisional plate numbers have different formats from the common ones. Moreover, there are cases when the same number is typed differently throughout the same decision (e.g., "GH13ABC" – "GH 13 ABC" – "GH-13-ABC"). The AUTO label is also used for other vehicle identification numbers, like chassis series, which have a different format than the plate numbers. Thus, the annotation of entity types that does not depend on the semantic context of occurrence can also be problematic at times, when formats are heterogeneous inside the same type.

4 Manual annotation in the RELATE platform

RELATE (Păiș et al., 2020) is a modern platform incorporating a large number of tools (Păiș, 2020) for processing the Romanian language. It was previously used for automatic annotation of large corpora, such as the MARCELL (Váradi et al., 2020; Tufiș et al., 2020) legislative corpus and the CURLICAT (Váradi et al., 2022) corpus and for creating Romanian language named entity corpora, such as MicroBloggingNERo (Păiș et al., 2022) and LegalNERo (Păiș et al., 2021b).

For the purpose of this work, we use a number of RELATE platform's modules, including: corpus management, manual annotation and basic language annotation resource kits. For security reasons, with regard to data access, the modules were deployed in the secure network of the Superior Council of Magistracy, and the web interface was made available to annotators via VPN connections. For manual annotation, the RELATE platform integrates the BRAT Rapid annotation tool (Stenetorp et al., 2012), connected to the platform's corpus management component. Annotators are shown one document at a time and must select, using the mouse, each NE text span. The platform remembers the last document worked on by each annotator, as well as documents not finalized, allowing smooth transition between documents. At this stage, the NEs are only marked in the documents and no anonymization takes place, as the corpus is intended for training automatic processes later. Following the span-level annotation, documents are processed using UDPipe (Straka et al., 2016) with a custom model (Păiș et al., 2021) trained on the Romanian RoRefTrees (RRT) corpus version 2.7 (Barbu Mititelu et al., 2016), available in the Universal Dependencies project. The resulting tokenized version is automatically aligned with the span-level NE annotations, using a BIO (begin/inside/outside) annotation format.

5 Preliminary corpus statistics

The manual annotation task (which is currently in progress and done by 38 annotators) is intended to cover 1,500 documents and double annotation was taken in consideration for inter-annotator agreement (IAA) analysis. At the moment, based on 5,563,617 tokens from documents doubly annotated, the IAA score, computed using Cohen's Kappa, is 0.94. According to Landis and Koch (1977), a Kappa value greater than 0.81 is indicative of an "almost perfect" agreement. The annotators are primarily judges with experience in anonymization requirements for legal documents, working under the coordination of the Superior Council of Magistracy. This accounts for the high agreement score. Two additional annotators with experience in creating annotated corpora were involved in order to better understand the data and clarify disagreements. Throughout the annotation process, periodic discussions took place to clarify any problems.

Entity Class	# entities
AUTO (car plates)	218
CASE (trial case number)	2,028
CNP (personal numeric code)	291
CUI (commercial unique identifier)	82
DATE	1,444
DECISION (trial decision number)	2,532
DOC(ument)**NUMBER**	3,151
E(uropean)**C**(ase)**L**(aw)**I**(dentifier)	157
EMAIL (address)	3
IBAN	2
I(dentification)**D**(ocument)	73
INITIALS	1,149
LOC(ation)	2,370
NCAD (land registry number)	167
ORG(anization)	3,662
PER(son)	19,557
PHONE (number)	28
TOTAL	36,914

Table 2: Preliminary statistics on 594 unique annotated files with 5,563,617 tokens

As shown in Table 2, the documents are very rich in personal names and the vast majority of them have to be annotated as entities to be anonymised (19,557 PER entities); on the other end, entities like EMAIL (3 occurences) and IBAN (2 occurences) are very rare.

6 Conclusion and future work

This paper introduced the work carried out for creating a corpus for the purpose of anonymizing the Romanian jurisprudence. It is a very challenging task, with its own peculiarities when it comes to automatic processing. Even though it is suitable for an NER approach, the fact that only entities requiring anonymization (not all the entities) are annotated makes it difficult to use readily available NER applications. Thus, a combination of different methods are explored, including a combination of algorithms based on traditional techniques (dictionary, regular expressions) and large language models. Even though completely annotating the corpus for NEs and marking those that require anonymization would have enabled additional uses for the corpus, given the annotators experience in anonymization (and not NER or other corpus building activities) it was decided to focus only on the anonymization task.

System development, including algorithm's implementation, is realized open source[4], but the corpus itself cannot be publicly released, due to the sensitivity of the information. We are also considering releasing pre-trained models (when this would not compromise privacy) and anonymized corpus samples. The end-result of the project, the anonymized jurisprudence, will be available from the ReJust portal[5].

Acknowledgements

This work was performed within the project "System for the anonymization of Romanian jurisprudence (SAROJ). The SAROJ project was carried out with funding from the Council of Europe, within the project "Foster Transparency of Judicial Decisions and Enhancing the National Implementation of the ECHR (TJENI)" funded by the EEA and Norway Grants Fund for Regional Cooperation. The views expressed herein can in no way be taken to reflect the official opinion of the Council of Europe.

References

Ting Wai Terence Au, Vasileios Lampos, and Ingemar Cox. 2022. E-NER — an annotated named entity recognition corpus of legal text. In *Proceedings of the Natural Legal Language Processing Workshop 2022*, pages 246–255, Abu Dhabi, United Arab Emirates (Hybrid). Association for Computational Linguistics.

Verginica Barbu Mititelu, Radu Ion, Radu Simionescu, Elena Irimia, and Cenel-Augusto Perez. 2016. The romanian treebank annotated according to universal dependencies. In *Proceedings of The Tenth International Conference on Natural Language Processing (HrTAL2016)*.

[4]https://github.com/racai-ai/saroj/

[5]https://rejust.ro

Jacob Devlin, Ming-Wei Chang, Kenton Lee, and Kristina Toutanova. 2019. BERT: Pre-training of deep bidirectional transformers for language understanding. In *Proceedings of the 2019 Conference of the North American Chapter of the Association for Computational Linguistics: Human Language Technologies, Volume 1 (Long and Short Papers)*, pages 4171–4186, Minneapolis, Minnesota. Association for Computational Linguistics.

Prathamesh Kalamkar, Astha Agarwal, Aman Tiwari, Smita Gupta, Saurabh Karn, and Vivek Raghavan. 2022. Named entity recognition in Indian court judgments. In *Proceedings of the Natural Legal Language Processing Workshop 2022*, pages 184–193, Abu Dhabi, United Arab Emirates (Hybrid). Association for Computational Linguistics.

J Richard Landis and Gary G Koch. 1977. The measurement of observer agreement for categorical data. *Biometrics*, pages 159–174.

Elena Leitner, Georg Rehm, and Julian Moreno-Schneider. 2019. Fine-grained named entity recognition in legal documents. In *Semantic Systems. The Power of AI and Knowledge Graphs*, pages 272–287, Cham. Springer International Publishing.

Elena Leitner, Georg Rehm, and Julian Moreno-Schneider. 2020. A dataset of German legal documents for named entity recognition. In *Proceedings of the Twelfth Language Resources and Evaluation Conference*, pages 4478–4485, Marseille, France. European Language Resources Association.

Vasile Păiș, Radu Ion, Andrei-Marius Avram, Maria Mitrofan, and Dan Tufiș. 2021. In-depth evaluation of Romanian natural language processing pipelines. *Romanian Journal of Information Science and Technology (ROMJIST)*, 24(4):384–401.

Vasile Păiș, Radu Ion, and Dan Tufiș. 2020. A processing platform relating data and tools for Romanian language. In *Proceedings of the 1st International Workshop on Language Technology Platforms*, pages 81–88, Marseille, France. European Language Resources Association.

Luc Plamondon, Guy Lapalme, and Frédéric Pelletier. 2004. Anonymisation de décisions de justice. In *Actes de la 11ème conférence sur le Traitement Automatique des Langues Naturelles. Articles longs*, pages 159–168, Fès, Maroc. ATALA.

Vasile Păiș. 2020. Multiple annotation pipelines inside the relate platform. In *The 15th International Conference on Linguistic Resources and Tools for Natural Language Processing*, pages 65–75.

Vasile Păiș, Maria Mitrofan, Verginica Barbu-Mititelu, Elena Irimia, Carol Luca Gasan, Roxana Micu, Laura Marin, Maria Dicusar, Bianca Florea, and Ana Badila. 2022. Romanian micro-blogging named entity recognition (MicroBloggingNERo).

Vasile Păiș, Maria Mitrofan, Carol Luca Gasan, Vlad Coneschi, and Alexandru Ianov. 2021a. Named entity recognition in the Romanian legal domain. In *Proceedings of the Natural Legal Language Processing Workshop 2021*, pages 9–18, Punta Cana, Dominican Republic. Association for Computational Linguistics.

Vasile Păiș, Maria Mitrofan, Carol Luca Gasan, Alexandru Ianov, Corvin Ghiță, Vlad Silviu Coneschi, and Andrei Onuț. 2021b. Romanian Named Entity Recognition in the Legal domain (LegalNERo).

Doaa Samy, Jerónimo Arenas-García, and David Pérez-Fernández. 2020. Legal-ES: A set of large scale resources for Spanish legal text processing. In *Proceedings of the 1st Workshop on Language Technologies for Government and Public Administration (LT4Gov)*, pages 32–36, Marseille, France. European Language Resources Association.

Pontus Stenetorp, Sampo Pyysalo, Goran Topić, Tomoko Ohta, Sophia Ananiadou, and Jun'ichi Tsujii. 2012. brat: a web-based tool for NLP-assisted text annotation. In *Proceedings of the Demonstrations at the 13th Conference of the European Chapter of the Association for Computational Linguistics*, pages 102–107, Avignon, France. Association for Computational Linguistics.

Milan Straka, Jan Hajič, and Jana Straková. 2016. Udpipe: trainable pipeline for processing conll-u files performing tokenization, morphological analysis, pos tagging and parsing. In *Proceedings of the 10th International Conference on Language Resources and Evaluation (LREC 2016)*, Portorož, Slovenia. European Language Resources Association.

Fernando Trias, Hongming Wang, Sylvain Jaume, and Stratos Idreos. 2021. Named entity recognition in historic legal text: A transformer and state machine ensemble method. In *Proceedings of the Natural Legal Language Processing Workshop 2021*, pages 172–179, Punta Cana, Dominican Republic. Association for Computational Linguistics.

Dan Tufiș, Maria Mitrofan, Vasile Păiș, Radu Ion, and Andrei Coman. 2020. Collection and annotation of the romanian legal corpus. In *Proceedings of The 12th Language Resources and Evaluation Conference*, pages 2766–2770, Marseille, France. European Language Resources Association.

Tamás Váradi, Svetla Koeva, Martin Yamalov, Marko Tadić, Bálint Sass, Bartłomiej Nitoń, Maciej Ogrodniczuk, Piotr Pęzik, Verginica Barbu Mititelu, Radu Ion, Elena Irimia, Maria Mitrofan, Vasile Păiș, Dan Tufiș, Radovan Garabík, Simon Krek, Andraz Repar, Matjaž Rihtar, and Janez Brank. 2020. The marcell legislative corpus. In *Proceedings of The 12th Language Resources and Evaluation Conference*, pages 3754–3761, Marseille, France. European Language Resources Association.

Tamás Váradi, Bence Nyéki, Svetla Koeva, Marko Tadić, Vanja Štefanec, Maciej Ogrodniczuk, Bartłomiej Nitoń, Piotr Pęzik, Verginica Barbu Mititelu, Elena Irimia, Maria Mitrofan, Vasile Păiș, Dan Tufiș, Radovan Garabík, Simon Krek, and Andraž Repar. 2022. Introducing the curlicat corpora: Seven-language domain specific annotated corpora from curated sources. In *Proceedings of the Language Resources and Evaluation Conference*, pages 100–108, Marseille, France. European Language Resources Association.

Class Balancing for Efficient Active Learning in Imbalanced Datasets

Yaron Fairstein
Amazon / yyfairstein@gmail.com

Oren Kalinsky
Amazon / orenkalinsky@gmail.com

Zohar Karnin
Amazon / zkarnin@amazon.com

Guy Kushilevitz
Amazon / guyk@amazon.com

Alexander Libov
Amazon / alibov@amazon.com

Sofia Tolmach
Amazon / sofiato@amazon.com

Abstract

Recent developments in active learning algorithms for NLP tasks show promising results in terms of reducing labelling complexity. In this paper we extend this effort to imbalanced datasets; we bridge between the active learning approach of obtaining diverse and informative examples, and the heuristic of class balancing used in imbalanced datasets. We develop a novel tune-free weighting technique that can be applied to various existing active learning algorithms, adding a component of class balancing. We compare several active learning algorithms to their modified version on multiple public datasets and show that when the classes are imbalanced, with manual annotation effort remaining equal the modified version significantly outperforms the original both in terms of the test metric and the number of obtained minority examples. Moreover, when the imbalance is mild or non-existent (classes are completely balanced), our technique does not harm the base algorithms.

1 Introduction

Pre-trained Language Models (PLMs) and Masked Language Models (Peters et al., 2018; Devlin et al., 2019; Liu et al., 2019) have revolutionized NLP by supplying meaningful contextual embeddings for tokens and sentences. These models pushed SoTA on many tasks, proving especially effective for text classification tasks (Sun et al., 2019). For many of these tasks, given enough labeled data for fine-tuning a PLM, satisfactory results can be achieved. On the other hand, due to the rapid growth in textual datasets, for many domains and tasks it is often the case that while a vast amount of textual data is available, only a small portion of the text-instances belong to a specific class of interest (Li et al., 2018; Padurariu and Breaban, 2019; Shaikh et al., 2021).

This sparsity makes annotation challenging because naive data sampling methods do not produce enough examples belonging to a class of interest. It is often possible to use some filtering heuristic before performing manual annotations, so that the percentage of data belonging to the class in question will rise. This approach however is not scalable, since it requires hand-crafting for each specific task or even class. In addition, when filtering is imperfect, the PLM may never observe an important cluster of examples, hurting its generalization capabilities. Therefore, It is essential to minimize the amount of human annotations needed in order to acquire labeled data that will be sufficient for the model to reach a satisfying performance. This calls for the use of Active Learning (AL) techniques. There are many works applying AL techniques for PLM fine-tuning (Gissin and Shalev-Shwartz, 2019; Ash et al., 2020; Dor et al., 2020) but most do not specifically consider the imbalanced dataset case.

Standard AL objectives include obtaining samples which the model is less certain about and increasing the diversity of the chosen sample set. Existing AL methods (C Lin, 2018; Kim and Yoo, 2022) aimed to handle imbalanced datasets suggest doing so by alternating between some approach designed to obtain positive examples[1], and another approach with standard AL objectives. The shortcoming of this alternating approach is that the exact balance of objectives, i.e., how many samples should be chosen aimed to be positive vs diverse, etc., is dependent on the imbalance of the dataset. As a result, existing methods either require a balancing hyperparameter that cannot be tuned in a practical[2] setting, or need to learn the correct balancing ratio over time, making the methods efficient only after a large amount of labelling.

In this work we take a different approach that modifies an AL algorithm to favor positive exam-

[1]Throughout this paper we assume w.l.o.g. that the positive class is the minority class.

[2]AL is most needed when labeled data is missing, therefore assuming a dev set is unpractical.

Proceedings of The 18th Linguistic Annotation Workshop (LAW-XVIII), pages 77–86
March 22, 2024

ples in a way that is self-tuned to obtain an equal amount of positive and negative samples. The core idea of our approach is to debias the inherent skew in the imbalanced dataset by utilizing the inverse-propensity score of the probability of a sample to be positive, according to the model obtained thus far. The simplest form of our algorithm is to sample according to these scores. Intuitively, once the model is reasonable, and this happens quickly in the era of pre-trained models, the amount of positive samples is in the same order of magnitude as the negative samples. We show that these scores can be used not only as a tool to modify the uniform sampling approach, but can be combined with other algorithms providing their own weights to the data points (Yuan et al., 2020), or clustering approaches aimed to maximize diversity (Gissin and Shalev-Shwartz, 2019; Ash et al., 2020).

We demonstrate that for the imbalanced setting, our adaptation of SoTA AL algorithms outperform their original counterparts in multiple datasets. We show that this behavior is consistent across various levels of data imbalance and that in the balanced setting, our adaptation is comparable to the original AL algorithms. The latter property is crucial from a practical perspective as the imbalance ratio of a dataset is rarely known in advance and can be difficult to estimate.

Concluding, we showcase a weakness of recent AL approaches when dealing with imbalanced datasets and devise a novel self-tuned reweighting solution that complements existing (including SoTA) AL algorithms, improving their performance on imbalanced datasets. We experiment on four imbalanced datasets from different tasks and domains. We publish our code and imbalanced datasets for reproducibilty and to encourage future research in this area[3].

2 Related Work

Conventional active learning. There is a myriad of works on active learning in different settings (Ren et al., 2021; Fu et al., 2013). Herein, we consider a pool-based active learning scenario where the algorithm has access to a large unlabeled dataset $\mathcal{U}$ that can be labeled through human annotations. As previously mentioned, our solution modifies existing active learning algorithms in order to better deal with imbalanced datasets. We identify three types of active learning algorithms: random, embedding-based, and score-based algorithms. Random sampling, the simplest approach, generates a distribution over $\mathcal{U}$ from which k distinct samples are randomly selected (e.g., uniform sampling).

Embedding-based algorithms embed unlabeled samples in a high dimensional space. A subset of samples is then selected for annotation using a clustering algorithm based on their embedding, to increase the sample diversity. BADGE (Ash et al., 2020) is an embedding-based algorithm where the sample gradient from the last layer of the model, taken from the log loss of the predicted label, is used as an embedding. ALPS (Gissin and Shalev-Shwartz, 2019) adopts a similar approach, but uses an embedding that captures the language model uncertainty of the different tokens in the sentence.

Score-based algorithms attach a model score to each sample. The most common score-based approach is Least Confidence (Lewis and Gale, 1994) which selects the top-K samples with the highest model uncertainty. A more recent work called DAL (Gissin and Shalev-Shwartz, 2019) trains a classifier to detect new samples dissimilar from the already labeled data.

Active learning in skewed datasets. Compared to active learning, relatively only a few studies have specifically addressed the issue of class imbalance. A common approach in handling class imbalance is to skew the active learning algorithm towards ranking positive samples higher. ODAL (Barata et al., 2021) is an extension of DAL that targets the cold-start setting using an outlier detection algorithm until a single positive sample is found. HAL (Kazerouni et al., 2020) suggests a Hybrid Active Learning algorithm that switches between selecting 'exploitation' that chooses points where the model is uncertain and 'exploration' that either chooses samples uniformly at random or according to how far they are from already chosen samples, yet this approach requires a hyperparameter determining how to balance exploration and exploitation, that is crucial to the performance, and setting it is said to be an open problem.

Recent works try to combine conventional active learning algorithms with positive-skewed sampling. C Lin (2018) explore a method that combines multiple strategies for selecting new examples such as standard active learning, sampling in a skewed way towards positive examples, and generating examples of the minority type (via manual annotators).

[3]https://github.com/balancingAL/ImbAL

They apply a Multi-armed bandit (MAB) algorithm (UCB) to balance between the strategies. Similarly, BMP (Kim and Yoo, 2022) defines two types of policies, one samples from the positive class and the other uses a standard AL algorithm such as random or VE (Beluch et al., 2018), and uses a MAB algorithm to dynamically allocate batches to the different policies. It is folklore knowledge that MAB algorithms require a large number of rounds (at least 10s) before they can learn anything meaningful[4], and indeed the number of rounds in the mentioned papers are 55 or more. Having a large number of rounds can be computationally expensive as SoTA active learning algorithms require applying a large ML model on all examples, as well as time consuming in a human annotation setting. We thus focus on a small number of rounds (say, 5), making these works less applicable.

3 Setting

We consider the pool-based active learning setting, where we are given a pool of unlabeled samples $\mathcal{U}$. At each iteration t, some subset $S_t \subset \mathcal{U}$ of size k is selected for annotation. This subset, sometimes together with $S_1, \dots, S_{t-1}$, is used to train a model M_t. The subset S_t is selected by a sampling algorithm $\mathcal{A}$, which is usually dependent on the model M_{t-1}. A formal description of this process is given in Algorithm 1. The goal in this setting is to select a subset $\mathcal{D} \subset \mathcal{U}$ to be labeled, such that a model trained on $\mathcal{D}$ optimizes some metric on a separate test set. We focus on the binary classification problem, as it includes multiple common and important imbalanced scenarios such as phishing attempts, fraud, etc. (Kazerouni et al., 2020; Barata et al., 2021; C Lin, 2018).

4 Our approach

Consider some iteration t where we have at our disposal a model M_{t-1} trained on samples labelled in previous iterations.[5] For a sample $x \in \mathcal{U}$, we consider $M_{t-1}(x)$ as an approximation of the probability of x being a positive example. If we utilize the naive random algorithm to select samples $x \in \mathcal{U}$, then $M_{t-1}(x)$ is a random variable in $[0, 1]$. Our goal is to construct a distribution p over $\mathcal{U}$ such that the resulting random variable $M_{t-1}(x)$ is uniformly distributed in $[0, 1]$. To motivate this idea, consider a case where the model is perfectly calibrated, meaning the probability it provides is correct. Here, if sampled according to p, half of the examples, in expectation, will be positive (in Observation 1 we provide an additional bound under a weaker assumption). Another advantage of such a distribution appears even in the case of balanced datasets. Consider a case where many of the examples are easy to classify. It is likely that in an early stage easy samples will be concentrated near 0 and 1 in the distribution of $M_{t-1}(x)$. This means that our sample strategy will upweight exactly the problematic points where the model is uncertain, such that we obtain the property of biasing towards informative examples.

Algorithm 1 Pool-based Active Learning

Input: Unlabeled data pool $\mathcal{U}$, number of samples per iteration k, number of iterations T, sampling algorithm $\mathcal{A}$, classifier model training algorithm $\mathcal{M}$ and seed samples $\mathcal{S}$.

$\mathcal{D} \leftarrow \mathcal{S}$
$M_0 = \mathcal{M}(\mathcal{D})$ ▷ Initiate classifier model
for $t \leftarrow 1 : T$ **do**
  $S_t = \mathcal{A}(M_{t-1}, \mathcal{U}, k)$ ▷ Sampling step
  Annotate S_t
  $\mathcal{U} \leftarrow \mathcal{U} \setminus S_t$
  $\mathcal{D} \leftarrow \mathcal{D} \cup S_t$
  $M_t = \mathcal{M}(\mathcal{D})$ ▷ Learning step
Return M_T

The distribution p described above can be achieved by weighting each sample inversely to its propensity results in a uniform sample. Thus, we call this method **InvProp**. In terms of implementation, we discretize the interval $[0, 1]$ into m bins uniformly, meaning $[0, \frac{1}{m}), [\frac{1}{m}, \frac{2}{m}), \dots, [\frac{m-1}{m}, 1]$, as can be seen in Figure 1(a). For bin i that contains b_i samples we give each sample a probability proportional to $\frac{1}{b_i}$ (see Figure 1(b)).

The following lemma demonstrates the robustness of InvProp-weights to the exact, and unknown, degree of imbalance in the data.

Lemma 1. *Let $\mathcal{A}$ be the random algorithm with InvProp weights defined over 2 bins, and let M be a model with precision α. Also, let $S = \mathcal{A}(M, \mathcal{U}, k)$*

[4]This follows from a simple statistics exercise showing that with a handful of rounds, the posterior distributions of the reward of each option is very close to the prior, or that the confidence intervals remain large.

[5]We assume that the process begins with a model trained on a handful of examples. This is a realistic setting, as it is rarely the case that a practitioner will aim to solve a classification problem without having a single labelled example. Alternatively, we can begin with uniform weights. We discuss this issue in Section 5.9.

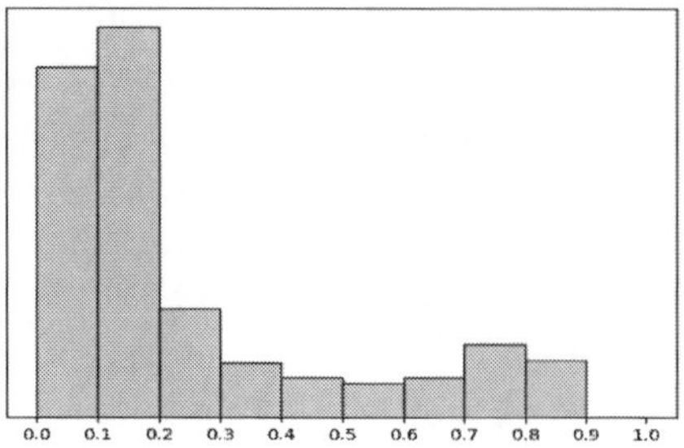

(a) Histogram of confidence scores $M_t(x)$.

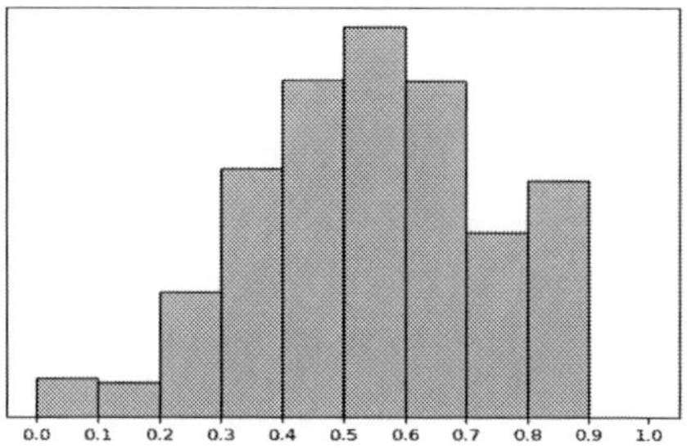

(b) Inverse propensity distribution p.

Figure 1: Confidence scores histogram and the probability fitting the InvProp-weights.

be the subset of size k sampled by $\mathcal{A}$. If the number of samples in bin $[1/2, 1]$ is at least $\beta \cdot k$ for $\beta > 0$, then the expected number of positive samples in S is $\mathbb{E}\big[\big|\{s \in S \mid y_s = 1\}\big|\big] \geq \frac{\alpha \cdot \gamma \cdot k}{2}$, where $\gamma = \beta/2$ if $\beta < 1$ and $\gamma = 1 - \frac{1}{2\beta}$ if $\beta \geq 1$.

The proof for the lemma can be found in Appendix A. The lemma does not directly translate to the setting with $m > 2$ bins, but by altering the precision assumption with that of the model being approximately calibrated, we keep the guarantee of obtaining a constant fraction of positive examples[6]. In our ablation studies (see section 5.8) we see that the precise number of bins has a small effect on the result, resulting in our decision to use an arbitrary default value (of $m = 10$) in our experiments.

4.1 Extending to SoTA algorithms

The random algorithm combined with the InvProp distribution, as described above, enjoys being skewed towards the minority class and informative samples. Nevertheless, recent AL algorithms have been able to provide additional benefit over the naive random approach. This leads us to incorporate our weighting scheme in SoTA AL algorithms. To this end, we consider the underlying distribution p of the InvProp method as a weighting function, assigning each point x a weight denoted by $w(x)$ (in the section above this is the probability of choosing x). For score based algorithms that choose samples based on a score $s(x)$, we modify the score to become $s_w(x) = w(x) \cdot s(x)$ (see Algorithm 2). For embedding-based algorithms that choose samples based on clustering, we modify the clustering procedure to be weighted according to $w(x)$ (see Algorithm 3). With this strategy, we are able to modify SoTA algorithms such as BADGE (Ash et al., 2020), ALPS (Yuan et al., 2020) and DAL (Gissin and Shalev-Shwartz, 2019) to be better suited to imbalanced datasets.

Algorithm 2 Weighted Score-based AL

Input: Unlabeled data pool $\mathcal{U}$, number of samples to select k, scoring function s, weight function w.

$s_w(x) = \sum_{x \in S} w(x) \cdot s(x)$
Return $\text{argmax}_{S \subseteq \mathcal{U}} \{s_w(x) \mid |S| = k\}$

Algorithm 3 Weighted Embedding-based AL

Input: Unlabeled data pool $\mathcal{U}$, number of samples to select k, embeddings e_x, weight function w.

Cluster $\{e_x\}_{x \in \mathcal{U}}$ with weights $w(x)$ into k clusters, pick S to be the samples nearest to the cluster centers.
Return S

5 Experiments

5.1 Datasets & Measure

We follow recent AL work (Ein-Dor et al., 2020; Yuan et al., 2020; Wang et al., 2021) and use 4 popular text classification datasets. **DBpedia-14** (Zhang et al., 2015) contains text snippets from 14 different DBpedia (Lehmann et al., 2015) classes. Each snippet's label is the ontology class it was taken from. **SST-2** (Socher et al., 2013) is a binary classification dataset containing sentences from movie reviews labeled by their sentiment. **PubMed-20K-RCT** (Dernoncourt and Lee, 2017) contains sentences from PubMed abstracts labeled by their role in the abstract. **AG_news** (Zhang et al., 2015) contains news snippets classified into 4 categories.

Binary-Imbalanced data. We generate several Binary-Imbalanced versions from each of the above

[6]The precise assumption is that for a bin $[\rho, \rho + 1/m]$, at least $\alpha\rho$ of the samples have a positive label. This property measures how calibrated the model is; indeed a perfectly calibrated model guarantee this with $\alpha = 1$. In this case we are guaranteed that in expectation, $\sum_{i=0}^{m-1} \frac{i\alpha\gamma k}{2m^2} = \frac{(m-1)}{4m}\alpha\gamma k \geq \alpha\gamma k/6$ samples are positive.

mentioned datasets. This is done by first selecting a class from the original dataset to serve as the positive (minority) class in the generated dataset. Samples from all other classes are regarded as negative. Both train and test sets are updated this way. For DBpedia-14, due to its larger number of classes and small variance we observe on this dataset, we randomly select 3 of the classes to serve as the minority class. For the rest of the datasets we use each of the original classes as a minority class. After selecting a positive class and updating the train and test sets, we sample positive examples from the training set so that the fraction of positive samples in the resulting dataset will be equal to the desired value. We construct datasets where the fraction of positives is $1/x$ for $x \in \{2, 10, 20, 50, 100\}$, i.e., 4 different imbalance ratios and a balanced dataset. See Table 1 for further details about the datasets.

Measure. As customary in studies related to imbalanced classes, we measure Balanced Accuracy and ROC-AUC, metrics that are insensitive to change in class distribution. Thus, the test set is not down-sampled, as this would only add noise to the evaluation. In addition, we compare the Positives Ratio, the fraction of minority samples found by each algorithm. This will allow us to evaluate the skew produced by our technique. Due to aggregations over different datasets, we found the standard deviations tend to be large, making confidence intervals uninformative. We thus measure statistical significance via p-values[7] and mark in **bold** results whose p-value is smaller than 5% for all compared results.

5.2 Active Learning Algorithms

We test our proposed weighting method by incorporating it into well established AL algorithms.

- **BADGE** (Ash et al., 2020) is an embedding-based algorithm. It generates a weak label according to the prediction of the current model. The weak label is used to calculate the gradient of the last layer of the model. The gradients are used as the embeddings.
- **ALPS.** (Yuan et al., 2020) Is an embedding-based algorithm. It generates an embedding according to the MLM objective. Some tokens are masked and predicted by the model. The embeddings are defined as the cross entropy distance between the prediction of the model and the actual masked tokens.
- **DAL.** (Gissin and Shalev-Shwartz, 2019) Is a score-based algorithm. It trains a classification model to predict whether a sample is labelled or unlabelled. The "top" unlabelled samples (the samples with the highest confidence score) are selected.
- **Random.** The naive random baseline which selects samples uniformly at random.

5.3 Weighting Methods

Other than our main approach of **InvProp**, we evaluate two additional weighting methods.

- **Uniform** ignores the imbalance issue and assigns the same weight to all samples, effectively running the original AL algorithm.
- **PosProb** assigns a point x the weight $M_{t-1}(x)$, meaning the probability according to the available model that the sample is positive. This option is explored as a strawman that promotes positive samples, but is not adaptive to the imbalance ratio.

We test 3 weighting methods (Uniform, PosProb, InvProp), incorporated into the 4 mentioned AL algorithms. Overall, 12 procedures are tested.

Previous studies came to the conclusion that even though AL algorithms improve over naive random sampling, there is no single algorithm which performs best for all models and tasks (Lowell et al., 2019; Dor et al., 2020). Hence, we do not aim to show that one algorithm outperforms another, we aim to test whether utilizing our weighting method improves the performance of each of the base algorithms when applied on imbalanced datasets.

5.4 Experimental Setup

We evaluate each algorithm on all Binary-Imbalanced datasets through 10 runs, each with a different random seed that determines the shuffling and random initialization. The results of these runs were averaged to produce the reported results. We ran the algorithms for 5 AL iterations, selecting 50 samples at each iteration.

We use the uncased bert-base model with 110M parameters[8] (Devlin et al., 2019) as the PLM, and set the maximum sequence length to 128 and the number of train epochs to 2. To cope with the imbalance of the data that was already labeled, we use oversampling to ensure that the positive samples

[7] The p-value is calculated using a relative t-test of the elements whose mean is calculated.

[8] https://huggingface.co/transformers/

Dataset	Classes	Original train/test	Selected minority classes
DBpedia-14	14	$560K/70K$	Company, Animal, Album
SST-2	2	$\sim 67K/872$	all classes
Pubmed-20K-RCT	5	$\sim 180K/30K$	all classes
AG_news	4	$120K/7.6K$	all classes

Table 1: **Dataset details.** Number of classes and train/test sizes in the original dataset, and the set of classes from the original dataset used as the minority class in the Binary-Imbalanced datasets we created (see section 5.1).

are at least a quarter of the training samples. This heuristic is known to vastly reduce the negative effects of the imbalance (Estabrooks and Japkowicz, 2001). At each iteration, we fine-tune the original pre-trained model using all examples, rather than fine-tuning the resulting model of a previous iteration, as this is known to provide better performance (Ash and Adams, 2020).

At the beginning of each run, we generate a random labeled subset of 5 negative and 5 positive samples that is given to the algorithm. An intuitive design would be that of a 'cold start', beginning with no labeled data. However, we found this setup to have a very high variance in terms of the final performance. In Section 5.9 we elaborate on the conjectured reason for this, provide experimental results to support our claim, and motivate our choice of starting with 5 examples of each class.

5.5 Main Results

In order to concisely compare between the weighting methods, we aggregate the results over either algorithms or datasets. Table 2 compares the performance of the InvProp and Uniform weighting method on the 4 datasets. A detailed comparison to PosProb can be found in Section 5.6. For each Binary-Imbalanced dataset and weighting method, we select the algorithm that performed best for the combination, based on its average score over 10 random seeds. We then take the average metric over Binary-Imbalanced variants of a dataset to obtain a single score for each (metric, dataset, weighting procedure) triplet. Here, we consider only Binary-Imbalanced datasets with an imbalance ratio of $\frac{1}{50}$. In both AUC and Balanced Accuracy, InvProp provides either superior or comparable results. As a justification, there is an overwhelming advantage to our weighting method in terms of positive ratio, nearly doubling the number of positive examples.

In Table 3 we compare the performance of the weighting methods between different AL algorithms. For each algorithm we average the score obtained by a specific weighting method over all

	Balanced Accuracy		AUC		Positives Ratio	
	InvProp	Uniform	InvProp	Uniform	InvProp	Uniform
AG_news	**0.7889**	0.7674	**0.9475**	0.9414	**0.3601**	0.2030
DBpedia	**0.9876**	0.9826	0.9983	0.9983	**0.4377**	0.2287
Pubmed	0.6338	0.6387	**0.8813**	0.8606	**0.2516**	0.1217
SST-2	0.6523	0.6299	**0.8709**	0.8538	**0.2045**	0.0989

Table 2: Comparison of InvProp with Uniform across multiple datasets (for an imbalance ratio of $\frac{1}{50}$).

	Balanced Accuracy		AUC		Positives Ratio	
	InvProp	Uniform	InvProp	Uniform	InvProp	Uniform
ALPS	**0.7002**	0.6887	0.8712	0.8625	**0.0368**	0.0271
BADGE	0.7203	0.7181	0.8914	0.8901	**0.2730**	0.1646
DAL	**0.7036**	0.6692	**0.8948**	0.8560	**0.2823**	0.0142
Random	**0.7248**	0.6763	**0.8986**	0.8681	**0.2442**	0.0196

Table 3: Comparison of InvProp and Uniform across multiple base algorithms (for an imbalance ratio of $\frac{1}{50}$).

Binary-Imbalanced datasets, averaged on 10 random seeds. Here we also consider an imbalance ratio of $\frac{1}{50}$. For both AUC and Balanced Accuracy we see a clear advantage to InvProp-weighting compared to Uniform weighting, in that it is either better or comparable for all algorithms. In terms of the Positives Ratio, the effect on the different algorithms varies, but we see a clear increase when using the InvProp weighting method. The method is able to produce more positives, and as shown in Appendix B is able to do this throughout the different iterations.

Two interesting insights that are not directly related to our study are (1) the algorithms differ in their robustness to imbalance, with BADGE proving to be quite robust, especially when Uniform weighting is applied; (2) the Random algorithm combined with our weighting method becomes a strong baseline and is in fact the leader w.r.t both Balanced Accuracy and AUC.

We ran a similar comparison against the PosProb baseline and concluded that for an imbalance ratio of $\frac{1}{50}$, the results are comparable. We provide the full experiments comparing all 3 weighting methods on multiple imbalance ratio combinations, on all datasets and base algorithms in Section 5.6. In

	Balanced Accuracy		AUC		Positives Ratio	
	InvProp	Uniform	InvProp	Uniform	InvProp	Uniform
2.0	0.9009	0.9029	0.9518	**0.9534**	0.4816	0.4855
10.0	**0.8253**	0.8149	**0.9348**	0.9306	**0.3259**	0.1436
20.0	**0.7709**	0.7519	**0.9175**	0.9061	**0.2779**	0.0946
50.0	**0.7122**	0.6881	**0.8890**	0.8692	**0.2091**	0.0564
100.0	**0.6839**	0.6612	**0.8552**	0.8454	**0.1692**	0.0375

Table 4: Comparison of InvProp with Uniform across multiple degrees of imbalance.

	Balanced Accuracy		AUC		Positives Ratio	
	InvProp	PosProb	InvProp	PosProb	InvProp	PosProb
2.0	**0.9009**	0.8313	**0.9518**	0.9442	0.4816	**0.6425**
10.0	**0.8253**	0.8155	**0.9348**	0.9310	0.3259	**0.3702**
20.0	0.7709	0.7744	**0.9175**	0.9140	0.2779	0.2821
50.0	0.7122	0.7128	**0.8890**	0.8833	**0.2091**	0.1831
100.0	0.6839	0.6800	0.8552	0.8513	**0.1692**	0.1273

Table 5: Comparison of InvProp with PosProb across multiple degrees of imbalance.

addition, a qualitative analysis of the informativeness of selected positive samples can be found in Appendix C.

5.6 Sensitivity to Imbalance Ratio

The main approach of techniques addressing dataset imbalance is to skew the sampling process towards positive samples. This leads to the question of when each technique should be applied; optimizing towards positive samples may have a negative effect on the results when the real-world distribution is almost balanced. Therefore, we evaluate the performance of InvProp-weighting on datasets with different imbalance ratios. As described in Section 5.1, we generated datasets with different imbalance ratios. Specifically, we use datasets with an imbalance ratio of $100, 50, 20, 10$ and 2 (i.e. balanced). As in earlier experiments, we repeat the experiment on each Binary-Imbalanced dataset with 10 different random seeds. For each imbalance ratio we compare the average performance of each weighting method over all AL algorithms and datasets (the results per dataset and algorithm appear in Appendix D). Results of this experiment are reported in Table 4; it is easy to see that the InvProp-weighting method outperforms the Uniform baseline across all imbalance ratios which represent an imbalanced dataset. In addition, even for the balanced scenario, the baseline slightly outperforms our method in only one metric, AUC, while being comparable in the Balanced Accuracy metric and in Positives Ratio. This allows us to recommend the usage of InvProp-weighting even if the imbalance ratio is unknown.

As mentioned in Section 5.5, the PosProb weighting method performance is comparable to InvProp when considering a dataset with an imbalance ratio of $\frac{1}{50}$. In Table 5 we extend this comparison and compare the effect of the imbalance ratio on these two weighting methods. This shows that InvProp either outperforms or is comparable to PosProb in both Balanced Accuracy and AUC. A deeper dive into the Balanced Accuracy scores shows that PosProb performs best (compared to InvProp) on datasets with an imbalance ratio of 20. Since the weights of PosProb are independent of the imbalance of the dataset, i.e., down-sampling the minority class does not affect the proportion between weights of two of the remaining samples, it is expected that the performance of PosProb will peak at some specific imbalance ratio and decline as the imbalance ratio changes further away from this peak.

Another important aspect of the results is the number of positive samples accumulated by each solution. For the balanced dataset, PosProb over-skews the selection toward the positive class, leading to more than 60% of positive selected samples. As the imbalance grows, this stabilizes, and for imbalance ratio of 50 and 100 InvProp is able to identify a larger number of positive samples. The higher AUC score of InvProp points toward PosProb finding less diverse positive samples due to the large weight it assigns to positive samples which the model is certain about.

5.7 Extreme imbalance

To further test the limits of our methods, we extend the imbalance ratios to 200 and 1000. Results are presented in Table 6. Interestingly, even though the InvProp and PosProb weighting schemes manage to produce more positive examples than the uniform scheme, the Balanced Accuracy and the AUC metrics are better for the uniform as the imbalance ratio reaches extremes such as 1000. This could be explained by the weighting methods choosing positive examples that are too similar which do not contribute to the efficacy of the model. In general, we believe that in such extreme cases, where positive examples are so scarce, the trained model is unable to learn and is under-performing, hindering the efficacy of any AL approach. The performance of all AL algorithms with the Uniform weighting scheme exemplifies this, where we see that random

	Balanced Accuracy			AUC			Positives Ratio		
	InvProp	PosProb	Uniform	InvProp	PosProb	Uniform	InvProp	PosProb	Uniform
200.0	**0.6619**	0.6543	0.6377	0.8244	0.8251	**0.8302**	**0.1263**	0.0886	0.0267
1000.0	0.6181	0.6154	0.6160	0.7821	0.7831	**0.8081**	**0.0535**	0.0304	0.0103

Table 6: Comparing the weighting schemes against extreme imbalance ratios.

sampling produces the highest AUC score all of the AL algorithms, with statistical significance (see Table 9, Appendix D).

5.8 Sensitivity to number of bins

One drawback of InvProp-weighting compared to Uniform and PosProb-weighting is the addition of a new parameter, the number of bins. We evaluate the effect of the number of bins on the performance of different AL algorithms (with InvProp-weights) on the Binary-Imbalanced variants of the AG_news dataset. We consider InvProp with $2, 5, 10, 15$ and 20 bins. Results appear in table 11 in Appendix D. In table 12 (Appendix D), we evaluate the sensitivity to the number of bins by measuring significance with a relative t-test. This table lists the p-value $p(m)$ of a test comparing AUC and Balanced Accuracy for the selection of m bins (for $m \in \{2, 5, 15, 20\}$) to that of 10, as 10 was our choice throughout the paper. The results demonstrate that our method is insensitive to the bin count hyper-parameter, as except for one outlier, all p-values fall in $[0.05, 0.95]$. This motivates our choice to avoid optimizing this parameter, thus fixing it to a single value throughout the paper. This experiment was performed for all imbalance ratios discussed in this paper $(2, 10, 20, 50, 100)$. For brevity, we report only on an imbalance ratio of 100, since for this value the affect of the number of bins parameter was the largest. Since we conclude that this parameter is not significant even for this imbalance ratio, this conclusion is relevant across all imbalance ratios.

5.9 Warm start

Recall that in lieu of starting the learning process with no examples (cold-start), we start the process with 5 examples from each class. In Table 10 (Appendix) we show the size of the confidence intervals for the BADGE algorithm over the different datasets, showing an increase of at least $1.5X$, sometimes over $10X$ when comparing the cold-start to the chosen warm-start scenario. A major cause of the cold-start variance is the time it takes the learner to achieve a handful of positive examples. Indeed, when the imbalance ratio is 50, a random selection is expected to obtain only 1 positive sample in each iteration, and in many runs the learner fails simply as it does not find a sufficient initial amount of positive examples. A full solution should discuss realistic methods for obtaining an initial seed of examples, but this challenge is outside the scope of this paper. In order to remove the noise in the evaluation process originating from the time it takes to obtain a handful of examples, we have all methods initialize with the mentioned warm-start. We chose to work with particularly 5 examples as this is a small enough number of samples for it to be easy to obtain even in the imbalance scenario, and on the other hand, the variance is significantly reduced compared to the 'cold-start' setting.

6 Conclusions

In this paper, we tackled the problem of AL in imbalanced datasets. We propose a novel weighting-technique, InvProp , and apply it to three recent AL algorithms (BADGE, APLS and DAL) as well as to naive random sampling. We show results for the PosProb weighting scheme in addition to InvProp and compare to a uniform weighting baseline on four datasets. We show that InvProp-weighting consistently finds more positive examples, and leads to better or comparable performance compared to other weighting schemes on all tested datasets and AL algorithms. We also test various imbalance settings showing that InvProp outperforms the Uniform baseline across all imbalance ratios which represent some imbalance. In addition, on a balanced dataset the Uniform baseline outperforms our method in only one metric, while being comparable in the rest. Compared to PosProb, our solution proved to be more robust to changes in the imbalance ratio. When testing extreme scenarios where the imbalance is less than 0.5%, all tested algorithms perform worse than the simple random sampling baseline, suggesting that AL algorithms are not advantageous given an uninformative model. Concluding, we show our novel weighting scheme improves several SoTA AL algorithms on various datasets and imbalance ratios.

References

Jordan Ash and Ryan P Adams. 2020. On warm-starting neural network training. *Advances in Neural Information Processing Systems*, 33:3884–3894.

Jordan T. Ash, Chicheng Zhang, Akshay Krishnamurthy, John Langford, and Alekh Agarwal. 2020. Deep batch active learning by diverse, uncertain gradient lower bounds. In *8th International Conference on Learning Representations, ICLR 2020, Addis Ababa, Ethiopia, April 26-30, 2020*. OpenReview.net.

Ricardo Barata, Miguel Leite, Ricardo Pacheco, Marco OP Sampaio, João Tiago Ascensão, and Pedro Bizarro. 2021. Active learning for imbalanced data under cold start. In *Proceedings of the Second ACM International Conference on AI in Finance*, pages 1–9.

William H Beluch, Tim Genewein, Andreas Nürnberger, and Jan M Köhler. 2018. The power of ensembles for active learning in image classification. In *Proceedings of the IEEE conference on computer vision and pattern recognition*, pages 9368–9377.

Mausam C Lin. 2018. Active learning with unbalanced classes & example-generated queries. In *AAAI Conference on Human Computation*.

Franck Dernoncourt and Ji Young Lee. 2017. Pubmed 200k RCT: a dataset for sequential sentence classification in medical abstracts. In *Proceedings of the Eighth International Joint Conference on Natural Language Processing, IJCNLP 2017, Taipei, Taiwan, November 27 - December 1, 2017, Volume 2: Short Papers*, pages 308–313. Asian Federation of Natural Language Processing.

Jacob Devlin, Ming-Wei Chang, Kenton Lee, and Kristina Toutanova. 2019. BERT: Pre-training of deep bidirectional transformers for language understanding. In *Proceedings of the 2019 Conference of the North American Chapter of the Association for Computational Linguistics: Human Language Technologies, Volume 1 (Long and Short Papers)*, pages 4171–4186, Minneapolis, Minnesota. Association for Computational Linguistics.

Liat Ein Dor, Alon Halfon, Ariel Gera, Eyal Shnarch, Lena Dankin, Leshem Choshen, Marina Danilevsky, Ranit Aharonov, Yoav Katz, and Noam Slonim. 2020. Active learning for bert: an empirical study. In *Proceedings of the 2020 Conference on Empirical Methods in Natural Language Processing (EMNLP)*, pages 7949–7962.

Liat Ein-Dor, Alon Halfon, Ariel Gera, Eyal Shnarch, Lena Dankin, Leshem Choshen, Marina Danilevsky, Ranit Aharonov, Yoav Katz, and Noam Slonim. 2020. Active learning for BERT: an empirical study. In *Proceedings of the 2020 Conference on Empirical Methods in Natural Language Processing, EMNLP 2020, Online, November 16-20, 2020*, pages 7949–7962. Association for Computational Linguistics.

Andrew Estabrooks and Nathalie Japkowicz. 2001. A mixture-of-experts framework for learning from imbalanced data sets. In *International Symposium on Intelligent Data Analysis*, pages 34–43. Springer.

Yifan Fu, Xingquan Zhu, and Bin Li. 2013. A survey on instance selection for active learning. *Knowledge and information systems*, 35(2):249–283.

Daniel Gissin and Shai Shalev-Shwartz. 2019. Discriminative active learning. *CoRR*, abs/1907.06347.

Abbas Kazerouni, Qi Zhao, Jing Xie, Sandeep Tata, and Marc Najork. 2020. Active learning for skewed data sets. *arXiv preprint arXiv:2005.11442*.

Gwangsu Kim and Chang D Yoo. 2022. Blending query strategy of active learning for imbalanced data. *IEEE Access*.

Jens Lehmann, Robert Isele, Max Jakob, Anja Jentzsch, Dimitris Kontokostas, Pablo N. Mendes, Sebastian Hellmann, Mohamed Morsey, Patrick van Kleef, Sören Auer, and Christian Bizer. 2015. Dbpedia - A large-scale, multilingual knowledge base extracted from wikipedia. *Semantic Web*, 6(2):167–195.

David D Lewis and William A Gale. 1994. A sequential algorithm for training text classifiers. In *SIGIR'94*, pages 3–12. Springer.

Yijing Li, Haixiang Guo, Qingpeng Zhang, Mingyun Gu, and Jianying Yang. 2018. Imbalanced text sentiment classification using universal and domain-specific knowledge. *Knowl. Based Syst.*, 160:1–15.

Yinhan Liu, Myle Ott, Naman Goyal, Jingfei Du, Mandar Joshi, Danqi Chen, Omer Levy, Mike Lewis, Luke Zettlemoyer, and Veselin Stoyanov. 2019. Roberta: A robustly optimized BERT pretraining approach. *CoRR*, abs/1907.11692.

David Lowell, Zachary C Lipton, and Byron C Wallace. 2019. Practical obstacles to deploying active learning. In *Proceedings of the 2019 Conference on Empirical Methods in Natural Language Processing and the 9th International Joint Conference on Natural Language Processing (EMNLP-IJCNLP)*, pages 21–30.

Cristian Padurariu and Mihaela Elena Breaban. 2019. Dealing with data imbalance in text classification. In *Knowledge-Based and Intelligent Information & Engineering Systems: Proceedings of the 23rd International Conference KES-2019, Budapest, Hungary, 4-6 September 2019*, volume 159 of *Procedia Computer Science*, pages 736–745. Elsevier.

Matthew E. Peters, Mark Neumann, Mohit Iyyer, Matt Gardner, Christopher Clark, Kenton Lee, and Luke

Zettlemoyer. 2018. Deep contextualized word representations. In *Proceedings of the 2018 Conference of the North American Chapter of the Association for Computational Linguistics: Human Language Technologies, NAACL-HLT 2018, New Orleans, Louisiana, USA, June 1-6, 2018, Volume 1 (Long Papers)*, pages 2227–2237. Association for Computational Linguistics.

Pengzhen Ren, Yun Xiao, Xiaojun Chang, Po-Yao Huang, Zhihui Li, Brij B Gupta, Xiaojiang Chen, and Xin Wang. 2021. A survey of deep active learning. *ACM computing surveys (CSUR)*, 54(9):1–40.

Sarang Shaikh, Sher Muhammad Daudpota, Ali Shariq Imran, and Zenun Kastrati. 2021. Towards improved classification accuracy on highly imbalanced text dataset using deep neural language models. *Applied Sciences*, 11(2).

Richard Socher, Alex Perelygin, Jean Wu, Jason Chuang, Christopher D. Manning, Andrew Y. Ng, and Christopher Potts. 2013. Recursive deep models for semantic compositionality over a sentiment treebank. In *Proceedings of the 2013 Conference on Empirical Methods in Natural Language Processing, EMNLP 2013, 18-21 October 2013, Grand Hyatt Seattle, Seattle, Washington, USA, A meeting of SIGDAT, a Special Interest Group of the ACL*, pages 1631–1642. ACL.

Chi Sun, Xipeng Qiu, Yige Xu, and Xuanjing Huang. 2019. How to fine-tune BERT for text classification? *CoRR*, abs/1905.05583.

Shuohang Wang, Yang Liu, Yichong Xu, Chenguang Zhu, and Michael Zeng. 2021. Want to reduce labeling cost? GPT-3 can help. In *Findings of the Association for Computational Linguistics: EMNLP 2021, Virtual Event / Punta Cana, Dominican Republic, 16-20 November, 2021*, pages 4195–4205. Association for Computational Linguistics.

Michelle Yuan, Hsuan-Tien Lin, and Jordan L. Boyd-Graber. 2020. Cold-start active learning through self-supervised language modeling. In *Proceedings of the 2020 Conference on Empirical Methods in Natural Language Processing, EMNLP 2020, Online, November 16-20, 2020*, pages 7935–7948. Association for Computational Linguistics.

Xiang Zhang, Junbo Jake Zhao, and Yann LeCun. 2015. Character-level convolutional networks for text classification. In *Advances in Neural Information Processing Systems 28: Annual Conference on Neural Information Processing Systems 2015, December 7-12, 2015, Montreal, Quebec, Canada*, pages 649–657.

When is a Metaphor Actually Novel? Annotating Metaphor Novelty in the Context of Automatic Metaphor Detection

Sebastian Reimann and **Tatjana Scheffler**
Ruhr University Bochum
Department for German Language and Literature
Bochum, Germany
{sebastian.reimann,tatjana.scheffler}@rub.de

Abstract

We present an in-depth analysis of metaphor novelty, a relatively overlooked phenomenon in NLP. Novel metaphors have been analyzed via scores derived from crowdsourcing in NLP, while in theoretical work they are often defined by comparison to senses in dictionary entries. We reannotate metaphorically used words in the large VU Amsterdam Metaphor Corpus based on whether their metaphoric meaning is present in the dictionary. Based on this, we find that perceived metaphor novelty often clash with the dictionary based definition. We use the new labels to evaluate the performance of state-of-the-art language models for automatic metaphor detection and notice that novel metaphors according to our dictionary-based definition are easier to identify than novel metaphors according to crowdsourced novelty scores. In a subsequent analysis, we study the correlation between high novelty scores and word frequencies in the pretraining and finetuning corpora, as well as potential problems with rare words for pre-trained language models. In line with previous works, we find a negative correlation between word frequency in the training data and novelty scores and we link these aspects to problems with the tokenization of BERT and RoBERTa.

1 Introduction

Most data for training and evaluating automatic metaphor detection systems contains binary labeling that only distinguishes between metaphoric and literal tokens. The distinction between novel and conventionalized metaphor has received some, albeit little attention in the context of annotating data for automatic metaphor detection (Do Dinh et al., 2018; Neidlein et al., 2020; Djokic et al., 2021). There is however still a lack of publicly available, large-scale annotations that make this distinction. So far, all existing work on novel metaphor in NLP has used crowdsourced annotations of metaphors from the VU Amsterdam Metaphor Corpus (VUAMC; Steen et al., 2010).

This lack of resources and research in general is problematic in several ways: Neidlein et al. (2020) suggest that considerable numbers of novel metaphors remain undetected by metaphor detection systems. What is more, the notion of when a metaphor can be considered *novel* varies in the literature. Besides crowdsourced novelty scores, dictionary-based approaches are frequently used. For example, Reijnierse et al. (2018) and Egg and Kordoni (2022) consider a metaphor to be not conventionalized, if the sense in which it is used cannot be found in a dictionary. Krennmayr (2006) already argued for the use of corpus-based dicitionaries in metaphor analysis since they provide transparency and replicability, which would also be an advantage in annotation of metaphor novelty. Do Dinh et al. (2018) even stress the need to compare their novelty scores with dictionary entries.

Identifying novel metaphors is especially important for computational approaches to figurative language, since other forms of metaphor can often be easily captured by distributional approaches to meaning. For example, depending on the subsection for the respective register, between 33% and 45% of the prepositions in the VUAMC were used in a metaphorical way (Steen et al., 2010). These are often temporal prepositions such as *in July*, which are seen as spatial words such as *in* transferred into a temporal sense. These highly conventionalized metaphors are not usually of interest in computational approaches to figurative language.

In this study, we evaluate crowdsourced novelty scores by investigating how well they align with dictionary-based definitions of *novel metaphor* (RQ1). We show that there are systematic discrepancies between these two definitions. Based on our findings, we develop a new label for novel metaphor and use this label to evaluate current

Proceedings of The 18th Linguistic Annotation Workshop (LAW-XVIII), pages 87–97
March 22, 2024 ©2024 Association for Computational Linguistics

state-of-the-art metaphor detection systems specifically on novel metaphors (RQ2). We will make these new annotations on metaphor novelty publicly available. We find that the systems appear to find a higher share of novel metaphors defined by our dictionary-based label, compared to a distinction based on the crowdsourced novelty score and a threshold. We link our results to the findings of Neidlein et al. (2020) and raise the concern that crowdsourced novelty scores may mainly trace the overall rarity of the words and should be replaced by deeper estimates of the unconventionality of metaphors in future work.

2 Previous Work

2.1 Metaphor Annotation

The Metaphor Identifcation Procedure Vrjie Universiteit Amsterdam (MIPVU; Steen et al., 2010) was widely used to obtain binary metaphor annotations. MIPVU identifies so-called metaphor related words (MRWs) and distinguishes between indirect and direct MRWs. Indirect MRWs are identified by comparing the contextual meaning of a word with available senses in the dictionary: if one semantically related meaning in the dictionary can be considered more "basic" (more concrete or human-related) than the contextual interpretation, the word is seen as potentially metaphoric. In (1), the meaning of the word *brilliant* equates to the sense *extremely clever or skillful* in the Longman Dictionary of Contemporary English (LDOCE) (Longman, 2023). The more concrete meaning is *brilliant light or colour is very bright and strong*. As both brightness and intelligence are seen as positive, we can conclude that *brilliant* is an MRW according to MIPVU.

(1) This was a brilliant move.

In direct MRWs, there is no contrast between the contextual and a more basic meaning of a word but the word still is part of a mapping between two domains. This is for example the case in metaphoric comparisons, like (2). Here *proud* and *man* are technically used in their most basic meaning. However, by comparison and lexical signals (*like*) the domain TREE is mapped onto the domain HUMAN/MAN.

(2) This tree stands like a proud man.

Steen et al. (2010) applied MIPVU to the BNC-Baby Corpus in order to create the VUAMC, which was then used as training and test data in the Metaphor Detection Shared Tasks 2018 and 2020 (Leong et al., 2018, 2020) and other studies on automatic metaphor detection.

There exist, however, approaches to metaphor annotation that go beyond a mere distinction between metaphoric and literal. The LCC dataset (Mohler et al., 2016) contains word pairs in four languages (English, Spanish, Russian and Farsi) annotated on a four-point-scale according to their metaphoricity. The judgement on *metaphoricity* includes how easy the source domain can be perceived by the senses, how vivid the used language is, how frequently the metaphor may be encountered. The degree of conventionalization is thus to some extent taken into account in this annotation of metaphoricity. However, it is only one of several factors that influence metaphoricity and Mohler et al. (2016) do not present annotations on degree of conventionalization of a metaphor isolated from the other aspects of metaphoricity.

Another fine-grained distinction can be drawn between deliberate metaphors, which are meant to be understood as metaphors (Reijnierse et al., 2018), and non-deliberate ones. The Deliberate Metaphor Identification Procedure (DMIP) of Reijnierse et al. (2018) is a way to systematically annotate an MRW (previously identified via MIPVU) on potential deliberateness by checking whether its source domain is needed to actually understand the metaphor in its context, which, according to Reijnierse et al. (2018), is always the case for novel and unconventionalized metaphors. Reijnierse et al. (2018) define *novel metaphor* based on whether the metaphoric sense of a word is represented in the dictionary. In Reijnierse et al. (2019), the entire VUAMC was annotated for potentially deliberateness of an MRW according to DMIP. The labels in Reijnierse et al. (2019) only present a binary distinction between *potentially deliberate* and *non-deliberate*.

The first approach to provide annotations on perceived metaphor novelty in the VUAMC was by Parde and Nielsen (2018), who obtained novelty annotations for syntactically related word pairs from the VUAMC. Here, on the one hand, a smaller dataset of about 3,000 pairs was annotated by trained annotators and a larger dataset (about 18,000 pairs) was annotated by crowdworkers. In both cases, annotators needed to rate the word pairs on a scale from 0 to 3, where 0 marks non-metaphoric instances and 3 highly novel instances. The disagreements for the trained annotators were resolved by discussion and a third annotator, whereas the crowdworkers' annotations were automatically aggregated to a final annotation on the same scale.

Do Dinh et al. (2018) also provided annotations on metaphor novelty for the VUAMC. They focused however on annotations for each token labeled as MRW and not on syntactic pairs. Here, crowdworkers were asked to rank MRWs from the VUAMC according to how novel they are. These annotations were aggregated and transformed into scores ranging from -1 (very conventionalized) to 1 (very novel). The authors moreover explored how their novelty scores correlate with word frequency, concreteness scores and potential for metaphoricity (POM) (Del Tredici and Bel, 2016), where they observed a correlation of novelty annotations with frequency and POM but not with concreteness.

For the distinction between metaphor and nonsense, Pedinotti et al. (2021) released a dataset of 300 items, 100 metaphoric sentences, 100 literal and 100 nonsensical statements. The metaphors in their dataset were also grouped into creative (i.e. novel) and conventional metaphors. Unfortunately, Pedinotti et al. (2021) did not explain further how they exactly defined the terms *creative* and *conventional*. Additionally, they provided annotations by crowdworkers on semantic plausibility, that is how meaningful a sentence is, and metaphoricity. Here, novel metaphors were considered less plausible than conventional metaphors by human judges and were rated more metaphorical than conventional metaphors.

2.2 Automatic Metaphor Detection and Novel Metaphor

In recent years, large pre-trained language models were dominating the field of automatic metaphor detection. This is exemplified by the results of the 2020 shared task on metaphor detection (Leong et al., 2020), where the five best-performing approaches all used some variation of BERT (Devlin et al., 2019) or RoBERTa (Liu et al., 2019). Approaches such as DeepMet by Su et al. (2020) that intends to simulate a reading comprehension with two RoBERTa encoder layers and linguistic features such as POS-tags, and MelBERT (Choi et al., 2021), which emulates two theoretical methods for identifying metaphors in text, Metaphor Identification Procedure (MIP) (Pragglejaz Group, 2007), a predecessor of MIPVU and Selectional Preference Violation (SPV) (Wilks, 1975), where metaphors are identified by looking at whether a word semantically matches its context, achieve impressive F1-scores of more then 75 on a binary distinction between MRW and literal use.

When it comes to finding novel metaphors, much less work has been carried out. One early attempt to detect novel metaphors was conducted by Haagsma and Bjerva (2016). They employ selectional preference violations (Wilks, 1975) by extracting the frequencies of verb-noun pairs from a large Wikipedia corpus, semantically clustering them and calculating selectional preference metrics. These serve as inputs for a logistic regression classifier that was then tested on detecting metaphors in VUAMC data. In the evaluation, they however conclude that, back then, they were not able to clearly state the effectiveness of their system for novel metaphors since labels on metaphor novelty were not available for the VUAMC.

Besides providing annotations on metaphor novelty, Do Dinh et al. (2018) also built a system to predict metaphor novelty scores. For this, they used a BiLSTM with dependency-based word embeddings that achieved a mean absolute error of 0.166. Adding the features with which novelty scores correlate (frequency and POM) however only led to an improved MAE of 0.163.

Neidlein et al. (2020) conducted an extensive analysis of metaphor detection systems based on large language models. One focus was on how well these models were able to handle novel metaphors. For this, they set various thresholds for the scores of Do Dinh et al. (2018) and looked at the accuracy for MRWs with a score higher than that threshold. They observed that the higher the threshold, the lower the accuracy, and concluded that novel metaphors are more difficult than conventionalized metaphors. They moreover looked at word frequencies in the training set and found that the performance is lower on metaphoric words that have rarely been seen in fine-tuning and that a high number of conventionalized metaphors have high word frequencies in the training data. Moreover, the models evaluated in (Neidlein et al., 2020) performed better if derivational variants (such as *warm* and *warmth*) have been seen in training before.

To see if BERT can distinguish between metaphors and nonsense, Pedinotti et al. (2021), on the one hand calculated the pseudo-log-likelihood (PLL) score (Wang and Cho, 2019) of metaphoric, literal and nonsensical sentences and the cosine similarity with so-called *landmarks*, words that are either from the same or a different semantic space than the metaphor in question (Kintsch, 2000). Based on the PLL scores, the model considers novel metaphor significantly more plausible than nonsensical sentences, however less plausible than conventional metaphors. Moreover, it struggles harder to interpret novel metaphor by comparing them with landmarks than to interpret conventional metaphors.

The only effort so far that actually made use of metaphor novelty in training was presented by Djokic et al. (2021). They used a BERT-based classifier that predicted novelty scores in a joint manner together with general binary labels on metaphor (MRW or not MRW). It was trained on data from the VUAMC and then applied to an unlabeled corpus of short stories, which unfortunately does not allow for a systematic evaluation. They only tested the score prediction on the VUAMC test data, which led to a slightly improved MAE of 0.142 compared to the baseline of Do Dinh et al. (2018).

3 Methodology

We systematically evaluate the crowdsourced novelty scores of Do Dinh et al. (2018) by comparing them with our own binary annotation of MRWs that uses a linguistic definition of novel metaphor, according to which a metaphor is considered novel if the contextual meaning of the MRW is not included in a standard dictionary for the language under investigation. Steen et al. (2010) and Reijnierse et al. (2018) used the MacMillan dictionary (Rundell, 2002) as a primary lexical resource in their metaphor annotation. Unfortunately, the online version of the MacMillan dictionary has been shut down in July 2023. In our annotation, we thus use the Longman Dictionary of Contemporary English (LDOCE), which was used by Steen et al. (2010) as a secondary source and which is also corpus-based, as our main resource for checking if the contextual meaning of a word is represented in the dictionary, either as a sense description in the entry of a word or as entry for a fixed expression.

DMIP, introduced in the previous section, considers metaphor novelty (via the availability of sense descriptions in dictionaries) as one criterion for potential deliberateness of a metaphor. It was applied to all MRWs in the VUAMC by Reijnierse et al. (2019). Unfortunately, the authors did not provide any further information on why they consider a metaphor potentially deliberate. Nevertheless, Reijnierse et al. (2019) present novel metaphors according to a dictionary-based definition as a subset of potentially deliberate MRWs. This provides a good heuristic to find MRWs that are potentially novel. We consequently check the contextual meaning in the dictionary for:

- MRWs that were annotated as potentially deliberate in Reijnierse et al. (2019) with the exception of direct MRWs, as their contextual meaning is not different from a basic meaning in the dictionary

- MRWs marked as non-deliberate but which received scores over the previously used threshold of 0.45 (a modification by Djokic et al. (2021) of the originally used threshold of 0.5 in Do Dinh et al. (2018)) for novelty. Since the annotations on potential deliberateness are supposed to include all novel metaphors, these cases already represent an interesting clash in annotations since the scores here suggest high novelty but the annotations of Reijnierse et al. (2019), which treat them as non-deliberate, suggest otherwise.

We consider MRWs with low novelty scores and which are not marked potentially deliberate to be not novel. Given the annotations of Reijnierse et al. (2019) we can assume that the availability of a dictionary entry was already considered for labeling them non-deliberate and thus also conventionalized.

All listed cases are manually checked by two annotators: a student assistant trained in metaphor annotation and the first author of this paper. If the contextual meaning of the MRW is not found in the dictionary, the MRW receives the label *novel*, otherwise it is considered *conventionalized*.

After our additional dictionary-based novelty annotation, we conduct a survey of model performance in a similar fashion to Neidlein et al. (2020). We conduct reruns of metaphor detection systems and then compare their performance. For this, we chose DeepMet (Su et al., 2020), because of its strong performance in the 2020 Metaphor Detection Shared Task. We moreover selected MelBERT (Choi et al., 2021) since it achieves competitive performance with DeepMet, while its architecture is more strongly motivated by linguistic theories on metaphor. Here, the layer inspired by SPV is particularly interesting, as already Haagsma and

Bjerva (2016) attempted to use SPV for the detection of novel metaphor. For MelBERT we therefore test the entire architecture as well as both layers in isolation. Finally, we considered the model used in Djokic et al. (2021), since it was designed with the specific goal of finding novel metaphors. We evaluate their model with both the joint objective as well as with only the metaphor detection task in training, in the following referred to as Djokic (joint pred.) and Djokic (met. only), respectively.

The models are trained on the binary classification task (metaphoric vs. literal), with the data from the VUAMC as in the 2020 Metaphor Detection Shared Task (including the same training-test splits) and the same hyperparameters as in the respective original papers. All models use the BERT and RoBERTa implementations from the HuggingFace Transformer library (Wolf et al., 2020): DeepMet and MelBERT use *roberta-base* and the models by Djokic et al. (2021) use *bert-base-cased*. In the evaluation, following Neidlein et al. (2020), we then look at the share of novel metaphors (both according to our definition and according to a novelty score threshold of 0.45) that was detected by the model.

4 Results

4.1 Dictionary-Based Annotation of Novel Metaphors

In total we re-annotated 1160 MRWs with our dictionary based definition of *novel metaphor*. When deciding on whether a dictionary entry for a specific contextual meaning exists or not, the two annotators reached relatively robust agreement of Cohen's $\kappa = 0.73$. Instances for which we disagreed were revisited on a case-to-case basis and a consensus decision was reached.

Table 1 shows the detailed results of our comparison. Overall, we can see that a substantial number of MRWs whose contextual meaning is not represented in the dictionary would be ignored if we applied a threshold of 0.45. We can however see that the share of novel metaphors according to the dictionary-based definition rises with higher crowdsourced novelty since the vast majority of MRWs with scores lower than 0.1 have a conventionalized sense description in the dictionary. This picture however changes with higher scores and for scores only slightly below the threshold, the majority may already be considered novel according to a dictionary-based definition. This suggests that, while there may be some correlation between the two ways of annotating metaphor novelty, defining novelty via crowdsourced scores and a set threshold ignores a wide range of metaphorically used words without a corresponding sense in the dictionary. Table 2 shows three such examples, where a dictionary entry for the respective meaning in the sentence was not found but which eventually would not be considered novel when only looking at novelty scores and the threshold.

The entry in the LDOCE for *pollution* refers either to the process or the substances that make the water, the air or the soil dirty and to the fixed expressions of *noise pollution* and *light pollution*. The author of the example sentence uses pollution to refer to something they perceive as immoral. The sense descriptions for *gulp* explicitly refer to a human activity, either to swallowing or taking in breaths. Here on the other hand, one of these activities is in a novel way ascribed to the *soil*. *Somersault* is in the dictionary described as a bodily movement by a person and not by an organ. *Soupy* only has one meaning (*having a thick liquid quality like soup*), which is obviously not fit to describe music as in the example.

The largest clash between the two definitions of metaphor novelty may however be observed through MRWs that were marked as non-deliberate in Reijnierse et al. (2019) but received novelty scores of over 0.45. Applying this threshold would consider them novel, but the overwhelming majority actually has a sense descriptions in the dictionary. This is illustrated by Example 3, which received a novelty score of 0.545 but for which it can be argued that the use of *gripped* is equivalent to the second entry in the LDOCE dictionary for *to grip* (power and control over someone or something), which would render it conventionalized.

(3) He rejects charges that he was partly responsible for the ‘ casino atmosphere ’ that **gripped** US corporate life in the early 1980s .

A final observation is that a dictionary-based definition leads to a lower number of novel metaphors, compared to defining novelty via crowdsourced scores and a threshold. The former would lead to 421 (318 in the training set and 103 in the test set), compared to 536 novel MRWs (385 in the training and 151 in the test set) according to scores only.

novelty score	potentially delib.	total	in dictionary	not in dictionary (%)
<0.1	yes	244	189	55 (22.54%)
0.1–0.2	yes	88	49	39 (44.31%)
0.2–0.45	yes	292	104	188 (64.38%)
>0.45	yes	113	27	86 (76.10%)
>0.45	no	423	370	53 (12.53%)

Table 1: Overview over MRWs that were annotated by us and if they were found in the dictionary.

Example Sentence	Novelty
The wastes include lindane [...] and even pornography (a different kind of **pollution**).	0.103
You can almost hear the soil **gulping**.	0.303
Paula 's stomach turned a **somersault** .	0.412
The voice of rock'n'roll, in contrast, is almost unrelievedly **soupy**.	0.441

Table 2: Examples of novel MRWs and their respective novelty scores, with metaphorically used words in bold.

4.2 Analysis of Model Performance on Novel Metaphors

Table 3 shows the results of our metaphor detection experiments. We first observe that novel metaphors according to our dictionary-based definition appear to be easier to find than novel metaphors based on crowdsourced scores. The recall for novel metaphors is still worse than the recall for all metaphors but higher that the recall for novel metaphors according to the crowdsourcing threshold.

This would suggest, on the one hand, that novel metaphors are less of a problem for metaphor detection systems than previously assumed by Neidlein et al. (2020). On the other hand, they still remain harder to find than conventionalized metaphors and especially the continued, mostly poor, results for words with high novelty scores hint at other problems. We discuss them in the next section.

Comparing the different model architectures to each other, we can see that DeepMet outperformed the other approaches. Interestingly, the joint prediction of novelty scores and metaphoricity did not help in finding metaphors since adding the loss from the novelty score prediction even led to a minor drop in overall performance for the model of Djokic et al. (2021). Moreover, contrary to previous assumptions, the linguistically motivated architecture of Choi et al. (2021) performed worse than the other models on novel metaphors. Despite previous assumptions that SPV might be suitable to detect metaphor novelty (Haagsma and Bjerva, 2016), MelBERT with only the SPV layer found the lowest share of novel metaphors.

One hypothesis for the poor recall of MelBERT's SPV layer when it comes to novel metaphors may lie in the particular implementation of SPV. It compares the representation of the word in its context with the embedding of the [CLS]-token, representing the entire sentence. This raises doubts about whether it is enough to represent a semantic clash between the word and the context in which it is used.

5 Discussion

5.1 Subjectivity

Our results have shown that perceived novelty and availability of dictionary entries indeed diverge. We now discuss reasons that may cause this difference. On the one hand, we raise the possibility that the perception of untrained annotators might still be too subjective to be solely taken into account when drawing conclusions on the novelty of a metaphor. This can be exemplified by the two instances of *block* in 4. MIPVU considers these two tokens to be separate MRWs and it can be assumed that they were treated separately in the crowdsourcing annotation of Do Dinh et al. (2018) and were annotated by separate annotators. The first *block* has received a novelty score of 0.176 whereas the second *block* received a novelty score of -0.029. This difference seems counterintuitive as they occur in the same context and are used with the same contextual meaning. This example shows that annotations by crowd workers may diverge wildly even for similar instances.

Model	F1	Recall (all metaphor)	Recall (novel/label)	Recall (novel/threshold)
DeepMet	**73.53**	**74.54**	**63.10**	**59.60**
MelBERT (all)	73.07	70.00	56.31	54.96
MelBERT (MIP)	71.77	68.58	57.28	52.98
MelBERT (SPV)	71.28	67.88	53.39	50.33
Djokic (joint pred.)	69.50	72.50	60.19	50.00
Djokic (met. only)	70.60	72.30	62.13	50.67

Table 3: Performance of the selected models, best performance for each metric in bold.

(4) In general, our policy should be to proceed with building our state block by block[...]

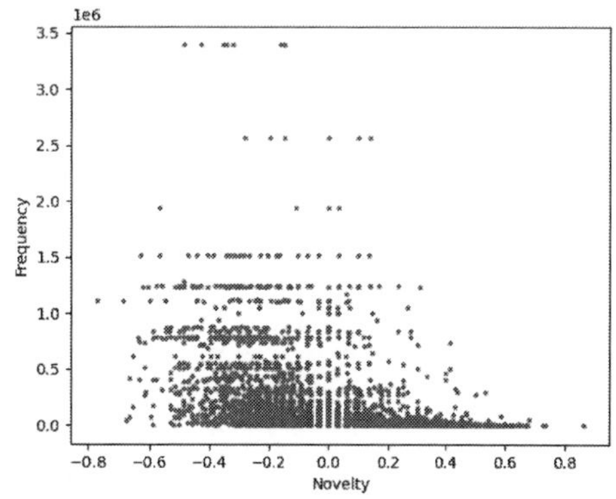

Figure 1: Plot showing the relation between novelty score of a metaphoric word and its frequency in the BookCorpus.

5.2 Word Frequency

Word frequency is another factor to be considered when explaining the discrepancy between crowdsourced and dictionary based definitions of metaphor novelty. Do Dinh et al. (2018) have demonstrated a negative correlation of the crowdsourced novelty score with word frequency in a Wikipedia dump. This suggests that a higher novelty score often indicates that a word is rare. In turn, rare words are rarely seen in the pre-training or fine-tuning process of metaphor detection systems. Neidlein et al. (2020) have already shown that pre-trained language models appear to have problems with rare words in the context of automatic metaphor detection. Their findings also indicate that words with low novelty scores have a tendency to occur frequently and, vice versa, words with high novelty scores occur rarely in the training data. Now, assuming that metaphoric words with novelty scores over 0.45 indeed have low frequencies in the training corpora, it seems logical that fewer of them are identified as metaphoric.

The Spearman correlation between frequencies in the training data from the VUAMC, used in fine-tuning the models, and the crowdsourced novelty scores indeed is $\rho = -0.612$, clearly supporting previous findings of Do Dinh et al. (2018) and Neidlein et al. (2020). Looking at the data used in pre-training, we conduct a similar analysis with the BookCorpus (Zhu et al., 2015), used for pre-training BERT and RoBERTa in addition to Wikipedia data. The Spearman correlation for both is similar, with $\rho = -0.601$ and the plot in Figure 1 is in line with the findings of Neidlein et al. (2020) and shows that metaphors with high novelty scores almost exclusively occur infrequently in the pre-training data. On the one hand, this suggests that annotators in crowdsourcing may have a higher tendency to classify metaphors that involve words they do not frequently encounter as novel, which may be problematic since the example of *pollution* in Table 1 shows that also relatively common words may be used with novel, metaphoric senses. A further investigation of this would however go beyond the scope of this paper.

On the other hand, this relation might have direct implications for model performance. To investigate how rare or unseen words in either pre-training or fine-tuning influence the task of automatic metaphor detection, we perform an error analysis on three examples with crowd sourced novelty scores over 0.45, which did not occur in the pre-training data and which were misclassified by all models. They are shown in Table 4. Indeed, none of these three words were present in the vocabulary files of the used BERT and RoBERTa models.

Moreover, the way how the respective tokenizers split these rare words up into subword tokens may be problematic. As Table 5 shows, the subword tok-

MRW	Sentence	Score
indistinguishable	Whatever else such a strategy may achieve, it certainly does not manage to produce a situation in which children are politically indistinguishable from adults and it rests on premises which, unless they can be defended, gain nothing for any defence to the charge of arbitrariness.	0.485
millipedes	After all, Mancunians and visitors to the Manchester conurbation are going to have to look at these mechanical millipedes for well into the twenty-first century.	0.531
Wriggling	Wriggling across country on the D216 to Port-d'Envaux, you come to two more chateaux : 18th-century Panloy, flaking romantically away on its hillock overlooking a bend in the Charente and, almost next door, the much older, moated Crazannes, half-smothered in amazing flamboyant Gothic carving.	0.625

Table 4: Wrongly classified examples by all model architectures.

MRW	Subwords (BERT)	Subwords (RoBERTa)
indistinguishable	in ##dis ##ting ##ui ##sha ##ble	ind ##ist ##inguishable
millipedes	mill ##ip ##ede ##s	mill ##ip ##edes
wriggling	w ##rig ##gling	w ##rig ##gling

Table 5: Output of the BERT and RoBERTa tokenizer for the MRWs presented in Table 4.

enization of the previously presented cases is not at all in line with the actual morphology of the words. *Distinguish* in *indistinguishable* for example is unrecognizable in the way it has been split into subword units. Neidlein et al. (2020) have shown that it may help if models have seen derivational variants of unseen words in training. However, if they are split like in this example, it is doubtful whether such knowledge can be transferred.

Nayak et al. (2020) have raised further doubts on how well the semantics of a word are represented if the subword tokenization does not fall in line with the actual constituents of the word. For instance, the cosine similarity between *unsaturated* (wrongly tokenized by BERT) and *saturated* is at only 0.30, whereas the cosine distance between *un saturated* (with a space and actually correctly tokenized) and *saturated* is at 0.81. Similar issues may have hurt the viability of the semantic representation for metaphor detection for the examples in Table 5.

In contrast, the MRW *drunkenly* in Example (5) received a relatively high novelty score (0.559) but was still correctly recognized by all models as metaphoric. The tokenizers of both BERT and RoBERTa split the word as *drunken ##ly*, thus retaining its derivational bases and suggesting that the more natural splitting may have played a role in the correct classification.

(5) The plane climbs reluctantly, one set of wings dipping **drunkenly**.

6 Conclusion and Future Work

We systematically compared the crowdsourced novelty scores of Do Dinh et al. (2018) with sense entries available in the dictionary. We evaluated state of the art systems for automatic metaphor detection on their performance on novel metaphor wrt. both score-based and dictionary-based labels. Finally, we discussed these results by taking word frequency as well as the underlying subword tokenization of BERT and RoBERTa into account.

We found that measuring novelty purely by crowdsourced scores and a set threshold ignores a wide range of metaphors for which no conventionalized sense descriptions are available, and in addition considers words used in actually conventionalized senses to be novel. As many theoretical approaches to metaphor use dictionaries as a tool for measuring the degree of conventionalization, we thus present new annotations of metaphor novelty for the widely used VUAMC that are more in line with these theoretical concepts. We moreover argue that our dictionary-based annotations are more transparent, compared to crowdsourced scores, where the perception of annotators sometimes appears to diverge greatly and where the overall rarity of a word may have a great impact on the annotator's perception of novelty.

Our evaluation of metaphor detection models suggests that rare words may present a larger problem than words used in unusual contexts or with novel meaning. This is reflected in a higher percentage of recognized novel metaphors according to our linguistically grounded label, compared with novelty defined via crowdsourced scores only. Moreover, we found that the underlying word representations of BERT and RoBERTa are often formed from sub-word units that do not reflect the actual morphology of derived words and consequently might not be fit for semantically complex tasks such as metaphor detection, especially when the words are used in unusual, novel contexts.

One potential line for future research would be a closer look at the perception of annotators in crowdsourcing on whether unusual words have a higher tendency to be perceived as novel metaphors, even though they are used in a relatively conventionalized way. Moreover, since the number of truly novel metaphors in the VUA corpus is quite small, further data sets that contain a higher share of novel metaphors and, consequently, evaluation on these data sets is necessary to better judge the performance of metaphor detection systems. Finally, we would like to propose to extend the task of automatic metaphor detection from a binary classification task to a three-way classification by further distinguishing between novel and conventionalized metaphors.

Limitations

One limitation of our study is that the number of novel metaphors in the test set is relatively small, especially for our own dictionary based definition of metaphor novelty. While our model evaluation shows a tendency when it comes to the performance on novel metaphors, a test set containing a larger number of novel metaphors would be needed in order to draw more reliable conclusions on the performance of current language models on detecting novel metaphors.

Finally, such a definition of metaphor novelty relies heavily on the availability of well-structured dictionaries. While this is not a problem for English, it may be difficult to obtain such resources for other languages, especially low-resource languages. Other ways to measure metaphor novelty need to be considered in those cases.

Ethics Statement

In our work we only used corpora that were already freely available. The student research assistant conducted the annotation work within a fixed work contract and was paid according to public pay scales.

Acknowledgements

We thank the reviewer for the valuable comments and Simon Kreutz for his annotation efforts. We moreover thank the PC^2(Paderborn Center for Parallel Computing) for granting us compute time on the Noctua 1 cluster. Funded by the Deutsche Forschungsgemeinschaft (DFG, German Research Foundation) – SFB 1475 – Project ID 441126958.

References

Minjin Choi, Sunkyung Lee, Eunseong Choi, Heesoo Park, Junhyuk Lee, Dongwon Lee, and Jongwuk Lee. 2021. MelBERT: Metaphor detection via contextualized late interaction using metaphorical identification theories. In *Proceedings of the 2021 Conference of the North American Chapter of the Association for Computational Linguistics: Human Language Technologies*, pages 1763–1773, Online. Association for Computational Linguistics.

Marco Del Tredici and Núria Bel. 2016. Assessing the potential of metaphoricity of verbs using corpus data. In *Proceedings of the Tenth International Conference on Language Resources and Evaluation (LREC'16)*, pages 4573–4577, Portorož, Slovenia. European Language Resources Association (ELRA).

Jacob Devlin, Ming-Wei Chang, Kenton Lee, and Kristina Toutanova. 2019. BERT: Pre-training of deep bidirectional transformers for language understanding. In *Proceedings of the 2019 Conference of the North American Chapter of the Association for Computational Linguistics: Human Language Technologies, Volume 1 (Long and Short Papers)*, pages 4171–4186, Minneapolis, Minnesota. Association for Computational Linguistics.

Vesna G. Djokic, Ekaterina Shutova, and Verna Dankers. 2021. Episodic memory demands modulate novel metaphor use during event narration. In *Proceedings of the Annual Meeting of the Cognitive Science Society*, volume 43.

Erik-Lân Do Dinh, Hannah Wieland, and Iryna Gurevych. 2018. Weeding out conventionalized metaphors: A corpus of novel metaphor annotations. In *Proceedings of the 2018 Conference on Empirical Methods in Natural Language Processing*, pages 1412–1424, Brussels, Belgium. Association for Computational Linguistics.

Markus Egg and Valia Kordoni. 2022. Metaphor annotation for German. In *Proceedings of the Thirteenth Language Resources and Evaluation Conference*, pages 2556–2562, Marseille, France. European Language Resources Association.

Hessel Haagsma and Johannes Bjerva. 2016. Detecting novel metaphor using selectional preference information. In *Proceedings of the Fourth Workshop on Metaphor in NLP*, pages 10–17, San Diego, California. Association for Computational Linguistics.

Walter Kintsch. 2000. Metaphor comprehension: A computational theory. *Psychonomic bulletin & review*, 7(2):257–266.

Tina Krennmayr. 2006. Using dictionaries in linguistic metaphor identification. *Selected Papers from the 2006 and 2007 Stockholm Metaphor Festivals*, page 95.

Chee Wee (Ben) Leong, Beata Beigman Klebanov, Chris Hamill, Egon Stemle, Rutuja Ubale, and Xianyang Chen. 2020. A report on the 2020 VUA and TOEFL metaphor detection shared task. In *Proceedings of the Second Workshop on Figurative Language Processing*, pages 18–29, Online. Association for Computational Linguistics.

Chee Wee (Ben) Leong, Beata Beigman Klebanov, and Ekaterina Shutova. 2018. A report on the 2018 VUA metaphor detection shared task. In *Proceedings of the Workshop on Figurative Language Processing*, pages 56–66, New Orleans, Louisiana. Association for Computational Linguistics.

Yinhan Liu, Myle Ott, Naman Goyal, Jingfei Du, Mandar Joshi, Danqi Chen, Omer Levy, Mike Lewis, Luke Zettlemoyer, and Veselin Stoyanov. 2019. Roberta: A robustly optimized bert pretraining approach.

Longman. 2023. *Longman Dictionary of Contemporary English (Online Edition)*. Pearson Education Limited.

Michael Mohler, Mary Brunson, Bryan Rink, and Marc Tomlinson. 2016. Introducing the LCC metaphor datasets. In *Proceedings of the Tenth International Conference on Language Resources and Evaluation (LREC'16)*, pages 4221–4227, Portorož, Slovenia. European Language Resources Association (ELRA).

Anmol Nayak, Hariprasad Timmapathini, Karthikeyan Ponnalagu, and Vijendran Gopalan Venkoparao. 2020. Domain adaptation challenges of BERT in tokenization and sub-word representations of out-of-vocabulary words. In *Proceedings of the First Workshop on Insights from Negative Results in NLP*, pages 1–5, Online. Association for Computational Linguistics.

Arthur Neidlein, Philip Wiesenbach, and Katja Markert. 2020. An analysis of language models for metaphor recognition. In *Proceedings of the 28th International Conference on Computational Linguistics*, pages 3722–3736, Barcelona, Spain (Online). International Committee on Computational Linguistics.

Natalie Parde and Rodney Nielsen. 2018. A corpus of metaphor novelty scores for syntactically-related word pairs. In *Proceedings of the Eleventh International Conference on Language Resources and Evaluation (LREC 2018)*, Miyazaki, Japan. European Language Resources Association (ELRA).

Paolo Pedinotti, Eliana Di Palma, Ludovica Cerini, and Alessandro Lenci. 2021. A howling success or a working sea? testing what BERT knows about metaphors. In *Proceedings of the Fourth BlackboxNLP Workshop on Analyzing and Interpreting Neural Networks for NLP*, pages 192–204, Punta Cana, Dominican Republic. Association for Computational Linguistics.

Pragglejaz Group. 2007. MIP: A Method for Identifying Metaphorically Used Words in Discourse. *Metaphor and Symbol*, 22(1):1–39.

W. Gudrun Reijnierse, Christian Burgers, Tina Krennmayr, and Gerard J. Steen. 2018. Dmip: A method for identifying potentially deliberate metaphor in language use. *Corpus Pragmatics*, 2(2):129–147.

W. Gudrun Reijnierse, Christian Burgers, Tina Krennmayr, and Gerard J. Steen. 2019. Metaphor in communication: the distribution of potentially deliberate metaphor across register and word class. *Corpora*, 14(3):301–326.

Michael Rundell, editor. 2002. *Macmillan English Dictionary for Advanced Learners*. Macmillan, Oxford.

Gerard J. Steen, Aletta G. Dorst, J. Berenike Herrmann, Anna A. Kaal, Tina Krennmayr, and Trijntje Pasma. 2010. *A Method for Linguistic Metaphor Identification: From MIP to MIPVU*, volume 14 of *Converging Evidence in Language and Communication Research*. John Benjamins Publishing Company, Amsterdam/Philadelphia.

Chuandong Su, Fumiyo Fukumoto, Xiaoxi Huang, Jiyi Li, Rongbo Wang, and Zhiqun Chen. 2020. DeepMet: A reading comprehension paradigm for token-level metaphor detection. In *Proceedings of the Second Workshop on Figurative Language Processing*, pages 30–39, Online. Association for Computational Linguistics.

Alex Wang and Kyunghyun Cho. 2019. BERT has a mouth, and it must speak: BERT as a Markov random field language model. In *Proceedings of the*

Workshop on Methods for Optimizing and Evaluating Neural Language Generation, pages 30–36, Minneapolis, Minnesota. Association for Computational Linguistics.

Yorick Wilks. 1975. A preferential, pattern-seeking, semantics for natural language inference. *Artificial intelligence*, 6(1):53–74.

Thomas Wolf, Lysandre Debut, Victor Sanh, Julien Chaumond, Clement Delangue, Anthony Moi, Pierric Cistac, Tim Rault, Remi Louf, Morgan Funtowicz, Joe Davison, Sam Shleifer, Patrick von Platen, Clara Ma, Yacine Jernite, Julien Plu, Canwen Xu, Teven Le Scao, Sylvain Gugger, Mariama Drame, Quentin Lhoest, and Alexander Rush. 2020. Transformers: State-of-the-art natural language processing. In *Proceedings of the 2020 Conference on Empirical Methods in Natural Language Processing: System Demonstrations*, pages 38–45, Online. Association for Computational Linguistics.

Yukun Zhu, Ryan Kiros, Richard Zemel, Ruslan Salakhutdinov, Raquel Urtasun, Antonio Torralba, and Sanja Fidler. 2015. Aligning books and movies: Towards story-like visual explanations by watching movies and reading books. In *arXiv preprint arXiv:1506.06724*.

Enhancing Text Classification through LLM-Driven Active Learning and Human Annotation

Hamidreza Rouzegar and **Masoud Makrehchi**

Department of Electrical, Computer and Software Engineering
Ontario Tech University
Oshawa, ON, Canada
hamidreza.rouzegar@ontariotechu.net
masoud.makrehchi@ontariotechu.ca

Abstract

In the context of text classification, the financial burden of annotation exercises for creating training data is a critical issue. Active learning techniques, particularly those rooted in uncertainty sampling, offer a cost-effective solution by pinpointing the most instructive samples for manual annotation. Similarly, Large Language Models (LLMs) such as GPT-3.5 provide an alternative for automated annotation but come with concerns regarding their reliability. This study introduces a novel methodology that integrates human annotators and LLMs within an Active Learning framework. We conducted evaluations on three public datasets. IMDB for sentiment analysis, a Fake News dataset for authenticity discernment, and a Movie Genres dataset for multi-label classification. The proposed framework integrates human annotation with the output of LLMs, depending on the model uncertainty levels. This strategy achieves an optimal balance between cost efficiency and classification performance. The empirical results show a substantial decrease in the costs associated with data annotation while either maintaining or improving model accuracy.

1 Introduction

Active learning allows machine learning algorithms to choose their learning data selectively. This methodology optimizes learning efficiency while reducing the need for labor-intensive labeled instances, often leading to enhancing the performance metrics with less training (Settles et al., 2008).

While Active Learning has been explored in research for over two decades, it has seen a resurgence of interest in Natural Language Processing (NLP), particularly around 2009-2010. This resurgence has been aligned with adopting neural models in NLP research (Zhang et al., 2022b). Recent trends suggest the advantageous pairing of Active Learning techniques with deep learning methodologies (Zhang et al., 2022b).

A prevalent strategy within Active Learning is uncertainty sampling. This technique involves the algorithm selecting instances in which the model might be least certain about their labels. For instance, in binary classification tasks, it might select an instance whose probability of belonging to the positive class is nearest to 0.5. This often employs a 'pool-based' approach where a human expert validates and assigns true labels to the selected samples, which are then used to update the classifier iteratively (Lewis and Gale, 1994). Additional approaches like Query-By-Committee (QBC) (Seung et al., 1992) and Expected Gradient Length (EGL) (Settles, 2009) offer alternative techniques in Active Learning.

Broadly speaking, Active Learning aims to reduce the expenses associated with human annotation, achieving this by strategically selecting the most informative data points for labeling (Hachey et al., 2005). However, Active Learning is not the only strategy employed to minimize human annotation costs. LLMs have been applied to various text annotation tasks such as political Twitter message categorization (Törnberg, 2023), relevance and topic detection in tweets (Gilardi et al., 2023), and hate speech classification (Huang et al., 2023). Some recent studies have also examined the potential of utilizing Active Learning in Prompt-Based Uncertainty sampling with LLMs (Yu et al., 2023).

In this study, we propose a novel pipeline for text classification focusing on three distinct, open-source datasets: IMDB for sentiment analysis, a dataset for identifying fake news, and another for classifying Movie Genres. We introduce a framework that integrates Active Learning based on uncertainty sampling with human and GPT-3.5 annotations. This integration is tailored to adaptively choose between human and machine annotators based on the uncertainty levels estimated from GPT-

Proceedings of The 18th Linguistic Annotation Workshop (LAW-XVIII), pages 98–111
March 22, 2024

3.5's annotation.

To the best of our knowledge, this is the first study that comprehensively evaluates the utility and efficiency of combining human annotators, Active Learning, and GPT-3.5 in a text classification task. We extend the traditional Active Learning methodologies by integrating uncertainty measurements from LLM, such as GPT-3.5, into our annotation selection process. This not only minimizes the costs of manual annotation but also capitalizes on the strengths of machine learning models for efficient and accurate text classification.

Our approach offers a nuanced trade-off analysis between cost and accuracy, using real-world pricing models for both human and machine annotation. The goal is to provide a robust, cost-effective, and scalable text classification pipeline that leverages the best of both human expertise and advanced machine learning techniques. The code provide in anonymous GitHub.[1]

In the subsequent sections, we explore a methodology that combines human expertise with LLMs in an Active Learning framework. We detail the experimental setup and methodologies, including uncertainty-based sampling and LLMs for data annotation. The results are analyzed for their accuracy and efficiency, leading to a discussion on the broader implications and future potential of this approach in text classification.

2 Related Works

Text classification is an instrumental task in Natural Language Processing (NLP) that uses methods ranging from traditional machine learning techniques to advanced neural networks such as Long Short-Term Memory (LSTM) (Qaisar, 2020) and Convolutional Neural Networks (CNN) (Haque et al., 2019). Although these methods primarily focus on improving model accuracy, our study diverges by emphasizing the reduction of labeled data through selective annotation, subsequently enhancing the model performance. We also manage the pool of unlabeled data by removing instances that have been labeled, thus continuously refining our dataset for model training.

2.1 Uncertainty-based Active Learning

Anderson et al. (Andersen and Zukunft, 2022) explored Active Learning based on uncertainty across different models, including support vector machines, logistic regression, and decision trees. They proposed a criterion for manual annotation that identifies a certain percentage of the most uncertain predictions for each model type as a stopping point for annotation. For example, they suggested a 12.71% threshold for logistic regression to achieve desired model performance.

In (Goudjil et al., 2018) Active Learning is applied on text analysis tasks. The authors used support vector machines and Active Learning-supported SVM (AL-SVM) models. They introduced a thresholding mechanism, such as setting a 70% threshold for AL-SVM, to select instances with less than 70% probability for annotation.

2.2 Advanced Active Learning Methods

In (Yuan et al., 2020), a range of Active Learning techniques, such as Active Learning by Processing Surprisal and Entropy, are examined. However, their work did not establish any clear stopping criterion to determine how many Active Learning iterations are necessary.

In the work by Zhang et al. (Zhang et al., 2022a), they proposed a method that uses local sensitivity and adversarial perturbations in the Active Learning loop. They aimed to alleviate the sampling bias that comes from selecting only the most uncertain examples. They used data augmentation and adversarial perturbation to measure the local sensitivity of instances, thereby picking examples that lie near the decision boundary. Their approach also incorporated a "learning hardness" criterion to sidestep examples that are hard to learn or potentially mislabeled.

2.3 Active Learning with Language Models

Yue Yu et al. (Yu et al., 2023) proposed a method called PATRON that integrates prompt-based techniques for cold-start data selection in Active Learning. Their method uses estimated uncertainty for data points, adopting two key design strategies—uncertainty propagation and a partition-then-rewrite (PTR) strategy to ensure a balance between informativeness and diversity in sample selection.

Building upon these foundations, recent studies have furthered our understanding of the potential of Active Learning when combined with LLMs. Zhang et al. (Zhang et al., 2023) introduced a framework where LLMs serve as active annotators, underscoring the efficiency of LLMs in reducing annotation costs while maintaining accuracy. "Beyond Labels" further expanded this concept by inte-

[1]GitHub Code

grating human annotators with machine-generated natural language explanations, demonstrating the potential for more informative annotations in low-resource settings.

In (Xiao et al., 2023), the authors proposed a novel collaborative learning approach, reducing the need for human annotation by leveraging LLMs as weak annotators. This framework indicates the potential of LLMs to enhance unsupervised performance in various NLP tasks. On the other side, Lu et al. (Lu et al., 2023) presented empirical evidence that smaller models trained with expert annotations can outperform LLMs in domain-specific tasks, highlighting the irreplaceable value of human expertise.

Furthermore, Margatina et al. (Margatina et al., 2023) explored selecting demonstrations for few-shot learning with LLMs, revealing that demonstrations semantically similar to test examples yield superior performance across tasks and model sizes. This finding supports our methodology of integrating human annotators and GPT-3.5 in a new Active Learning paradigm evaluated across multiple open-source datasets.

Lastly, in (Margatina and Aletras, 2023), the authors critically examined the challenges in Active Learning research, especially in simulated environments. They emphasize the need for realistic, transparent, and reproducible Active Learning research, aligning with our approach of combining human expertise with the capabilities of LLMs to address the challenges in text classification and Active Learning.

While these works have significantly advanced the field of Active Learning, there remains a gap in leveraging the power of LLMs like GPT-3.5 for both annotation and uncertainty estimation in an integrated Active Learning framework. Our work aims to bridge this gap by using both human annotators and GPT-3.5 in a novel Active Learning paradigm, which we evaluate across multiple open-source datasets.

3 Methodology

This section details the methodology employed for text classification, emphasizing the integration of Large Language Models in data annotation. The approach encompasses an Active Learning framework, applying uncertainty-based sampling across varied datasets to enhance accuracy and efficiency.

Algorithm 1 Procedure for Collecting Sentiment Label and Confidence

Require: Movie review text $X[i]$

Ensure: Sentiment label and confidence level in JSON format

1: **Prompt:** "What is the sentiment of the following movie review, and how confident are you about this 'sentiment'?"

2: **Instructions:** "Give your answer as a single word, either 'positive' or 'negative' and a single percentage in JSON format delimited with space."

3: **Display:** "Review text: ''' $X[i]$ '''"

3.1 Active Learning based on uncertainty sampling

Our Active Learning approach revolved around the concept of uncertainty sampling. In each iteration of the Active Learning process, we used an iterative strategy to select the most uncertain data points from the unlabeled data pool, employing the logistic regression model's predicted probabilities. The ranking of data points based on their predicted probabilities provided a measure of uncertainty or confidence measure for each sample. This ranking helps to identify and select the data points for which the classifier was most uncertain, enabling the model to learn from these challenging instances and refine its classification performance.

Data Selection: In each Active Learning iteration, the data samples with the highest uncertainty scores from the pool of unlabeled data are selected, adding these data samples to the training set for the next iteration. This process of focusing on high-information gain data allowed the model to learn from its previous mistakes and incrementally improve its overall performance with each iteration. By iteratively selecting and incorporating informative data, the Active Learning approach optimizes the learning process efficiently, requiring significantly fewer labeled samples compared to conventional supervised learning methods.

Pool Initiation: We initiated the Active Learning process by creating an initial set of data that incorporated a small fraction of the entire data available for the classification task. This set served as the starting point for the learning process, enabling the model to make its initial predictions. The rest of the data, not included in the initial set, constituted the 'unlabeled pool.' This pool continuously

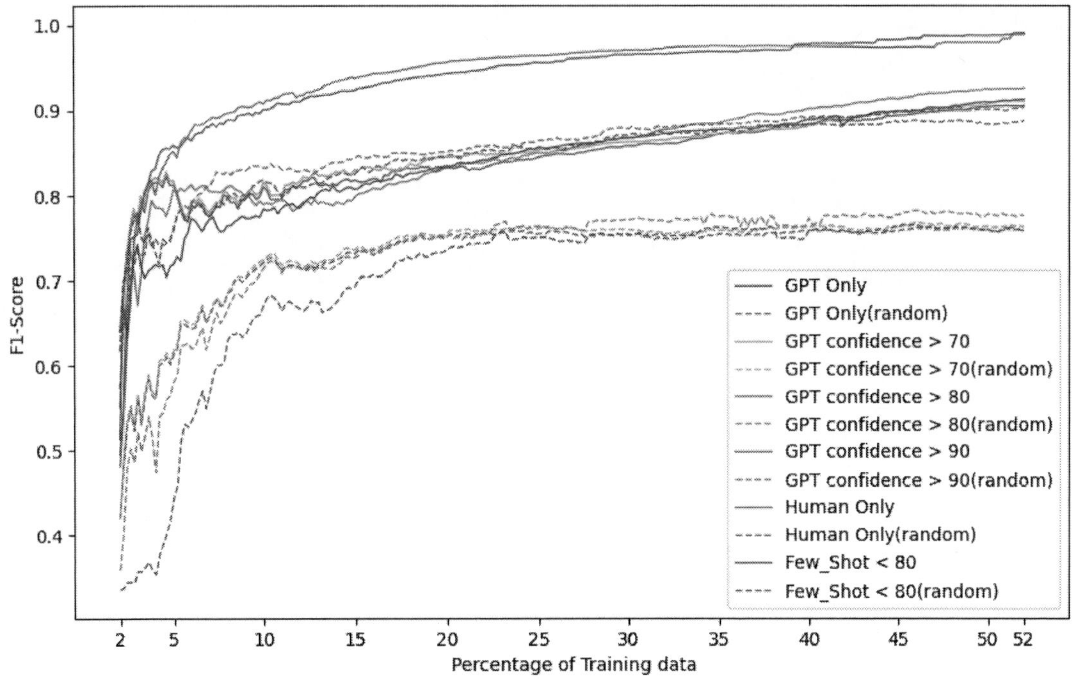

Figure 1: F1 Score Progression from 2% to 52% Training Data Portions in the Fake News Dataset. This figure visualizes the evolution of F1 scores across different training data portions, ranging from 2% to 52%, for various annotation methods, including GPT-only, Hybrid models, Human-only, Few-shot learning, and a baseline of random sampling. Each incremental step represents an increase in the training dataset size, highlighting the performance changes in F1 scores across the experiments.

provided a source of uncertain samples to be selected and labeled during each iteration of the Active Learning process.

3.2 Proxy-Validation Set

One of the key contributions of our work is the creation of a 'proxy-validation' set. This set, which is a subset of the total data, served to estimate the model's performance at each iteration of the Active Learning process, acting as a set of labeled samples. It also emulated the statistical distribution presented in the main unlabeled pool, undergoing updates alongside each iteration.

During each Active Learning iteration, we computed the model's accuracy on the proxy-validation set. To ensure consistency, we applied the same percentage of confidence for low-confidence data removal to the proxy-validation set as we did to the main unlabeled pool. The remaining data in the proxy-validation set provided us with an estimation of the main pool's accuracy, a crucial measure when true labels for the pool were unavailable.

3.3 LLM-based Data Annotation

We employed the GPT-3.5 API to annotate our dataset, increasing the overall efficiency of the Active Learning process. A set of prompts is designed for GPT-3.5 to predict the sentiment of movie reviews and to report confidence in each prediction. The use of LLM for annotation allowed us to obtain sentiment labels and corresponding confidence scores for each data, opening the way for several experimental conditions. The procedure for IMDB datasets is illustrated in Algorithm 1.

Adaptation of Active Learning to Prompt Engineering: Building on the foundational concepts of Active Learning, a new approach is introduced to apply the components mentioned above in a solution based on LLMs such as GPT-3.5.

Unlike usual Active Learning methods, which often require retraining models with carefully chosen labeled data, our method takes a different path by focusing on improving the prompts given to GPT-3.5. This approach makes the most of the model's pre-existing knowledge and avoids the need for retraining. Instead, GPT-3.5's responses carefully crafted the prompts.

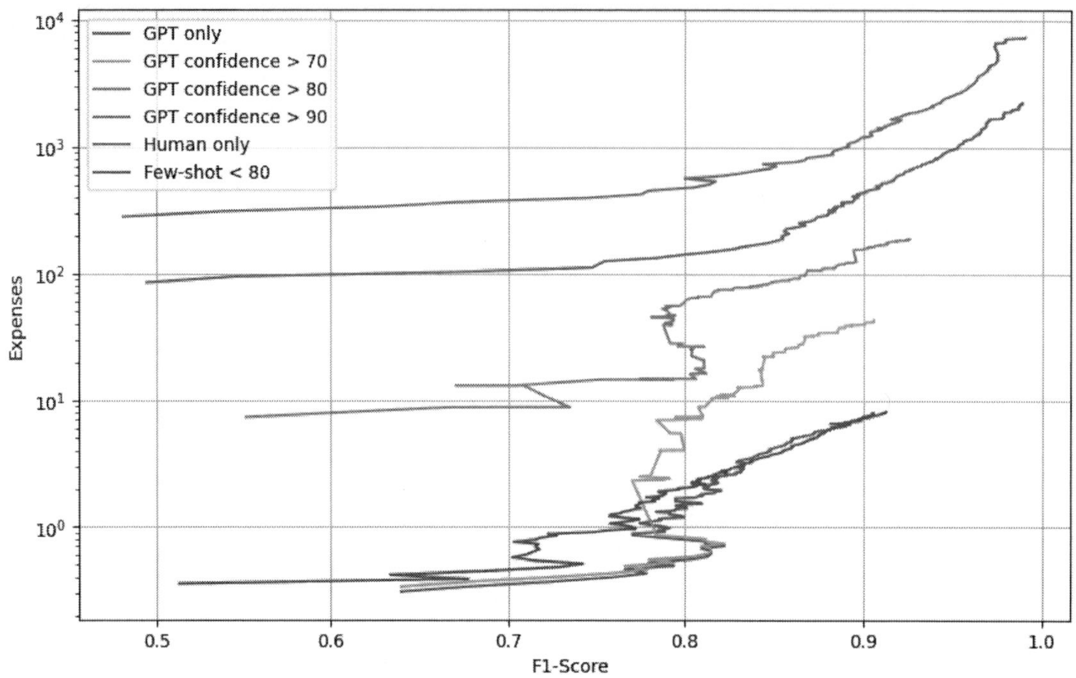

Figure 2: Cost per F1 Score Analysis During Iterative Training Data Increments in the Fake News Dataset. This figure illustrates the cost efficiency (cost per F1 score) for different annotation strategies as the training data portion increases from 2% to 52%. It compares the cost-effectiveness of GPT-only, Hybrid models, Human-only, and Few-shot learning methods, providing insights into the financial implications of each annotation approach over the iterative training process.

Initially, we utilize zero-shot learning, presenting tasks to GPT-3.5 without any specific examples. The model's response and associated confidence scores provide an initial measure of its proficiency in the given task. These confidence scores are analogous to uncertainty measures in traditional Active Learning, guiding our subsequent steps.

In instances where GPT-3.5 exhibits lower confidence (below 70% in the IMDB dataset and below 80% in two other datasets), we transition to a few-shot learning approach. This progression involves providing the model with low-confidence tasks. These thresholds were chosen based on an analysis of our datasets, which revealed that lower thresholds did not significantly change many labels, while higher thresholds led to an excessively large portion of the data being re-annotated. With these thresholds, we managed to target approximately 10 to 15 percent of the IMDB and Movie Genres datasets and about 4 percent of the fake news dataset, ensuring a manageable yet effective scope for applying few-shot learning.

This methodology effectively replicates the essence of Active Learning, where the model iteratively improves by focusing on the most informative or uncertain samples. By applying this approach to prompt design, we leverage the innate capabilities of LLMs for more efficient and targeted learning.

4 Experimental Setup

In the experimental setup, we explore the impact of using GPT-3.5 for data annotation under various scenarios, including different confidence thresholds and combinations of human and GPT-3.5 annotations. The experiments were conducted across three datasets: IMDB, Movie Genress, and fake news.

GPT-3.5 Labels Only Our first experiment investigates the feasibility of employing an LLM for data annotation using only the labels provided by GPT-3.5.

Human Labels Only As a baseline, our second experiment involves using human annotations exclusively. This experiment serves as a control to measure the effectiveness of GPT-3.5's annotations against traditional human annotation.

Hybrid Labels: Confidence Threshold Exper-

Portion	10%		20%		30%		40%		50%	
Method	Cost	F1	Cost	F1	Cost	F1	Cost	F1	Cost	F1
GPT only	0.46	0.8201	0.92	0.8651	1.3809	0.9152	1.84	0.9439	2.30	0.9629
GPT conf > 70	74.44	0.8548	170.45	0.9077	283.37	0.9446	373.04	0.9671	442.42	0.978
GPT conf > 80	219.04	0.8522	476.13	0.908	733.22	0.9469	958.60	0.9696	1151.85	0.9802
GPT conf > 90	369.12	0.8533	750.09	0.9112	1139.51	0.9495	1517.10	0.9700	1873.55	0.9800
Human only	423.24	0.8597	846.49	0.9085	1269.73	0.9475	1692.98	0.9693	2116.22	0.9796
Few-shot <70	0.95	0.8469	1.77	0.8973	2.60	0.9407	3.33	0.9631	4.07	0.9773

Table 1: IMDB Dataset Results: F1 Scores and Costs (in USD) for Various Annotation Methods on the IMDB Dataset. This table illustrates the comparative performance and cost-efficiency of different annotation approaches, including GPT-only, Hybrid models with varying confidence thresholds, Human-only, and Few-shot learning strategies across 10% to 50% data portions.

Portion	10%		20%		30%		40%		50%	
Method	Cost	F1	Cost	F1	Cost	F1	Cost	F1	Cost	F1
GPT only	1.53	0.8099	3.06	0.8339	4.59	0.8576	6.12	0.8837	7.66	0.9041
GPT conf > 70	7.16	0.8099	12.91	0.8394	25.70	0.8573	34.27	0.8764	41.44	0.9028
GPT conf > 80	39.53	0.7889	77.66	0.8319	97.49	0.8675	159.54	0.9017	187.82	0.9243
GPT conf > 90	437.85	0.9007	843.33	0.9426	1289.63	0.9646	1714.82	0.9771	2156.90	0.9871
Human only	1409.02	0.9074	2818.04	0.956	4227.07	0.9701	5636.09	0.9745	7045.11	0.9791
Few-shot <70	1.59	0.7838	3.14	0.8335	4.69	0.8667	6.24	0.8888	7.81	0.9092

Table 2: Fake News Dataset Results: Comparative Analysis of F1 Scores and Annotation Costs (in USD) for the Fake News Dataset. The table presents a detailed breakdown of the performance metrics and financial implications of using GPT-only, various Hybrid models, Human-only, and Few-shot annotations at different data portions.

iments These experiments explore the efficacy of combining GPT-3.5's predictions with human annotations at various confidence levels set by GPT-3.5.

Confidence Threshold 90 For data points where GPT-3.5's confidence score exceeds 90%, we utilize the labels provided by the model. If the confidence score is below 90%, human annotations are used. This experiment aims to evaluate the performance and cost-effectiveness of relying predominantly on AI annotations at a high confidence level.

Confidence Threshold 80 In this setup, GPT-3.5's labels are adopted for data points with a confidence score above 80%. For those below this threshold, human annotations are employed. This approach aims to balance AI efficiency and human accuracy at an intermediate confidence level.

Confidence Threshold 70 Here, the threshold is set at 70% confidence. GPT-3.5's labels are used for data points above this level, while human annotations supplement the lower-confidence points. The objective is to assess the impacts of a lower threshold on annotation efficiency and accuracy.

GPT-3.5 with Few-Shot Learning for Active Learning This experiment investigates the application of GPT-3.5's few-shot learning for data annotation in an Active Learning context, specifically focusing on data points with varying confidence levels. Unlike the hybrid approach that combines human and GPT-3.5 annotations, this setup utilizes GPT-3.5's few-shot learning capabilities exclusively. The aim here is to assess how GPT-3.5's few-shot learning can enhance the model's annotation performance, particularly for data points where it initially shows low confidence. The strategy involves:

One-Shot Learning for Higher Confidence Data Points: For data points where GPT-3.5's confidence score is above a certain threshold, we employ one-shot learning. GPT-3.5 is provided with a single relevant example to refine its understanding and improve annotations.

Few-Shot Learning for Lower Confidence Data Points: For data points with confidence scores below the threshold, few-shot learning is implemented, where GPT-3.5 is given three examples to

Portion	10%		20%		30%		40%		50%	
Method	Cost	F1	Cost	F1	Cost	F1	Cost	F1	Cost	F1
GPT only	0.81	0.3530	1.62	0.4066	2.43	0.4236	3.24	0.4233	4.05	0.4337
GPT conf > 70	6.01	0.3767	8.31	0.4056	17.31	0.4235	25.56	0.4308	31.58	0.4364
GPT conf > 80	125.82	0.2688	169.79	0.4806	233.10	0.4998	299.39	0.5053	347.83	0.5358
GPT conf > 90	263.48	0.6212	534.40	0.716	809.79	0.7513	1078.48	0.7959	1353.87	0.8271
Human only	744.92	0.6039	1489.84	0.711	2234.77	0.7520	2979.69	0.8099	3724.61	0.8443
Few-shot <70	0.88	0.37	1.74	0.4223	2.60	0.4726	3.4615	0.4761	4.31	0.4996

Table 3: Movie Genres Dataset Results: Performance Metrics and Costs (in USD) Across Different Annotation Methods for the Movie Genres Dataset. This table compares the F1 scores and associated costs for GPT-only, Hybrid annotation at different confidence levels, Human-only, and Few-shot learning across incremental portions of the dataset.

assist its annotations.

Confidence Thresholds: In the IMDB Dataset, A 70% confidence threshold is used. Data points above this threshold receive one-shot learning, while those below it are processed with few-shot learning. However, for Movie Genres and Fake News Datasets, An 80% confidence threshold is applied. Similarly, data points above this threshold are handled with one-shot learning and those below it with few-shot learning.

Baseline Comparison (Random Data Addition): Each experimental setup includes a component where data points are added to the training set randomly, serving as a baseline for comparison. This strategy illustrates the advantages of our more targeted Active Learning approaches.

Comparison and Cost Estimation: We evaluate each experimental setup based on two main metrics: the F1 score and the associated annotation costs. The focus is on finding the optimal balance between accuracy and cost-efficiency, particularly in the hybrid annotation and few-shot learning scenarios. The results highlight the trade-offs involved in using GPT-3.5's annotations to reduce costs.

Cost Estimation: For a more thorough understanding of the feasibility of each approach, the annotation costs associated with each experiment were evaluated. These costs were computed based on the pricing structure provided by the AI Platform Data Labeling Service for human labels[2], and the pricing for the GPT-3.5 API [3] for LLM generated labels. For human annotation costs, we referred to the AI Platform Data Labeling Service pricing, which uses units per human labeler, with each unit encompassing a fixed number of words. The total cost of human annotation was calculated by multiplying the total number of units labeled by human annotators with the per-unit price. For LLM annotation costs, we utilized the pricing structure provided for the GPT-3.5 API, which charges based on the number of tokens processed. The total cost of machine annotation was determined by multiplying the total number of tokens processed by GPT-3.5 with the cost per token. By taking both F1-Score and cost into consideration, we established a comprehensive comparison of each experiment. This comparison provided insights into the trade-off between cost and accuracy, allowing us to identify the most economically efficient approach that does not compromise the performance of our Active Learning model. This comprehensive evaluation and comparison serve as a valuable guide in implementing Active Learning strategies for text classification tasks.

5 Analysis and Results

The methodology exhibited notable scalability across three distinct datasets, each presenting unique classification challenges: IMDB Reviews: This dataset involved a binary classification task, determining the sentiment of movie reviews as either positive or negative. Fake News: Another binary classification task where the variability in text lengths presented an additional layer of complexity. Movie Genres: This dataset represented a more intricate four-class classification based on movie plots. The consistent application of the methodology across these datasets underscores its adaptability and versatility in handling varying text lengths and classification complexities.

[2]https://cloud.google.com/ai-platform/data-labeling/pricing

[3]https://openai.com/pricing

The F1 scores and costs associated with each experimental setup were analyzed. For instance, in the IMDB dataset, GPT-only annotations demonstrated a progressive increase in F1 scores from 0.8201 at 10% to 0.9629 at 50%, with corresponding costs ranging from 0.4603 to 2.3015. Conversely, the human-only approach showed F1 scores from 0.8597 to 0.9796, with significantly higher costs.(Table 1)

Critically, Figure 1 demonstrates that all annotation methods significantly outperform random sampling. This superiority is evident across various metrics, particularly as the training data incrementally increases from 2% to 52%. These findings underscore the effectiveness of structured annotation strategies over random approaches in enhancing the efficiency and accuracy of text classification.

Confidence thresholds played a crucial role in balancing automated and manual annotations. In the IMDB dataset, a 70% threshold was used, where data points above this threshold received one-shot learning, and those below it were processed with few-shot learning. For the Movie Genres and Fake News datasets, an 80% threshold was applied. These thresholds were determined based on the datasets' characteristics, targeting approximately 10 to 15 percent of the IMDB and Movie Genres datasets and about 4 percent of the Fake News dataset for few-shot learning. This strategy effectively replicated the essence of Active Learning, focusing on the most informative or uncertain samples.

The cost implications of each setup were a focal point. For instance, the Hybrid 80 model for IMDB and the Hybrid 90 for Movie Genres demonstrated significant cost-efficiency while achieving comparable accuracies to human-only labels but at a fraction of the cost. This was effectively illustrated through logarithmic scale representations, Figure 2 highlighting stark cost disparities and indicating the practicality of the chosen thresholds and annotation strategies.

The concept of proxy validation emerged as a crucial aspect of the study. Analysis revealed a notable correlation between the F1 score of the proxy validation and the remaining pool, indicating that proxy validation serves as a reliable indicator of the overall pool quality. Though some variations between the F1 score of proxy validation and the actual pool were observed, these discrepancies were minimal. Detailed examples and a deeper analysis of this phenomenon are provided in the appendix. Increasing the size of the proxy validation compared to pool data might lead to even more similar F1 scores between proxy validation and the pool, enhancing the reliability of this method as an indicator.

The study also delved into the analysis of GPT-3.5's output confidence scores. In the IMDB dataset, 11% of the annotations were found to be incorrect overall. However, in instances where GPT-3.5's confidence was below 70%, the rate of incorrect annotations rose to nearly 50%. Similar trends were observed in the Movie Genres dataset (33% overall inaccuracies, rising to 50% for data under 80% confidence) and the Fake News dataset (27% overall inaccuracies, increasing to nearly 50% for data under 80% confidence). These findings suggest that the model's confidence score can be a reliable indicator of uncertainty and the likelihood of annotation errors.

These results have significant implications for the application of Active Learning models, particularly in how confidence scores can be interpreted and used. The observed correlation between lower confidence scores and higher rates of annotation errors supports the idea that GPT-3.5's confidence can be treated similarly to uncertainty measures in traditional Active Learning models. This insight opens up new avenues for utilizing LLMs in Active Learning frameworks, where confidence scores can guide the annotation process more effectively.

Conclusion

The paper demonstrates that combining Large Language Models (LLMs), such as GPT-3.5, with human annotators in an Active Learning framework significantly enhances text classification tasks. This hybrid approach, which selectively employs either GPT-3.5 or human annotations based on confidence thresholds, efficiently balances cost and accuracy. The methodology reduces data annotation expenses while maintaining or even improving model performance compared to traditional human-only annotation methods. The study also introduces the concept of proxy validation, which effectively estimates the quality of the entire unlabeled dataset, proving useful in optimizing the annotation process. Overall, the research highlights the benefits of integrating advanced AI models with human insights to create more efficient, accurate, and scalable solutions for text classification.

References

Jakob Smedegaard Andersen and Olaf Zukunft. 2022. Towards more reliable text classification on edge devices via a human-in-the-loop. In *ICAART (2)*, pages 636–646.

Fabrizio Gilardi, Meysam Alizadeh, and Maël Kubli. 2023. Chatgpt outperforms crowd-workers for text-annotation tasks. *arXiv preprint arXiv:2303.15056*.

Mohamed Goudjil, Mouloud Koudil, Mouldi Bedda, and Noureddine Ghoggali. 2018. A novel active learning method using svm for text classification. *International Journal of Automation and Computing*, 15:290–298.

Ben Hachey, Beatrice Alex, and Markus Becker. 2005. Investigating the effects of selective sampling on the annotation task. In *Proceedings of the Ninth Conference on Computational Natural Language Learning (CoNLL-2005)*, pages 144–151, Ann Arbor, Michigan. Association for Computational Linguistics.

Md Rakibul Haque, Salma Akter Lima, and Sadia Zaman Mishu. 2019. Performance analysis of different neural networks for sentiment analysis on imdb movie reviews. In *2019 3rd International conference on electrical, computer & telecommunication engineering (ICECTE)*, pages 161–164. IEEE.

Fan Huang, Haewoon Kwak, and Jisun An. 2023. Is chatgpt better than human annotators? potential and limitations of chatgpt in explaining implicit hate speech. *arXiv preprint arXiv:2302.07736*.

David D. Lewis and William A. Gale. 1994. A sequential algorithm for training text classifiers. In *SIGIR '94*, pages 3–12, London. Springer London.

Yuxuan Lu, Bingsheng Yao, Shao Zhang, Yun Wang, Peng Zhang, Tun Lu, Toby Jia-Jun Li, and Dakuo Wang. 2023. Human still wins over llm: An empirical study of active learning on domain-specific annotation tasks. *arXiv preprint arXiv:2311.09825*.

Katerina Margatina and Nikolaos Aletras. 2023. On the limitations of simulating active learning. *arXiv preprint arXiv:2305.13342*.

Katerina Margatina, Timo Schick, Nikolaos Aletras, and Jane Dwivedi-Yu. 2023. Active learning principles for in-context learning with large language models. *arXiv preprint arXiv:2305.14264*.

Saeed Mian Qaisar. 2020. Sentiment analysis of imdb movie reviews using long short-term memory. In *2020 2nd International Conference on Computer and Information Sciences (ICCIS)*, pages 1–4. IEEE.

Burr Settles. 2009. Active learning literature survey. Computer Sciences Technical Report 1648, University of Wisconsin–Madison.

Burr Settles, Mark Craven, and Lewis Friedland. 2008. Active learning with real annotation costs. In *Proceedings of the NIPS workshop on cost-sensitive learning*, volume 1. Vancouver, CA:.

H Sebastian Seung, Manfred Opper, and Haim Sompolinsky. 1992. Query by committee. In *Proceedings of the fifth annual workshop on Computational learning theory*, pages 287–294.

Petter Törnberg. 2023. Chatgpt-4 outperforms experts and crowd workers in annotating political twitter messages with zero-shot learning. *arXiv preprint arXiv:2304.06588*.

Ruixuan Xiao, Yiwen Dong, Junbo Zhao, Runze Wu, Minmin Lin, Gang Chen, and Haobo Wang. 2023. Freeal: Towards human-free active learning in the era of large language models. *arXiv preprint arXiv:2311.15614*.

Yue Yu, Rongzhi Zhang, Ran Xu, Jieyu Zhang, Jiaming Shen, and Chao Zhang. 2023. Cold-start data selection for better few-shot language model fine-tuning: A prompt-based uncertainty propagation approach. In *Proceedings of the 61st Annual Meeting of the Association for Computational Linguistics (Volume 1: Long Papers)*, pages 2499–2521, Toronto, Canada. Association for Computational Linguistics.

Michelle Yuan, Hsuan-Tien Lin, and Jordan Boyd-Graber. 2020. Cold-start active learning through self-supervised language modeling. In *Proceedings of the 2020 Conference on Empirical Methods in Natural Language Processing (EMNLP)*, pages 7935–7948, Online. Association for Computational Linguistics.

Ruoyu Zhang, Yanzeng Li, Yongliang Ma, Ming Zhou, and Lei Zou. 2023. Llmaaa: Making large language models as active annotators. *arXiv preprint arXiv:2310.19596*.

Shujian Zhang, Chengyue Gong, Xingchao Liu, Pengcheng He, Weizhu Chen, and Mingyuan Zhou. 2022a. Allsh: Active learning guided by local sensitivity and hardness. *arXiv preprint arXiv:2205.04980*.

Zhisong Zhang, Emma Strubell, and Eduard Hovy. 2022b. A survey of active learning for natural language processing. In *Proceedings of the 2022 Conference on Empirical Methods in Natural Language Processing*, pages 6166–6190, Abu Dhabi, United Arab Emirates. Association for Computational Linguistics.

A Appendix

In this appendix, additional figures and detailed explanations to supplement the findings and methodologies presented in the main body of the study are provided. These supplementary materials are crucial for a deeper understanding of the performance and efficiency of our proposed Active Learning framework, as well as the effectiveness of our proxy validation approach and prompt design strategy in handling various text classification tasks. Each section of the appendix is dedicated to a specific aspect of our research, offering visual representations, example prompts, and thorough descriptions of the datasets and Active Learning process used in our study.

A.1 Additional Figures of Active Learning Performance and Cost

This part presents visual representations to further elucidate our model's performance across different datasets. These figures are integral to understanding the effectiveness and efficiency of the proposed Active Learning framework in handling varied text classification tasks.

Figure 5 presents a detailed comparison of the model's performance on the IMDB dataset across various methods, including the proposed Active Learning framework and a baseline method of random data addition. The figure illustrates the F1 scores as a percentage for each method, showcasing the effectiveness of selective data addition in enhancing model accuracy and precision over iterative learning processes.

Similarly, Figure 6 provides a comparative analysis for the Movie Genres dataset. It juxtaposes the results of the Active Learning framework against the baseline random data addition method. This comparison is crucial in demonstrating the model's capability to handle different classification tasks and the superiority of the selective addition approach in improving performance metrics.

A.2 Proxy Validation Correlation Examples

This section of the appendix illustrates through examples the effectiveness of using a small subset of the data (5% of the entire dataset) as a proxy validation tool. These figures demonstrate how the proxy validation F1 scores serve as reliable indicators of the overall pool quality, which is particularly important in real-world scenarios where access to the complete pool labels is not feasible.

Figure 9 showcases the correlation for the IMDB dataset. It compares the F1 scores obtained from GPT-3.5 annotations (with confidence > 90%) and GPT-3.5 only annotation to the F1 scores from the proxy validation set. The key observation here is the trend alignment between the proxy validation scores and the overall pool quality. This figure serves as an empirical example to demonstrate how effectively the proxy validation set can estimate the model's performance and help in determining an optimal stopping point for the Active Learning process.

Figure 10 focuses on the Movie Genres dataset and presents a similar analysis. It contrasts the F1 scores for GPT-3.5 annotations with confidence levels > 70% and GPT-3.5 only against the proxy validation F1 scores. Despite the varying confidence levels, both scenarios consistently correlate with the proxy validation scores. This figure highlights the effectiveness of the proxy validation in mirroring the potential performance of the model in the broader dataset, thus serving as a guide for the continuation or cessation of data annotation efforts.

A.3 Prompt Design

To illustrate the type of prompt used for GPT-3.5 annotation, consider the example shown in Figure 3 for the IMDB dataset.

```
prompt = f"""
    What is the sentiment of the
        following movie review,
    and how confident you are about this
        'sentiment',
    which is delimited with triple
        backticks?

    Give your answer as a single word,
        either 'positive'
    or 'negative' and a single
        percentage in JSON format
        delimited with space.

    Review text: '''{X[i]}'''
    """
```

Figure 3: Example of a GPT-3.5 prompt for sentiment analysis in movie reviews, formatted to request output in JSON format.

This prompt was designed to be straightforward, directing GPT-3.5 to classify a given movie review as either Positive or Negative. The simplicity of the prompt ensures clarity in the task, allowing GPT-3.5 to focus solely on the sentiment analysis of the provided review text.

The example provided in Figure 4 shows a few-shot prompt used in the study for the Movie Genres dataset.

```
prompt = f"""
  Determine the genre of the movie based
       on the following plot:

  For the plot provided, classify its
      genre as a single word (without
      other marks or words like 'genre
      :'), either "comedy", "action", "
      drama", or "horror".

  Use the few-shot learning examples
      below to improve your prediction:

  Few-shot Examples:
  '''{newsetX.iloc[0]}''' genre:{newsetY
      .iloc[0]}
  '''{newsetX.iloc[1]}''' genre:{newsetY
      .iloc[1]}
  '''{newsetX.iloc[2]}''' genre:{newsetY
      .iloc[2]}
  Movie plot:
  '''{newsetX.iloc[i]}'''
  """
```

Figure 4: Example of a GPT-3.5 few-shot learning prompt for Movie Genres classification.

This prompt provides GPT-3.5 with a few examples to illustrate the task, followed by a new description for classification. The structure of the prompt is key in 'teaching' the model and the nature of the task, using just a few examples, enabling it to apply this understanding to new, unseen descriptions.

A.4 Dataset and Active Learning details

Figure 7 and Figure 8 delve into the cost implications associated with achieving different F1 scores in the IMDB dataset Movie Genres dataset, respectively. These figures provide a detailed breakdown of the costs incurred in each experiment, offering insights into the economic feasibility and efficiency of models in achieving high levels of accuracy at a reduced cost.

The sizes of the datasets used in our research were carefully chosen to ensure a comprehensive analysis while maintaining manageability. The IMDB dataset consisted of 10,000 entries, providing a rich source of movie reviews for sentiment analysis. The fake news dataset comprised 5,000 entries, offering a diverse range of articles for the identification of veracity in news content. Lastly, the Movie Genres dataset included 4,000 entries, encompassing various movie descriptions for genre classification. A critical aspect of our dataset selection was the balance in each dataset. We ensured that each dataset was carefully balanced to represent a wide range of scenarios and conditions. This balance was crucial in avoiding biases and ensuring that the results of our study were fair and unbiased.

The Active Learning phase of our study began with an initial dataset comprising 2% of the total data for each dataset. This initial selection served as the baseline for our model. From this point, we engaged in a systematic and incremental learning process, expanding the dataset by 0.002% in each iteration. This process was repeated over a total of 250 iterations. By the end of these iterations, we had cumulatively added an additional 50% of data to our initial pool, bringing the total data utilized to 52%. This gradual and iterative approach was critical in optimizing the learning curve of the model, allowing it to progressively improve its classification accuracy while being exposed to more data samples.

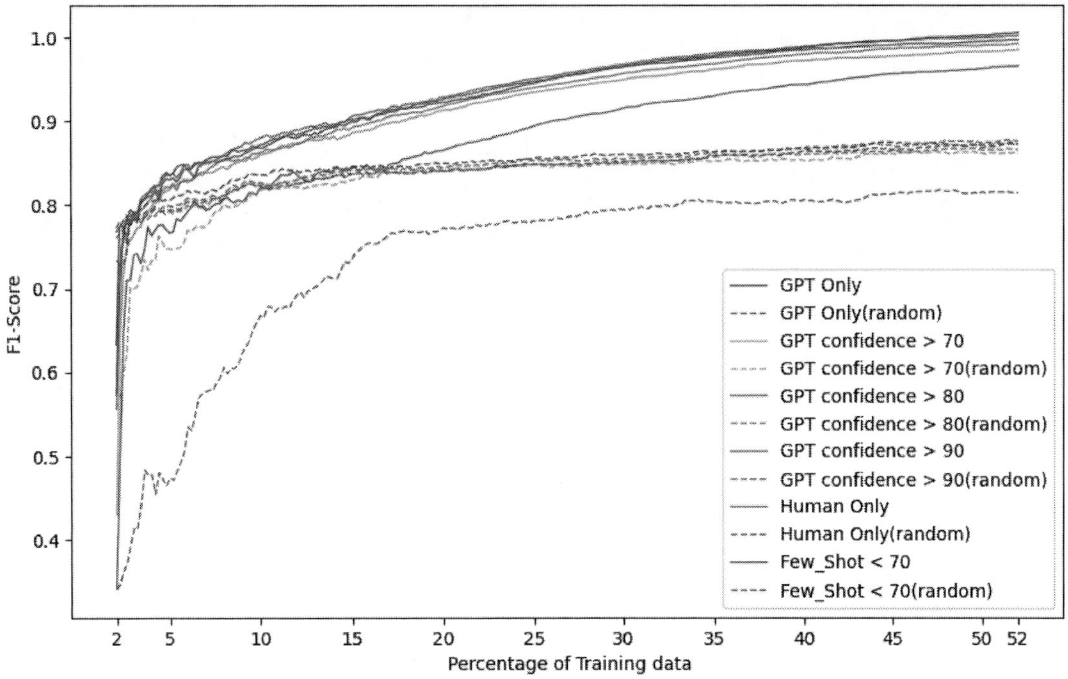

Figure 5: F1 Score Progression from 2% to 52% Training Data Portions in the IMDB Dataset. This figure visualizes the evolution of F1 scores across different training data portions for various annotation methods, including GPT-only, Hybrid models, Human-only, Few-shot learning, and a baseline of random sampling.

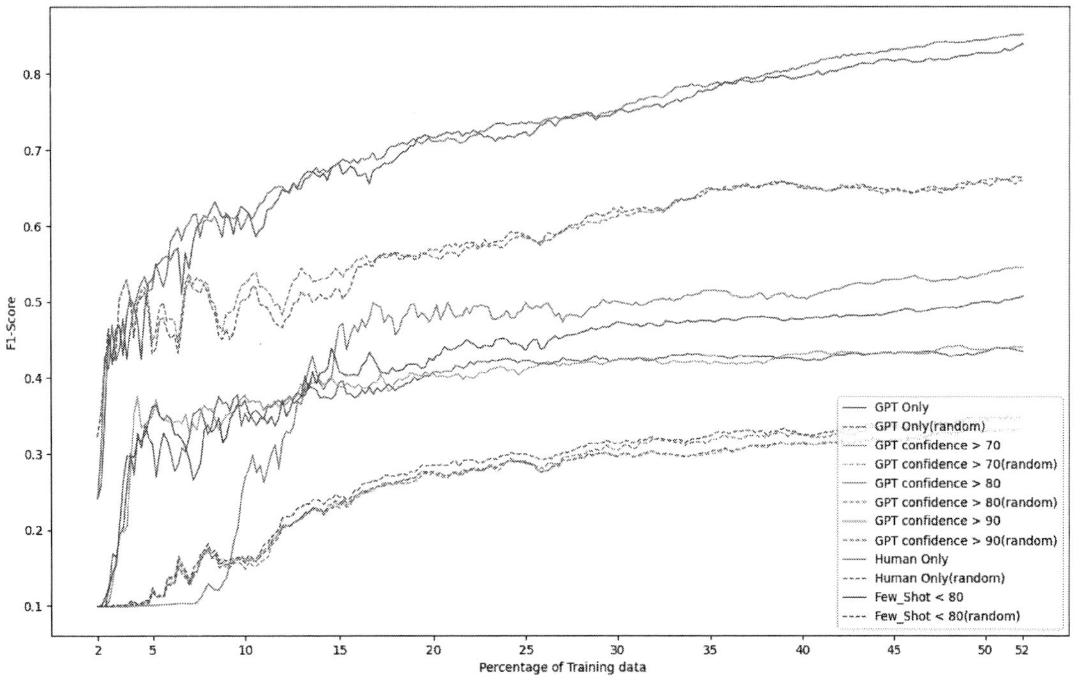

Figure 6: This figure shows the visualization and evolution of F1 scores of the Movie Genres Dataset across different training data portions for various annotation methods compared with a baseline of random sampling.

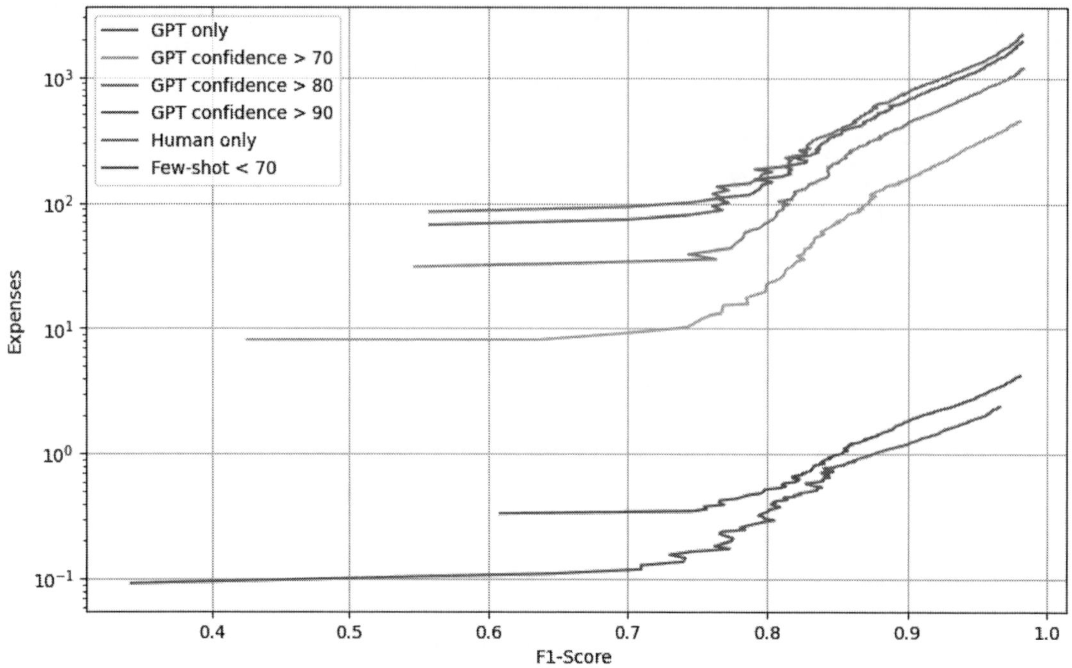

Figure 7: Cost per F1 Score Analysis During Iterative Training Data Increments in the IMDB Dataset. This figure illustrates the cost efficiency (cost per F1 score) for different annotation strategies as the training data portion increases from 2% to 52%. It compares the cost-effectiveness of GPT-only, Hybrid models, Human-only, and Few-shot learning methods.

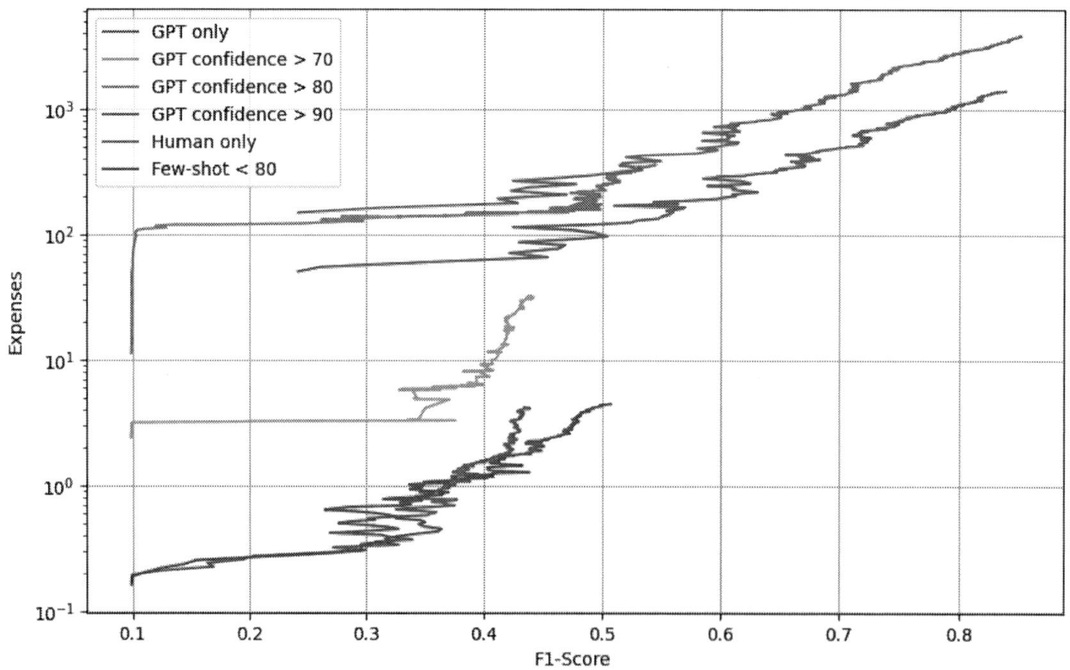

Figure 8: Cost per F1 Score Analysis During Iterative Training Data Increments in the Movie Genress Dataset. This figure shows the cost efficiency (cost per F1 score) for different annotation strategies as the training data portion. .

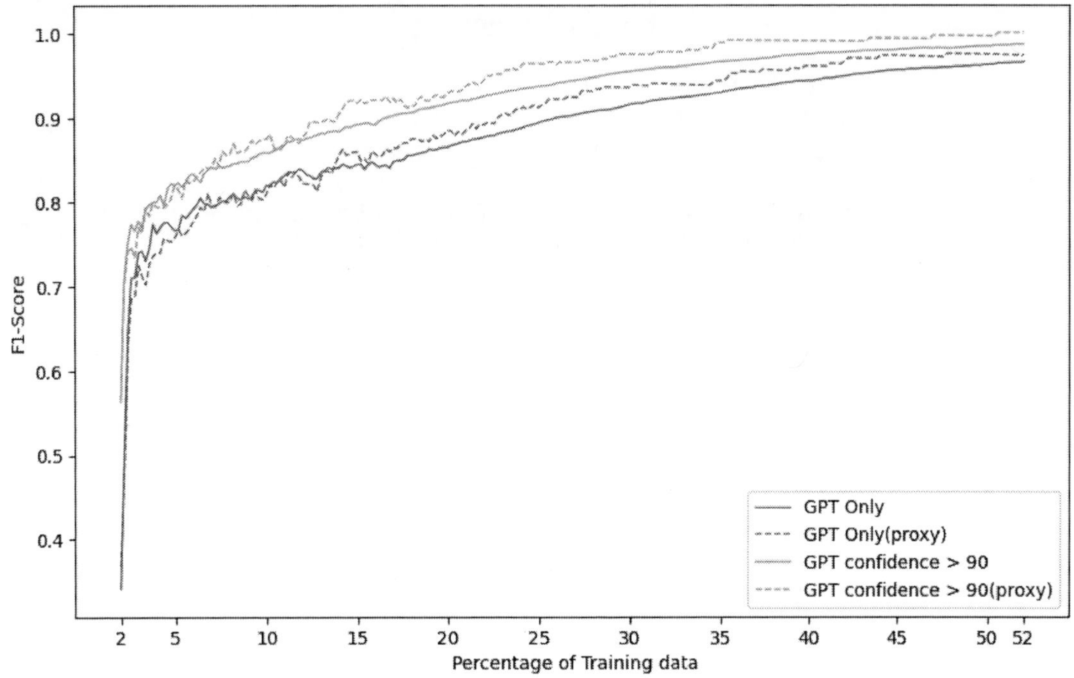

Figure 9: Correlation Between GPT-3.5 Annotation Confidence and Proxy Validation in IMDB Dataset: This figure illustrates the alignment of proxy validation F1 scores with GPT-3.5 annotations at confidence levels above 90% and GPT-3.5-only annotation.

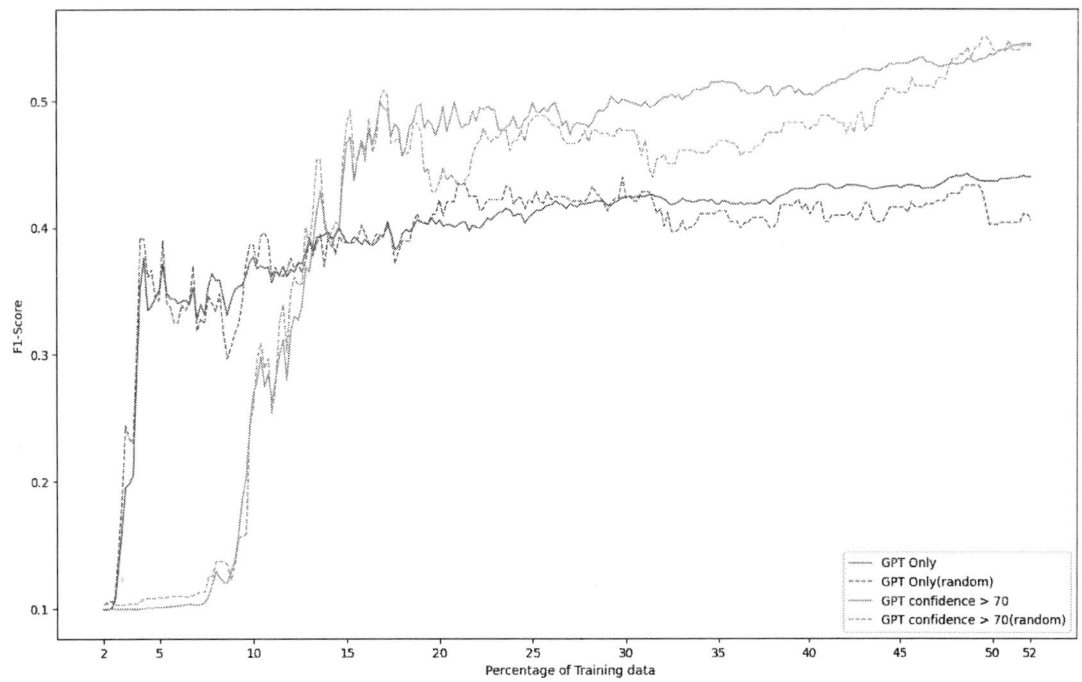

Figure 10: Proxy Validation F1 Score Trends for Different GPT-3.5 Confidence Levels in Movie Genre Dataset: Displaying the trend similarity in proxy validation F1 scores for GPT-3.5 annotations with confidence levels above 70% and GPT3.5 only.

Using ChatGPT for Annotation of Attitude within the Appraisal Theory: Lessons Learned

Mirela Imamović
University of Hildesheim
imamovic@uni-hildesheim.de

Silvana Deilen
University of Hildesheim
deilen@uni-hildesheim.de

Dylan Glynn
University of Paris 8
dsg.up8@gmail.com

Ekaterina Lapshinova-Koltunski
University of Hildesheim
lapshinovakoltun@uni-hildesheim.de

Abstract

We investigate the potential of using ChatGPT to annotate complex linguistic phenomena, such as language of evaluation, attitude and emotion. For this, we automatically annotate 11 texts in English, which represent spoken popular science, and evaluate the annotations manually. Our results show that ChatGPT has good precision in itemisation, i.e. detecting linguistic items in the text that carry evaluative meaning. However, we also find that the recall is very low. Besides that, we state that the tool fails in labeling the detected items with the correct categories on a more fine-grained level of granularity. We analyse the errors to find systematic errors related to specific categories in the annotation scheme.

1 Introduction

The present paper investigates the potential of using large language models (LLMs), specifically ChatGPT for annotating pragmatic categories. Recent advances in Artificial Intelligence (AI), propelled by LLMs such as ChatGPT, have led to substantial improvements in automating complex linguistic tasks such as coherent text generation, text simplification, machine translation, error detection, and question answering. They have produced unprecedented results in a wide range of applications including linguistic annotations.

We focus on the feasibility of using ChatGPT to annotate linguistic items expressing evaluation, attitude and emotion according to the framework based on Appraisal Theory (Martin and White, 2005). More specifically, we probe the tool for the annotation of evaluative language in spoken popular science discourse. To this end, we automatically annotate selected English texts extracted from a dataset of TED talks and evaluate the annotation results manually to see how well ChatGPT can recognise linguistic items carrying the pragmatic meaning under analysis and if these items were correctly classified according to the pre-defined categories of the Appraisal Theory. We also analyse erroneous cases to find the systematic failure of the tool in assigning specific categories.

So far, especially when investigating complex pragmatic and discourse features, most of the annotation work is still done manually. However, manual corpus annotation is time-consuming and requires specialised skills and training. Automating this task would significantly reduce the annotator's workload, save resources and costs, and would allow researchers to build and annotate larger and thus more representative corpora. Moreover, manual annotation is error-prone and is subject to inconsistencies which can be avoided by automatic or semi-automatic procedures integrated into the process of annotation.

Thus, our aim is two-fold. On the one hand, we aim to evaluate ChatGPT in a demanding annotation task of complex linguistic phenomena. On the other hand, we want to learn about the challenges present in the data at hand. This knowledge will allow us to detect phenomena that are particularly hard to annotate, which in turn will allow us to create better guidelines for human annotators.

The remainder of the paper is structured as follows. In Section 2, we outline the basic principles of the Appraisal Theory and present the categories we consider in our analysis. Section 3 describes related works that utilise LLMs for annotating. In Section 4, we provide details on the data used for this study, as well as procedures to annotate the data. We present and discuss our results in Section 5. An outlook for future work is given in Section 6. We discuss the limitations of our work in Section 7.

2 Theoretical Background

We use Appraisal Theory (Martin and White, 2005) developed under the general framework of Sys-

Proceedings of The 18th Linguistic Annotation Workshop (LAW-XVIII), pages 112–123
March 22, 2024

temic Functional Linguistics (SFL, Halliday and Matthiessen, 2014). Appraisal is related to the interpersonal metafunction of language and it consists of three interrelated domains: Attitude (expressions of opinions and feelings), Engagement (positioning of the writer/speaker toward other voices within the discourse) and Graduation (intensifying or down-toning attitude and engagement). We focus on the three sub-types of Attitude: Affect (emotions), Judgement (moral judgements about human behaviours) and Appreciation (evaluations of objects, products and processes). We use the original appraisal annotation scheme and consider these three sub-types of Attitude as the main semantic categories (level 1). Furthermore, we focus on the sub-categories of Attitude on a more fine-grained level (level 2) and their related sub-values that represent the finest level of granularity (level 3). The categories on levels 2 and 3 include (with the 3rd level given in brackets): for Affect DIS/INCLINATION (fear; desire), UN/HAPPINESS (misery, antipathy; cheer, affection), IN/SECURITY (disquiet, apprehension; confidence, trust), and DIS/SATISFACTION (ennui, displeasure; interest, pleasure), for Judgement SOCIAL ESTEEM (normality, capacity, tenacity), and SOCIAL SANCTION (veracity, propriety), and for Appreciation REACTION (impact, quality), COMPOSITION (balance, complexity), and VALUATION. Our detailed scheme is presented in Figure 1.

3 Related Work

3.1 Annotating Appraisal

Appraisal Theory for annotation of evaluative language in English book reviews was used by Read et al. (2007). The authors proposed a multi-step strategy and analysed the inter-annotator agreement (IAA) for both itemisation and category assignment. The agreement varied depending on the level of abstraction in the Appraisal hierarchy, with a better result (a mean F-score of 0.698) for the highest level and a much worse result (a mean F-score of 0.395) at the most fine-grained level. Interestingly, the authors reported that the agreement was dependent on the category annotated: a better agreement was achieved for Attitude if compared to Engagement or Graduation. In our work, we focus on Attitude only.

Mora and Lavid-López (2018) also used Appraisal theory to annotate English and Spanish reviews. The authors stated some problematic issues in the application of the categories in Appraisal theory for the specific dataset at hand. The reported IAA was very high in both itemisation and classification of the main categories tasks. However, the authors also stated problematic cases, e.g. in the case of long and complex sentences that need contextualisation to convey an evaluative meaning. The agreement on a more fine-grained level was much lower and contrary to the findings of Read et al. (2007), the main problems here were caused by the subtypes of Attitude.

More recent work on annotation using Appraisal Theory includes (Dong and Fang, 2023). However, they do not report any agreement scores. In our study, we analyse the agreement between the automatic annotation by ChatGPT and a human evaluator. We expect that the results for categories on the higher level of granularity will be higher.

3.2 LLMs for annotation tasks

The potential of large language models (LLMs) for data annotation has been explored in some recent studies. For instance, some authors tested the potential of LLMs for crowd-sourcing approaches. Testing LLMs (with a focus on ChatGPT) against crowd-workers, Gilardi et al. (2023) showed that for most of the annotation tasks, ChatGPT's accuracy was higher than that of crowd-workers. The models' IAA also exceeded that of both trained annotators and crowd-workers. As using ChatGPT is more cost-effective than hiring professional annotators and even crowd-workers, the authors conclude that LLMs have a significant potential to transform common text-annotation procedures and to increase their efficiency. This was also confirmed by Ostyakova et al. (2023) who compared ChatGPT with not only crowd-workers but also human experts. The authors stated that in some cases LLMs could achieve human-like performance following a multi-step pipeline on complex discourse annotation.

However, for efficient crowd-sourced annotation procedures, LLMs should be provided with sufficient guidance and demonstrated examples as it was shown by He et al. (2023). The authors proposed a two-step approach called 'explain-then-annotate'. They created prompts for every demonstrated example, which they then subsequently utilized to prompt the language model GPT-3.5 to provide an explanation for why the specific ground truth answer/label was chosen for that particular example. Following this, they constructed the

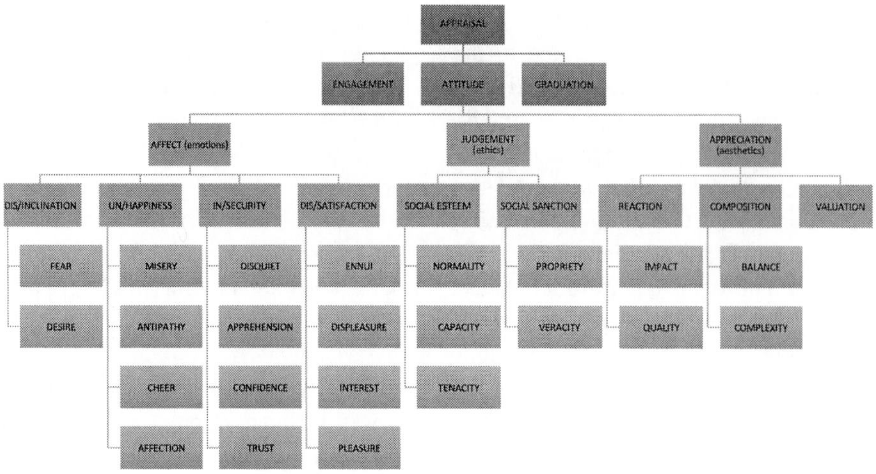

Figure 1: Analysis scheme according to Appraisal Theory, based on Martin and White (2005)

few-shot chain-of-thought prompt with the self-generated explanation and employed it to annotate the unlabeled data. The authors conducted experiments on three tasks and their results were that for the two out of the three tasks, GPT-3.5 achieved results that were comparable to those obtained through crowd-sourced annotation.

This was also confirmed by Ding et al. (2023) who found that LLMs have the potential to accurately annotate data for different NLP tasks while requiring only a fraction of the time and cost of human annotators.

The range of annotation tasks for LLMs, i.e. linguistic categories in focus, is varying from named entity recognition and relation extraction (Zhang et al., 2023), semantic verb classes (Straková et al., 2023), sentence meaning structure (Ettinger et al., 2023) to more complex task of pragmatic annotation. For instance, Yu et al. (2023) explored the feasibility of using LLMs in the annotation of apologies. Their study showed that the models were able to identify key features of apologies with high accuracy. The models seemed to achieve results comparable with human annotations.

In another study (Nedilko, 2023), ChatGPT was used for emotion detection by leveraging the prompt engineering and zero-shot as well as few-shot learning methodologies based on multiple experiments showing improvement over their baseline model. However, the authors state that although ChatGPT provides stable results, especially if asked for a specific output format, there is still an element of volatility due to the conversational nature of the model. They also note that the context window limitation does not allow for working with larger datasets. Furthermore, the authors admit that the emotion detection task remains challenging for machines in general.

In our study, we use ChatGPT for a pragmatic annotation task, which is challenging not only for machines but also for humans.

4 Research Design

4.1 Data

For this study, we selected 11 texts (25,117 words) from a dataset of TED talks collected for a bigger project on the analysis of evaluative language[1]. These texts cover talks in eleven disciplines (Arts, Business, Education, Entertainment, History, Medicine, Natural science, Philosophy, Politics and Law, Psychology, and Technology). The individual text size is given in Appendix B. The communicative aim of the talks is two-fold. On the one hand, they serve for the knowledge transfer between experts and laypeople. On the other hand, they also aim at entertaining the audience. We assume that evaluative language is used for both better knowledge transfer and entertainment purposes. The texts are transcripts of speeches available on the TED website[2]. We selected talks by both female and male native speakers of North American English. For all the selected texts, there are also translations into German available. However, their analysis remains beyond the scope of this paper.

[1]The data used for the current study including the annotation results is provided in the GitHub repository `https://github.com/katjakaterina/chatgptanno`.

[2]`https://www.ted.com`

4.2 Data Analysis

The annotation task was conducted using the large language model ChatGPT[3]. ChatGPT was used via the chat interface with default settings (temperature = 1).

In our prompt, we first included information on Appraisal Theory and then asked the tool (in the same prompt) to annotate all the evaluative linguistic instances of Affect, Judgement and Appreciation in the given text. We also requested to only assign one value to each evaluative linguistic instance. Another request (still the same prompt) was to focus on verbs, nouns, adjectives and adverbs, i.e. explicit (directly inscribed) attitudes and to only annotate the linguistic instances that correspond to Affect, Judgement and Appreciation and its sub-values instead of annotating the whole sentence. The exact prompt we used is given in the Appendix A. As we added basic information on Appraisal Theory to our prompt, our prompting can be classified as instruction-based or context-based prompting, rather than zero-shot prompting. The human annotator followed the same guidelines given in the prompt. The annotation scheme used is presented in Section 2.

5 Results

5.1 Itemisation

In the first step, we experimented with running the same prompt several times. More precisely, we ran it two times for each text and observed diverging results. In some cases, the output did not contain the actual items that were supposed to be tagged as instances of Appraisal, i.e. the output would not contain any data. In this case, we ran the prompt again. The number of items identified in subsequent queries varied, even though the prompts were run within minutes of each other. The fact that we used ChatGPT via the chat interface and with the default setting (temperature = 1) might explain why the system created very different outputs in the two runs.

Table 1 presents the numbers of items returned for each text for the first two successful prompts (with the same prompt formulation).

The differences in the number of items returned were significant (Chi^2, df = 10, $p = 4.575^{-10}$) and the discrepancy for the texts Art, Med, and Pol[4] is, perhaps, noteworthy. These differences may inform the results concerning the classification of items, reported below. The ensuing results on the accuracy of the itemisation, i.e. identification of evaluative items, are all based exclusively on the returns for the first query.

In the second step, we analysed the output annotated by ChatGPT in terms of item recognition precision – if all instances marked by the tool were correctly marked as evaluative. A human annotator, a trained linguist with a theoretical background in Appraisal Theory, evaluated the output of ChatGPT. The results showed that out of 381 items tagged by the tool, 21 were false positives, which means that ChatGPT achieved a high precision (94.49%) in itemisation.

Then, the human annotator analysed a subsample of 5 texts (Art, Bus, Edu, Ent, His) to assess the itemisation results in terms of recall (the number of evaluative items in the texts missed by ChatGPT). The results showed that a total of 485 evaluative instances remained undetected. The number of the automatically detected items (true positives) in these five texts comprises 177, so the tool achieves a recall of 26.74%, which is rather low.

5.2 Error analysis

To determine if some types of evaluation were more problematic than others, the items missed by ChatGPT in the five texts were manually annotated for the most coarse-grained level of evaluative distinction, namely Affect, Judgement and Appreciation. The results showed that in total, Appreciation was most frequently missed (230 items) followed by Judgement (159) and Affect (96). We also noticed that this tendency was not the same across the texts. While in Bus, the erroneous tagging was more evenly distributed across the categories (20 Affect, 16 Judgement and 19 Appreciation), in His, Judgement was much more frequently missed than the other two categories (27 Affect, 76 Judgement and 45 Appreciation) and in Edu, it was Appreciation where ChatGPT most frequently failed to detect evaluative meaning (15 Affect, 37 Judgement and 88 Appreciation). However, to be able to relate this

[3]Our study was conducted in November 2023, i.e., the results are based on GPT-4 Turbo, the latest version of ChatGPT available at the time of writing.

[4]The text IDs represent disciplines: Art=Arts, Bus=Business, Edu=Education, Ent=Entertainment, His=History, Med=Medicine, NatSci=Natural Science, Phil=Pilosophy, Pol=Politics and Law, Psy=Psychology, Tech=Technology. However, the analysis of disciplines remains beyond the scope of this study.

Prompt run/Text	Art	Bus	Edu	Ent	His	Med	NatSci	Phil	Pol	Psy	Tech
1st run	48	22	35	63	29	46	37	21	26	33	30
2nd run	20	28	21	30	50	75	16	27	50	16	16

Table 1: Number of items retrieved in two runs of the prompt per text.

Text part/Text	Art	Bus	Edu	Ent	His
Full-length	35	21	35	59	27
Two-part	59	62	61	45	50
Three-part	82	50	107	105	92

Table 2: Number of items retrieved for two-part and three-part text-splitting procedure for 5 texts versus full-length texts.

variation in the results to the domain effects, we need to analyse more texts per discipline.

An example of a missed item representing Affect is illustrated in (1) and another example illustrating several Attitude types missed by the tool is shown in (2).

(1) *They felt science had stagnated since the days of the scientific revolution that had happened in the 17th century.*

(2) *A couple of years ago, I put a video on Youtube, and in the video, I acted out every terrible [Judgement] conference call you've ever been on. It goes on for about five minutes, and it has all the things that we hate [Affect] about really bad [Appreciation] meetings.*

In the next step, we experimented further with the prompts and inputs. For instance, we noticed that ChatGPT could not deal with longer texts returning approximately the same number of items for each text (around 30). So, we split each of the 5 texts (that we manually analysed) into two and three parts. The text parts were run in separate sessions. Table 2 shows the number of items (both true and false positives) returned for the two-part and three-part text-splitting procedure in comparison to the output for full-length texts (true positives). We also slightly modified the prompt and asked the tool to include the context around the identified evaluative instances. Splitting the texts into two halves doubled the output in terms of the number of identified items (both true and false positives). Splitting the texts into three parts returned the highest amount of identified items (the highest being 107). We assume that ChatGPT can deal better with shorter texts. An example of an item which was missed in the first prompt but captured in the three-part-split text is illustrated in (3) (with the item in question marked in bold). It also correctly marked *immoral* as Judgement: PROPRIETY. However, the tool still failed to identify other evaluative items (as those underlined that were tagged by the human annotator) within the same context.

(3) *And there's a lot to be overwhelmed [Affect] about, to be fair [Judgement] – an environmental crisis [Judgement], wealth disparity [Judgement] in this country unlike we've seen since 1928, and globally, a totally* ***immoral*** *[Judgement] and ongoing wealth disparity [Judgement]. Xenophobia's [Judgement] on the rise. The trafficking [Judgement] of women and girls. It's enough to make you feel very overwhelmed [Affect].*

As an example, one text (that was also used for the analysis) in our data set had a total of 148 false negatives in the first prompt. The number of true positives in this output was 27. In the experiments with two- and three-part-split texts, the tool returned 50 and 92 items (both true and false positives) respectively. In another text, the number of detected items increased from 35 (true positives) to 59 (two-part-split) and 82 (three-part-split) (both true and false positives). However, even with the increased number of detected items, there are still many false negatives left, hence the recall remaining low. Another issue is the linguistic context, i.e. the tool coming up with evaluative items based on the contextual information as illustrated in examples (4), (5) and (6). Those phrases (*astounding, revolutionary, unequal*) do not appear in the original text. However, the tool listed them as evaluative based on the context (the sentences in quotation marks). ChatGPT also wrongly classified the items as Attitude.

(4) *astounding - "how could the word 'scien-*

tist' not have existed until 1833?" [Appreciation: IMPACT*].*

(5) *revolutionary - "pledged to bring about, and what's so amazing about these guys is, not only did they have these grandiose undergraduate dreams" [Appreciation:* VALUATION*].*

(6) *unequal - "wealth disparity in this country" [Judgement:* PROPRIETY*].*

Although the prompt we used explicitly stated that only evaluative instances that appear in the text should be listed, ChatGPT still performed this surprising action. The fact that the tool can "retrieve" an evaluative expression based on the contextual information is indicative of potentially recognising implicit evaluation/attitude. However, more studies are needed to confirm this assumption.

Interestingly, the output also contained 15 items that did not occur in the text. This is not a definite number, as checking each instance manually would be laborious. This is an indicator of hallucinations observed by other existing studies using ChatGPT for NLP applications (Zhang et al., 2023; Peng et al., 2023; Guerreiro et al., 2023).

5.3 Classification

We start with the analysis of the main categories of Attitude from the Appraisal scheme (Affect, Judgement, Appreciation) as defined in Section 2. The tool recognised 360 items in total (160 Affect, 89 Judgement and 108 Appreciation, 2 were marked as "difficulty" and 1 as "ease"). The categories assigned by the human annotator were 95 Affect, 101 Judgement and 164 Appreciation. The level of IAA between the tool and human annotator at this 1st level of abstractness was calculated using Cohen's weighted Kappa (Cohen, 1968). The human classification for these three nominal categories was done independently of the tool and resulted in a Kappa of 0.52 (lower.bound = 0.43, upper.bound = 0.61, $p < .0001$). As a general guide, values between 0.4 and 0.75 are taken to be indicative of a fair level of agreement that is above chance. However, given that we are only dealing with three categories and at a level of abstractness that is normally unproblematic for human raters, this score should not be indicative of successful categorisation on the part of ChatGPT.

At the second and intermediary level of abstractness, ChatGPT classified the following Appraisal categories: DISINCLINATION (19), INCLINATION (8), UNHAPPINESS (16), HAPPINESS (33), INSECURITY (17), SECURITY (16), DISSATISFACTION (20), SATISFACTION (31), SOCIAL ESTEEM (49), SOCIAL SANCTION (40), REACTION (65), COMPOSITION (25), VALUATION (18). The tool also marked "difficulty" (2) and "ease" (1) that were not given in the prompt and are not considered as original appraisal categories. The classifications of the human annotator are DISINCLINATION (10), INCLINATION (1), UNHAPPINESS (14), HAPPINESS (19), INSECURITY (16), SECURITY (14), DISSATISFACTION (11), SATISFACTION (10), SOCIAL ESTEEM (57), SOCIAL SANCTION (44), REACTION (76), COMPOSITION (23), VALUATION (65).

At the third and finest level of abstractness, 133 (34.91%) labels matched between ChatGPT and the human annotator. The tool incorrectly classified 248 (65.09%) labels. The second and third levels of abstractness resulted in Kappas of 0.39 (lower.bound = 0.024, upper.bound = 0.75, $p < .0001$) and 0.34 (lower.bound = -0.10, upper.bound = 0.78, $p < .0001$), respectively. Although the third level of abstractness has 24 categories[5], in contrast to the second level which has 13, the IAA was marginally better. Given that only the 1st level of abstractness produced results that show any workable degree of agreement between ChatGPT and the human annotator, we restricted further investigation to this level. Two examples of a disagreement between the tool and the human annotator are shown in (7) and (8).

(7) *And I'm talking about something far more valuable than office furniture. I'm talking about time* (tagged as Judgement: CAPACITY by ChatGPT and as Appreciation: VALUATION by the human annotator).

(8) *If you're a doctor, you can do some good things, but if you're a caring doctor, you can do some other things* (tagged as Affect: TRUST by ChatGPT and as Judgement: PROPRIETY by the human annotator).

These examples show a strong disagreement in the classification of attitude types at the highest level of granularity, i.e. the most abstract attitude categories between the tool and the human annotator. Looking at the context, it becomes clear that

[5]The third level originally contains 23 categories, as indicated in Figure 1. However the label "valuation" is used at both the second and the third level.

valuable does not judge someone's capacity to do something, but evaluates the worth of something and that being *caring* is not a direct expression of emotion, but rather a moral judgement of someone.

As expected, some categories revealed a higher rate of agreement between ChatGPT and the human annotator than others. Table 3 presents the residuals of a Pearson's Chi^2 test for independence between the human and machine classification.

Examining the residuals of a Chi^2 test for independence between the human and machine classification results show that the highest level of agreement was for Judgement, followed by Affect and then Appreciation, but the differences between them were not particularly remarkable. We can also see that none of the mismatches between machine and human were particularly noteworthy. The residuals suggest that there might be two exceptions to this. Firstly, it appears to be relatively unlikely that if ChatGPT classifies an instance as Appreciation that the human will classify it as Affect, a mismatch between Appreciation and Judgement being much more likely. Secondly, the most likely mismatches do occur when ChatGPT classifies the instance as Affect, but the human as Appreciation or when ChaptGPT classifies it as Appreciation, but the human as Judgement. These potential exceptions aside, the results overall suggest relatively random errors in classification, with none of the categories at level 1 abstractness proving substantially easier or more difficult to classify.

5.4 Individual text effects on classification

Having established that a pairwise comparison between ChatGPT and human annotator produces classification only weakly in agreement, the next step is to determine whether this is equally the case for different texts. Of particular interest are the potential effects that domain variation, often associated with different disciplines, may have on ChatGPT's ability to accurately classify certain categories. Although our sample does not allow any claims concerning specific domain effects of certain disciplines, we do observe significant differences between the texts for the level of IAA relative to the different classifications at the 1st level of abstractness.

To determine for which categories agreement or disagreement between the human and machine classifications were significantly higher or lower than chance, we ran a log-linear analysis looking at the number of classifications for each 1st-level category for each text. Figure 2 presents the results in the form of a mosaic plot. Each box represents the classification for the machine and human annotator for each text. The size of the box represents the relative frequency and, based on Pearson residuals, the colour indicates whether the the combination is significantly higher or lower than expected. When both ChatGPT and the human propose the same category and that combination is blue, especially dark blue, this represents a noteworthy and high level of agreement. If the box is blue but the two annotators classified the categories differently, it represents a high level of disagreement. Red indicates a lower number of that combination that would be expected and grey boxes simply indicate that the frequency of that combination is not noteworthy. To interpret the plot, one looks at the top row of the top line of boxes for agreement on Affect, the middle row of the middle line for Appreciation and the bottom row of the bottom line of boxes for agreement on Judgement. For instance, for Affect, we have a substantial agreement for the texts His, Med and Pol, but substantial disagreement for Ent where ChatGPT classifies instances as Affect, but the human as Appreciation and then again for Psy, where the ChatGPT classifies Affect, but the human as Judgement. Looking across the three categories for the 11 texts, we see that the best agreement is for Judgement with six texts (Edu, Ent, NatSci, Phil, Pol and Psy). In contrast, in only 3 texts is there significant agreement for Appreciation and Affect. The two red boxes are difficult to interpret but indicate that ChatGPT and the human are less likely to disagree with the combination of Affect and Appreciation. Psy and Pol are the only two texts where two of the categories are classified in a significantly similar way. In all the other texts, it is only one category or none that reveals significant agreement for a category. Art and Tech reveal no significant agreement for any of the categories. Although clear patterns are difficult to discern, it is only for Affect that we see significant disagreements, neither Appreciation nor Judgement revealing any at all. Although Appreciation has no significant agreement, it only has three texts where there is significant agreement. Judgement has six texts with agreement and none with significant disagreement. These results appear to contradict the results presented in Table 3 where Judgement is best and Appreciation is worse in terms of agreement. The difference in the results indicates that text variation does have a significant effect on the IAA of the classification.

	Human Affect	Human Appreciation	Human Judgement
ChatGPT Affect	6.639010	-2.611789	-3.187939
ChatGPT Appreciation	-4.649263	5.560443	-2.457828
ChatGPT Judgement	-3.668086	-3.668086	6.928130

Table 3: Pearson residuals for Chi^2 test of independence between raters for level 1.

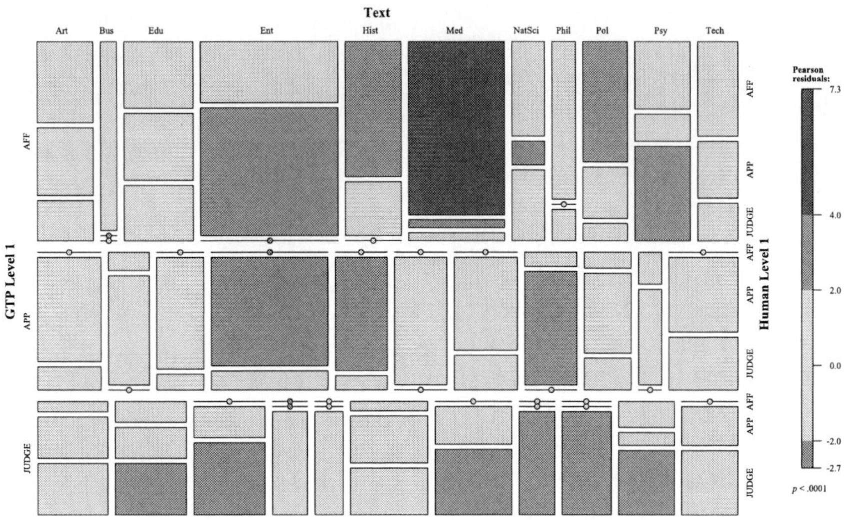

Figure 2: Text variation and inter-annotator level 1 classification

Lastly, in the previous section, we saw that ChatGPT itemisation, when run more than once, showed substantially different numbers of items for texts Art, Med and Pol. It is possible, therefore, that ChatGPT struggled more with these texts. If that is the case, we do not see it reflected at the stage of classification for level 1.

6 Conclusion and Future Work

The present paper evaluates the use of ChatGPT as an annotation tool for evaluative language in spoken popular science discourse. Our results showed that while the concordance rate between the tool and the human annotator in terms of itemisation precision was rather high (94,49%), it was rather low in terms of the sub-category label classification (35%). Although the tool succeeds in recognising evaluative items, it fails in retrieving all of them (as shown by the low recall) and in correctly classifying them.

Also, the tool produced hallucinations in the output. This is especially problematic as human annotators not only have to manually check the results in terms of recall and the assigned category, but they also have to double-check if the annotated item appears in the text at all. This problem could be eliminated by changing the form of the output (see discussion of limitations below).

Our observations also show that most of the recognised evaluative items (58,89%) were adjectives. However, a more detailed analysis of part-of-speech (pos) categories would be an asset. For this, we plan to automatically pos-tag and parse the corpus, which will also help us to define systematic morpho-syntactic patterns of explicit evaluative expressions. However, it would be also interesting to find out if ChatGPT could identify and annotate implicit (indirect) attitudes in texts which is a task demanding even for human annotators, which is also amongst the tasks for our future work.

Besides that, the tool performed better on some texts than on others. However, as we only analysed one text per discipline we cannot determine if the varying results depend on the text discipline or other factors, such as the speaker's style or the topic of the text.

Interestingly, regardless of the text length, the number of instances annotated by ChatGPT was more or less the same (approximately 30 instances per text). Our results show that splitting the texts and performing the annotation task on shorter parts improves the output. This suggests that text length could potentially have an impact on the results. With this assumption, the recall rate of future studies could be improved by adjusting the text length. This, however, does not guarantee that some items will not be missed out completely or not be false positives.

We also found that the output varied across several runs of the same prompt. This means that the results of the automatic annotation are not reliable in terms of consistency, which is in line with other studies. While other existing annotation projects found that GPT-4 was more reliable in annotation than other GPT models (e.g. Pérez et al., 2023), we conclude that even the latest model GPT-4 Turbo exhibits low consistency compared to human annotator for the annotation of evaluative language. We explain the inconsistency of ChatGPT as an annotator of complex linguistic phenomena by the non-deterministic nature of LLM: identical input with minor word alterations in prompts leads to different outputs (see Reiss, 2023, for more details). Thus, improving and designing effective prompts is important for optimal model performance. We will also explore and compare different prompting strategies (few-shot vs. zero-shot). By doing so, we will investigate whether the tool's ability of in-context learning through prompting can increase the concordance rate. Moreover, we will test and compare further existing LLM tools (e.g. Bard[6]).

We also plan to collect annotations by multiple human annotators and compare them with those of ChatGPT and other LLMs. We will use the findings of this study to improve the annotation guidelines for human annotators in terms of itemisation and classification of appraisal categories. Crucially, we will follow up on the evaluative items that ChatGPT incorrectly assigned and observe if the human annotators also tend to disagree regarding those linguistic items, explaining what kind of tasks the tool performs best on. We will also analyse the evaluation span as its length seems to have an impact on the ChatGPT's output and may also cause inconsistencies in human annotator decisions.

Besides, we will annotate several texts of the same discipline which will allow us to identify tendencies in terms of stylistic or domain-specific variation. Therefore, we plan to analyse texts from different genres and compare the results for different text types. Further, we will cross-lingually test ChatGPT's annotation of evaluation in German translations of the analysed texts by comparing originals with translations and exploring how evaluation is translated and if pragmatic meaning is altered.

[6]https://bard.google.com/chat.

7 Discussion of Limitations

Our work has several limitations. First of all, only one human annotator evaluated the output of ChatGPT and performed the manual annotation of the texts. Evaluation by multiple human annotators would provide us with information if there is a correlation between erroneous classification by ChatGPT and disagreement of Appraisal classification between human annotators.

Second, labelling evaluative items directly in the input texts (e.g. by marking the items with XML tags) would be more advantageous instead of listing out single linguistic instances such as nouns or adjectives. In this way, the context of the evaluative instances was not contained in the output. An example of the ChatGPT output generated using our prompt is given in Figure 3 in the Appendix.

Third, we did not split the texts into 2 and 3 parts from the very beginning which could have potentially given us a higher recall.

Besides that, our analysis is limited in terms of genre and language, as we analysed texts of TED talks in English only. The performance of ChatGPT may vary across different text types and also across different topics. Since our dataset contains one text per discipline, we are not able to correlate the performance of the tool with genres or disciplines.

Also, our analysis is restricted to one LLM only. Testing more LLM-based tools would give us a better idea of their usability for our annotation tasks.

Ethics Statement

The data used in this study are collected from the TED website, which is publicly available. The texts are anonymised and do not contain any personal information.

References

Jacob Cohen. 1968. Weighted kappa: Nominal scale agreement provision for scaled disagreement or partial credit. *Psychological Bulletin*, 70:213–220.

Bosheng Ding, Chengwei Qin, Linlin Liu, Yew Ken Chia, Boyang Li, Shafiq Joty, and Lidong Bing. 2023. Is GPT-3 a Good Data Annotator? In *Proceedings of the 61st Annual Meeting of the Association for Computational Linguistics (Volume 1: Long Papers)*, pages 11173–11195, Toronto, Canada. Association for Computational Linguistics.

Min Dong and Alex Fang. 2023. Appraisal Theory and the Annotation of Speaker-Writer Engagement. In *Proceedings of the 19th Joint ACL-ISO Workshop on Interoperable Semantics (ISA-19)*, pages 18–26, Nancy, France. Association for Computational Linguistics.

Allyson Ettinger, Jena D. Hwang, Valentina Pyatkin, Chandra Bhagavatula, and Yejin Choi. 2023. "You Are An Expert Linguistic Annotator": Limits of LLMs as Analyzers of Abstract Meaning Representation. *arXiv preprint*, 2310.17793.

Fabrizio Gilardi, Meysam Alizadeh, and Maël Kubli. 2023. ChatGPT outperforms crowd workers for text-annotation tasks. *Proceedings of the National Academy of Sciences of the United States of America*, 120.

Nuno M Guerreiro, Duarte Alves, Jonas Waldendorf, Barry Haddow, Alexandra Birch, Pierre Colombo, and André FT Martins. 2023. Hallucinations in large multilingual translation models. *arXiv preprint arXiv:2303.16104*.

M.A.K. Halliday and C.M.I.M. Matthiessen. 2014. *Halliday's Introduction to Functional Grammar*, 4 edition. Routledge.

Xingwei He, Zheng-Wen Lin, Yeyun Gong, Alex Jin, Hang Zhang, Chen Lin, Jian Jiao, Siu Ming Yiu, Nan Duan, and Weizhu Chen. 2023. AnnoLLM: Making Large Language Models to Be Better Crowdsourced Annotators. *ArXiv*, abs/2303.16854.

JR Martin and Peter Robert Rupert White. 2005. *The Language of Evaluation: Appraisal in English*. Palgrave MacMillan.

Natalia Mora and Julia Lavid-López. 2018. Building an annotated dataset of app store reviews with appraisal features in English and Spanish. In *Proceedings of the Second Workshop on Computational Modeling of People's Opinions, Personality, and Emotions in Social Media*, pages 16–24, New Orleans, Louisiana, USA. Association for Computational Linguistics.

Andrew Nedilko. 2023. Generative pretrained transformers for emotion detection in a code-switching setting. In *Proceedings of the 13th Workshop on Computational Approaches to Subjectivity, Sentiment, & Social Media Analysis*, pages 616–620, Toronto, Canada. Association for Computational Linguistics.

Lidiia Ostyakova, Veronika Smilga, Kseniia Petukhova, Maria Molchanova, and Daniel Kornev. 2023. ChatGPT vs. crowdsourcing vs. experts: Annotating open-domain conversations with speech functions. In *Proceedings of the 24th Meeting of the Special Interest Group on Discourse and Dialogue*, pages 242–254, Prague, Czechia. Association for Computational Linguistics.

Keqin Peng, Liang Ding, Qihuang Zhong, Li Shen, Xuebo Liu, Min Zhang, Yuanxin Ouyang, and Dacheng Tao. 2023. Towards making the most of ChatGPT for machine translation. *arXiv preprint arXiv:2303.13780*.

Anxo Pérez, Marcos Fernández-Pichel, Javier Parapar, and David E Losada. 2023. DepreSym: A Depression Symptom Annotated Corpus and the Role of LLMs as Assessors of Psychological Markers. *arXiv preprint arXiv:2308.10758*.

Jonathon Read, David Hope, and John Carroll. 2007. Annotating expressions of appraisal in English. In *Proceedings of the Linguistic Annotation Workshop*, pages 93–100, Prague, Czech Republic. Association for Computational Linguistics.

Michael V Reiss. 2023. Testing the reliability of ChatGPT for text annotation and classification: A cautionary remark. *arXiv preprint*, arXiv:2304.11085.

Jana Straková, Eva Fučíková, Jan Hajič, and Zdeňka Urešová. 2023. Extending an event-type ontology: Adding verbs and classes using fine-tuned LLMs suggestions. In *Proceedings of the 17th Linguistic Annotation Workshop (LAW-XVII)*, pages 85–95, Toronto, Canada. Association for Computational Linguistics.

Danni Yu, Luyang Li, Hang Su, and Matteo Fuoli. 2023. Assessing the potential of AI-assisted pragmatic annotation: The case of apologies. *arXiv: 2305.08339*.

Ruoyu Zhang, Yanzeng Li, Yongliang Ma, Ming Zhou, and Lei Zou. 2023. LLMaAA: Making Large Language Models as Active Annotators. *arXiv:2310.19596*.

A Appendix: The Prompt

Do you know Appraisal Theory developed my Martin and White (2005)? Appraisal Theory consists of Attitude, Engagement and Graduation. Attitude consists of Affect, Judgement and Appreciation. Affect consists of these values: inclination (sub-value desire), disinclination (sub-value fear), happiness (sub-values cheer and affection), unhappiness (sub-values misery and antipathy), security (sub-values confidence and trust), insecurity (sub-values disquiet and apprehension), satisfaction (sub-values interest and pleasure), dissatisfaction (sub-values ennui and displeasure). Judgement consists of these values: social esteem (sub-values normality, capacity and tenacity) and social sanction (sub-values veracity and propriety). Appreciation consists of these values: reaction (sub-values impact, quality), composition (sub-values balance and complexity) and valuation. Can you annotate all the evaluative linguistic instances of Affect, Judgement and Appreciation in this text and create a list for me? Assign one of the sub-values of Affect, Judgement and Appreciation that are in brackets to evaluative linguistic instance. Please assign only one value to each evaluative linguistic instance. Focus on verbs, nouns, adjectives and adverbs. Do not annotate the whole sentence. Please annotate only the linguistic instances that correspond to Affect, Judgement and Appreciation and its sub-values. This is the text:

B Appendix: The Dataset

Topic	Text ID	Words
Art	Art	2,268
Business	Bus	1,209
Education	Edu	3,096
Entertainment	Ent	3,215
History	His	1,809
Medicine	Med	1,906
Natural Science	NatSci	3,233
Philosophy	Phil	1,693
Politics & Law	Pol	4,501
Psychology	Psy	1,177
Technology	Tech	1,010

Table 4: Details on the dataset.

C Appendix: ChatGPT Output

Affect
1. fascinating (happiness - cheer)
2. surprised (insecurity - disquiet)
3. interesting (satisfaction - interest)
4. magical (happiness - cheer)
5. nice (happiness - cheer)
6. cool (satisfaction - pleasure)
7. impressive (satisfaction - interest)
8. fail (dissatisfaction - displeasure)
9. fun (happiness - cheer)
10. love (inclination - desire)
11. wrong (dissatisfaction - displeasure)
12. love (inclination - desire)
13. fallible (insecurity - disquiet)
14. err (dissatisfaction - displeasure)
15. mistakes (dissatisfaction - displeasure)
16. biased (dissatisfaction - displeasure)
17. genius (security - confidence)

Judgement
1. logical (social esteem - capacity)
2. right (social sanction - veracity)
3. wrong (social sanction - veracity)
4. impressive (social esteem - capacity)
5. powerful (social esteem - capacity)
6. genius (social esteem - capacity)
7. elegant (social sanction - propriety)
8. quirky (social sanction - propriety)
9. buggy (social sanction - propriety)
10. rational (social sanction - veracity)

Appreciation
1. powerful (valuation)
2. remarkable (valuation)
3. extraordinary (impact - quality)
4. staggering (valuation)
5. sophisticated (composition - complexity)
6. innovative (composition - complexity)
7. technological (composition - complexity)
8. insightful (composition - complexity)

Figure 3: Visualisation of the output by ChatGPT

Are You Serious?
Handling Disagreement When Annotating Conspiracy Theory Texts

Ashley Hemm, Sandra Kübler[†], Michelle Seelig, John Funchion,
Manohar Murthi, Kamal Premaratne, Daniel Verdear, Stefan Wuchty
University of Miami, [†]Indiana University
ashleyhemm@miami.edu, skuebler@iu.edu,
{mseelig,jfunchion,mmurthi,kamal,dverdear,s.wuchty}@miami.edu

Abstract

We often assume that annotation tasks, such as annotating for the presence of conspiracy theories, can be annotated with hard labels, without definitions or guidelines. Our annotation experiments, comparing students and experts, show that there is little agreement on basic annotations even among experts. For this reason, we conclude that we need to accept disagreement as an integral part of such annotations.

1 Introduction

In typical linguistic annotation projects, such as for part of speech tags or for dependency syntax, we assume that there is a single correct analysis, which can be determined reliably by trained annotators (e.g. Kübler and Zinsmeister, 2014). For phenomena such as hate speech or conspiracy theories (CTs), we tend to follow the same model without reflecting on the tasks. We assume that we know what hate speech or CTs are, asking our annotators to proceed without providing a definition of the phenomenon or guidelines. Another way of creating corpora of annotated data consists of using search terms to find examples of the phenomenon, where the search term (or the website from which the example was retrieved) serves as an approximation of the gold standard annotation. For example, a research team from the RAND Corporation, investigating the automatic detection of "conspiracy theory language" (Marcellino et al., 2021), used search terms to find examples of CT texts from social media. They created a machine learning classifier for which such texts were to be distinguished from "a baseline sample of 'normal' non-conspiracy talk". The CT texts covered alien visitation, vaccine dangers, the origins of COVID-19, while the non-CT texts were sampled from topics such as 'sports', 'movies', 'holidays', etc. Similarly, Miani et al. (2021) created a large corpus of CT texts, LOCO. It provides CTs and mainstream texts on the same topics. To gather CT texts, they used a list of CT websites based on scores from mediabiasfactcheck[1]. To retrieve mainstream documents, the authors used Google to search for the seeds. Work by Mompelat et al. (2022), who re-annotated parts of the LOCO corpus, shows that the original distinction of conspiracy and mainstream texts is reasonably reliable, but they also found that in some cases, it was difficult to decide whether a CT was perpetuated in a text. Note that any bias introduced by annotation or corpus creation will automatically be perpetuated into any machine learning model trained on such a corpus.

In the work presented here, we delve deeper into the distinction of CT and mainstream texts. In the first experiment, we asked students to annotate texts to determine how CTs were propagated. They were first trained on a set of texts, after having been provided with annotation guidelines. The results showed low inter-annotator agreement (IAA). In a follow-up study, we decided to redo the experiment with CT experts. These results were slightly improved but still did not meet the threshold of acceptable IAA, which raises the question of whether we need better annotation guidelines or whether the CT phenomenon is highly subjective. After a thorough evaluation of the two separate sets of annotations (students and experts), we come to the conclusion that the latter is the case. This suggests that we cannot expect a single gold standard annotation, and consequently cannot use IAA as a measure of the annotation quality. We finally provide a discussion of the consequences of our findings for annotation projects concerned with highly subjective phenomena.

Our work is closely aligned with other work on annotator disagreement and perspectivist approaches to NLP. Thus, our insights are not novel in NLP; we are adding to the discussion by

[1] https://mediabiasfactcheck.com/conspiracy/

Proceedings of The 18th Linguistic Annotation Workshop (LAW-XVIII), pages 124–132
March 22, 2024

adding conspiracy annotation/detection to the list of subjective tasks, which require perspectivist approaches.

2 Disagreement in Annotation

Early work on disagreement in linguistic annotations (Passonneau, 2004; Poesio and Artstein, 2005) introduced Krippendorff's alpha (Krippendorff, 2019) as a metric to measure inter-annotator agreement and introduced the notion of explicit and implicit ambiguity in annotations, the latter referring to ambiguity revealed through annotator disagreement. More recent work has started looking into disagreement in annotations beyond measuring it, instead accepting it as a necessary phenomenon in the annotation of subjective tasks for a range of tasks: for example, POS tagging (Plank et al., 2014), textual inference (Pavlick and Kwiatkowski, 2019), sexism (Almanea and Poesio, 2022), toxicity (Sap et al., 2022), and hate speech detection (Akhtar et al., 2020; Mostafazadeh Davani et al., 2022).

3 Annotating Conspiracy Theories

A CT refers to a story or narrative that claims a small group or 'deep state' has control over the government and is involved in harmful activities aimed at causing widespread harm (e.g. Enders et al., 2021). This includes doubting scientific evidence of climate change and vaccinations, believing that elections are rigged, and fearing that immigrants, Black individuals, or Jewish people pose a threat to the rights, freedom, and culture of white people (Enders et al., 2021). Empirical evidence-based research from a variety of disciplines seeks to explain why people believe in certain CTs (e.g. Daniel and Harper, 2022; Lewandowsky et al., 2013; Uscinski et al., 2020, 2022).

Neville-Shepard (2018) and Serazio (2016) assert that creators of CT text use language familiar to audiences attracted to conspiracism, and conspiratorial text is grounded in a small amount of 'evidence' that encourages a 'leap of faith' by the audience to reach conclusions. This suggests that conspiratorial discourse caters to people in the know and, therefore, does not explicitly convey a premise, rather, the audience completes the argument based on prior knowledge. Reyes and Smith (2014) further assert that creators of CT text depend on audiences already familiar with similar ideas. This means that these theories tap into a broader culture of belief in conspiracies and act as a way for people to find others who share their beliefs and reinforce their convictions. However, this makes it difficult to classify conspiratorial text because, without an explicit claim, it is up to the audience to 'leap' to conclusions based on the familiar tropes presented in the text.

Mompelat et al. (2022) have reannotated parts of the LOCO corpus (Miani et al., 2021) to determine how reliable the automatic corpus collection was. They started with a simple definition of what they considered a CT text, namely a text that propagated a *conspiracy belief*, defined as: "A conspiracy belief is the belief that an organization made up of individuals or groups was or is acting covertly to achieve some malevolent end. It depicts causal narratives of an event as a covert plan orchestrated by a secret cabal of people or organizations instead of a random or natural happening" (Seelig et al., 2022). Their first round of annotations showed high IAA for mainstream texts, but the IAA for CT was 0.47. As a consequence, they adjusted the guidelines and added that in order for a text to be considered a CT text, the following had to hold: "A document is considered CT if and only if such a belief is manifested in the text via specific expressions" (Mompelat et al., 2022). They also identified a set of textual and verbal cues that triggered a reading of conspiracy, e.g., all caps texts, paraphrases, questions. The revised guidelines resulted in a higher IAA for conspiracy texts of 0.70. However, when they used the same annotation scheme for a different conspiracy theory, the results for CT texts was considerably lower (0.58), thus showing that robust annotations are difficult, even with trained annotators.

4 The Annotation Study

We conducted an annotation study to determine which circumstances (in terms of training) we need to reliably annotate a range of phenomena. More specifically, the annotations covered identifying similarities in main themes, structures, rhetorical forms, and tropes. For the annotation samples, we revisited the LOCO corpus to draw a sample of CTs. We only extracted documents identified as a conspiracy, representing a broad range of topics, using the seeds Covid-19, Pizzagate, Climate change, JFK assassination, 9/11, Illuminati, and Flat Earth. Our non-experts are graduate students without prior knowledge of the literature on CTs. The experts are researchers who have worked on CTs for at least 2 years. We report both Fleiss' kappa (Fleiss, 1971) and Krippendorff's alpha (Krippendorff, 2019).

The annotation scheme is based on past research on hate speech, CT text, and populist rhetoric (Bastos and Farkas, 2019; Rieger et al., 2021; Seelig et al., 2022). We used the following questions:

1. Presence of a CT in the text (e.g., causal narratives of an event as a covert plan orchestrated by a secret cabal of people/organizations).
2. Main or dominant CT narrative (e.g., Flat Earth, Moon Landing, White Genocide, etc.).
3. Treatment of the CT: document supports, endorses, and/or reinforces a CT; or refutes or debunks it.
4. Leap of faith: narrative takes accepted facts and makes a leap of faith to reach conclusions that are not supported by the facts.
5. Type of argument: syllogism (a deductive scheme of a formal argument consisting of a major and a minor premise and a conclusion) or enthymeme (an argument in which one premise is not explicitly stated).
6. Sentiment of narrative (e.g., positive, neutral, or negative).
7. Pathos: appealing to audience's emotions (e.g., humor and sarcasm; inspiration and hope; sadness; sympathy and pity; courage and strength; hatred; love; fear; anger).
8. Logos: rational basis for an argument/reason (e.g., statistics; recorded evidence; historical data or facts; studies, surveys, or academic papers; personal experience/testimony; hearsay; or not applicable).
9. Ethos: the credibility of the speaker or poster (e.g., celebrity; authority figure; credible or public figure; animals; inanimate objects; a person in the street excluding celebrity/ authority/credible figures).
10. Fearmongering (e.g., mentioning fatalities caused by natural disasters, crime, acts of terrorism, civil unrest, or accidents).
11. Emotional spectrum: use of emotional words (e.g., afraid, excited, sweet, and jealous), exclamation marks (e.g., they are crying!), or emojis.

	Non-experts		Experts	
	κ	α	κ	α
CT present	0.10	0.37	-0.12	-0.71
Main CT present	0.22	0.58	0.07	0.25
Treatment of CT	0.13	0.46	0.01	-0.01
Leap of faith	0.09	0.11	0.10	0.02
Type of arg.	0.03	0.34	-0.09	0.28
Sentiment	0.02	0.30	-0.05	0.05
Pathos	0.07	0.33	0.06	0.51
Logos	0.03	0.23	0.01	0.29
Ethos	0.04	0.28	0.02	0.41
Fearmongering	0.15	0.48	-0.07	-0.28
Emotional spect.	0.06	0.34	-0.13	-0.38
Real-world	0.13	0.43	0.03	-0.10

Table 1: Inter-annotator agreement for CTs comparing non-experts and expert.

12. Real-world issues (e.g., politics, economy, military conflict, crime, local affairs, weather, public health, education, protest, ethnocultural minorities, or terrorism).

We first trained the non-expert annotators on a sample of 11 conspiracy documents selected from the seven CTs (Covid-19, Pizzagate, Climate change, JFK assassination, 9/11, Illuminati, and Flat Earth). After training, they independently annotated a random sample of 472 CT texts representing the same conspiracy topics. The annotations were conducted by two MA students and three PhD students without prior knowledge of research on CTs. The results are shown in Table 1. The analysis yielded poor IAA, even for the most basic question of whether a CT was present ($\kappa = 0.10$).

Given the low IAA of the non-experts, we conducted a similar, but smaller experiment with a group of 4 experts as annotators. We used the same annotation scheme on a sub-sample of 25 CTs from the same sample the students annotated. The results of this experiment are shown in the second column in Table 1. We notice that there are several negative values. Similar to the findings of Mompelat et al. (2022), the reason for this can be found in the very high expected values. Neither metric is useful for data with very high agreement and small sample size (Zhao et al., 2013). If we interpret these values as reasonably high agreement, we see that the experts tend to agree on whether a CT is present, how the CT is treated, and on fearmongering, the emotional spectrum, and real-

	κ	α
CT present	0.403	0.827
Main CT present	0.298	0.217
Treatment of CT	0.383	0.795

Table 2: Inter-annotator agreement for CTs for experts using the simplified annotation scheme.

world issues present. The remaining numbers are lower in comparison to the non-experts, including for the questions which CT was present and its treatment, thus showing that prior research experience on CTs is not helpful.

As part of this second round of annotations, we added questions to capture experts' certainty of their annotation for items flagged controversial (e.g., very certain, pretty sure, not sure, I have no idea/guessed). The answers show that while the experts never guessed, the majority were only pretty sure (61-84%) or not sure (3-18%).

Due to the lack of agreement for non-experts and experts, we decided to simplify the coding scheme to the first three questions, but to clarify and extend the guidelines, to see if more explicit instructions would increase IAA. The modifications were based on a discussion of the experts of which uncertainties they faced during the annotation process. We used another sub-sample of 10 CTs from the same sample the students annotated. The results are based on 6 expert annotators and are shown in Table 2. We see that these numbers are higher than for the previous experiment, but the agreement is still far from what is generally considered reliable: when asked whether the text contains a CT, we obtained $\kappa = 0.403$; for "main conspiracy present?" $\kappa = 0.298$; and for "treatment of conspiracy" $\kappa = 0.383$.

During the last experiment, we also asked the larger group of experts to describe any difficulty they had determining the answers. We show sample responses in Table 3. These responses show that even experts struggle with basic questions such as whether a CT is present, which we interpret as an indication that there do not exist clear boundaries.

Q1	Text read as if an excerpt from a news story [Text 1]
Q1	The overall passage read as if not true, but hard to discern a specific CT
Q1	Unsure if this is a CT or simple a dispute [Text 2]
Q2	sounds like a movie plot [Text 2]
Q2	This one was difficult because it's describing a real thing that happened in language that's a bit bombastic, and also acknowledges an offshoot that may or may not actually exist. [Text 3]
Q2	Illuminati is mentioned, but the main text assumes the reader knows the Illuminati are perpetrating mind control and other atrocities.
Q3	needs fact checking
Q3	narrative was about combating the spread of COVID-19 [Text 1]
Q3	Unsure about this one - it mentions misinformation but is it a CT?
Q3	It engages with CTs and seems to endorse them, but it is more about getting you to pay attention and stay.

Table 3: Sample responses describing difficulties in answering questions. Text numbers refer to Appendix A.

5 Consequences for Annotation Projects

Our results above show clearly that it is extremely difficult to reach high IAA on even basic questions such as whether a text contains a CT, even when experts are used as annotators. It is possible that agreement metrics can be increased by further extending the instructions for annotations and by training annotators to respond in a specific way to specific texts. However, such a setup may encourage annotators to annotate what experimenters want to hear instead of annotating what they see as being present in the text. A closer look at the texts and the annotations shows that these decisions depend on prior knowledge and on how the text is interpreted. If we streamline the annotations too rigidly, then we create the possibility that annotators try to guess what the experimenters want to see as answers, thus clouding legitimate interpretations of the text. For example, the decision whether Text 3 in Appendix A propagates a CT will depend not only on how much the annotator knows about the case, but also on how much they trust the source of this text.

A closer look at the texts and the annotations allows us to conclude that the annotations are and need to be subjective. We cannot have a single gold standard annotation; rather, we must be prepared to accept a range of answers. This conclusion leads to several consequences, partly for the definition of the problem, and partly for modeling the problem computationally.

1. Disagreement between annotators is not a sign of lack of clarity in the annotation scheme but a direct consequence of the phenomenon to be annotated. One reason is that belief in CTs is not monolithic, but rather faceted, where individuals belief in subsets of factoid of a range of CTs. Another reason is that we need to model the preception of standard readers, and their interpretation will depend on prior knowledge as well as prior bias.
2. We cannot expect a single "correct" answer; rather, we need to accept ranges of answers. This is in line with other subjective tasks such as hate speech annotation or sentiment annotation.
3. Metrics such as Fleiss' kappa and Krippendorff's alpha cannot be used to evaluate the quality of annotations. More specifically, such tasks cannot be evaluated based on consistency.
4. Machine learning (ML) approaches to model the phenomenon should not define it as a classification task but instead need to predict the range and distribution of answers.
5. ML models based on gold standard annotations may be severely biased.
6. The lack of agreement requires a shift in machine learning paradigm, taking learning from disagreement (Mostafazadeh Davani et al., 2022; Uma et al., 2021) more seriously since the variability in annotations can significantly affect the task (classification vs. predicting a distribution). Thus, it needs to be integrated more closely in the training regime.

6 Limitations

Our comparative annotation study is based on a small number of annotators since it was supposed to serve as a pilot stud for a larger annotation project. However, the students went through a thorough training session, and the number of experts is naturally limited by availability. All expert annotators are also co-authors on this report, our expertise ranges over a wide array of fields, which ensures a wide disciplinary stance.

7 Ethical Considerations

Working with CTs tends to be difficult for the annotators. For this reason, we concentrated on a set of different CTs that are less prone to explicit hatred that is often present in CTs targeting specific minority groups (e.g., white genocide). However, despite this careful selection, the chosen texts can contain content that may upset annotators.

Acknowledgments

This work is based on research supported by US National Science Foundation (NSF) Grants #2123635 and #2123618.

We are grateful to all our annotators and to the reviewers for their comments, which helped strengthen the paper.

References

Sohail Akhtar, Valerio Basile, and Viviana Patti. 2020. Modeling annotator perspective and polarized opinions to improve hate speech detection. In *Proceedings of the AAAI Conference on Human Computation and Crowdsourcing*, pages 151–154.

Dina Almanea and Massimo Poesio. 2022. ArMIS - the Arabic Misogyny and Sexism Corpus with annotator subjective disagreements. In *Proceedings of the Thirteenth Language Resources and Evaluation Conference*, pages 2282–2291, Marseille, France.

Marco Bastos and Johan Farkas. 2019. "Donald Trump is my President!": The internet research agency propaganda machine. *Social Media + Society*, 5(3).

Lauren Daniel and David J. Harper. 2022. The social construction of conspiracy beliefs: A Q-methodology study of how ordinary people define them and judge their plausibility. *Journal of Constructivist Psychology*, 35(2):564–585.

Adam Enders, Joseph Uscinski, Casey Klofstad, Michelle Seelig, Stefan Wuchty, Manohar Murthi, Kamal Premaratne, and John Funchion. 2021. Do conspiracy beliefs form a belief system? Examining the structure and organization of conspiracy beliefs. *Journal of Social and Political Psychology*, 9(1):255–271.

Joseph L. Fleiss. 1971. *Statistical Methods for Rates and Proportions*. John Wiley.

Klaus Krippendorff. 2019. *Content Analysis: An Introduction to Its Methodology*. SAGE.

Sandra Kübler and Heike Zinsmeister. 2014. *Corpus Linguistics and Linguistically Annotated Corpora*. Bloomsbury.

Stephan Lewandowsky, Klaus Oberauer, and Gilles E. Gignac. 2013. NASA faked the moon landing – therefore, (climate) science is a hoax: An anatomy of the motivated rejection of science. *Psychological Science*, 24(5):622—633.

William Marcellino, Todd C. Helmus, Joshua Kerrigan, Hilary Reininger, Rouslan I. Karimov, and Rebecca Ann Lawrence. 2021. Detecting conspiracy theories on social media. Technical Report RR-A676-1, The RAND Corporation.

Alessandro Miani, Thomas Hills, and Adrian Bangerter. 2021. LOCO: The 88-million-word language of conspiracy corpus. *Behavior Research Methods*.

Ludovic Mompelat, Zuoyu Tian, Matthew Luettgen, Amanda Kessler, Aaryana Rajanala, Sandra Kübler, and Michelle Seelig. 2022. How "loco" is the LOCO corpus? Annotating the language of conspiracy theories. In *Proceedings of the Sixteenth Linguistic Annotation Workshop*, Marseille, France.

Aida Mostafazadeh Davani, Mark Díaz, and Vinodkumar Prabhakaran. 2022. Dealing with disagreements: Looking beyond the majority vote in subjective annotations. *Transactions of the Association for Computational Linguistics*, 10:92–110.

Ryan Neville-Shepard. 2018. Paranoid style and subtextual form in modern conspiracy rhetoric. *Southern Communication Journal*, 83(2):119–132.

Rebecca Passonneau. 2004. Computing reliability for coreference annotation. In *Proceedings of the Fourth International Conference on Language Resources and Evaluation (LREC)*, Lisbon, Portugal.

Ellie Pavlick and Tom Kwiatkowski. 2019. Inherent disagreements in human textual inferences. *Transactions of the Association for Computational Linguistics*, 7:677–694.

Barbara Plank, Dirk Hovy, and Anders Søgaard. 2014. Linguistically debatable or just plain wrong? In *Proceedings of the 52nd Annual Meeting of the Association for Computational Linguistics*, pages 507–511, Baltimore, MD.

Massimo Poesio and Ron Artstein. 2005. The reliability of anaphoric annotation, reconsidered: Taking ambiguity into account. In *Proceedings of the Workshop on Frontiers in Corpus Annotations II: Pie in the Sky*, pages 76–83, Ann Arbor, MI.

Ian Reyes and Jason K. Smith. 2014. What they don't want you to know about planet X: Surviving 2012 and the aesthetics of conspiracy rhetoric. *Communication Quarterly*, 62(4):399–415.

Diana Rieger, Aanna Sophie Kümpel, Maximilian Wich, Toni Kiening, and Groh Groh. 2021. Assessing the extent and types of hate speech in fringe communities: A case study of alt-right communities on 8chan, 4chan, and Reddit. *Social Media + Society*, 7(4).

Maarten Sap, Swabha Swayamdipta, Laura Vianna, Xuhui Zhou, Yejin Choi, and Noah A. Smith. 2022. Annotators with attitudes: How annotator beliefs and identities bias toxic language detection. In *Proceedings of the 2022 Conference of the North American Chapter of the Association for Computational Linguistics: Human Language Technologies*, pages 5884–5906, Seattle, WA.

Michelle Seelig, John Funchion, Ruth Trego, Sandra Kübler, Daniel Verdear, Stefan Wuchty, Joseph Uscinski, Casey Klofstad, Manohar Murthi, Kamal Premaratne, and Amada Diekman. 2022. The dark side of Twitter: A framing analysis of conspiratorial rhetoric stoking fear. Presentation at the 72nd Annual ICA Conference: One World, One Network? Online.

Michael Serazio. 2016. Encoding the paranoid style in American politics: "Anti-establishment" discourse and power in contemporary spin. *Critical Studies in Media Communication*, 33(2):181–194.

Alexandra Uma, Tommaso Fornaciari, Dirk Hovy, Silviu Paun, Barbara Plank, and Massimo Poesio. 2021. Learning from disagreement: A survey. *Journal of Artificial Intelligence Research*, 72.

Joseph Uscinski, Adam Enders, Amanda Diekman, John Funchion, Casey Klofstad, Sandra Kübler, Manohar Murthi, Kamal Premaratne, Michelle Seelig, Daniel Verdear, and Stefan Wuchty. 2022. The psychological and political correlates of conspiracy theory beliefs. *Scientific Reports*, 12(21672).

Joseph E Uscinski, Adam M Enders, Casey Klofstad, Michelle Seelig, John Funchion, Caleb Everett, Stefan Wuchty, Kamal Premaratne, and Manohar Murthi. 2020. Why do people believe covid-19 conspiracy theories? *Harvard Kennedy School Misinformation Review*, 1(3).

Xinshu Zhao, Jun S Liu, and Ke Deng. 2013. Assumptions behind intercoder reliability indices. *Annals of the International Communication Association*, 36(1):419–480.

A Appendix

Text 1:

Mainland China reported 30 new coronavirus cases on Saturday, up from 19 a day earlier as the number of cases involving travellers from abroad as well as local transmissions increased, highlighting the difficulty in stamping out the outbreak.

The National Health Commission said in a statement on Sunday that 25 of the latest cases involved people who had entered from abroad, compared with 18 such cases a day earlier.

Five new locally transmitted infections were also reported on Saturday, all in the southern coastal province of Guangdong, up from a day earlier.

The mainland has now reported a total of 81,669 cases, while the death toll has risen by three to 3,329.

Though daily infections have fallen dramatically from the height of the epidemic in February, when hundreds of new cases were reported daily, Beijing remains unable to completely halt new infections despite imposing some of the most drastic measures to curb the virus spread.

The so-called imported cases and asymptomatic patients, who have the virus and can give it to others but show no symptoms, have become among Chinas chief concerns in recent weeks. The country has closed off its borders to almost all foreigners as the virus spread globally, though most of the imported cases involve Chinese nationals returning from overseas.

The platinum standard of advanced multivitamin formulations is back in stock! Order Vitamin Mineral Fusion at 50% off with double Patriot Points and free shipping today!

Text 2:

Between 542 and 66 million years ago — long before the "supervolcano" became part of Yellowstone's geologic story — the area was covered by inland seas.

NPS/Jim Peaco

Most of Earth's history (from the formation of the earth 4.6 billion years ago to approximately 541 million years ago) is known as the Precambrian time. Rocks of this age are found in northern Yellowstone and in the hearts of the Teton, Beartooth, Wind River, and Gros Ventre ranges. During the Precambrian and the subsequent Paleozoic and Mesozoic eras (541 to 66 million years ago), the western United States was covered at times by oceans, sand dunes, tidal flats, and vast plains. From the end of the Mesozoic through the early Cenozoic, mountain-building processes formed the Rocky Mountains.

During the Cenozoic era (approximately the last 66 million years of Earths history), widespread mountain-building, volcanism, faulting, and glaciation sculpted the Yellowstone area.

Magma (molten rock from Earth's mantle) has been close to the surface in Yellowstone for more than 2 million years. Its heat melted rocks in the crust, creating a magma chamber of partially molten, partially solid rock. Heat from this shallow magma caused an area of the upper crust to expand and rise. The Yellowstone Plateau became a geomorphic landform shaped by episodes of volcanic activity. Stress also caused rocks overlying the magma to break, forming faults and causing earthquakes. Eventually, these faults reached the deep magma chamber. Magma oozed through these cracks, releasing pressure within the chamber and allowing trapped gases to expand rapidly. A massive volcanic eruption then occurred along vents, spewing volcanic ash and gas into the atmosphere and causing fast super-hot debris (pyroclastic) flows on the ground. As the underground magma chamber emptied, the ground above it sunk, creating the first of Yellowstones three calderas.

This diagram shows the general ideas behind two theories of how magma rises to the surface. Adapted with permission from Windows into the Earth by Robert Smith and Lee J. Siegel, 2000.

Researchers found that the changes leading up to an eruption may happen in a matter of decades rather than thousands of years in advance as previously thought.

Based on minerals from the last major eruption, the Supervolcanoes are characterized as volcanic centers that have had eruptions that covered more than 240 cubic miles. The US has two: one in Yellowstone and another in Californias Long Valley. An eruption could emit ash that would expand over 500 miles. The eruption would likely cover the ground with as much as 4 inches of gray ash, which could be detrimental to crops growing in the Midwest. Another less worrisome concern is the 1,000 degree F molten lava that could ooze out. Gases, including sulfur dioxide, which contributes to acid rain would be spewed from the supervolcano and the global cooling issues associated with reflecting sunlight away from the Earth are also concerns.

But there are other supervolcanos in the world with sooner predictions than Yellowstones. Campi Flegri, a name that aptly translates as burning fields, is in a critical state, according to researchers in Italy. It consists of a vast and complex network of underground chambers that formed hundreds of thousands of years ago, stretching from the outskirts of Naples to underneath the Mediterranean Sea. Though its last eruption was in 1538, its due for an eruption soon. It would be a minor event compared to the 72 cubic miles of molten rock it spewed in its most notorious eruption 39,000 years ago, called Campanian Ignimbrite, that likely contributed to the extinction of the Neanderthals.

Fortune website article reported that if the Yellowstone supervolcano erupts, it could shoot out more than 1,000 cubic kilometers of rock and ash into the air. Thats 250 cubic miles. Thats more than three times as large as the Campanian Ignimbrite eruption in Italy, which created a sulfurous cloud that floated more than 1,200 miles away to hang over Russia. Thats 2,500 times more material than Mount St. Helens expelled in 1980, killing 57 people. An eruption at Yellowstone would result in a cloud of ash more than 500 miles wide, stretching across nearly the entire western United States.

NASA has a plan to neutralize supervolcano threats however. They believe the most viable solution could be to drill up to 6 miles down into the supervolcano, and pump down water at high pressure. The circulating water would return at a temperature of around 662F, thus slowly day by day extracting heat from the volcano. And while such a project would come at an estimated cost of around $3.46 billion, it comes with an enticing catch which could convince politicians to make the investment. It would become a source of geothermal energy. But there are considerable risks, too. It could trigger the eruption its meant to save us from.

Historically, four types of volcanic events have taken place in Yellowstone (you may click on each one to learn more):

1. Caldera Forming Eruptions – 2.1 and 1.3 million years ago

2. Lava Flows – about 30 between 640,000 and 70,000 years ago

3. Earthquakes – 1000 to 3000 yearly; last notable quake was in 1959

4. Hydrothermal (Steam) Explosions – small explosions in the 20th century; a dozen or so major explosions between 14,000 and 3,000 years ago

The likelihood of an eruption in the near future is still low. However those who instigate such a project will never see it to completion, or even have an idea whether it might be successful within their lifetime. Cooling Yellowstone in this manner would happen at a rate of 3.2808399 feet a year, taking of the order of tens of thousands of years until just cold rock was left.

Featured Image: Yellowstone harbours a giant magma chamber that will blow one day if we dont act (Credit: iStock)

Text 3:

The victim was kept in a chemically induced sleep for weeks and subjected to rounds of electroshocks, experimental drugs and tape-recorded messages played non-stop.

CBC News recently reported that the Canadian government reached an out-of-court settlement of $100,000 with Allison Steel, the daughter of Jean Steel, a woman who was subjected to horrific brainwashing experiments funded by the CIA.

The settlement was quietly reached in exchange for dropping the legal action launched by Allison Steel in September 2015. The settlement includes a non-disclosure agreement prohibiting Steel from talking about the settlement itself. However, the existence of the settlement and its total amount appeared in public accounts released by the federal government in October.

Jean Steels ordeal began in 1957, at the age of 33. She was admitted at the Allan Memorial Institute in Montreal after being diagnosed with manic depression and delusional thinking.

In the following months, Steel became a victim of CIA-funded MKULTRA experiments conducted by Dr. Ewen Cameron.

Camerons experiments aimed to de-pattern the victims mind through intense trauma in order to re-pattern it afterward. In other words, he was researching the basis of Monarch Programming the mind control program that is often discussed on Vigilant Citizen.

Cameron believed a combination of chemically induced sleep for weeks at a time, massive electroshock treatments, experimental hallucinogenic drugs like LSD and techniques such as psychic driving through the repeated playing of taped messages could de-pattern the mind, breaking up the brain pathways and wiping out symptoms of mental illnesses such as schizophrenia. Doctors could then re-pattern patients. However, the de-patterning also wiped out much the patients memory and left them in a childlike state. In some cases, grown adults forgot basic skills such as how to use the bathroom, how to dress themselves or how to tie their shoes.

CBC News, Federal government quietly compensates daughter of brainwashing experiments victim

Hundreds of pages detail the horrific experiments Jean Steel was subjected to.

According to a report written by Cameron, Steel was kept in a chemically induced sleep for weeks. One series lasted 29 days. A second lasted 18 days. The sleep therapy was accompanied by a series of electroshocks. She was extremely confused and disoriented but much more co-operative, Cameron wrote in his report. Nurses notes on her charts detail repeated doses of sodium amytal, and how Steel would pace the hall and rail about feeling like a prisoner: Its just like being buried alive. Somebody please do something. This was all said screaming at the nurse and doctor, one note said.

Steel then began to exhibit bizarre behavior. Her daughter recounts:

When you wanted to talk with her about something emotional she just could not do it, Steel said. Her emotions were stripped. It took away her soul. Her mother would sit alone in the dark, writing codes and numbers on the walls. One time I came home and the ceiling was spray-painted with red swirls all over it, Steel said. She would take wallpaper and cut out little sections of it and she would pin it to the whole room.

While MKULTRA is viewed by mass media as a shameful episode of the past, it is also part of our present. The program still exists in a much more refined version under the name of Monarch programming.

Heres an interesting 1980 documentary about MKULTRA experiments in Canada produced by the CBC:

A GPT among Annotators: LLM-based Entity-Level Sentiment Annotation

Egil Rønningstad and **Erik Velldal** and **Lilja Øvrelid**
University of Oslo, Language Technology Group
{egilron,erikve,liljao}@ifi.uio.no

Abstract

We investigate annotator variation for the novel task of Entity-Level Sentiment Analysis (ELSA) which annotates the aggregated sentiment directed towards volitional entities in a text. More specifically, we analyze the annotations of a newly constructed Norwegian ELSA dataset and release additional data with each annotator's labels for the 247 entities in the dataset's test split. We also perform a number of experiments prompting ChatGPT for these sentiment labels regarding each entity in the text and compare the generated annotations with the human labels. Cohen's Kappa for agreement between the best LLM-generated labels and curated gold was 0.425, which indicates that these labels would not have high quality. Our analyses further investigate the errors that ChatGPT outputs, and compare them with the variations that we find among the 5 trained annotators that all annotated the same test data.

1 Introduction

Sentiment analysis constitutes an annotation task that is highly subjective in nature, typically with moderate inter-annotator agreement levels (Bobicev and Sokolova, 2017; Provoost et al., 2019; Kim and Klinger, 2018; Barnes et al., 2021). Recently, Gilardi et al. (2023) and Alizadeh et al. (2023) compare the label quality of crowd workers to the labels generated by a large language model (LLM). They show how annotations by a LLM can surpass the quality obtained from crowd workers, for certain annotation tasks for the English language. Šmíd and Přibáň (2023) employ multilingual generative language models (mT5 and mBART) for other sentiment analysis tasks through prompts and fine-tuning for Czech sentiment analysis. They find that prompting these types of models can be a potentially promising avenue for few-shot or zero-shot scenarios.

An important direction in recent work on sentiment analysis focuses on analysis of longer texts (Dufraisse et al., 2023; Rønningstad et al., 2022). Our task of Entity-Level Sentiment Analysis (ELSA) follows in this direction. It was introduced and motivated by Rønningstad et al. (2022) and can be defined as providing one sentiment score for each volitional entity in a text, the reader's total impression from reading the entire text. The overall, entity-wise sentiment is central to this work, since the annotated texts are quite long, containing several different entities, whereby each entity may be referenced in several sentences in separate parts of the text. A volitional entity, or just "entity" in our context, is a person or organization mentioned by its proper name in the text. We recently released a manually annotated dataset for the ELSA task where the overall sentiment conveyed in the text towards each volitional entity is annotated.[1] Figure 1 shows an example text with ELSA annotations.

In this paper we present a number of experiments attempting to generate ELSA sentiment annotations by prompting ChatGPT, and we perform an in-depth comparison between the LLM-generated labels, and the labels provided by five human annotators that all labeled the test-split of our dataset in parallel. With this paper we also make available the annotators' labels for each entity in the test set. We believe that the ELSA annotation task offers a challenging testbed for LLM-based annotation due to the following characteristics:

Longer texts The texts are professional published reviews with a mean sentence count of 27.5.

Norwegian language The texts are in the Norwegian language, a small language which amounts to a minuscule portion of the GPT pre-training data;

[1] https://github.com/ltgoslo/ELSA

Proceedings of The 18th Linguistic Annotation Workshop (LAW-XVIII), pages 133–139
March 22, 2024 ©2024 Association for Computational Linguistics

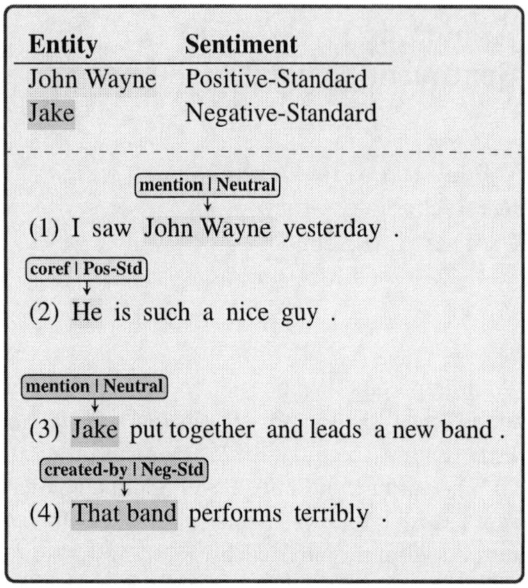

Figure 1: Toy example of one text containing two entities and their overall sentiment classification (top), together with their references in the text, with sentiment classifications. The sentiments here are not expressed directly towards the entity mention, but towards a coreference in sentence 2 and towards something "created by" the entity in question, in sentence 4. The reader considers sentence 4 to convey a negative sentiment with respect to the entity "Jake", since he appears to be so central to it.

New task definition The specific sentiment analysis task (ELSA) is to the best of our knowledge not annotated in other publicly available datasets that could have been seen during pretraining;

Long distance relations The task requires filtering sentiment expressions with regards to the entity in question, to connect all relevant expressions of the document and aggregate this into a sentiment label from the provided set.

2 ELSA annotation

The newly created ELSA dataset contains the texts of the NoReC_{fine} dataset (Øvrelid et al., 2020) – a subset of the Norwegian Review Corpus (NoReC; (Velldal et al., 2018)) of professional reviews from a variety of domains, e.g. screen, music, restaurants and literature. The ELSA annotations adds sentiment information at the sentence- and document-level for each volitional entity in a given text; entities of the types Person (PER) and Organization (ORG). The texts contain on average mentions of 6 different entities, and each entity is assigned an individual sentiment label based on the reader's overall impression from the text. Sentiment polarity is classified with two intensity levels, providing a set of five possible labels: "Positive-Standard", "Positive-Slight", "Neutral", "Negative-Slight", and "Negative-Standard".

The ELSA dataset is annotated by 5 annotators, all native Norwegian undergraduate NLP-students. After introductory training and fine-tuning of the guidelines, the annotators (single-)annotated separate parts of the main body of the dataset, i.e. the training and development splits. The test set, consisting of 44 documents with a total of 1252 sentences and annotated sentiment toward 247 unique entities, was subsequently annotated by all five annotators. The entire dataset was manually curated by the project leader. Curation consisted mainly of error-correction and assigning the majority vote, which was accepted for 90% of the entities. An English translation of the annotator guidelines is found in the supplementary materials.

2.1 Individual variations

Since all five annotators labeled the sentiment regarding all 247 entities in the test set, we can study the variation between well-informed human readers regarding perceived sentiment presented in a longer text. The bottom rows of Table 2 shows the variations between annotators and the curated version. We consider the views and findings of Pavlick and Kwiatkowski (2019) to be relevant when studying the inter-annotator agreement in our dataset. They find that for Natural Language Inference annotations, it is hard to support the view that disagreement between annotators should be dismissed as annotation "noise". For our dataset, we do consider the manually expert-curated gold to be the best available single representation of the sentiment expressed in the texts regarding each entity. But we also consider each annotator's labels to represent a valid reading of the text and of that annotator's classification of the sentiment perceived. We find that the average κ score is .68 which can be characterised as moderate/good, however, also observe that there is considerable variation between the annotators, and in particular one annotator (ann_1) represents an outlier with diverging annotations.

3 LLM-based annotation

We employ OpenAI's ChatGPT (OpenAI, 2023) in order to explore whether a widely used LLM can provide sentiment labels for volitional entities in longer Norwegian texts, similar to that of native human annotators. We here present the alternatives explored in our experiments. The results from the various experiments can be found in Table 1.

The model prompted was GPT-4, `gpt-4-1106-preview`. For all our experiments, we instructed the model to output both a justification regarding the sentiment of each entity, and to provide the concluded labels separately in structured format (JSON). The prompts used in the experiment yielding best results can be found in the appendix. The instructions, prompts and replies for one text during the earlier "gpt06" experiment, can be found in the supplementary material.

Norwegian or English prompting We experimented with both Norwegian and English prompts. We always specified in the instructions that the texts would be in Norwegian, and we mostly got Norwegian text back.

Requesting one or many analyses per prompt As mentioned above, each document contains on average six entities to label. We experimented with either listing all entities to label in one prompt per document, but also in one case to submit one prompt per entity. The chosen variant is shown in the "Entities per prompt" column in Table 1.

Adding knowledge For our two last experiments, gpt0801 and gpt0802, we experimented with the addition of more information to the system instructions. For gpt0801, a condensed version of the Norwegian annotation guidelines were uploaded and referenced in the system instructions. For gpt0802, we additionally added a text file containing three texts, with their entities and each entity's sentiment label annotated, thus corresponding to a few-shot scenario.

4 Findings

Table 1 presents our experiments and the evaluation results for the labels generated by ChatGPT. We here discuss the impact from alternating the options listed in Table 1, and our analysis of the labels generated by the best performing setup.

4.1 Best model

The annotations resulting from the experiment "gpt0802", i.e. the few-shot scenario described above, shows the best accuracy and weighted F_1, measured against the curated gold standard, and we choose these results for further analyses. We find that only 62.8% of the best GPT-generated labels are correct. The Cohen's Kappa (κ) agreement is 42.5%. When we compare with the mean values for the five annotators, we find that the GPT-generated labels perform noticeably poorer than the annotators' average. However, when we compare the GPT-generated labels with each of the five annotators' scores, we find that, by some metrics, one annotator deviates more from the curated gold than the GPT output does.

4.2 Adding knowledge helps

From our results in Table 1 we see that the two final experiments, gpt0801 and gpt0802, resulted in better annotations than the previous experiments. One example where the outputs in gpt0802 were accurate, while earlier experiments produced an incorrect label is found in a movie review where the entity "Hitler" is mentioned. The reference is used to place the the events of the movie in space and time, during the last days of Hitler. The text does not attribute the horrors of war directly towards this entity. Previous GPT-experiments yielded the label "Negative-Standard", while the label for "Hitler" in gpt0802 is "Neutral". The curated gold value for the entity is "Neutral". We speculate that the model tends to employ too much previous knowledge about the entity from its pretraining, while with the more thorough instructions given in the annotators' guidelines and in the examples, the model aligned to this information and yielded a label derived more from the text in question only.

4.3 Evaluation against curated

The lower part of Table 2 shows the gap between GPT-generated labels and annotators' average in terms of accuracy, κ and Mean Squared Error (MSE). MSE is calculated using the numerical mappings for the sentiment labels provided in Table 3, and indicates the distance with which a label deviates from the curated gold. We find that the generated labels are generally further away from the true labels, once again with the exception of the outlier annotator.

4.4 Majority, Within range or Outside

An interesting question in the current context relates to whether the LLM-based annotation errors are qualitatively different than the observed annotator variation. In order to assess this we computed

Configuration	Prompt language	Entities per prompt	Accuracy	W. F1	System files
gpt06	Norwegian	document	0.53	0.6	
gpt07	English	individual	0.49	0.54	
gpt0701	English	document	0.37	0.41	
gpt0801	Norwegian	document	0.58	0.61	guidelines
gpt0802	Norwegian	document	0.63	0.65	guidelines + 3 examples

Table 1: Our experimental setups with accuracy and weighted F_1 measured against curated gold data. Section 3 explains the various design options. Under "Entities per prompt", "document" indicates that all entities in one document were submitted in one prompt. "individual" means we submitted one prompt per entity in the document. The "Configuration" columns apply the working title for each experiment as identification. The five first experiments were considered to be introductory and are not reported on.

	ann_avg	gpt	ann_1	ann_2	ann_3	ann_4	ann_5	curated
Majority	0.816	0.623	0.623	0.895	0.806	0.842	0.915	0.907
Within range	0.089	0.219	0.117	0.061	0.121	0.089	0.057	0.093
Outside	0.095	0.158	0.259	0.045	0.073	0.069	0.028	0.000
Accuracy	0.804	0.628	0.684	0.862	0.818	0.789	0.866	1.000
κ	0.683	0.425	0.543	0.764	0.712	0.625	0.771	1.000
MSE	0.144	0.220	0.237	0.103	0.096	0.165	0.116	0.000

Table 2: For the upper part of the table, we have counted for each label assigned by the annotators, whether it agrees with the majority of annotators, within the label span created by the other annotators, or outside this span. Further discussion of these values is found in Section 4.4. The lower part of the table shows Accuracy, Cohen's Kappa, and Mean Squared Error for each annotator, measured against curated.

Label	Numerical
Negative-Standard	-1.0
Negative-Slight	-0.5
Neutral	0.0
Positive-Slight	0.5
Positive-Standard	1.0

Table 3: Numerical mapping for the sentiment labels, in order to calculate mean square errors.

for each of the annotators, the one or two labels assigned by a majority of the four other annotators. If the label assigned by the annotator in question equaled such a majority vote, the label was counted as "Majority". If not, we examined the maximum and minimum value for the labels assigned by the other annotators, using the conversion table in Table 3. If the label was within the range defined by the labels of the other annotators, we counted this label as "Within range". The labels that were outside the labels range of other annotators, were counted as "Outside". The results are shown in the upper part of Table 2. Note that each annotator was evaluated by the 4 other annotators, while the GPT-generated labels were evaluated against the labels from all 5 annotators. We see in Table 2 for the row "Outside", that 15.8% of the labels generated by GPT was deviating more from the majority vote than any annotator. This is more than 50% more than the annotator average (9.5%), but not more than for the outlier Annotator 1 (25.9%).

4.5 Post-processing GPT outputs

We find in general that the generated texts from our interaction with GPT are not always consistent with the instructions, neither in repeating the entity name, in the labels assigned, nor in the formatting of the requested JSON output. After implementing a post-processing heuristics for extracting the entity name and sentiment label in accordance with the standard GPT reply, we aligned the GPT output with our annotated data by inspecting each format error and creating a rule-based conversion script. Each experiment with its variations in system instructions and prompt wordings, yielded different format variations in the output. For the given dataset with 247 entities, this post-processing was manageable. For a larger dataset, tested for more variations in the setup, this will be a non-negligible part of the task.

5 Suggestions for future work

From the findings reported in this paper, we are personally not encouraged to undertake new annotation projects using LLM-based annotation only. But we see a potential for augmenting datasets using a similar approach. When it comes to modelling, both the ELSA dataset and other SA datasets may benefit from being extended by LLM annotations. Including more open source instruction-tuned LLMs would then be essential. Modelling with LLMs is also highly relevant, and the experiments reported here can be used as the starting point for further experiments in that direction.

6 Conclusions

We have presented and analyzed a dataset of annotators' agreement for the task of Entity-Level Sentiment Analysis in Norwegian, and studied how well GPT-generated labels compare with labels produced by five different human annotators for this particular task. We consider the ELSA task to be interesting for such comparisons since the entire text needs to be analyzed for each entity, and the texts are lengthy, varying around a mean of 27.5 sentences per text. We find that the GPT-generated labels have lower accuracy and Cohen's Kappa than any annotator. But when we try to quantify the magnitude of the deviations, *e. g.* through MSE, we find that one "outlier" annotator has stronger deviations from gold that the GPT-generated labels. This represents new insights for us, since it has been assumed that the errors made by an llm could be more dramatic than those made by humans.

Similar approaches may therefore be well worth exploring for other sentiment analysis tasks in other languages similarly related to English. Particularly in parallel with human annotators. The only method we are aware of which serves to explore how a LLM could help with a certain new task, is by annotating data manually, since the task is to identify the sentiment as perceived by humans.

7 Limitations

7.1 Norwegian Language

We have analyzed a Norwegian dataset. We find in general that ChatGPT does a decent job in translating between Norwegian and English. We believe that the ChatGPT performance we found, might be matched or surpassed by other languages related to English, *e. g.* Germanic or Italic languages, with a similar or stronger web presence than Norwegian.

7.2 Model limitations

There are clear limitations connected with the use of a closed, commercial model such as ChatGPT. There is limited knowledge concerning its training data and the model weights are not shared openly. This means that there is a certain possibility of data leakage and there are also no possibilities for further fine-tuning of the model and subsequent evaluation. Unfortunately there are currently no freely available Norwegian instruction-tuned generative models, however, in future efforts we do aim to experiment with other openly available multilingual models. As mentioned above, since the ELSA dataset has only recently been released, there is no possibility for data leakage of the specific labels annotated there.

Acknowledgements

The work documented in this publication has been carried out within the NorwAI Centre for Research-based Innovation, funded by the Research Council of Norway (RCN), with grant number 309834.
We would like to thank the anonymous reviewers for their helpful comments, and Håkon Liltved Hyrve for research assistance.

References

Meysam Alizadeh, Maël Kubli, Zeynab Samei, Shirin Dehghani, Juan Diego Bermeo, Maria Korobeynikova, and Fabrizio Gilardi. 2023. Open-source large language models outperform crowd workers and approach chatgpt in text-annotation tasks. *ArXiv*, abs/2307.02179.

Jeremy Barnes, Lilja Øvrelid, and Erik Velldal. 2021. If you've got it, flaunt it: Making the most of fine-grained sentiment annotations. In *Proceedings of the 16th Conference of the European Chapter of the Association for Computational Linguistics: Main Volume*, pages 49–62, Online. Association for Computational Linguistics.

Victoria Bobicev and Marina Sokolova. 2017. Inter-annotator agreement in sentiment analysis: machine learning perspective. In *International Conference Recent Advances in Natural Language Processing*, pages 97–102.

Evan Dufraisse, Adrian Popescu, Julien Tourille, Armelle Brun, and Jerome Deshayes. 2023. MAD-

TSC: A multilingual aligned news dataset for target-dependent sentiment classification. In *Proceedings of the 61st Annual Meeting of the Association for Computational Linguistics (Volume 1: Long Papers)*, pages 8286–8305, Toronto, Canada. Association for Computational Linguistics.

Fabrizio Gilardi, Meysam Alizadeh, and Maël Kubli. 2023. Chatgpt outperforms crowd workers for text-annotation tasks. *Proceedings of the National Academy of Sciences of the United States of America*, 120.

Evgeny Kim and Roman Klinger. 2018. Who feels what and why? annotation of a literature corpus with semantic roles of emotions. In *Proceedings of the 27th International Conference on Computational Linguistics*, pages 1345–1359, Santa Fe, New Mexico, USA. Association for Computational Linguistics.

OpenAI. 2023. Gpt-4 technical report. *ArXiv*, abs/2303.08774.

Lilja Øvrelid, Petter Mæhlum, Jeremy Barnes, and Erik Velldal. 2020. A fine-grained sentiment dataset for Norwegian. In *Proceedings of the Twelfth Language Resources and Evaluation Conference*, pages 5025–5033, Marseille, France. European Language Resources Association.

Ellie Pavlick and Tom Kwiatkowski. 2019. Inherent disagreements in human textual inferences. *Transactions of the Association for Computational Linguistics*, 7:677–694.

Simon Provoost, Jeroen Ruwaard, Ward van Breda, Heleen Riper, and Tibor Bosse. 2019. Validating automated sentiment analysis of online cognitive behavioral therapy patient texts: An exploratory study. *Frontiers in Psychology*, 10.

Egil Rønningstad, Erik Velldal, and Lilja Øvrelid. 2022. Entity-level sentiment analysis (ELSA): An exploratory task survey. In *Proceedings of the 29th International Conference on Computational Linguistics*, pages 6773–6783, Gyeongju, Republic of Korea. International Committee on Computational Linguistics.

Jakub Šmíd and Pavel Přibáň. 2023. Prompt-based approach for Czech sentiment analysis. In *Proceedings of the 14th International Conference on Recent Advances in Natural Language Processing*, pages 1110–1120, Varna, Bulgaria. INCOMA Ltd., Shoumen, Bulgaria.

Erik Velldal, Lilja Øvrelid, Eivind Alexander Bergem, Cathrine Stadsnes, Samia Touileb, and Fredrik Jørgensen. 2018. NoReC: The Norwegian review corpus. In *Proceedings of the Eleventh International Conference on Language Resources and Evaluation (LREC 2018)*, Miyazaki, Japan. European Language Resources Association (ELRA).

A Experiment gpt0802

The following are the Assistant instructions and the prompt used for retrieving a replay containing a JSON-formatted segment with the sentiment labels for each pre-identified entity in one text. All files referenced in the system instructions and the prompts, were uploaded with the parameter `purpose="assistants"`.

A.1 Assistant instructions

```
instructions=f"You are a helpful assistant designed to output sentiment classification labels. All questions are about entity-wise sentiment analysis on Norwegian texts. You will analyze the sentiment regarding one volitional entity at the time, inspecting a Norwegian text that is provided as the introduction. The reply should contain the analysis of the sentiment towards the entity submitted in the first reply, and a second reply should contain the sentiment label only, chosen from this list: '['Positive-Standard', 'Positive-Slight', 'Neutral', 'Negative-Slight', 'Negative-Standard' ]'. 'Neutral' is the most common label. 'Positive-Slight' and 'Negative-Slight' are used if an entity receives slight, vague or uncertain sentiment. Otherwise, the 'Positive-Standard' and 'Negative-Standard' labels are used for all clear sentiments expressed towards the entity. You should not refer to common knowledge about an entity, but strictly analyze the sentiment conveyed in the given text. If both positive or negative sentiments exist, you must decide what is the prevalent or overall strongest sentiment conveyed in the text regarding the enity in question. You should make use of the instructions in the file {instructions.id} for determining the sentiment and give a json with the entities and their corresponding sentiments. In {pretraining.id} you will find some gold examples of this analysis."
```

A.2 Example prompt

The prompts were given in Norwegian. The following is a simple translation into English for one example text and the relevant entities in the document:
We are going to analyze the entities in the document 'file-OtlWmi9LJgyOMsB3dKelNDZK'. The text mentions these 8 entities: [Jamie, Jared Fraser, Claire, Caitriona Balfe, Diana Gabaldons, Black Jack Randalls, Ludvig XV of France, Sam

Heughan]. Your task is to assign a sentiment label that the text in file-OtlWmi9LJgyOMsB3dKelNDZK communicates regarding each entity, according to the system instructions for the assistant.

Datasets Creation and Empirical Evaluations of Cross-Lingual Learning on Extremely Low-Resource Languages: A Focus on Comorian Dialects

Abdou Mohamed Naira[1,2], **Abdessalam Bahafid**[1,2], **Zakarya Erraji**[1], **Imade Benelallam**[1,2]
[1] INSEA, Rabat, Morocco [2] ToumAI Analytics, Rabat, Morocco
{nabdoumohamed,i.benelallam,a.bahafid,zerraji}@insea.ac.ma
{naira,imade,abahafid}@toum.ai

Abstract

In this era of extensive digitalization, there are a profusion of Intelligent Systems that attempt to understand how languages are structured for the aim of providing solutions in various tasks like Text Summarization, Sentiment Analysis, Speech Recognition, etc. But for multiple reasons going from lack of data to the nonexistence of initiatives, these applications are in an embryonic stage in certain languages and dialects, especially those spoken in the African continent, like Comorian dialects. Today, thanks to the improvement of Pre-trained Large Language Models, a spacious way is open to enable these kind of technologies on these languages. In this study, we are pioneering the representation of Comorian dialects in the field of Natural Language Processing (NLP) by constructing datasets (Lexicons, Speech Recognition and Raw Text datasets) that could be used on different tasks. We also measure the impact of using pre-trained models on languages closely related to Comorian dialects to enhance the state-of-the-art in NLP for these latter, compared to using pre-trained models on languages that may not necessarily be close to these dialects. We construct models covering the following use cases: Language Identification, Sentiment Analysis, Part-Of-Speech Tagging, and Speech Recognition. Ultimately, we hope that these solutions can catalyze the improvement of similar initiatives in Comorian dialects and in languages facing similar challenges.

1 Introduction

The Comoros are an archipelago composed of four islands in the Indian Ocean. Approximately 850,000 people are living there (Worldometers), speaking four dialects belonging to the Bantu Language family (Atlasocio). These dialects are consequently impacted by geo-spatial features that progressively increase or eliminate similarities between them as shown in (Maurizio and Michele, 2021; Chamanga, 2022) and according to the ORELC[1] lexicon (See Fig. 1) in which we can observe that in a dictionary of 7,386 entries, 15.38% of the words are shared by all the dialects, 6.47% by three and 16.10% by two dialects. Indeed, these dialects can be divided into two groups: Eastern group (ShiNdzuani and ShiMaore) and Western group (ShiNgazidja and ShiMwali). Moreover, a part of the experiments conducted in (Maurizio and Michele, 2021) has shown through lexical distances calculation that these dialects could be classified into two other different groups, the first one composed of the ShiNgazidja while the second one contains the other three dialects.

The arrival of Transformers (Vaswani et al., 2017) was a real breakthrough in Artificial Intelligence (AI). This architecture allows us to better represent the context within texts which is a major spearhead in Language Understanding. Pre-trained Language Models like Bidirectional Encoder Representations from Transformers (BERT) (Devlin et al., 2019) have encapsulated this architecture, paving the way to better representation of multiple languages in all around the world (Pikuliak et al., 2021) through Cross-Lingual Learning. In multilingual scenarios, this latter allows languages that suffer from data scarcity to learn from the others owing to a sort of transfer learning. This becomes more interesting when working on close languages as demonstrated in (Tebbifakhr et al., 2020) where a Machine Translation system was adapted to a language close to the source language used on training.

The aim of this work is to contribute on the pioneering of Natural Language Processing (NLP) on Comorian dialects by (a) constructing datasets that could be used on different downstream tasks for future works and (b) experimenting the impact of using a cross-multilingual approach on close lan-

[1] https://orelc.ac/academy/ShikomoriWords/?i=kmWords

Proceedings of The 18th Linguistic Annotation Workshop (LAW-XVIII), pages 140–149
March 22, 2024 ©2024 Association for Computational Linguistics

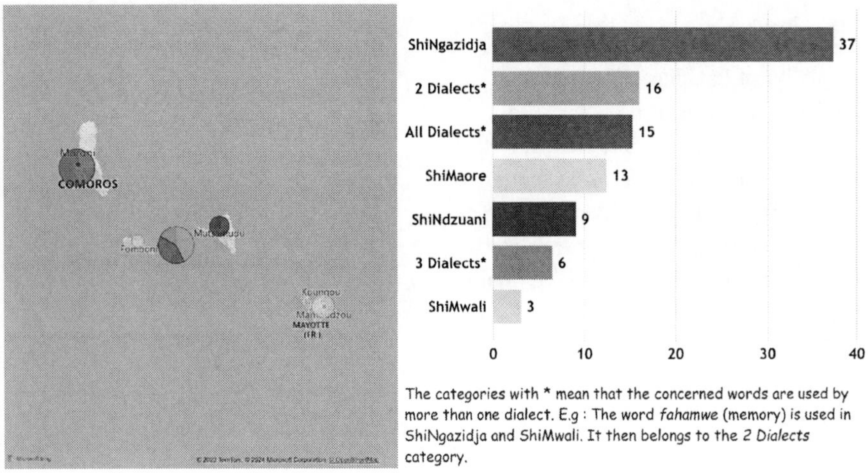

Figure 1: Dialects Varieties.

guage to leverage NLP solutions on low-resource scenarios. The rest of this study is structured as follows: We first present in Section 2 notable previous works in these dialects, then we describe in Section 3 the data collection methodologies that we adopted to collect the different datasets, Section 4 shows the experiments that we conducted to evaluate the constructed datasets while Section 5 presents the future work that could result from this study following a final conclusion.

2 Related Work

One thing to know about these works is that only few of them use NLP approaches and the data used or resulted from them are not publicly available. This make it more interesting the data retrieving and the resorting to recent NLP solutions in order to contribute to the digital representation of these dialects, hoping that this could be helpful in different upcoming use cases by researchers, institutions, companies or particulars.

2.1 Old Resources

In this section, we compile studies that have significantly influenced the advancement of Comorian dialects processing. These earlier resources predominantly employed linguistic and manual methodologies, primarily focusing on proposing structural frameworks for the written forms of these dialects and translations into foreign languages like French:

- **The Kamar-Eddine system**: In the 1960s, as described in (Lafon, 2007), Said Kamar-Eddine proposed a writting system of Comorian dialects using Arabic scripts. This notable work allowed several people to learn how to write their language and is used until now.
- **French-Comorian dictionnaries**: These dictionaries were published in 1979 (Sacleux et al., 1979) and 1997 (Chamanga, 1997). Other initiatives like ORELC followed and allow until now many people to learn these idioms.
- **Introduction to Shikomori**: A structural grammar books (Ahmed-Chamanga, 2010; Chamanga and national de documentation et de recherche scientifique , Comoros) written by the linguist Mohamed Ahmed Chamanga.

2.2 Modern NLP-specific Resources

After the democratization occuring since these recent years of solutions based on recent information technologies, the necessity to resort to these approaches for low-resource languages has become apparent. For Comorian dialects, among the few solutions that consider them, we emphasize:

- **Machine Translation dataset**: To the best of our knowledge, the work described in (Abdourahamane et al., 2016) is one of the first attempts to manage Comorian dialects through NLP. The corpus was created based on a Transfer Learning from Swahili due to the similarities between these languages.
- **Language Identification**: In (Adebara et al., 2022), Comorian dialects were added to a massive corpus for Language Identification in several African Languages.

3 Datasets

Ensuring the quality of data has always been at the center of concerns when designing AI solutions, especially in NLP (Sonntag, 2004; Nesca, 2021). This is more important in low-resource scenarios to the point that before trying to understand which model architecture could be more appropriate for a given task in a given language, ensuring quality and sufficiency of data is crucial.

Following the experiments conducted in (Artetxe et al., 2022), interesting propositions were advanced. In fact, the experiments consisted of measuring the impact of focusing on data processing in the Basque language. They first estimated with native Basque speaker the quality of three datasets (mC4, CC100 and EusCrawl) then trained different models (Topic Classification, Sentiment Analysis, Stance Detection, Named Entity Recognition and Question Answering) with the same parameters for each dataset. One of the main conclusions resulted from this study was that in language understanding on low-resource scenario, the quantity of data could be more helpful than its quality, even if this latter is a crucial feature to take into account when managing natural language.

We consider two observations (the data quality and quantity importance) when constructing Comorian datasets for the aim to manage different NLP tasks. For that we resort to different methodologies depending on the task, the nature of data and from each source the data was initially retrieved. We also investigate the effectiveness of using advance processing approaches like transfer learning from close languages and data augmentation in possible cases.

3.1 Lexicons

3.1.1 Lexicon Processing Pipeline

The pipeline described in Figure 2 aims to process a given lexicon in order to make usable in different downstream task like Sentiment Analysis (SA) and Part-Of-Speech (POS) tagging.

To enhance SA tasks, we employ pseudo-labeling using the Valence Aware Dictionary for sEntiment Reasoning (VADER) (Hutto and Gilbert, 2014). This is an English lexicon-based SA model constructed using existing human-validated sentiment lexicons, to which additional lexicons used in Social Media, such as emoticons, slang, etc., were added. The annotation was done through a wisdom-of-the-crowd approach, involving human raters who rated each lexicon on a scale ranging from -4 (extremely negative) to 4 (extremely positive), with 0 indicating a neutral sentiment. The average sentiment of the words within a given text is considered as the sentiment of that text. VADER has proven to be more efficient than many state-of-the-art models.

If, instead of utilizing a lexicon with English translations, we have a different language, such as French, two approaches can be employed: adopting a method similar to VADER for this language or translating the lexicon into English and then applying VADER. For instance, when dealing with French, we opt for the latter approach due to the absence of a cost-effective solution in lexicon-based SA. Our suggestion is to leverage NLLB (Team et al., 2022) for translating French words into English. NLLB, short for No Language Left Behind, is an extensive multilingual machine translation model that supports pairs of 200 languages. We simply configure French as the input language and English as the output in its parameters.

The last module of the pipeline comes into play to complete the outputs and to enrich the dataset. In fact, at the end of the previous modules, we observe that some words are not mapped to a tag. We retrieve some of these tags using the Swahili POS dataset proposed in (Dione et al., 2023) by simply searching the non-mapped words in this dataset. Moreover, since in the dictionary names, places and punctuation are nonexistent, we add to the dataset all the corresponding entries in the Swahili dataset.

3.1.2 Bahari Foundation

We use here the ShiNgazidja-English dictionary (Thrower) written by Bahari Foundation. After transforming the PDF file into text, we apply several processing procedures. In fact, for some entries, we can found the three particularities: the existence of words variants (madjana, madjanaza, etc.), variant spellings (djando $\rightarrow$ mdjando) or implosive consonants (ɗ and ɓ). For word plurals and variant spellings, we simply consider them as new entries that taking the same translations as their associated words. As for the implosive consonants, we add new entries by just replacing them with their similar letters (ɗ $\rightarrow$ d, ɓ $\rightarrow$ b). In fact, despite the fact that these consonants are the correct spellings, they are infrequently used. For example, they are not used in the JW datasets (Section 3.2.1). We then consider the two orthographies, with and

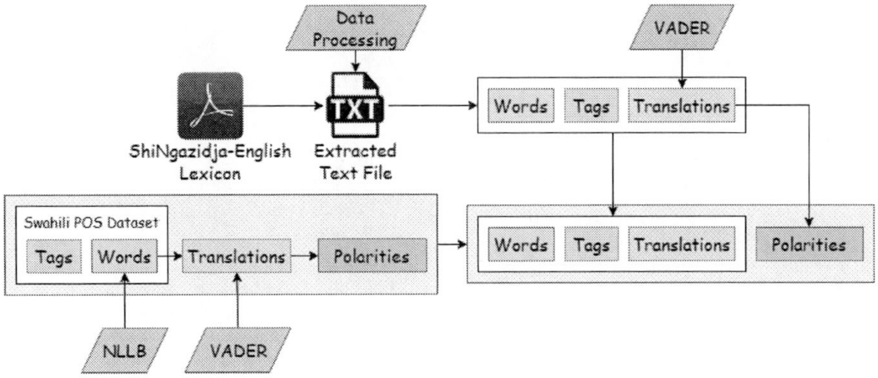

Figure 2: Lexicon Processing Pipeline.

without the implosive consonants.

Finally, in Table 1, a sample of the dictionary can be found. The lexicon contains three columns: the ShiNgazidja word, the Noun Class, and the English translation. In the latter, we can find the POS of the word such as adjective, adverb, noun, etc. We separate the POS tags from the English words, and then we apply the pipeline to these to generate the sentiments.

3.1.3 Ylangue e-langue

Ylange e-langue is an online ShiMaore-French lexicon[2]. We manually concatenate all the entries into the same text file then we apply the previous pipeline. We use NLLB to translate the French lexicon into English so that we can apply VADER and proceed to the rest of the pipeline.

3.2 Parallel Texts

3.2.1 Jehovah Witnesses

For Machine Translation, we retrieve data from the Jehovah Witnesses website[3]. ShiNgazidja and ShiMaore are one of the languages present in this platform. We can find there different PDF files containing texts in these two dialects. We can also find the French corresponding PDF (a sentence-by-sentence translation) when filtering on French data. After converting the documents into text files, we chunk the dialectal and French texts into sentences by considering dots as separators. Finally, we map each sentence to its French translation and we end with approximately 4,000 sentences for ShiNgazidja and 2,000 sentences for ShiMaore.

[2] http://ylangue.free.fr/lexique/index-french/main.htm

[3] https://www.jw.org

3.2.2 Bloom Library

The Bloom Library (Leong et al., 2022) is a multilingual dataset covering 363 languages and 32 language families. An educational web platform resulted from this initiative, in which 15 ShiNdzuani books[4] translated into English can be found. We concatenate the content of these books and we finally end with a corpus of 1,000 sentences with their translations.

3.2.3 Bible.com

The Bible.com website[5] contains all of the bible books translated into several languages including ShiMaore. In the website there are the possibility to visualize at the same time the bible translated verse by verse in two languages as we can see in Figure 3. We use Selenium[6] to perform bitext mining then we end with a total of 7,643 verses.

3.3 Speech Recognition

The Pangloss Collection[7] is a project initiated to archive speech documents in different languages with a special focus on the low-resourced ones. The initiative covers 43 countries and contains 1,120 hours of audios spread over 240 languages and dialects. The corpus contains 1h30min of ShiMaore audios and 12min of ShiNgazidja with their transcriptions. We apply a speech processing pipeline (See Fig. 4) to make the dataset easily manageable using two task: (a) audio segmentation and down-sampling. In fact, the audio transcriptions are stored in XML files with the timestamps of

[4] https://bloomlibrary.org/language:wni

[5] https://www.bible.com/

[6] https://selenium-python.readthedocs.io/

[7] https://pangloss.cnrs.fr/?mode=normal&lang=en

Table 1: ShiNgazidja-English Dictionary.

ShiNgazidja	Noun Class	English
-a ɗaima	-	Adj. eternal
-a ɗini	-	Adj. religious
-a ɗiwara	-	Adj. round
-adabisha	15	V. to correct a child, to punish
-adabishiwa	15	V. to be punished
-adhini	15	(ar.) V. to call to prayer
-adiana	15	V. to promise
-airisha	15	V. to postpone, to delay, to bargain
-alfuɓesha	15	(fr. alphabétiser) V. to teach literacy
(...)	(...)	(...)
djana (madjana)	5-6	N. one-hundred (number)
djanaza (madjanaza)	5-6	N. board for carrying dead body
djando (madjando) / mdjando (midjando)	5-6, 3-4	N. deceit

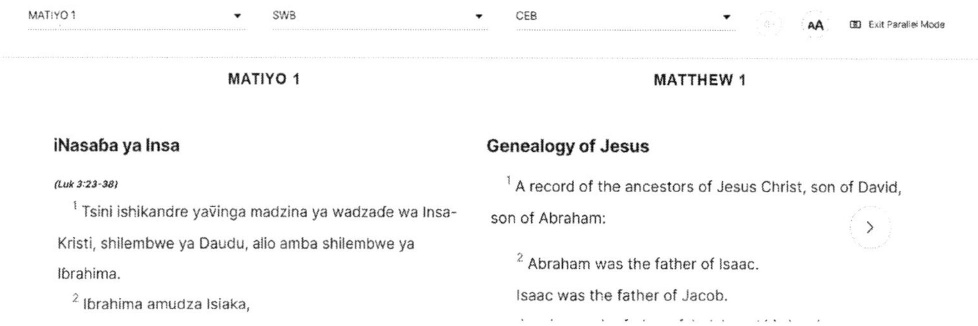

Figure 3: ShiMaore and English translations of the Bible.

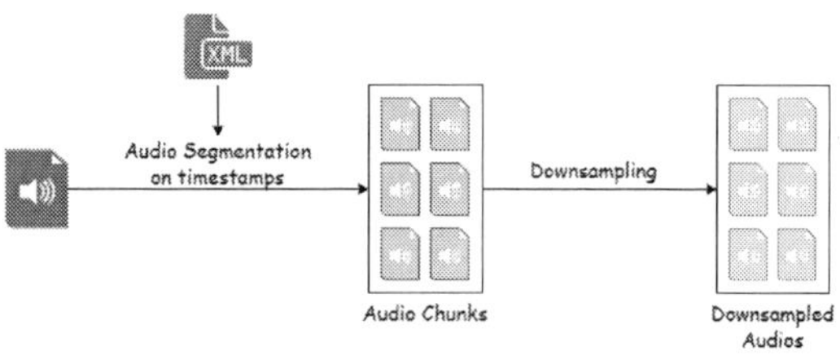

Figure 4: Speech Processing.

each sentence. We then use The AudioSegment[8] module of the Python package Pydub to segment the audios into different chunks. The final dataset contains 1.9 hours and 800 sentences.

3.4 Data-Centric Experiments

3.4.1 Sentiment Pseudo-Labeling

Here, we are proposing to create from scratch supervised datasets using transfer learning from various existing works. For that we consider the Jehovah Witnesses and Bloom Library datasets. Additionally, we employ an approach close to the one used in the lexicons to obtain the sentiments associated to each sentence using VADER. But since VADER works only on English, we translate before pseudo-labeling the French translations in the Jehovah Witnesses dataset into English.

One thing to notice here is that the choice of VADER was because of its ability to detect sentiment on single words. But when dealing with long texts, attention-based model like BERT perform generally well (Devlin et al., 2019) precisely because of its ability to understand the text. For that we use an SA fine-tuned BERT model[9] to detect the polarities of the English translated sentences. We finally consider the average sentiments between VADER and BERT for sentence labeling.

3.4.2 Audio Data Augmentation

In Automatic Speech Recognition (ASR), Data Augmentation on audio allows to better improve the models performances (Rebai et al., 2017) especially in low-resourced languages (Bartelds et al., 2023). We use the SpeechBrain toolkit (Ravanelli

[8] https://audiosegment.readthedocs.io/en/latest/audiosegment.html

[9] https://huggingface.co/nlptown/bert-base-multilingual-uncased-sentiment

et al., 2021) to augment the speech dataset that we constructed by corrupting the audio following four steps:

- **Speed Perturbation**: We change a bit the sampling rate to make the audio a bit slower or faster than the original audio.
- **Time Dropout**: This consists of replacing random chunks within the raw waveform of audio by zeros. The idea is to allow the Neural Network to better process the data even if such information are not found.
- **Frequency Dropout**: Here, the zeros are added into the frequency domain.
- **Clipping**: It is a saturation effect that is added to the signal.

3.5 Data Availability

We leave all the datasets that we have constructed throughout this work available to the public. They can be found on Table 2.

4 Evaluations

4.1 Evaluation Metrics

We assess the Text and Token Classification model performances using these classical four metrics classification problems: Accuracy, F1-score, Recall and Precision. For ASR, we resort to the Word Error Rate (WER) and Character Error Rate (CER). WER measures the percentage of word errors in the generated transcription compared to a reference transcription. It is calculated by comparing the total number of substitutions, deletions, and insertions needed to align the generated to the reference transcriptions. CER operates similarly but measures the percentage of character errors rather than word errors. It is often used to assess the quality of transcriptions on a character-by-character basis.

4.2 Models

We conduct all the training model experiments in Google Colaboratory[10] on a machine with 12GB of RAM, powered by a Tesla T4 GPU. Since the default data storage is not persistent, we connect the environment to a Google Drive storage. During the model training process, we first shuffle the datasets (sentences, words, or audio) before splitting into training and testing sets. We then set 80% for training and we test on the remaining 20%.

4.2.1 Language Identification

We use here the dataset described in 3.2.1, not for a Machine Translation task, but rather for a two-classes classification for Language Identification purpose. We compare three models: (a) mBERT, the multilingual version of BERT, trained on 104 languages and introduced in the original BERT paper (Devlin et al., 2019), (b) AfriBERTa (Ogueji et al., 2021), a model designed to understand several African languages and (c) BantuLM (Abdou Mohamed et al., 2023b), a multilingual model oriented towards Bantu languages.

On Table 3, we find the results obtained at the end of the three experiments. Indeed, we see that the BantuLM model trained specifically on Bantu languages returns better performance than the other two, especially mBERTs. This could partially confirms the hypothesis according to which the transfer of knowledge between different languages is quite important when dealing with closely related languages.

4.2.2 Sentiment Analysis

Our approach is inspired by previous work that has used language models based on BERT to improve the state of the art in SA on African languages (Martin et al., 2021; Muhammad et al., 2023). We actually apply the pseudo labeling methodology introduced in 3.4.1 on parallel corpora. We end up with 15,000 sentences and words accompanied by their polarities.

Finally, we train a multilingual SA model that enhance at the same time all the dialects. Table 4 summarizes the final results of the three approaches.

4.2.3 Part-Of-Speech Tagging

To establish the Part-Of-Speech (POS) Tagging experiment in ShiNgazidja, we use two datasets described in the previous sections: the Jehovah Witnesses sentences and the Bahari Foundation lexicon. In POS, the dataset must have several sentences with their tags. For that we use the python-Levenshtein[11] library to match the lexicon entries to each word in the sentences. In fact, the idea is to find the most similar words in the sentences to the ones in the lexicon. For the couples in which we have a mapping ratio more than 80% we attribute the lexicon tag to the word in the sentence and we attribute a default tag (*"n"*, as in *"noun"*) for the rest. The final dataset contains 23,454 tokens structured as presented in Table 5.

[10] https://colab.research.google.com/

[11] https://pypi.org/project/python-Levenshtein/

Table 2: Data Repositories.

URL	Type	Dialects	Size
ShiNgazidja Lexicon	Lexicon	ShiNgazidja	5,714 words
ShiMaore Lexicon	Lexicon	ShiMaore	2,161 words
ShiKomori Sentiment	Raw text	ShiMaore, ShiNgazidja and ShiNdzuani	17,419 sentences+words
ShiKomori ASR	Audios+Transcriptions	ShiMaore, ShiNgazidja	1.9 hours
ShiKomori ASR Augmented	Audios+Transcriptions	ShiMaore, ShiNgazidja	9 hours

Table 3: Language Identification Results.

Model	Accuracy	F1-score	Recall	Precision
mBERT	0.940574	0.932762	0.928240	0.937825
AfriBERTa	0.945403	0.940489	0.926131	0.948652
BantuLM	**0.963798**	**0.959927**	**0.957621**	**0.962378**

Table 4: SA Results.

Model	Accuracy	F1-score	Recall	Precision
mBERT	0.7623	0.7251	0.7227	0.7388
AfriBERTa	**0.7793**	**0.7577**	**0.7580**	**0.7592**
BantuLM	0.7704	0.7366	0.7342	0.7511

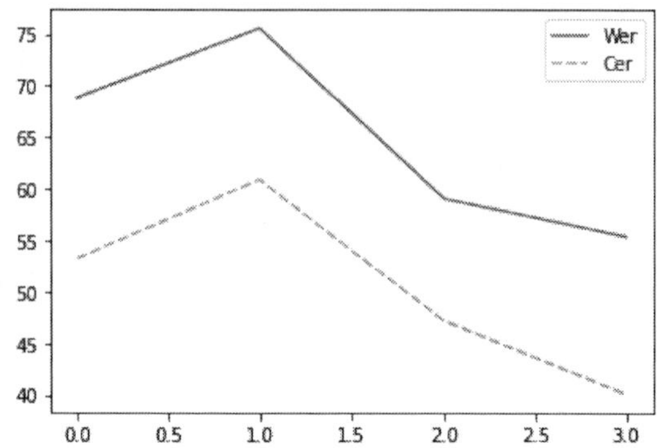

Figure 5: WER and CER Evolutions during Training.

We then fine-tune BantuLM for a Token Classification task. Table 6 resumes the results obtained throw these experiments. Here, we observe once again that AfriBERTa and BantuLM perform slightly better than mBERT. One thing to notice is that, unlike sentence classification tasks such as Language Identification, the POS tagging process depends particularly on the tokens used in the pre-training of the model. This is because of the fact that out-of-vocabulary words impacts severely the tags recognition (Horsmann and Zesch, 2016). For that, the absence of Comorian dialects in the pre-training data of the three models definitely plays a major role in the token classification. This is why in the examples presented in the Table 6 we can observe wrong words truncation.

4.2.4 Speech Recognition

For Speech Recognition, we also resort to multilingual models to leverage the state-of-the-art NLP on low-resource languages. Notable previous works have used similar approaches on several African languages (Abdou Mohamed et al., 2023a) or on specific language family like Bantu (Elamin et al., 2023). The first approach is based on Wav2vec (Babu et al., 2021), a cross-lingual pre-trained ASR model, while the second resort to Conformer (Gulati et al., 2020). These both models were initially designed like textual pre-trained language model to enhance several languages including ones that are not present on the pre-training corpus.

In our case, after proceeding to Data Augmentation, we use Whisper (Radford et al., 2022), one of the most current innovative ASR solutions. More precisely, we use *whisper-small*[12], a distilled checkpoint that has 244 millions parameters and which is trained on 680,000 hours of labeled data for the aim of enhancing multiple tasks in Speech Processing like ASR, Speech Translation or Speech Generation. Despite the fact that the checkpoint is multilingual, it was not initially trained to enhance Comorian dialects. But Swahili was in the pre-training corpus. When choosing the language on fine-tuning, we then select Swahili.

The WER and CER evolutions shown in Figure 5 are quite interesting knowing the size of the data. In fact, the high final WER of 55.42% is an expected score because of the fact that the transcribed texts are not sufficient to facilitate the model generalization. Indeed, the training dataset has a very limited vocabulary composed of only 2,216 unique words, which leads to this high score. Unlike that, we observe a low final CER of 40.11% suggesting that the model has the ability to detect the granular sounds within the audio.

[12]https://huggingface.co/openai/whisper-small

Table 5: POS Tokens Frequencies.

adv	adj	v	n	loc	prep	int	plac	conj	pron
Adverb	Adjective	Verb	Noun	Locution	Preposition	Interjection	Place	Conjunction	Pronoun
866	1,788	6,669	11,161	96	677	9	960	1,195	33

5 Conclusion and Future Work

The work presented in this article had two main objectives: contributing to the community by proposing datasets that can be used to advance the state-of-the-art on under-represented languages, particularly Comorian dialects and assessing the impact in terms of transfer learning on different pre-trained models. We evaluated the constructed datasets on four tasks: Language Identification, SA, Part-of-Speech Tagging and Speech Recognition. But before we conducted Data-Centric experiments consisting of Pseudo-Labeling and Data Augmentation respectively for SA and Speech Recognition.

Promising results have been obtained, opening the door to the representation of Comorian dialects in the field of Artificial Intelligence. However, a long way remains to be covered in order to make this representation more effective. It would be interesting in future work to experiment with other areas that we have not been able to cover due to lack of data such as Automatic Translation, Speech Generation, etc. For the downstream tasks already supported, we propose in future work to see how we could best refine them by facilitating their generalization. This could be made possible by enriching and diversifying the data or by experimenting with other models.

References

Naira Abdou Mohamed, Imade Benelallam, Anass Allak, and Kamel Gaanoun. 2023a. Multilingual speech recognition initiative for african languages.

Naira Abdou Mohamed, Imade Benelallam, Abdessalam Bahafid, and Zakarya Erraji. 2023b. Bantulm: Enhancing cross-lingual learning in the bantu language family.

Moneim Abdourahamane, Christian Boitet, Valérie Bellynck, Lingxiao Wang, and Hervé Blanchon. 2016. Construction d'un corpus parallèle français-comorien en utilisant de la TA français-swahili. In *TALAf (Traitement Automatique des Langues africaines)*, Paris, France.

Ife Adebara, AbdelRahim Elmadany, Muhammad Abdul-Mageed, and Alcides Alcoba Inciarte. 2022. Afrolid: A neural language identification tool for african languages.

M. Ahmed-Chamanga. 2010. *Introduction à la grammaire structurale du comorien: Le shiNgazidja*. Number vol. 1 in Ya Mkobe publications. Komedi.

Mikel Artetxe, Itziar Aldabe, Rodrigo Agerri, Olatz Perez-de Viñaspre, and Aitor Soroa. 2022. Does corpus quality really matter for low-resource languages? In *Proceedings of the 2022 Conference on Empirical Methods in Natural Language Processing*, pages 7383–7390, Abu Dhabi, United Arab Emirates. Association for Computational Linguistics.

Atlasocio. Classement des langues bantoues (et autres langues bantoïdes) par nombre de locuteurs. `https://atlasocio.com/classements/langues/familles/classement-langues-bantoues-par-nombre-locuteurs-total-monde.php`. (Accessed on 11/06/2023).

Arun Babu, Changhan Wang, Andros Tjandra, Kushal Lakhotia, Qiantong Xu, Naman Goyal, Kritika Singh, Patrick von Platen, Yatharth Saraf, Juan Pino, Alexei Baevski, Alexis Conneau, and Michael Auli. 2021. Xls-r: Self-supervised cross-lingual speech representation learning at scale.

Martijn Bartelds, Nay San, Bradley McDonnell, Dan Jurafsky, and Martijn Wieling. 2023. Making more of little data: Improving low-resource automatic speech recognition using data augmentation.

M.A. Chamanga. 1997. *Dictionnaire français-comorien: dialecte shindzuani*. Archipel des Comores. CEROI-INALCO.

M.A. Chamanga and Centre national de documentation et de recherche scientifique (Comoros). 2010. *Introduction à la grammaire structurale du comorien: Le shiNdzuani*. Introduction à la grammaire structurale du comorien. Komedit.

Mohamed Ahmed Chamanga. 2022. ShiKomori, the bantu language of the comoros: Status and perspectives. In *Handbook of Language Policy and Education in Countries of the Southern African Development Community (SADC)*, pages 79–98. BRILL.

Jacob Devlin, Ming-Wei Chang, Kenton Lee, and Kristina Toutanova. 2019. Bert: Pre-training of deep bidirectional transformers for language understanding.

Cheikh M. Bamba Dione, David Adelani, Peter Nabende, Jesujoba Alabi, Thapelo Sindane,

Table 6: Part-Of-Speech Tagging Results (n, prep, v, plac, conj).

Model	Accuracy	F1-score	Recall	Precision	Example: mister said forced the child to go to school to learn
mBERT	0.955857	0.937806	0.930366	0.945369	mze said ha trendeza ye moi na yende shi yoni ili yende ya some
AfriBERTa	**0.971986**	**0.967411**	**0.965182**	**0.969650**	mze said ha trende za ye mo ina yende shiyo ni ili yende ya some
BantuLM	0.957343	0.937451	0.924731	0.950526	mze said hu trendeza ye moin a yende shiyoni ili yende ya some

Happy Buzaaba, Shamsuddeen Hassan Muhammad, Chris Chinenye Emezue, Perez Ogayo, Anuoluwapo Aremu, Catherine Gitau, Derguene Mbaye, Jonathan Mukiibi, Blessing Sibanda, Bonaventure F. P. Dossou, Andiswa Bukula, Rooweither Mabuya, Allahsera Auguste Tapo, Edwin Munkoh-Buabeng, victoire Memdjokam Koagne, Fatoumata Ouoba Kabore, Amelia Taylor, Godson Kalipe, Tebogo Macucwa, Vukosi Marivate, Tajuddeen Gwadabe, Mboning Tchiaze Elvis, Ikechukwu Onyenwe, Gratien Atindogbe, Tolulope Adelani, Idris Akinade, Olanrewaju Samuel, Marien Nahimana, Théogène Musabeyezu, Emile Niyomutabazi, Ester Chimhenga, Kudzai Gotosa, Patrick Mizha, Apelete Agbolo, Seydou Traore, Chinedu Uchechukwu, Aliyu Yusuf, Muhammad Abdullahi, and Dietrich Klakow. 2023. Masakhapos: Part-of-speech tagging for typologically diverse african languages.

Moayad Elamin, Yonas Chanie, Paul Ewuzie, and Samuel Rutunda. 2023. Multilingual automatic speech recognition for kinyarwanda, swahili, and luganda: Advancing ASR in select east african languages. In *4th Workshop on African Natural Language Processing*.

Anmol Gulati, James Qin, Chung-Cheng Chiu, Niki Parmar, Yu Zhang, Jiahui Yu, Wei Han, Shibo Wang, Zhengdong Zhang, Yonghui Wu, and Ruoming Pang. 2020. Conformer: Convolution-augmented transformer for speech recognition.

Tobias Horsmann and Torsten Zesch. 2016. LTL-UDE \$@\$ EmpiriST 2015: Tokenization and PoS tagging of social media text. In *Proceedings of the 10th Web as Corpus Workshop*. Association for Computational Linguistics.

C. Hutto and Eric Gilbert. 2014. VADER: A parsimonious rule-based model for sentiment analysis of social media text. *Proceedings of the International AAAI Conference on Web and Social Media*, 8(1):216–225.

Michel Lafon. 2007. Le système Kamar-Eddine : une tentative originale d'écriture du comorien en graphie arabe. *Ya Mkobe*, 14-15:29–48.

Colin Leong, Joshua Nemecek, Jacob Mansdorfer, Anna Filighera, Abraham Owodunni, and Daniel Whitenack. 2022. Bloom library: Multimodal datasets in 300+ languages for a variety of downstream tasks. In *Proceedings of the 2022 Conference on Empirical Methods in Natural Language Processing*, pages 8608–8621, Abu Dhabi, United Arab Emirates. Association for Computational Linguistics.

Gati L. Martin, Medard E. Mswahili, and Young-Seob Jeong. 2021. Sentiment classification in swahili language using multilingual bert.

Serva Maurizio and Pasquini Michele. 2021. The sabaki languages of comoros | serva | indian ocean review of science and technology (iorst). http://www.iorst.net/index.php/paper/view/10. (Accessed on 11/06/2023).

Shamsuddeen Hassan Muhammad, Idris Abdulmumin, Abinew Ali Ayele, Nedjma Ousidhoum, David Ifeoluwa Adelani, Seid Muhie Yimam, Ibrahim Sa'id Ahmad, Meriem Beloucif, Saif M. Mohammad, Sebastian Ruder, Oumaima Hourrane, Pavel Brazdil, Felermino Dário Mário António Ali, Davis David, Salomey Osei, Bello Shehu Bello, Falalu Ibrahim, Tajuddeen Gwadabe, Samuel Rutunda, Tadesse Belay, Wendimu Baye Messelle, Hailu Beshada Balcha, Sisay Adugna Chala, Hagos Tesfahun Gebremichael, Bernard Opoku, and Steven Arthur. 2023. Afrisenti: A twitter sentiment analysis benchmark for african languages.

Marcello Nesca. 2021. *Measuring the quality of unstructured text in routinely collected electronic health data: a review and application*. Ph.D. thesis.

Kelechi Ogueji, Yuxin Zhu, and Jimmy Lin. 2021. Small data? no problem! exploring the viability of pretrained multilingual language models for low-resourced languages. In *Proceedings of the 1st Workshop on Multilingual Representation Learning*, pages 116–126, Punta Cana, Dominican Republic. Association for Computational Linguistics.

Matúš Pikuliak, Marián Šimko, and Mária Bieliková. 2021. Cross-lingual learning for text processing: A survey. *Expert Systems with Applications*, 165:113765.

Alec Radford, Jong Wook Kim, Tao Xu, Greg Brockman, Christine McLeavey, and Ilya Sutskever. 2022. Robust speech recognition via large-scale weak supervision.

Mirco Ravanelli, Titouan Parcollet, Peter Plantinga, Aku Rouhe, Samuele Cornell, Loren Lugosch, Cem Subakan, Nauman Dawalatabad, Abdelwahab Heba, Jianyuan Zhong, Ju-Chieh Chou, Sung-Lin Yeh, Szu-Wei Fu, Chien-Feng Liao, Elena Rastorgueva, François Grondin, William Aris, Hwidong Na, Yan Gao, Renato De Mori, and Yoshua Bengio. 2021. Speechbrain: A general-purpose speech toolkit.

Ilyes Rebai, Yessine BenAyed, Walid Mahdi, and Jean-Pierre Lorré. 2017. Improving speech recognition using data augmentation and acoustic model fusion. *Procedia Computer Science*, 112:316–322.

C. Sacleux, M.A. Chamanga, and N.J. Gueunier. 1979. *Le dictionnaire comorien-français et français-comorien*. Number vol. 1 in Asie et Monde Insulindien Series. SELAF.

Daniel Sonntag. 2004. Assessing the quality of natural language text data. In *GI Jahrestagung*.

NLLB Team, Marta R. Costa-jussà, James Cross, Onur Çelebi, Maha Elbayad, Kenneth Heafield, Kevin Heffernan, Elahe Kalbassi, Janice Lam, Daniel Licht, Jean Maillard, Anna Sun, Skyler Wang, Guillaume Wenzek, Al Youngblood, Bapi Akula, Loic Barrault, Gabriel Mejia Gonzalez, Prangthip Hansanti, John Hoffman, Semarley Jarrett, Kaushik Ram Sadagopan, Dirk Rowe, Shannon Spruit, Chau Tran, Pierre Andrews, Necip Fazil Ayan, Shruti Bhosale, Sergey Edunov, Angela Fan, Cynthia Gao, Vedanuj Goswami, Francisco Guzmán, Philipp Koehn, Alexandre Mourachko, Christophe Ropers, Safiyyah Saleem, Holger Schwenk, and Jeff Wang. 2022. No language left behind: Scaling human-centered machine translation.

Amirhossein Tebbifakhr, Matteo Negri, and Marco Turchi. 2020. Machine-oriented NMT adaptation for zero-shot NLP tasks: Comparing the usefulness of close and distant languages. In *Proceedings of the 7th Workshop on NLP for Similar Languages, Varieties and Dialects*, pages 36–46, Barcelona, Spain (Online). International Committee on Computational Linguistics (ICCL).

Joshua Thrower. Shingazidja english dictionary. `https://fr.scribd.com/document/619345660/ShiNgazidja-English-Dictionary`. (Accessed on 11/06/2023).

Ashish Vaswani, Noam Shazeer, Niki Parmar, Jakob Uszkoreit, Llion Jones, Aidan N Gomez, Ł ukasz Kaiser, and Illia Polosukhin. 2017. Attention is all you need. In *Advances in Neural Information Processing Systems*, volume 30. Curran Associates, Inc.

Worldometers. Population by country (2023) - worldometer. `https://www.worldometers.info/world-population/population-by-country/`. (Accessed on 11/06/2023).

Prompting Implicit Discourse Relation Annotation

Frances Yung[1] **Mansoor Ahmad**[1] **Merel Scholman**[1,2] **Vera Demberg**[2]
[1]Saarland University, Saarbrücken, Germany
[2]Utrecht University, Utrecht, Netherlands
{frances, mahmad, m.c.j.scholman, vera}@coli.uni-saarland.de

Abstract

Pre-trained large language models, such as ChatGPT, archive outstanding performance in various reasoning tasks without supervised training and were found to have outperformed crowdsourcing workers. Nonetheless, ChatGPT's performance in the task of implicit discourse relation classification, prompted by a standard multiple-choice question, is still far from satisfactory and considerably inferior to state-of-the-art supervised approaches. This work investigates several proven prompting techniques to improve ChatGPT's recognition of discourse relations. In particular, we experimented with breaking down the classification task that involves numerous abstract labels into smaller subtasks. Nonetheless, experiment results show that the inference accuracy hardly changes even with sophisticated prompt engineering, suggesting that implicit discourse relation classification is not yet resolvable under zero-shot or few-shot settings.

1 Introduction

Pre-trained language models have demonstrated superior performance in various NLP tasks for years, and recently prompt-tuning instead of fine-tuning has become the dominant framework to make efficient use of large language models (LLMs). LLMs such as ChatGPT have demonstrated human-level performance in various reasoning tasks under zero-shot or few-shot settings using natural language prompts as inputs (see e.g., OpenAI, 2023; Bang et al., 2023). This has led to a wave of research in prompt engineering to elicit the prediction potential of LLMs (such as Wei et al., 2022; Kojima et al., 2022).

In order to create metadata for textual analysis or to train models for specific NLP tasks, researchers have been relying on the annotation performed by trained annotators or crowdsourced workers. Recently, ChatGPT was shown to outperform crowdsourced workers in annotating political topics, affiliation, and policy frames (Gilardi et al., 2023; Törnberg, 2023). However, it is not yet clear whether a similar prompting approach can also be successful for classifying what discourse relation holds between two text spans. Discourse relations (DRs) are semantic-pragmatic links between clauses and sentences. They can be explicitly marked by discourse connectives (DCs), such as *however* and *in addition*, or they can be inferred from the text without relying on a specific marker – such cases are referred to as implicit relations. For example, there is a `causal` relation between the following sentences: *Mary lost her keys. Therefore, she could not enter her office.*, and the same relation can still be inferred without the DC *therefore*.

Discourse relation analysis is useful for various downstream tasks, such as summarization (Xu et al., 2020; Dong et al., 2021) and relation extraction (Tang et al., 2021), and discourse-annotated data serves as the basis of various linguistic research (e.g. Sanders and Spooren, 2010). However, classifying implicit DRs involves cognitive processing that is difficult even for humans in different languages (Oza et al., 2009; Zhou and Xue, 2012; Poláková et al., 2013; Zeyrek et al., 2020; Hoek et al., 2021) and poses a challenge for NLP (e.g., 64.58% accuracy and 49.03% F1 on PDTB 2.0 in Chan et al., 2023b), even with powerful LLMs.

Chan et al. (2023a) evaluated ChatGPT's ability to infer implicit DRs. They used a multiple-choice prompt that lists all options of DR labels and included in-context samples. They found that pairing the DR options with typical DCs improves the performance. However, even then, accuracy is still far behind (e.g., 24.54% accuracy and 16.20% F1 on PDTB 2.0) the performance of state-of-the-art supervised models. There could be several reasons for this: the chosen prompts might not be optimal, the LLM may not be able to deal well with a 14-way classification, or it may fail to build good representations of discourse relations.

Proceedings of The 18th Linguistic Annotation Workshop (LAW-XVIII), pages 150–165
March 22, 2024

The current work tests whether alternative prompt designs, using formulations that have been shown to work well in crowdsourced annotation tasks with untrained humans, can produce more accurate implicit DR annotation. First, we replicate the methodology used by Chan et al. (2023a) with the latest *gpt-4* model and analyse the strengths and weaknesses of the predictions. We then explore the benefits of breaking down the multi-way classification task into individual prompts. We hypothesize that this might be beneficial because a) it reduces a choice between 14 options per prompt into multiple prompts that each contain a binary choice and b) because implicit DRs are inherently ambiguous and multiple interpretations are often possible depending on the reader's perspective and context (Rohde et al., 2016; Scholman et al., 2022).

We however found that sophisticated prompt strategies did not improve the performance of ChatGPT's inference of implicit DRs and the accuracy still largely lags behind the state-of-the-art supervised models. This suggests that the implicit DR recognition task is not yet solvable under a zero-shot or few-shot setting.

2 Related Work

2.1 Lexicalized DR annotation

DCs are natural language signals for DRs, and have been used by annotators to classify originally implicit DRs. For example, the DC *nevertheless* can be inserted between the two text spans that make up a DR (known as the *Arg1* and *Arg2*) to indicate a `concession` relation. This approach has been used in the creation of manually annotated resources including the Penn Discourse Treebank (PDTB, Prasad et al., 2008, 2019) and DiscoGeM (Scholman et al., 2022).

A complicating factor in the annotation of DRs is the fine-grainedness between DR types. Compared with typical text classification tasks such as entailment and stance detection, DR classification involves a considerably larger range of labels, making the task particularly challenging. For example, the DR framework PDTB (Prasad et al., 2008, 2019) defines 36 DR sense labels arranged in a three-level hierarchy, which can be lexicalized by one of 184 connectives. Previous annotation efforts for implicit relations report inter-annotator agreement scores of κ=0.58 (Hoek et al., 2021) and κ=0.47 (Zikánová et al., 2019) between expert annotators, and κ=0.55 between aggregated crowdsourced and expert annotation (Scholman et al., 2022).

Untrained human annotators also struggle when given a large choice of different relations or connectives. The DiscoGeM corpus was therefore annotated using a "two-step DC insertion method" (Yung et al., 2019), where the crowd annotators first freely type a linking phrase that represents the relation between two consecutive sentences and then disambiguate this intuitive choice by selecting from a list of DC options dynamically generated based on the first DC. This approach lexicalizes DRs into natural language for untrained workers who are not familiar with DR labels.

While general-purpose generative LLMs such as ChatGPT might have seen discourse relation labels as part of their training data, they could nevertheless profit from a connective-based annotation approach, as their exposure to connectives in natural language is much higher. We thus evaluate the two-step DC insertion method on generative LLMs.

2.2 Supervised models for DR recognition

Given that explicit as well as originally implicit relations are annotated with a connective in the PDTB, earlier work has explored the use of both explicit and annotated DCs for implicit DR recognition (e.g., Marcu and Echihabi, 2002; Sporleder and Lascarides, 2008; Xu et al., 2012; Rutherford and Xue, 2015; Ji et al., 2015). In combination with modern LLMs, DC prediction was found to be an effective sub-task for which the LLMs are fine-tuned to identify implicit DRs (Shi and Demberg, 2019; Kishimoto et al., 2020; Jiang et al., 2021; Kurfalı and Östling, 2021; Liu and Strube, 2023).

Recent improvements in supervised implicit DR recognition use prompt tuning based on pre-trained LLMs. Typically, the prompt includes a template where the connective between two input sentences is to be predicted (Xiang et al., 2022; Zhao et al., 2023; Wu et al., 2023). Other works also evaluated left-to-right generational prompts such as *the connective between Arg1 and Arg2 is ...* (Zhou et al., 2022) or *the sense between Arg1 and Arg2 is ...* (Xiang et al., 2023). A list of less ambiguous connectives were selected to verbalize each DR sense label. In addition to DCs, hierarchical information of the sense labels was also found to be effective to classify DR senses (Zhao et al., 2023; Chan et al., 2023b; Jiang et al., 2023).

2.3 Natural language prompts for zero/few-shot inferences

LLMs have demonstrated impressive performance in reasoning tasks with/without in-context examples. This has fostered extensive research on effective ways to design natural-language prompts to query LLMs. For example, it was found that prompting the LLMs to provide explanations is useful (Reynolds and McDonell, 2021; Lampinen et al., 2022). In particular, the generation of intermediate reasoning steps before the final answer (*Chain-of-Thought*, Wei et al., 2022) can significantly improve the performance, even without few-shot examples (Kojima et al., 2022). Subsequent works further investigated how the reasoning steps could be verified (Wang et al., 2022; Wang and Zhao, 2023) and decomposed (Yao et al., 2023; Besta et al., 2023). In particular, Dhuliawala et al. (2023) found that verification questions are typically answered with higher accuracy than the original question. The current work therefore also investigates the effectiveness of formulating DR classification prompts directly as verification questions.

It is yet unclear if zero-shot prompting approaches can also be applied to abstract and subtle linguistic interpretations, which additionally require world knowledge, like discourse coherence. Related to our work, Ostyakova et al. (2023) compare human and ChatGPT's annotations of dialogue functions. They found that decomposing the 32-way classification task to a tree of binary questions largely improves the inference performance. However, the development of the structural prompts involves heavy engineering, and the methodology was only evaluated on a small subset of 189 utterances. We investigate alternative methods to disassemble the established task of implicit DR recognition and evaluate the LLM's performance against large samples of expert-annotated and crowdsourced data.

2.4 Zero / few-shot DR annotation

To our knowledge, Chan et al. (2023a) is the only work that has investigated the zero-shot performance of LLMs in DR recognition. They evaluated ChatGPT's performance in the classification of DRs in PDTB 2.0 and DiscoGeM using a multiple-choice template that lists the 11 Level-2 and 18 Level-3 DR label options of the two corpora respectively. It was found that most explicit DRs could be recognized correctly (F1 > 60% for most DR types). However, the performance for implicit DRs was much poorer. It achieved 16.20% F1 and 24.54% accuracy on 11-way Level-2 classification of the PDTB 2.0 Ji-test set and F1 < 15% for most DR types, considerably lagging behind the SOTA supervised model (49.03% F1 and 64.58% accuracy, Chan et al., 2023b). Pairing the relation label options with typical DCs was shown to improve the performance while the few-shot performance varied depending on the in-context examples provided and could degrade the performance significantly. We re-ran their prompts using GPT-4 for comparison.

In addition, the performance of prompt-based inference has been shown to differ strongly between different relation subsets. Among the DRs defined in PDTB (see Table 1), causal and temporal relation reasoning are established as separate tasks with dedicated datasets, such as COPA (Gordon et al., 2012) for causal relations and TB-Dense (Cassidy et al., 2014) for temporal relations. The formats and designs of these tasks and datasets are not the same as the DR recognition tasks: typically, the task asks for more fine-grained causal or temporal relations, given that the relations are present in the text. Chan et al. (2023a) showed that ChatGPT outperforms supervised baselines in causal relation detection, but underperforms in temporal relation classification. Gao et al. (2023) instead reported that ChatGPT can be biased to over-predict causality, depending on the prompting format, and can only capture explicit causality.

3 Methodology

Prompting LLMs to classify among specific labels typically requires listing all valid options. The input becomes even longer when an example per class is included for in-context learning. Instead, we propose several methods to break down the 14-way DR classification task into smaller sub-tasks, which are described in details below.

3.1 Two-step DC insertion prompt

This approach adapts the two-step method used to crowdsource DR annotations Yung et al. (2019) into a two-step prompt. In the first step, the LLM is prompted to generate a word or phrase that represents the relation between two given arguments. As a continuous conversation, a second prompt asks for a forced choice among a subset of options. The provided options are based on the free insertion in the first step, following the mapping used in the original crowdsourcing method. For example, *however* could be generated in the first task, but it can ambiguously signal a CONTRAST or CONCESSION relation. The second step, which is a forced choice between *despite* and *in contrast*, serves as a verification question to identify fine-grained DRs. An example of the input and output is shown in Figure 6 in Appendix B.

This method assumes that DRs can be interpreted and produced through the lexical semantics of DCs and does not require specific training about the definitions of the DRs. As in the original crowdsourcing method, we did not include in-context examples in the prompt[1].

3.2 Per-class binary prompt

This method decomposes the multi-way DR classification task into independent binary prompts, e.g., *"does the discourse relation between the provided arguments represent a* ASYNCHRONOUS *relation?"*. One binary question is used for each class, so 14 prompts are necessary for each instance of DR (for the 14 Level-2 DR sense defined in PDTB 3.0). A short description of the relation type, taken from the annotation manual (Prasad et al., 2007), is also included (see Figure 7 for an example). For each binary question, one positive and one negative example, also taken from the annotation manual, of the particular relation are provided in the prompt: the positive example is the demonstrative example of the relation and the negative example is the demonstrative example of another relation type that has a different top-level sense category.

This method can produce multiple labels because the GPT model can answer *yes* to several of the binary prompts. This is particularly relevant to DR inference because multiple DRs can co-occur and simultaneously be interpreted by different reasoning traits (Scholman and Demberg, 2017). In the crowdsourced DiscoGeM corpus, most relations are annotated with two or more DR senses (see Table 3), against which the multiple predicted labels can be compared.

It is nonetheless necessary to combine the answers of the binary prompts into a single DR label in order to compare with the single gold labels in PDTB. We use the multiple-choice (MC) prompt (Chan et al., 2023a) that lists all DR options that were answered with *"yes"* in the binary questions and ask for the best choice among the given options. In case all DR senses were answered with *"no"*, all the options are provided in the MC step. The input and output of all the binary questions are included in the context. An example of the input and output is shown in Figure 7 in Appendix B. We also tried asking for a confidence score for the answer to the binary questions, as documented in Figure 7. However, since nearly all answers were assigned the same confidence score, we ignored these scores in the subsequent analyses.

3.3 Per-class verification prompt

This method also breaks down the multi-way classification task into individual per-class prompts, but instead of a straightforward yes-no question, we formulate the binary question as a verification question. To do so, we make use of the hierarchical nature of the DR senses. For example, to classify whether an instance is a ASYNCHRONOUS relation, we ask *"which argument (Arg1 or Arg2) describes an event that precedes the other? Options: Arg1, Arg2, None"*, where the answers Arg1 and Arg2 correspond to the ASYNCHRONOUS sub-classes SUCCESSION and PRECEDENCE respectively[2]. The instance is classified as a ASYNCHRONOUS relation if either ARG1 or ARG2 is generated.

In other words, the answer to the verification question provides an explanation to justify the sense of the DR without stating the label, e.g. *Arg1 describes an event that precedes Arg2, (that's why the relation between Arg1 and Arg2 is* CAUSAL*).*

Similarly, one positive and one negative example, in the form of the verification questions, are included in each binary prompt and a multiple-choice prompt is used to choose the best option from the multiple positive answers. An example of the per-class verification prompt is shown in Figure 8 in Appendix B.

4 Experiment

We conduct our experiment using the state-of-the-art version GPT model from OpenAI gpt-4 (queried in December 2023). The experiments are implemented using the API provided by OpenAI.

[1]This decision is also because we found that, as reported in previous work (Chan et al., 2023b), the LLM's prediction varies a lot depending on the examples provided in the prompt, adding more uncertainty to the effectiveness of the prompt.

[2]For the non-directional senses such as CONJUNCTION and SYNCHRONOUS, we derived verification questions based on finer-grained definitions of these senses, e.g., *are the situations in Arg1 and Arg2 completely, partially or not overlapped in terms of time?*

We evaluate the results against the annotations in PDTB 3.0 and DiscoGeM.

4.1 Data

PDTB 3.0 is the largest discourse-annotated resource in English. The texts are news articles from the Wall Street Jounals. We evaluate our method to classify 14 Level-2 relation types with more than 10 instances in the sections 21 and 22 of the PDTB3.0 (i.e. the Ji-testset), following the setup of previous works (Kim et al., 2020; Xu et al., 2023). Most items in the PDTB 3.0 are labelled with a single DR labels but a number of relations are annotated with two labels.

DiscoGeM 1.0 is a crowdsourced discourse resource in English that includes texts from multiple genres: European Parliament preceedings, Wikipedia articles, and literature. Each implicit DR in the corpus was labelled by 10 crowdworkers, following the sense definitions of PDTB 3.0 and using the two-step DC insertion method (Yung et al., 2019). We evaluate our method to classify Level-2 relation types with over 10 instances in the test set of the corpus,[3] excluding instances with the majority label DIFFERENTCON, which means the DR sense is undetermined.

The predicted DR sense of each instance is compared against 1) the single majority label, which is the label that has the most votes. In case of a tie, one of the most voted labels are randomly selected; and 2) the multiple majority labels, which is the set of labels that have two or more votes. If none of the labels have two or more votes, the single majority label is used. The distributions of the labels in both test sets are shown in Table 1.

Level-1.Level-2 labels	PDTB	DG sing	multi.
Comparison.Concession	96	77	16
Comparison.Contrast	53	26	6
Contingency.Cause	384	402	116
Contingency.Cause+Belief	14	-	-
Contingency.Condition	14	-	-
Contingency.Purpose	59	-	-
Expansion.Conjunction	236	382	125
Expansion.Equivalence	30	-	-
Expansion.Instantiation	123	58	5
Expansion.Level-of-detail	208	207	48
Expansion.Manner	17	-	-
Expansion.Substitution	25	-	-
Temporal.Asynchronous	102	100	27
Temporal.Synchronous	35	-	-
2 labels	67	0	589
3 labels	0	0	282
4 labels	0	0	38
Total	1463	1252	1252

Table 1: Distribution of the level-2 labels in the PDTB 3.0 Ji testset and the DiscoGeM 1.0 testset

4.2 Baseline

Chan et al. (2023a) evaluated the MC prompt on 11 PDTB 2.0 Level-2 relations and 18 DiscoGeM Level-3 relations, using the *gpt-3.5-turbo* model of ChatGPT. We reran this standard prompt to classify 14 PDTB 3.0 Level-2 senses and 7 DiscoGem Level-3 senses, using *gpt-4*. Specifically, we use the classification prompt where each DR option is paired with a typical DC. Since the performance with in-context examples was found to be unstable and would require extra long inputs, we did not include examples in this implementation. We modified the options from the 11 PDTB 2.0 Level-2 labels to the 14 PDTB 3.0 labels and refined the DCs attached to the DR options, by including DCs for both sub-types of Level-2 labels (e.g., *before / after* for a ASYNCHRONOUS relation); or using less ambiguous connectives (e.g., *in contrast* instead of *however* for CONCESSION). The prompt template is shown in Figure 5 in Appendix B.

Following Chan et al. (2023a) and other previous works on supervised implicit DR classification, we prompt the LLM to generate DR labels given the two identified arguments according to the original corpus annotation. The retrieval of implicit DR arguments in DiscoGeM is trivial, because they are defined as two consecutive sentences that are not connected by an explicit DC. PDTB 3.0, however, also includes *intrasential* implicit DRs and the identification of these DRs and their arguments require another annotation step. Before validating the possibility of a fully automated discourse annotation pipeline, we focus on implicit DR annotation under a simplified setup.

4.3 Results

4.3.1 Evaluation on single-sense DRs

First, we look at the comparison of different methods evaluated against PDTB 3.0, which is shown in Table 2. In addition to the baseline MC prompt, we also compare the results with three generic baselines: random, always CONJUNCTION, and always CAUSE. The latter two DR types are the most common categories of implicit DRs in both corpora. In addition, the performance of state-of-the-art su-

[3]The count is based on the single majority label. The included 7 Level-2 relation types are also the most frequent relation types in the whole corpus.

pervised models for implicit DR classification are listed as a reference.

The following can be observed from Table 2:

1. inference by *gpt-4* achieves only about half of the performance of the supervised models (36.84% vs. 67.84% on Level-2 accuracy);

2. the two-step DC insertion prompt performs poorly, achieving less than half of the performance of other prompts (15.52%);

3. the per-class verification + MC aggregation method performs similarly with the baseline 14-way MC prompt (36.98% vs 36.84%), while the per-class binary method significantly underperforms (30.69%).

Chan et al. (2023a) reported that the per-class predictions by the standard multi-way MC prompt achieved an accuracy of 20.31% and F1 of 10.73% for the 11-way classification of Level-2 senses in PDTB 2.0, using *gpt-3.5-turbo*. For the 14-way classification of the PDTB 3.0 senses, using *gpt-4*, the accuracy and F1 are 36.84 and 26.12 respectively, which have considerably improved but are still far from a level of satisfactory reliability.

Table 3 compares the per-class precision, recall and F1 scores between the 14-way MC prompt and the per-class verification + MC aggregation prompt, and Figure 1 shows the corresponding confusion matrices of the predicted and gold labels in the PDTB 3.0 test set items. It can be observed that the precisions are generally higher than the recalls, but the performances are drastically different among different classes, ranging from 0% F1 for MANNER to $61 - 68\%$ F1 for PURPOSE. The per-class performance of the two methods is similar. The main difference is the better performance of the MC method on CAUSE and of the verification method on CONJUNCTION.

Some confusion patterns are similar to those of humans (Robaldo and Miltsakaki, 2014; Sanders et al., 1992; Scholman and Demberg, 2017). For example, the confusion between CONTRAST and CONCESSION and CAUSE and CAUSE+BELIEF – CONCESSION and CAUSE+BELIEF were hardly predicted at all. In general, there is particular confusion with CAUSE and LEVEL-OF-DETAIL relations (darker column on these two relations in the left matrix, Figure 1). Specific verification prompts to tease apart these easily confused relations could potentially improve the performance.

The poor performance of the two-step DC insertion method suggests that ChatGPT cannot infer DRs in a fully lexicalized manner based on DCs similar to humans. It is necessary to explicitly specify the link between the DCs and the DR labels, as in the MC prompts.

The underperformance of the per-class binary prompt is due to too many labels being rejected in the binary question step. The soft-match accuracy of 53.79 means that in nearly half of the questions, ChatGPT answered *"no"* to the correct relation in the first step. In fact, in about one-tenth of the questions in the PDTB data, all relation senses received the output *"no"*. This suggests that it is necessary to adjust the threshold of detecting a particular relation sense, which is not trivial to prompt.

The performances of the MC prompt and the per-class verification prompt were found to be similar, as seen in Table 3 and Figure 1 and 2. However, the MC prompt should be preferred since the cost of using the API, based on the number of prompts or the input tokens required for each item, is 15 times less. While the F1 scores suggest that the MC-prompt is stronger in detecting CONJUNCTION and the per-class verification method is stronger in CAUSE, the accuracies of both methods are too low to produce useful inferences for downstream tasks.

4.3.2 Evaluation on multi-sense DRs

One potential advantage of the per-class prompting methods over the MC prompt is the possibility of producing multiple labels by skipping the last MC step. It is not uncommon that several DR senses can be interpreted depending on the reader's perspective and multiple DR sense labels represent the semantics of the DR better.

In Table 2, we see that the per-class verification method, without the multi-way MC step, reaches soft-match accuracy of 89.33%. However, 7.67 labels are predicted on average, and it is unclear how many of the predicted senses are actually valid. To further analyze the performance of ChatGPT's inference multi-sense DRs, we turn to the results of the crowdsourced DiscoGeM data.

Table 4 compares the MC prompt and the per-class verification prompt with various baselines[5] and Table 5 compares the per-class F1s of the two

[4]https://github.com/openai/tiktoken

[5]Few supervised models have been evaluated on DiscoGeM and none of them are on a 7-way setting.

Models	per-item prompts	avg. input tokens	PDTB 3.0 (Ji-test) Level-1 4-way macro F1	Acc.	Level-2 14-way macro F1	Acc.
supervised models						
GOLF$_{large}$ (Jiang et al., 2023)	-	-	74.21	76.39	60.11	66.42
PEMI (Zhao et al., 2023)	-	-	69.06	73.27	52.73	63.09
CP-KD$_{large}$ (Wu et al., 2023)	-	-	75.52	78.56	52.16	67.84
baseline						
random	-	-	24.24	33.08	6.34	7.66
all CONJUNCTION	-	-	15.75	47.44	1.97	16.20
all CAUSE	-	-	12.68	35.89	3.04	27.75
1) 14-way MC (Chan et al., 2023a)	1	245	45.80	50.03	26.12	36.84
2) two-step DC insertion	2	99	23.44	30.49	6.02	15.52
3) per-class binary (avg. 3.62 labels)	14	2597	-	(61.52)	-	(53.79)
+ multi-way MC	1	120	41.76	47.16	19.66	30.69
4) per-class verification (avg. 7.67 labels)	14	3873	-	(95.56)	-	(89.33)
+ multi-way MC	1	167	47.53	52.84	25.77	36.98

Table 2: Results of the PDTB 3.0 Ji-testset. The average input token counts are calculated using the BPE tokenizer provided by OpenAi[4]. The 4-way Level-1 evaluation is calculated by mapping the Level-2 predictions to Level-1 based on the sense hierarchy. To calculate the accuracy, a prediction is counted as correct if it matches one of the gold labels.Values in brackets refer to soft-match scores: any overlap between the predicted multiple labels and the gold labels is counted as correct.

labels	14-way MC P	R	F1	per-class vf. P	R	F1
Conjunction	.52	.27	.36	.50	.49	.49
Cause	.49	.45	.47	.49	.37	.42
Cause+Belief	.10	.07	.08	.00	.00	.00
Condition	.02	.07	.03	.02	.07	.03
Purpose	.55	.90	.68	.50	.79	.61
Contrast	.14	.54	.22	.14	.42	.21
Concession	.17	.01	.02	.14	.03	.05
Asynchronous	.23	.60	.33	.26	.58	.36
Synchronous	.14	.28	.19	.12	.21	.15
Level-of-detail	.56	.11	.18	.48	.10	.17
Instantiation	.50	.51	.51	.44	.51	.47
Equivalence	.55	.20	.29	.24	.33	.28
Manner	.00	.00	.00	.00	.00	.00
Substitution	.27	.32	.29	.45	.30	.36
macro F1			.26			.26

Table 3: F1 scores on PDTB 3.0 Level-2 label prediction with the 14-way MC prompt and the per-class verification + MC aggregation method

prompting methods evaluated against the single gold sense label. In addition, we also evaluated the predictions against multiple gold sense labels. In the DiscoGeM test set, each item has one to three labels (see Table 1). We calculate the per-item F1 score, which is the harmonic mean of precision and recall of the multiple predicted labels compared with multiple gold labels of each item[6].

It can be observed in Table 4 that:

1. the accuracy of ChatGPT's prediction is even lower in DiscoGeM, compared with PDTB 3.0 (32.67% v.s. 36.84% with the MC prompt), and is similar to the *all* CONJUNCTION and *all* CAUSE baselines;

2. the per-class verification + MC aggregation method underperforms the 7-way MC prompt (30.83% v.s. 32.67%);

3. the multiple predicted labels by the per-class verification without MC aggregation method considerably overlap with the multiple gold labels (average per-item F1 50.63%).

The lower accuracy on DiscoGeM can be attributed to the highly skewed label distribution, as seen in Table 1. CAUSE and CONJUNCTION each covers one-third of the relations in the data, such that the accuracy of these relations is highly reflected in overall accuracy despite similar per-class performance. On the other hand, the lower accuracy of the results by the per-class verification is due to the lower F1 scores of the LEVEL-OF-DETAIL and CONCESSION in this dataset.

Evaluation against the single majority label of DiscoGeM involves a certain level of randomness since one of the majority labels is randomly selected when two or more labels have the maximum number of votes. The multiple gold labels, on the other hand, are based on a threshold; they include all labels receiving 20% or more votes among the 10 votes per item. We thus turn to the evaluation

[6]The average per-item F1 equals the accuracy if there are always one gold label and one predicted label. The macro F1 score, which is the arithmetic mean of all the per-class F1s, could not be calculated when most labels have multiple gold classes. In Table 3 and Figures 1 and 2, items with two gold labels (< 5% in the PDTB 3.0 test set) were treated as two separated items.

Models	per-item prompt	avg. input tokens	DiscoGeM testset Level-1 single 4-way macro F1	Acc.	Level-2 single 7-way macro F1	Acc.	Level-2 multi avg. per-item F1	Acc.
baseline								
random	-	-	24.20	29.63	12.99	13.18	17.22	(26.99)
all CONJUNCTION	-	-	17.12	51.68	6.76	30.51	36.91	(55.27)
all CAUSE	-	-	12.12	32.11	6.93	32.11	34.91	(52.72)
7-way MC (Chan et al., 2023a)	1	231	41.21	45.52	27.87	32.67	35.28	(52.16)
per-class verif. (avg. 3.87 labels)	7	2473	-	(90.34)	-	(80.51)	50.63	(92.81)
+ multi-way MC	1	184	37.68	44.41	24.08	30.83	32.61	(47.84)

Table 4: Results of the DiscoGeM test set. The predicted Level-2 labels are evaluated against the single majority labels at two levels (Level-1 single and Level-2 single), and against the multiple majority labels at Level-2. Values in brackets refer to soft-match scores: any overlap between the predicted multiple labels and the gold labels is counted as correct. *Average per-item F1* is the F1 score of the multiple predicted labels compared with the multiple gold labels of each item, averaged by the total number of items.

labels	7-way MC P	R	F1	per-class vf. P	R	F1
Conjunction	.53	.29	.38	.56	.35	.43
Cause	.58	.30	.39	.58	.23	.33
Contrast	.05	.62	.10	.09	.54	.15
Concession	.24	.10	.14	.0	.0	.0
Asynchronous	.31	.76	.44	.21	.91	.33
Level-of-detail	.32	.33	.33	.26	.10	.15
Instantiation	.21	.16	.18	.20	.59	.29
macro F1			.28			. 24

Table 5: F1 scores on DiscoGeM Level-2 label prediction with the 14-way MC prompt and the per-class verification + MC aggregation method

against the multiple Level-2 gold labels of DiscoGeM, which is shown in the right two columns of Table 4.

The soft-match accuracies, in brackets, are not directly comparable with the accuracies of single prediction against single gold labels because the chance agreement is higher. Nonetheless, the soft-match accuracy of the multiple labels, which are 3.87 labels on average, reaches 92.83%. This means that in most cases the predicted labels overlap with the senses of the DRs. The average per-item F1 is 50.63%, which is not too far from that between crowdsourced and expert multi-label annotations, which was found to be 58% in a subset of the DiscoGeM corpus.

5 Discussion and conclusion

We set out to test ChatGPT's ability to infer implicit DR senses with the latest model and carefully engineered prompts. Unfortunately, the low performance of implicit DR recognition could not be improved by sophisticated prompt engineering techniques that were successful in other tasks. This points to the fact that either other prompting techniques are needed, or that implicit DR recognition simply cannot be solved under zero-shot or few-shot settings. Knowledge acquired in other reasoning tasks does not seem to be transferrable to this task and supervised guidance to map the semantics of the arguments to the ambiguous and abstract DR labels is necessary.

We also performed smaller-scale experiments with other LLMs such as LLaMA (Touvron et al., 2023) but the performance was substantially worse even than *gpt-3.5*. The training data of these other LLMs do not include PDTB nor DiscoGeM. We found that ChatGPT is able to produce PDTB 2.0 labels even when the options are not provided in the prompt, suggesting that its training data should have at least included texts related to PDTB-style DR analysis (e.g., possibly an annotation manual or research article). Therefore, strictly speaking, the inference made by ChatGPT is not completely zero-shot because it is informed about the DR labels. This may explain why the two-step DC insertion prompt, which does not involve any DR labels at all, totally failed in the task.

The underperformance of the per-class binary prompt suggests that prompting the discriminative comparison among all possible options at once is more accurate than separate detection of individual DR sense. Too many relation senses were rejected when the model was presented with the binary choice of *yes/no*; some of these rejected senses have been accepted when compared with an even more unlikely sense.

The per-class approach, nevertheless, provides a framework to collect multi-label annotations, which is not only important to DR annotations but also to other tasks like natural language inference and sentiment analysis. We also experimented with running the MC prompts multiple times with a higher temperature setting, or explicitly asking for multiple labels in the prompt. ChatGPT only occasionally produced multiple labels in these cases, possibly due to the dominance of single-label annotated data in its training history.

The better performance of the per-class verification approach compared with binary questions shows that the verification questions actually worked. This approach is related to chain-of-thought prompting (Wei et al., 2022); the identification of the arguments of the Level-3 sense justifies the presence of the Level-2 relation. We will experiment using this approach to refine the MC prompt.

Another direction is to develop other approaches to disassemble the DR annotation task. Breaking down the multi-way classification task into smaller tasks was successful in dialogue structure annotation (Ostyakova et al., 2023), using a heavily engineered step-by-step scheme (e.g. > 6 steps, each asking for specific features of the input). Such a tailored annotation scheme might also be necessary to prompt implicit DR annotations.

6 Limitations

One of the limitations of the experiments is that we only queried the API once. There could be variation in output between queries. In addition, the findings of the prompting techniques are limited to PDTB-styled DRs, and may not be generalized to other frameworks or tasks. The experiment results are based on the specific templates we used. We did not implement nor compare other modifications, such as the choice of DCs in the options, which could potentially have an impact on the overall findings.

7 Ethical consideration

OpenAI's data collection complies with privacy laws[7]. The PDTB 3.0 corpus is licensed under the LDC User Agreement. The text comes from the Wall Street Journal, which is publicly purchasable. DiscoGeM is publicly available on GitHub. The text comes from publicly available European parliament proceedings, Wikipedia articles, and novels. The annotation crowd-sourcing was approved by the Deutsche Gesellschaft für Sprachwissenschaft ethics committee. However, we did not check whether any of the raw texts contained any information that names or uniquely identifies individual people or offensive content, nor did we take any steps to anonymize it.

[7] https://help.openai.com/en/articles/7842364-how-chatgpt-and-our-language-models-are-developed

Acknowledgements

This project is supported by the German Research Foundation (DFG) under Grant SFB 1102 ("Information Density and Linguistic Encoding", Project-ID 232722074).

References

Yejin Bang, Samuel Cahyawijaya, Nayeon Lee, Wenliang Dai, Dan Su, Bryan Wilie, Holy Lovenia, Ziwei Ji, Tiezheng Yu, Willy Chung, et al. 2023. A multitask, multilingual, multimodal evaluation of chatgpt on reasoning, hallucination, and interactivity. *arXiv preprint arXiv:2302.04023*.

Maciej Besta, Nils Blach, Ales Kubicek, Robert Gerstenberger, Lukas Gianinazzi, Joanna Gajda, Tomasz Lehmann, Michal Podstawski, Hubert Niewiadomski, Piotr Nyczyk, et al. 2023. Graph of thoughts: Solving elaborate problems with large language models. *arXiv preprint arXiv:2308.09687*.

Taylor Cassidy, Bill McDowell, Nathanael Chambers, and Steven Bethard. 2014. An annotation framework for dense event ordering. In *Proceedings of the 52nd Annual Meeting of the Association for Computational Linguistics (Volume 2: Short Papers)*, pages 501–506, Baltimore, Maryland. Association for Computational Linguistics.

Chunkit Chan, Jiayang Cheng, Weiqi Wang, Yuxin Jiang, Tianqing Fang, Xin Liu, and Yangqiu Song. 2023a. Chatgpt evaluation on sentence level relations: A focus on temporal, causal, and discourse relations. *arXiv preprint arXiv:2304.14827*.

Chunkit Chan, Xin Liu, Jiayang Cheng, Zihan Li, Yangqiu Song, Ginny Wong, and Simon See. 2023b. DiscoPrompt: Path prediction prompt tuning for implicit discourse relation recognition. In *Findings of the Association for Computational Linguistics: ACL 2023*, pages 35–57, Toronto, Canada. Association for Computational Linguistics.

Shehzaad Dhuliawala, Mojtaba Komeili, Jing Xu, Roberta Raileanu, Xian Li, Asli Celikyilmaz, and Jason Weston. 2023. Chain-of-verification reduces hallucination in large language models.

Yue Dong, Andrei Mircea, and Jackie Chi Kit Cheung. 2021. Discourse-aware unsupervised summarization for long scientific documents. In *Proceedings of the 16th Conference of the European Chapter of the Association for Computational Linguistics: Main Volume*, pages 1089–1102.

Jinglong Gao, Xiao Ding, Bing Qin, and Ting Liu. 2023. Is chatgpt a good causal reasoner? a comprehensive evaluation. *arXiv preprint arXiv:2305.07375*.

Fabrizio Gilardi, Meysam Alizadeh, and Maël Kubli. 2023. Chatgpt outperforms crowd-workers for text-annotation tasks. *arXiv preprint arXiv:2303.15056*.

Andrew Gordon, Zornitsa Kozareva, and Melissa Roemmele. 2012. SemEval-2012 task 7: Choice of plausible alternatives: An evaluation of commonsense causal reasoning. In **SEM 2012: The First Joint Conference on Lexical and Computational Semantics – Volume 1: Proceedings of the main conference and the shared task, and Volume 2: Proceedings of the Sixth International Workshop on Semantic Evaluation (SemEval 2012)*, pages 394–398, Montréal, Canada. Association for Computational Linguistics.

Jet Hoek, Merel CJ Scholman, and Ted JM Sanders. 2021. Is there less annotator agreement when the discourse relation is underspecified? In *Proceedings of the First Workshop on Integrating Perspectives on Discourse Annotation*, pages 1–6.

Yangfeng Ji, Gongbo Zhang, and Jacob Eisenstein. 2015. Closing the gap: Domain adaptation from explicit to implicit discourse relations. In *Proceedings of the 2015 Conference on Empirical Methods in Natural Language Processing*, pages 2219–2224, Lisbon, Portugal. Association for Computational Linguistics.

Congcong Jiang, Tieyun Qian, Zhuang Chen, Kejian Tang, Shaohui Zhan, and Tao Zhan. 2021. Generating pseudo connectives with mlms for implicit discourse relation recognition. In *PRICAI 2021: Trends in Artificial Intelligence: 18th Pacific Rim International Conference on Artificial Intelligence, PRICAI 2021, Hanoi, Vietnam, November 8–12, 2021, Proceedings, Part II 18*, pages 113–126. Springer.

Yuxin Jiang, Linhan Zhang, and Wei Wang. 2023. Global and local hierarchy-aware contrastive framework for implicit discourse relation recognition. In *Findings of the Association for Computational Linguistics: ACL 2023*, pages 8048–8064, Toronto, Canada. Association for Computational Linguistics.

Najoung Kim, Song Feng, Chulaka Gunasekara, and Luis Lastras. 2020. Implicit discourse relation classification: We need to talk about evaluation. In *Proceedings of the 58th Annual Meeting of the Association for Computational Linguistics*, pages 5404–5414, Online. Association for Computational Linguistics.

Yudai Kishimoto, Yugo Murawaki, and Sadao Kurohashi. 2020. Adapting BERT to implicit discourse relation classification with a focus on discourse connectives. In *Proceedings of the Twelfth Language Resources and Evaluation Conference*, pages 1152–1158, Marseille, France. European Language Resources Association.

Takeshi Kojima, Shixiang Shane Gu, Machel Reid, Yutaka Matsuo, and Yusuke Iwasawa. 2022. Large language models are zero-shot reasoners. *Advances in neural information processing systems*, 35:22199–22213.

Murathan Kurfalı and Robert Östling. 2021. Let's be explicit about that: Distant supervision for implicit discourse relation classification via connective prediction. In *Proceedings of the 1st Workshop on Understanding Implicit and Underspecified Language*, pages 1–10, Online. Association for Computational Linguistics.

Andrew Lampinen, Ishita Dasgupta, Stephanie Chan, Kory Mathewson, Mh Tessler, Antonia Creswell, James McClelland, Jane Wang, and Felix Hill. 2022. Can language models learn from explanations in context? In *Findings of the Association for Computational Linguistics: EMNLP 2022*, pages 537–563, Abu Dhabi, United Arab Emirates. Association for Computational Linguistics.

Wei Liu and Michael Strube. 2023. Annotation-inspired implicit discourse relation classification with auxiliary discourse connective generation. In *Proceedings of the 61st Annual Meeting of the Association for Computational Linguistics (Volume 1: Long Papers)*, pages 15696–15712, Toronto, Canada. Association for Computational Linguistics.

Daniel Marcu and Abdessamad Echihabi. 2002. An unsupervised approach to recognizing discourse relations. In *Proceedings of the 40th Annual Meeting of the Association for Computational Linguistics*, pages 368–375, Philadelphia, Pennsylvania, USA. Association for Computational Linguistics.

OpenAI. 2023. Gpt-4 technical report.

Lidiia Ostyakova, Veronika Smilga, Kseniia Petukhova, Maria Molchanova, and Daniel Kornev. 2023. ChatGPT vs. crowdsourcing vs. experts: Annotating open-domain conversations with speech functions. In *Proceedings of the 24th Meeting of the Special Interest Group on Discourse and Dialogue*, pages 242–254, Prague, Czechia. Association for Computational Linguistics.

Umangi Oza, Rashmi Prasad, Sudheer Kolachina, Suman Meena, Dipti Misra Sharma, and Aravind Joshi. 2009. Experiments with annotating discourse relations in the hindi discourse relation bank. In *Proceedings of the 7th International Conference on Natural Language Processing (ICON-2009), Hyderabad, India.*

Lucie Poláková, Jiří Mírovskỳ, Anna Nedoluzhko, Pavlína Jínová, Šárka Zikánová, and Eva Hajicová. 2013. Introducing the prague discourse treebank 1.0. In *Proceedings of the Sixth International Joint Conference on Natural Language Processing*, pages 91–99.

Rashmi Prasad, Nikhil Dinesh, Alan Lee, Eleni Miltsakaki, Livio Robaldo, Aravind Joshi, and Bonnie Webber. 2008. The Penn Discourse TreeBank 2.0. In *Proceedings of the Sixth International Conference on Language Resources and Evaluation (LREC'08)*, Marrakech, Morocco. European Language Resources Association (ELRA).

Rashmi Prasad, Eleni Miltsakaki, Nikhil Dinesh, Alan Lee, Aravind K. Joshi, Livio Robaldo, and Bonnie Webber. 2007. *The Penn Discourse Treebank 2.0 annotation manual.*

Rashmi Prasad, Bonnie Webber, Alan Lee, and Aravind Joshi. 2019. Penn Discourse Treebank Version 3.0.

Laria Reynolds and Kyle McDonell. 2021. Prompt programming for large language models: Beyond the few-shot paradigm. In *Extended Abstracts of the 2021 CHI Conference on Human Factors in Computing Systems*, pages 1–7.

Livio Robaldo and Eleni Miltsakaki. 2014. Corpus-driven semantics of concession: Where do expectations come from? *Dialogue & Discourse*, 5(1):1–36.

Hannah Rohde, Anna Dickinson, Nathan Schneider, Christopher Clark, Annie Louis, and Bonnie Webber. 2016. Filling in the blanks in understanding discourse adverbials: Consistency, conflict, and context-dependence in a crowdsourced elicitation task. In *Proceedings of the 10th Linguistic Annotation Workshop (LAW X)*, pages 49–58, Berlin, Germany.

Attapol Rutherford and Nianwen Xue. 2015. Improving the inference of implicit discourse relations via classifying explicit discourse connectives. In *Proceedings of the 2015 Conference of the North American Chapter of the Association for Computational Linguistics: Human Language Technologies*, pages 799–808, Denver, Colorado. Association for Computational Linguistics.

Ted Sanders and Wilbert Spooren. 2010. Discourse and text structure.

Ted J. M. Sanders, Wilbert P. M. S. Spooren, and Leo G. M. Noordman. 1992. Toward a taxonomy of coherence relations. *Discourse Processes*, 15(1):1–35.

Merel C. J. Scholman and Vera Demberg. 2017. Examples and specifications that prove a point: Identifying elaborative and argumentative discourse relations. *Dialogue & Discourse*, 8(2):56–83.

Merel C. J. Scholman, Tianai Dong, Frances Yung, and Vera Demberg. 2022. Discogem: A crowdsourced corpus of genre-mixed implicit discourse relations. In *Proceedings of the Thirteenth International Conference on Language Resources and Evaluation (LREC'22)*, Marseille, France. European Language Resources Association (ELRA).

Wei Shi and Vera Demberg. 2019. Learning to explicitate connectives with Seq2Seq network for implicit discourse relation classification. In *Proceedings of the 13th International Conference on Computational Semantics - Long Papers*, pages 188–199, Gothenburg, Sweden. Association for Computational Linguistics.

Caroline Sporleder and Alex Lascarides. 2008. Using automatically labelled examples to classify rhetorical relations: An assessment. *Natural Language Engineering*, 14(3):369–416.

Jialong Tang, Hongyu Lin, Meng Liao, Yaojie Lu, Xianpei Han, Le Sun, Weijian Xie, and Jin Xu. 2021. From discourse to narrative: Knowledge projection for event relation extraction. In *Proceedings of the 59th Annual Meeting of the Association for Computational Linguistics and the 11th International Joint Conference on Natural Language Processing (Volume 1: Long Papers)*, pages 732–742.

Petter Törnberg. 2023. Chatgpt-4 outperforms experts and crowd workers in annotating political twitter messages with zero-shot learning. *arXiv preprint arXiv:2304.06588*.

Hugo Touvron, Thibaut Lavril, Gautier Izacard, Xavier Martinet, Marie-Anne Lachaux, Timothée Lacroix, Baptiste Rozière, Naman Goyal, Eric Hambro, Faisal Azhar, et al. 2023. Llama: Open and efficient foundation language models. *arXiv preprint arXiv:2302.13971*.

Xuezhi Wang, Jason Wei, Dale Schuurmans, Quoc V Le, Ed H Chi, Sharan Narang, Aakanksha Chowdhery, and Denny Zhou. 2022. Self-consistency improves chain of thought reasoning in language models. In *The Eleventh International Conference on Learning Representations*.

Yuqing Wang and Yun Zhao. 2023. Metacognitive prompting improves understanding in large language models. *arXiv preprint arXiv:2308.05342*.

Jason Wei, Xuezhi Wang, Dale Schuurmans, Maarten Bosma, Fei Xia, Ed Chi, Quoc V Le, Denny Zhou, et al. 2022. Chain-of-thought prompting elicits reasoning in large language models. *Advances in Neural Information Processing Systems*, 35:24824–24837.

Hongyi Wu, Hao Zhou, Man Lan, Yuanbin Wu, and Yadong Zhang. 2023. Connective prediction for implicit discourse relation recognition via knowledge distillation. In *Proceedings of the 61st Annual Meeting of the Association for Computational Linguistics (Volume 1: Long Papers)*, pages 5908–5923, Toronto, Canada. Association for Computational Linguistics.

Wei Xiang, Chao Liang, and Bang Wang. 2023. TEPrompt: Task enlightenment prompt learning for implicit discourse relation recognition. In *Findings of the Association for Computational Linguistics: ACL 2023*, pages 12403–12414, Toronto, Canada. Association for Computational Linguistics.

Wei Xiang, Zhenglin Wang, Lu Dai, and Bang Wang. 2022. ConnPrompt: Connective-cloze prompt learning for implicit discourse relation recognition.

In *Proceedings of the 29th International Conference on Computational Linguistics*, pages 902–911, Gyeongju, Republic of Korea. International Committee on Computational Linguistics.

Jiacheng Xu, Zhe Gan, Yu Cheng, and Jingjing Liu. 2020. Discourse-aware neural extractive text summarization. In *Proceedings of the 58th Annual Meeting of the Association for Computational Linguistics*, pages 5021–5031.

Jing Xu, Ruifang He, Haodong Zhao, Huijie Wang, and Lei Zeng. 2023. Dual hierarchical contrastive learning for multi-level implicit discourse relation recognition. In *CCF International Conference on Natural Language Processing and Chinese Computing*, pages 55–66. Springer.

Yu Xu, Man Lan, Yue Lu, Zheng Yu Niu, and Chew Lim Tan. 2012. Connective prediction using machine learning for implicit discourse relation classification. In *The 2012 international joint conference on neural networks (ijcnn)*, pages 1–8. IEEE.

Shunyu Yao, Dian Yu, Jeffrey Zhao, Izhak Shafran, Thomas L Griffiths, Yuan Cao, and Karthik Narasimhan. 2023. Tree of thoughts: Deliberate problem solving with large language models. *arXiv preprint arXiv:2305.10601*.

Frances Yung, Vera Demberg, and Merel Scholman. 2019. Crowdsourcing discourse relation annotations by a two-step connective insertion task. In *Proceedings of the 13th Linguistic Annotation Workshop*, pages 16–25, Florence, Italy. Association for Computational Linguistics.

Deniz Zeyrek, Amália Mendes, Yulia Grishina, Murathan Kurfalı, Samuel Gibbon, and Maciej Ogrodniczuk. 2020. Ted multilingual discourse bank (tedmdb): a parallel corpus annotated in the pdtb style. *Language Resources and Evaluation*, 54:587–613.

Haodong Zhao, Ruifang He, Mengnan Xiao, and Jing Xu. 2023. Infusing hierarchical guidance into prompt tuning: A parameter-efficient framework for multilevel implicit discourse relation recognition. In *Proceedings of the 61st Annual Meeting of the Association for Computational Linguistics (Volume 1: Long Papers)*, pages 6477–6492, Toronto, Canada. Association for Computational Linguistics.

Hao Zhou, Man Lan, Yuanbin Wu, Yuefeng Chen, and Meirong Ma. 2022. Prompt-based connective prediction method for fine-grained implicit discourse relation recognition. In *Findings of the Association for Computational Linguistics: EMNLP 2022*, pages 3848–3858, Abu Dhabi, United Arab Emirates. Association for Computational Linguistics.

Yuping Zhou and Nianwen Xue. 2012. Pdtb-style discourse annotation of chinese text. In *Proceedings of the 50th Annual Meeting of the Association for Computational Linguistics (Volume 1: Long Papers)*, pages 69–77.

Šárka Zikánová, Jiří Mírovský, and Pavlína Synková. 2019. Explicit and implicit discourse relations in the prague discourse treebank. In *Text, Speech, and Dialogue: 22nd International Conference, TSD 2019, Ljubljana, Slovenia, September 11–13, 2019, Proceedings 22*, pages 236–248. Springer.

A Appendix

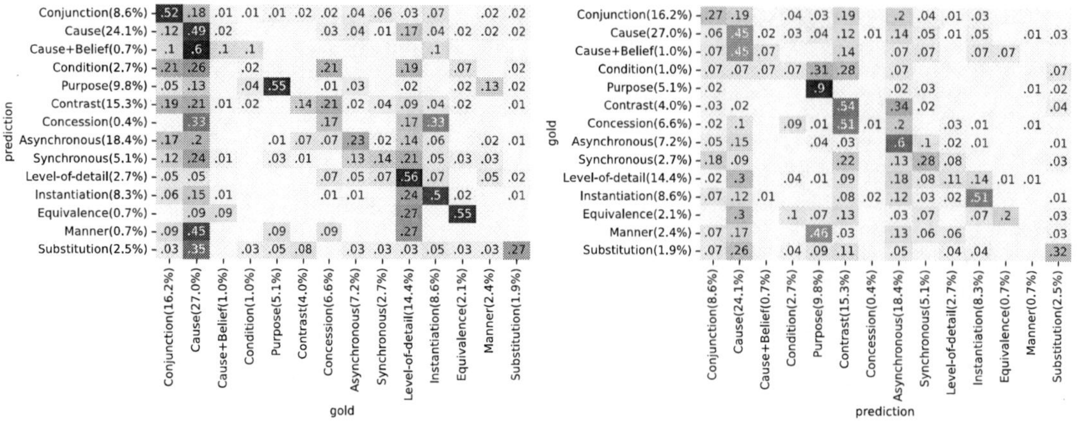

Figure 1: Confusion matrices comparing the gold and predicted labels in the **PDTB 3.0 test set** using the **MC prompt**. The distribution in the left figure is normalized by the predicted class, i.e. the diagonal corresponds to the **precision**; while the distribution on the right is normalized by the gold class, i.e. the diagonal corresponds to the **recall**. The percentages in brackets are the overall distributions of the predicted and gold labels respectively.

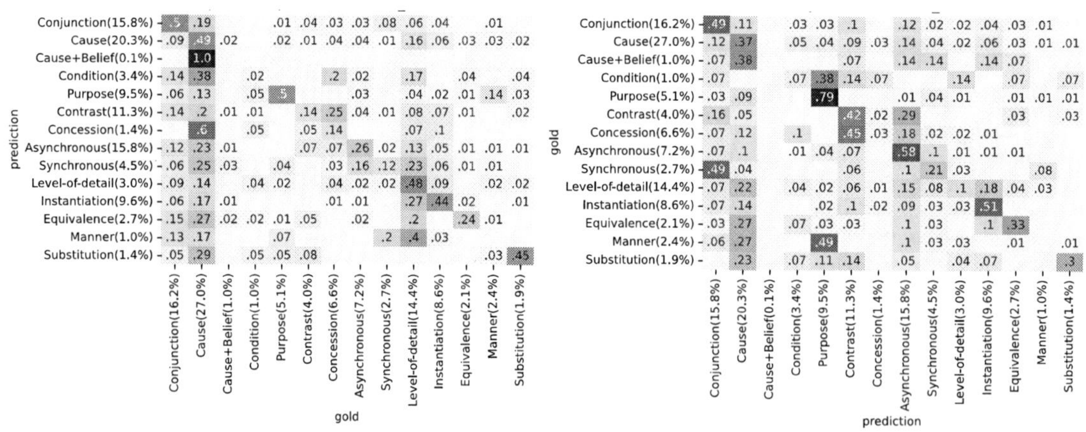

Figure 2: Confusion matrices comparing the gold and predicted labels in the **PDTB test set** using the **per-class verification prompt** with the MC aggregation step.

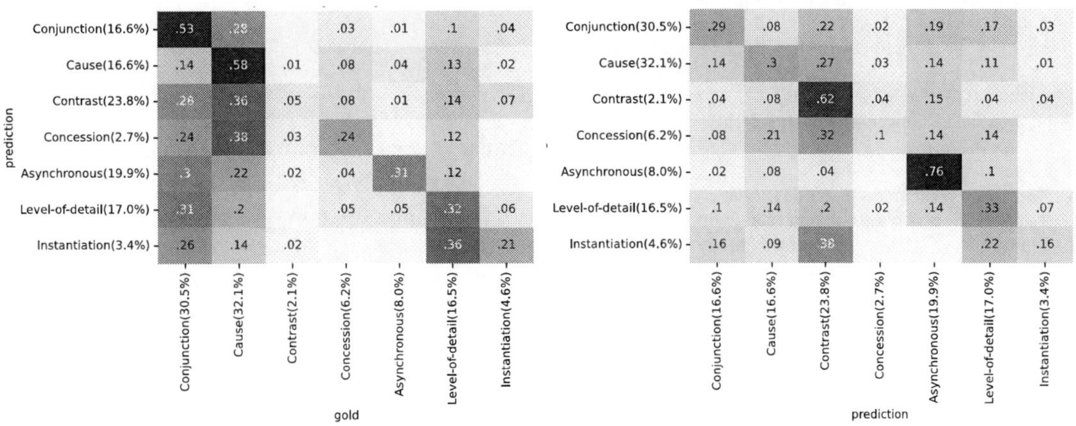

Figure 3: Confusion matrices comparing the **single** gold and predicted labels in the **DiscoGeM** test set using the **MC prompt**.

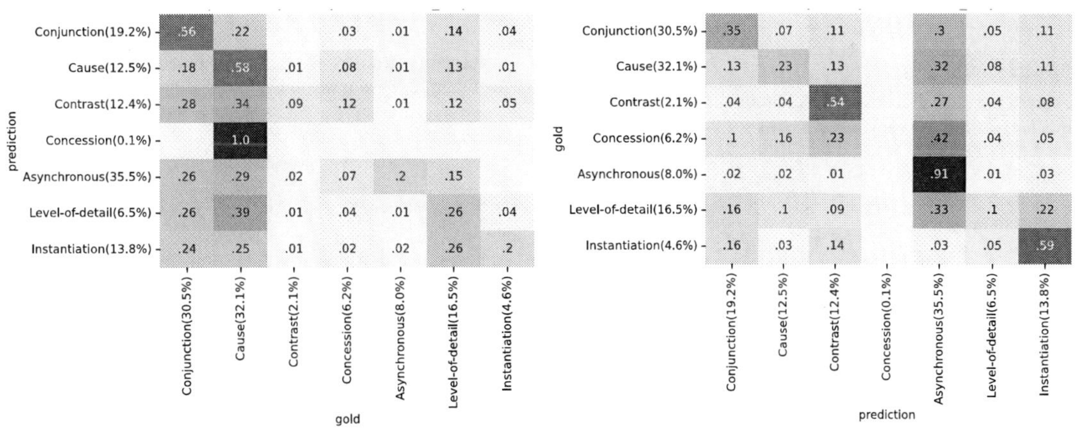

Figure 4: Confusion matrices comparing the **single** gold and predicted labels in the DiscoGeM test set using the **per-class verification prompt** with the MC aggregation step.

B Appendix

All prompts have *"You are a language expert."* as the system content.

Task: Identify the most suitable option from the list below that describes the discourse relationship between the following pair of arguments.

Argument 1: We've got a product.
Argument 2: If you want it, you can get it.

Options:
1. Temporal.Asynchronous, before / after
2. Temporal.Synchronous, at that time / while
3. Contingency.Cause, consequently / therefore
4. Contingency.Cause+Belief, considering this
5. Contingency.Condition, in that case / if
6. Contingency.Purpose, in order to / such that
7. Comparison.Contrast, on the contrary / in contrast
8. Comparison.Concession, despite this / even though
9. Expansion.Conjunction, in addition / also
10. Expansion.Instantiation, for example / for instance
11. Expansion.Equivalence, in other words
12. Expansion.Level-of-detail, specifically / in short
13. Expansion.Manner, how? / thereby
14. Expansion.Substitution, instead / rather

Answer: ?

Figure 5: MC prompt adapted from Chan et al. (2023a)

Free insertion step:

Write down the connective word/phrase that best reflects the logical connection between these two arguments.

Argument 1: You build up a lot of tension.
Argument 2: Working at a terminal all the day.

Answer: ?

Forced-choice step:

Select an option from the below list that best expresses the meaning of the phrase you have chosen in the first step.

Options:
1. in short
2. for the reason that
3. also

Answer: ?

Figure 6: Two-step prompt for implicit DR identification. Step 2's options are generated based on the free generation of Step 1.

Binary step: one prompt is used for each DR class (i.e. 14 prompts per each item. Here is an example of the prompt for ASYNCHRONOUS).

Question: Does the discourse relationship between the provided arguments represent an Asynchronous relation?

Description: Asynchronous relation describes a situation where one event is presented as preceding the other.

Argument 1: The Artist sticks to a daily routine...
Argument 2: At night he returns to the condemned...
Answer: Yes

Argument 1: The battle exceeds Justin's...
Argument 2: "I had no idea I was getting in so deep," says...
Answer: No

Argument 1: Capture the gaseous substance
Argument 2: And transport it to recycling center
Answer: ?

On a scale of 1-10, 1 being the lowest and 10 being the highest, Please express your confidence level in the prediction.

Multi-way MC step

Task: Identify the most suitable option from the list below that describes the discourse relationship between the following pair of arguments.

Argument 1: Capture the gaseous substance
Argument 2: And transport it to recycling center

Options:
1. Contingency.Cause, consequently / therefore
2. Expansion.Conjunction, in addition / also
3. Temporal.Synchronous, at that time / while

Answer: ?

Figure 7: Per-class binary prompt. Corresponding options (same as Figure 5) to the DRs answered with *"yes"* in the binary step are listed as option in the MC step.

Verification question step: one prompt is used for each DR class (i.e. 14 prompts per each item. Here is an example of the prompt for CAUSAL.)

```
Consider the discourse relation between Arg1 and Arg2, where Arg1 is "I trusted in his lordship's wisdom" and Arg2 is "I can't even say I made my own mistakes." Which argument (Arg1 or Arg2) gives the reason, explanation or justification of the effect described in the other argument?
Options: Arg1, Arg2, None
Answer: Arg1

Consider the discourse relation between Arg1 and Arg2, where Arg1 is 'What is greatness?' and Arg2 is "What is dignity?" Which argument (Arg1 or Arg2) gives the reason, explanation or justification of the effect described in the other argument?
Options: Arg1, Arg2, None
Answer: None

Consider the discourse relation between Arg1 and Arg2, where Arg1 is 'The chain is reviewing its product list' and Arg2 is 'to avoid such problems' Which argument (Arg1 or Arg2) gives the reason, explanation or justification of the effect described in the other argument?
Options: Arg1, Arg2, None
Answer: ?
```

Multi-way MC step

```
Task: Identify the most suitable option from the list below that describes the discourse relationship between the following pair of arguments.

Argument 1: The chain is reviewing its product list
Argument 2: to avoid such problems

Options:
1. Comparison.Contrast, on the contrary / in contrast
2. Expansion.Conjunction, in addition / also
3. Contingency.Purpose, in order to / such that

Answer: ?
```

Figure 8: Per-class binary prompt. Corresponding options (same as Figure 5) to the DRs *not* answered with *"none"* in the verification question step are listed as options in the MC step.

PropBank goes Public: Incorporation into Wikidata

Elizabeth Spaulding[1], **Kathryn Conger**[1], **Anatole Gershman**[2], **Mahir Morshed**[3], **Susan Windisch Brown**[1], **James Pustejovsky**[4], **Rosario Uceda-Sosa**[5], **Sijia Ge**[1] and **Martha Palmer**[1]

[1]University of Colorado Boulder, [2]Language Technologies Institute, Carnegie Mellon University, [3]University of Illinois Urbana-Champaign, [4]Brandeis University, [5]IBM Research, T.J.Watson

{elizabeth.spaulding,kathryn.conger,martha.palmer}@colorado.edu

Abstract

This paper presents the first integration of PropBank role information into Wikidata, in order to provide a novel resource for information extraction, one combining Wikidata's ontological metadata with PropBank's rich argument structure encoding for event classes. We discuss a technique for PropBank augmentation to existing eventive Wikidata items, as well as identification of gaps in Wikidata's coverage based on manual examination of over 11,300 PropBank rolesets. We propose five new Wikidata properties to integrate PropBank structure into Wikidata so that the annotated mappings can be added en masse. We then outline the methodology and challenges of this integration, including annotation with the combined resources.

1 Introduction

Recent work (Spaulding et al., 2023) has explored how Wikidata (Vrandečić and Krötzsch, 2014) can be adapted as an ontology for information extraction by: (1) providing an external resource that augments existing eventive Wikidata items with PropBank (Kingsbury and Palmer, 2002; Gildea and Palmer, 2002; Palmer et al., 2005) role information; and (2) documenting gaps of event coverage in Wikidata, where a PropBank concepts have no corresponding Wikidata items. For each PropBank predicate, annotators have been asked to identify a matching concept in Wikidata. All 11,300+ PropBank rolesets have been subject to at least one pass of this task, so that each PropBank predicate has either a Wikidata mapping or a flag indicating a missing concept in Wikidata. This paper outlines the methodology and challenges of integrating the project into Wikidata itself, including filling those gaps in event coverage. The paper will also document the unique annotation challenges faced in attempting to join the two different resources.

2 Background

Wikidata[1] is a large, crowd-sourced, multilingual knowledge base hosted by the Wikimedia Foundation. Originally created to support Wikipedia by serving as a repository linking matching articles of different languages together, it proliferated into a true knowledge graph of its own. It is now the centralized location for data in Wikipedia infoboxes, and is used for various natural language processing applications requiring the use of real-world knowledge. For example, Wikidata is often used as a source of facts to probe (Petroni et al., 2019) or update the knowledge (Meng et al., 2023) of large language models (LLMs). Knowledge bases generally have been used for search and question answering in large, industry-scale search engines (Noy et al., 2019). A major issue in using knowledge bases is quality and long-term maintenance (Piscopo and Simperl, 2019). While Wikidata is relatively reliable compared to other similar knowledge bases, there is still room for improvement in quality control (Shenoy et al., 2022) and coverage of event concepts (Spaulding et al., 2023).

Each item in Wikidata refers to either a concept ("planet") or a real-world instantiation of a concept ("Earth"), and is uniquely identified by a *Q* followed by a string of digits. Relations are called *properties* in Wikidata, and are uniquely identified by a *P* followed by a string of digits. Wikidata items can have statements, which are a property and a value (usually another item or a static data point such as a string or numerical quantity). Thus, <subject, relation, object> triples are <item, property, value> triples in Wikidata nomenclature. Statements can be annotated with qualifiers—for example, specifying the start and end time that a relation holds—and references, making Wikidata an extremely rich, detailed, and verifiable source of knowledge for natural language processing ap-

[1]https://www.wikidata.org/

Proceedings of The 18th Linguistic Annotation Workshop (LAW-XVIII), pages 166–175
March 22, 2024

plications. Additionally, Wikidata is a multilingual resource. Users can browse and add data to Wikidata in their preferred language, so concepts can be described by labels written in a broad range of languages, with an average of around 8 labels[2] per Wikidata Item.

2.1 The DWD Overlay

The DARPA Wikidata Overlay (DWD overlay; Spaulding et al. 2023) serves as an external resource augmenting Wikidata items with event role information drawn from PropBank (Kingsbury and Palmer, 2002; Gildea and Palmer, 2002; Palmer et al., 2005), natural language templates for how each event can prototypically be used in a sentence, and temporal relation mappings for event-to-event relations. The overlay currently contains 5,764 eventive Wikidata Items, 2,224 of which have hand-curated PropBank roleset mappings (the rest have semi-automatic PropBank mappings). 9,011 PropBank rolesets are currently documented as having no matching Wikidata Item, and thus, are not in the overlay. It is contained in a JSON file and hosted on Github, and must be continually updated as Wikidata changes. Because it can be edited by anyone with an internet connection, Wikidata is constantly changing, making the maintenance of the overlay, which relies on Wikidata, untenable in the long-term. Wikidata is also far more desirable as a host of this information for computing applications, as Wikidata provides support for large-scale projects with a SPARQL query service, and already has a large community of dedicated contributors which maintain it. Once the mappings contained in the overlay are fully integrated into Wikidata, overlay users can reconstruct the overlay from Wikidata itself by querying the PropBank additions.

2.2 Role of PropBank

PropBank is the source of participant roles for incorporation of events into Wikidata. PropBank is a verb lexicon initially annotated over the Wall Street Journal sentences in the Penn Treebank (Taylor et al., 2003), which separates verbs (and event nominalizations) into coarse senses, each with a set of verb-specific semantic roles (the "roleset"). While the roles are verb-specific, they are numbered 0-6, with ARG0 typically corresponding to Proto-Agent and ARG1 corresponding to Proto-Patient, allowing for some amount of generalization across verbs. An example of a PropBank roleset can be found in Table 1. PropBank was chosen because of its wide coverage of verbs and eventive nouns that could be easily matched to Wikidata concepts and because its roles could be represented as both broad, general roles (e.g., ARG0, ARG1) and as more event-specific (e.g., attacker, victim).

2.3 Use of the Overlay in Systems

Since the DWD Overlay covers eventive Wikidata concepts, it has been adapted for use as an event ontology in GLEN (Li et al., 2023). In particular, the mapping between Wikidata entities and PropBank rolesets was utilized to create distantly supervised training data by re-purposing PropBank annotation. In addition, the event detection model computed event type representations from Wikidata Item labels and descriptions. The DWD Overlay greatly accelerated the development of this general-purpose event detection model that now supports over 3000 event types.

In terms of argument extraction, the event templates (e.g., {A0_pag_transporter} transported {A1_ppt_thing_transported} from {A2_dir_source} to {A3_gol_destination} {A4_loc_path} at {AM_loc}) can be utilized to guide the extraction of arguments by formulating the argument extraction task as conditional generation (Li et al., 2021). Besides text generation, the argument extraction task can also be transformed into structured code generation (Wang et al., 2023) which takes advantage of the argument names and their type constraints.

The Wikidata labels and descriptions also contribute greatly to the schema matching and prediction component in the RESIN event extraction, tracking, and prediction system (Du et al., 2022). RESIN defines the similarity between an event mention and a schema event type as the WordNet (Miller, 1995) similarity between their corresponding Wikidata labels. Then, the matching is conducted based on these pairwise item similarities.

3 The Events and Role Frames WikiProject

To address the issues discussed in Section 2.1, a WikiProject has been created to integrate several thousand PropBank-Wikidata mapping annotations into Wikidata itself. This project merges together

[2]Although this average may be inflated due to some labels being the same in different languages—for example, when the label is a person's name.

ID	combust.01
Description	cause to burn
Roles	ARG0-PAG: agent/cause of combustion ARG1-PPT: thing combusting ARG2-MNR: instrument
Example	[$_{\text{ARG1}}$ Most fossil fuels] are combusted [$_{\text{ARG2}}$ with ambient air].

Table 1: The PropBank roleset for `combust.01`.

several proposals for how to format the integration, including introducing a handful of new properties. While our event mappings are only for generic event types (e.g., "eating" in Table 2), the proposed properties *can* be extended to instances (e.g., "assassination of Abraham Lincoln" in Table 4).

3.1 Goals and Motivation

The coverage of event classes and their role structures in Wikidata is limited. For example, some of the most common verbs in most languages are the verbs of perception, e.g., "to see" ("I see a house", "je vois une maison", "minä näen taloa", "ich sehe ein Haus"), "to hear" ("I hear the rain", "minä kuulen sadetta"), "to smell" ("I smell the coffee", "je sens le café"), etc. Wikidata has related concepts: visual perception (`Q162668`) "ability to interpret the surrounding environment using light in the visible spectrum"; hearing (`Q160289`), sense of smell (`Q1541064`), etc. We argue that an ability to do something is distinct from actually doing it which is an event in space-time. We examined over 11,300 rolesets contained in PropBank that describe English predicates (mostly verbs) and identified over 7,500 potentially missing Wikidata items. Each of these "gaps" needs to be further examined to determine if it warrants a new item, but the list gives us a starting point.

All action events have core semantic roles: "eating" has the "eater" and the "eaten"; "throwing" has the "thrower", the "target" and the "projectile". These roles are not optional. Every act of "eating" has an "eater" and the "eaten" independently of how and in which language it is expressed. However, most of the existing Wikidata items for action classes do not mention these roles. For example, throwing (`Q12898216`) "launching of a ballistic projectile by hand" does not have any statements that indicate the existence of the thrower, the target, or the projectile, let alone the specifications of the kinds of entities these attributes are likely to be.

Thus, the goal of the "Wikidata Events and Role Frames" project[3] is to use PropBank and other sources to fill these gaps in Wikidata and provide event items with role frames.

3.2 Proposed Properties

Event Role The key to our proposal is the new Wikidata property which we propose to call "event role" whose value is a Wikidata Item that describes the role in greater detail. For example, eating (`Q213449`) would have two statements, exemplified in Table 2. In this example, we used the existing Wikidata items for the "eater" and "eaten" roles. However, in most cases, such items do not currently exist and must be created.

Based on the number of PropBank predicates and roles per predicate, we currently estimate adding up to 25,000 – 30,000 event role items. It might also be possible to cluster multiple event role items and create a "subclass of" event concept hierarchy, using other event lexicon resources such as FrameNet (Baker et al., 1998) and VerbNet (Schuler, 2005). We want to stress that although we start from the English PropBank, the proposed event role items are not lexical or grammatical constructs. The existence of a killer in a killing event is not tied to any language or grammar. It is a part of the "killing" concept.

Selectional Preference Whether existing or newly created, event role items serve as anchors for whatever information we want to associate with the role. For example, we may specify that the eater is expected to be an organism. The existing item, eater (`Q20984678`), does not specify that. We propose to introduce another property "selectional preference" which we show in Table 3.

Multiple statements with "selectional preference" should be interpreted as an "OR", i.e., the filler of the role slot is likely to "descend from" at least one of the selectional preference items. The meaning of

[3] `http://www.wikidata.org/wiki/Wikidata:WikiProject_Events_and_Role_Frames`

eating (Q213449)	
ingestion of food to provide for all organisms their nutritional or medicinal needs	
event role	eater (Q20984678)
	food (Q2095)

Table 2: Sample usage of the proposed property "event role," using already-existing Wikidata items. Proposed additions to Wikidata in *italics*.

eater (Q20984678)	
human or other live being who eats something	
selectional preference	organism (Q7239)

Table 3: Sample usage of the proposed property "selectional preference." Proposed additions to Wikidata in *italics*.

"descend" could be application-specific, but, generally, we mean a combination of "subclass of", "parent taxon" and "instance of" properties. Violations of selectional preferences often signal metaphoric use as in "the house ate the savings". Other information such as dietary restriction statements can also be attached to the event role items.

Event Argument and Argument Role The proposed "event role" property applies only to event classes, not instances. For example, the assassination of Abraham Lincoln (Q1025404) is an instance of assassination (Q3882219). Our proposal will create the "assassin" and the "assassinate" event role items. We propose to create a new property "event argument", together with a qualifier "argument role", in order to represent the roles in an event instance, as shown in Table 4.

One might object that in this example, these properties convey the same information as "target" (P533) and "perpetrator" (P8031). Unfortunately, many instances of "assassination" use different properties or none at all to indicate the assassin and the victim. We propose to use a uniform approach even if it causes some redundancy.

We are aware that creating new properties in Wikidata is a time-consuming and difficult process. Our proposal involves one new property for event classes, two for event roles, and one property and one qualifier for event instances.

3.3 Aligning with Wikidata Standards and Structure

The incorporation of events and relationships from PropBank into Wikidata has the potential to greatly benefit the Abstract Wikipedia project under development (Vrandečić, 2020, 2021). The "abstract content" this project will use requires that information be stored in a language-independent fashion, so that anyone can edit it regardless of their spoken language. Hence, for this information to be grounded in terms of Wikidata entities, individual statements about event occurrences must not only have Wikidata items for particular participants, but also items for events and the roles those participants play in those events. Moreover, for a particular concept (such as PropBank's see.01) and predicates representing this concept across different languages (such as English "see", Finnish "nähdä", and Turkish "görmek"), an important goal is the ability to align the same semantic roles across languages, regardless of their syntactic expression in that language. For example, the syntactic object of English "see" and the subject of the isiZulu passive verb "bonwa" should both refer to the thing being viewed.

There has been one attempt to (1) map items for events to individual senses on Wikidata lexemes using the property "predicate for" (P9970), (2) map event roles for a given event across different languages' predicates using the property 'has thematic relation' (P9971) and (3) use these mappings in generating natural language text (Morshed, 2023).

Project Discussion Wikidata provides spaces for the discussion of the proposed properties[4] and of the project as a whole[5]. On top of the linguistic challenges found in annotating the mapping between PropBank and Wikidata, an essential component is negotiating the incorporation of these properties into Wikidata with the Wikidata community. Many annotation projects in natural language processing are developed within a team of perhaps a dozen researchers with relatively similar goals and interests. Due to the public nature of Wikidata, we must "convince" Wikidata users who may not

[4]e.g. https://www.wikidata.org/wiki/Wikidata:Property_proposal/event_role

[5]http://www.wikidata.org/wiki/Wikidata:WikiProject_Events_and_Role_Frames

assassination of Abraham Lincoln (Q1025404)		
1865 murder of the 16th President of the United States		
event argument	Abraham Lincoln (Q91)	
	argument role	*assassinated*
	John Wilkes Booth (Q180914)	
	argument role	*assassin*

Table 4: Sample usage of the proposed property "event role" and the proposed qualifier "argument role", using already-existing Wikidata Items. Proposed additions to Wikidata in *italics*.

share the same goals and interests that our proposal will benefit the wider community. We invite anyone who is interested to join the discussion of the many challenges in this project, some of which are described in the next section.

4 Challenges to Incorporation of PropBank into Wikidata

An inherent challenge to integration is inevitable discrepancies between projects. As a database of coarse-grained, predicate-specific semantic frames, PropBank entries are eventive in nature. While entries may be nominal, adjectival, or verbal, the majority are verbal. By contrast, the Wikidata database includes comparatively fine-grained entries for events and entities, in addition to a number of other types of Items. The majority of Wikidata entities are nominal and often non-eventive in nature. Differences in Item granularity and Item type necessitate careful comparisons of the scope of a roleset to the scope of an Item. Sometimes Items have better mappings to predicate arguments than to the predicates themselves, raising the question of whether such argument mappings are useful. Managing these differences has been largely guided by the utility of the overlay in downstream tasks.

4.1 Identifying Events

Because all PropBank entries are predicates, it is crucial that they are mapped to eventive Items. In some cases, the line between an event and a non-event in Wikidata is clear. For example, bathe.01 is defined as "have a bath, giving or having a bath" and can be used for verbs (e.g., *The place was* ***bathed*** *in sunlight*), eventive nouns (e.g., ***bathing*** *of the infant*), or light verb constructions (e.g., *I* ***gave*** *the dog a* ***bath***). Wikidata has entries for bathing (Q327651) "washing of the body with a liquid" and bathtub (Q152095) "large container for holding water in which a person may bathe". "Bathing" clearly refers to the event while "bathtub" refers to the physical item in which the event takes place. The line is less clear in cases such as signature (Q1373131) "mark of the creator on a work to identify themselves as such (name, initials, monogram)". The definition of "signature" suggests that the Item refers to the artifact itself but does not seem to preclude a signing event during which one creates or affixes a signature. However, the statements about "signature" indicate that this Item refers to artifact only; its subclass membership precludes extension to the event. Thus, we recommended that a new Item be created for the act of signing. There are many such process-result "logical polysemies" (Pustejovsky, 1995) that can be handled in a similar fashion.

4.2 Item Extensibility

A second consideration comes from differing levels of Item granularity, particularly with respect to the scope and extensibility of an Item. For example, see.01 is defined as "view" but is used for literal instances of visual perception (e.g., *I see you*), instances of observation (e.g., *They saw the value of their stocks decline*), and figurative extensions (e.g., *I see your point*). Wikidata has entries for sighting (Q52266213) "occurrence where a region of land is spotted from a ship" and "visual perception" (Q162668) "ability to interpret the surrounding environment using light in the visible spectrum".

While "sighting" does involve an act of seeing, it is very narrowly defined. "Visual perception" seems like a better match for literal instances. However, it is defined as an ability, specifying a capability rather than the active use of the ability that occurs during a seeing event. Given the specificity of Wikidata entries and the inherent differences between capabilities and actions, "visual perception" should not be extended to cover literal instances of the act of "seeing". Instead, a new Item is needed. This new Item for "seeing" can be linked to "visual perception" using the "uses" (P2283) property. There are no existing Item options for figurative instances of "see". Given the narrow construal of Items in general, the lack of figurative Items is challenging as many PropBank rolesets are typically extended to include figurative usages.

A major goal of the mapping is to create full correspondences between PropBank and Wikidata. In some cases, this can be accomplished with a one-to-one correspondence between a single roleset and a single Item. However, as long as the full scope of a roleset is accounted for, 1-many or many-1 mappings are also acceptable.

Where Wikidata has gaps, new items can be created. However, accounting for figurative language, which is often language specific, may be more appropriately handled through the use of Wikidata Lexemes (language-specific Wikidata entities whose IDs begin with 'L') rather than concept Items. Thus, we propose the alternative solution of adding figurative senses of terms like "see" to Wikidata Lexemes, rather than creating concept Items for these and other such multi-sense English lexemes.

4.3 Multiple Mappings

For full project compatibility, one should be able to do semantic role annotation on text by using PropBank practices but replacing the rolesets with their mapped Items, thus linking the events in the text to associated world knowledge. This is similar to the use case employed by Li et al. (2023) in their usage of the overlay (see Section 2.3). Similarly, a Wikidata user should be able to substitute a PropBank roleset for an Item, allowing for the incorporation of predicate-specific thematic role information into their Wikidata-based project. A prerequisite for this compatibility is very precise mappings that preserve the scope of the roleset without incidentally adding extraneous meaning, hence the 1-many or many-1 mappings discussed above. However, multiple mappings require careful consideration. Multiple mappings can be added for two reasons.

Two or more Items are indistinguishable First, if two or more Items are identical or would be indistinguishable in underspecified contexts, both are retained for consideration as mappings to rolesets. For example, death (`Q4`) "permanent cessation of vital functions" and dying (`Q267505`) "final process of life" are potential mappings to die.01 which represents the "dying or death" sense of the lexeme "die". "Dying" is a subtype of change of state and is, therefore, more applicable to verbal instances when it is clear that the dying event is actively occurring. However, die.01 can account for the verb "die" and the eventive nouns "die", "dying", and "death" where the ability to differentiate between applicability of "death" and "dying" is difficult. Rather than making an arbitrary decision, both are mapped to die.01.

An Item covers only a portion of the scope of a roleset The second reason for multiple mappings is when an Item covers a portion of the scope of a roleset and one or more Items cover the remaining scope of the sense. For example, physical contact (`Q38183514`) is defined as the "state of physical items and materials with no spatial separation, in which surface interactions may occur" and touch (`Q877674`) is defined as "physical contact involving one or more sentient agents (for contact between non-sentient objects, use (`Q38183514`)".

Both were evaluated as potential matches for touch.01, which refers to the "come into contact with" sense. "Physical contact" is a member of the subclass "intentional human activity" and specifies the involvement of one or more sentient agents. "Touch" is complementarily distributed relative to "physical contact" as it is used in cases of physical contact that do *not* involve sentient agents. Touch.01 does not differentiate between sentient and non-sentient agents, so, individually, these Items are more narrowly defined than the roleset. Together, their scope is similar to that of touch.01, so they are both mapped.

In the case of death (`Q4`) and dying (`Q267505`), the Items have a similar scope. However, in the case of physical contact (`Q38183514`) and touch (`Q877674`), touch covers a larger portion of the scope of touch.01 than physical contact. Weight is assigned to this Item via representation in a prioritized slot in the overlay, with additional Items added based on the degree of coverage they contribute. Additionally, future releases hope to include methods to add weights to these slots.

A mapping is considered "complete" when the collectively mapped Items can account for at least 90% of the scope of the roleset and the collectively mapped Items do not add additional information that the roleset is unable to account for. If no complete mapping (one-to-one or otherwise) can be identified, we recommend that a new Item be created.

Synchronizing argument structures for multi-roleset mappings Expanding to multiple-roleset-to-one-Item mappings also required a modification to the DWD Overlay to accommodate them. Mappings between a single Item and multiple rolesets presented a more serious challenge as they have the potential to attach conflicting argument structures to the Item.

For example, attempt (Q12897867) "action whose success is not guaranteed" is highly related to try.01 ("attempt") and attempt.01 ("try"). These rolesets share an argument structure, enriching the Item with consistent argument structure information. By contrast, want.01 and wish.01, which can both be mapped to wish (Q241625) "desire for a specific item or event", have different argument structures. Specifically, want.01 has two additional roles missing from the wish.01 frame – ARG3-PPT *in-exchange-for* and ARG4-DIR: *from*. Mapping them both to a single Item presents conflicting argument information.

One solution could be to supply the maximal number of arguments and then specify verb-specific selectional preferences. However, this issue cannot be entirely solved by simply increasing the valence of all co-mapped items to that of the largest structure as numbered arguments may be present in both rolesets but used differently. For example, issue.02 and problematic.01 "constituting a problem" (mapped to problem (Q621184) "situation that invites resolution") both have an ARG1. For issue.02, the ARG1 is an experiencer. For problematic.01, the ARG1 is a further description of the nature of the problem and the ARG2 is used for the experiencer. This requires encoding a more detailed set of specifications for the mapping between the rolesets and the Item within Wikidata to ensure backwards compatibility.

4.4 Predicate-level versus Argument-level Applicability

To aid in the identification of likely sense matches, annotators were given a list of automatically identified candidate Items as a starting point for evaluation. For opine.01, this list included opinion (Q3962655) (see Table 5). "Opinion" is listed as a type of entity, precluding it from mapping to the predicate. This information is important as full compatibility between projects will require mapping coverage at the argument-level in addition to predicate-level coverage.

Thus, we have begun this effort by mapping Items such as "opinion" at the argument level (in this case, to the ARG1 of opine.01). Identification of argument-level versus predicate-level applicability is critical, as failure to do so would introduce annotation circularity. Thus, not only have we increased the number of Items evaluated as potential mappings to a roleset, we have begun argument-level annotation efforts that can be used for richer capabilities of inference in information extraction tasks, argument extraction tasks, and future annotation refinement.

4.5 Eventiveness

In some cases, Items that map at the argument level are non-eventive. With the exception of noting Items that map to an argument of a predicate, this research has focused on events, as non-events cannot be mapped at the predicate level. Research collaborators sharing curated data have a similar focus. As such, we removed non-eventive Items from the shared DWD overlay so that they would not be considered as a potential predicate mapping. It should be noted that we take a conservative approach to the removal of non-eventive Items. For example, Items such as bathtub (Q152095) can safely be removed. However, alliance (Q878249) "coalition made between two or more parties to secure common interests" was not removed, despite the fact that its statements indicate it represents organizations.

4.6 Constraints

Another useful aspect of argument mapping is the ability to add in automatic, more fine-grained sense disambiguation, particularly when training data is limited. This can be seen in the case of contain.02 "restrain, halt the spread of", which has an ARG0: entity restraining ARG1 and an ARG1: thing being restrained, halted. Contain.02 is used for all types of restraint, including things such as diseases, chemicals as in the case of an oil spill, non-toxic items such as water, or more abstract items such as news or information. Because PropBank does not differentiate between these subtypes of containment, mapping at the predicate level can supply an argument structure for a general restricting event but cannot further enrich the event description.

However, the selectional preferences discussed in Section 3.2 can be added to the arguments. Selectional preferences specify the kind of information commonly associated with our containment subtypes (e.g., disease, chemicals, information, etc.). For example, see the usage of the predicate "contain" in Sentence 1:

Opine.01 argument structure	Candidate Item
ARG0-PAG: speaker ARG1-PPT: opinion ARG2-GOL: hearer	Opinion (Q3962655) "judgment, viewpoint, or statement that is not conclusive; may deal with subjective matters in which there is no conclusive finding"

Table 5: Opine.01 and Opinion *Q3962655*

(1) Public health officials are working to **contain** the spread of COVID-19, in part by using contact tracing.

We know from the predicate that this is interpreted as a general "halt the spread of" event. To this, we add a selectional preference to the ARG1, indicating that it should be an illness or malady. Such information would stand in contrast to the selectional preferences associated with chemicals, or news. For chemicals, we add a selectional preference of "geographic area" to the ARG0 and "non-infectious contaminant" to the ARG1. For news, we add the selectional preference of "information, communicated item, statement, or belief" to the ARG1, which does not preclude selection of misinformation.

Crucially, selectional preferences are intended as optional tools. They do not restrict the kinds of information that can fulfill a numbered argument role. Instead, they attempt to characterize frequent scenarios to aid in more fine-grained sense disambiguation.

5 Improving DWD Utility

The overlay's development has been closely guided by feedback from users of the overlay. Currently, the overlay is used for event extraction on newstext, so many of the changes and additions made to the overlay have been informed by the effect the change might have on that task.

5.1 Sentence Templates

To improve the clarity of the given roles for an event and to supply additional means for matching text instances of events and their arguments to a DWD event type, we added sentence-like templates to every event type. These templates place every PropBank argument role assigned to an event in an English language sentence with the event type expressed as the main verb for the sentence. For example, the roles for *combust.01* (see Table 1), mapped to Q133235, are incorporated into the following sentence template:

(2) {A0_pag_agent/cause_of_combustion} combusted {A1_ppt_thing_combusting} with {A2_mnr_instrument}.

These templates were created automatically using simple heuristics based on typical syntactic realizations of combinations of PropBank roles. For those Wikidata items that were easily converted to English verbs, this method worked fairly well, although some hand-correction was needed. However, for event types best expressed in English with nouns, such as coup d'etat (Q45383) or earthquake (Q7944), the sentence template needed additional manual curation. In many cases, a light verb or other multiword construction expressed the concept in a way that best allowed the incorporation of all roles into a sentence template. For the coup d'etat type, for example, we used

(3) {A0_pag_agent_coup_stager} staged a coup against {A1_ppt_theme_overthrown_government} at {AM_loc}.

5.2 Aligning with GLEN

The GLEN event-detection dataset was created using 3,465 event types drawn from the DWD ontology (Li et al., 2023). The dataset takes advantage of the DWD mappings between the Wikidata event Items and PropBank rolesets, which allowed them to build upon the extensive existing PropBank annotation. The resulting dataset, with 205K event mentions, has the broadest event-type coverage, 20x larger than the MAVEN dataset, which is based on 168 event types.

Li et al. (2023) selected a subset of DWD event types for GLEN, eliminating cognitive types like BELIEF, very fine-grained types like STAPEDECTOMY, and very low-frequency types like SINTERING. We are partially aligning the DWD with GLEN by eliminating the same fine-grained and low-frequency types. However, we are keeping the cognitive types for those who might need an expanded set of general-purpose types.

5.3 Concept Hierarchy

While Wikidata is not an ontology, some of the properties that describe relations between items can be used to construct domain-specific ontologies. The most obvious of these are “subclass of” (P279) and “instance of” (P31). There are, however, issues with this in practice. For example, no “subclass of” chain relates tiger (Q19939) to animal (Q729). Tigers are instead “instances of” taxon (Q16521) that are related through “parent taxon” (P171) and the concept “animal" is not in the “parent taxon” taxonomy. Another challenge is the length of the “subclass of" chain and the intermediate concepts it includes. These can be esoteric and not necessarily helpful for drawing the types of inferences NLP systems rely on. For the DWD overlay, an ontology with multiple inheritance using a “parent” relation was created. A parent of concept A is concept B in DWD such that there is a Wikidata chain of concepts $< A, c_0, ...c_k, B >$, where the intermediate concepts c_i are not in DWD and are connected via either “subclass of” or “parent taxon” properties. The last connection in the chain can also be “instance of”.

6 Conclusion

The project of merging PropBank into Wikidata presents unique annotation challenges. Wikidata is highly entity-centric, making it difficult to identify good candidates for mapping to PropBank: moreover, differing granularity between verb senses in PropBank and concepts in Wikidata has proved to be one of the foremost challenges of mapping between resources, even when an eventive Wikidata item exists. Our approach to managing many of these challenges has been to prioritize feedback from the users of the overlay, allowing the needs of the information extraction use case to guide us.

On top of the linguistic challenges, organizational and logistical challenges abound. PropBank is a relatively static resource that was annotated by linguistic experts. Wikidata is a constantly changing project maintained and compiled by anyone with an internet connection. While the overlay has a well-defined use case—event and argument extraction from natural language text—Wikidata has so many different users and stakeholders that it is difficult to claim that there is any one use case for the resource. Our current approaches for managing the challenges of PropBank-Wikidata linking, therefore, may need to be adjusted as we work with the Wikidata community to integrate our mappings into Wikidata itself.

Acknowledgements

We gratefully acknowledge the support of DARPA FA8750-18-2-0016-AIDA – RAMFIS: Representations of vectors and Abstract Meanings for Information Synthesis and a sub award from RPI on DARPA KAIROS Program No. FA8750-19-2-1004. Any opinions, findings, and conclusions or recommendations expressed in this material are those of the authors and do not necessarily reflect the views of DARPA or the U.S. government. We especially want to thank Zixuan Zhang for his contributions to Section 2.3.

References

Collin F. Baker, Charles J. Fillmore, and John B. Lowe. 1998. The Berkeley FrameNet Project. In *36th Annual Meeting of the Association for Computational Linguistics and 17th International Conference on Computational Linguistics, Volume 1*, pages 86–90, Montreal, Quebec, Canada. Association for Computational Linguistics.

Xinya Du, Zixuan Zhang, Sha Li, Pengfei Yu, Hongwei Wang, Tuan Lai, Xudong Lin, Ziqi Wang, Iris Liu, Ben Zhou, Haoyang Wen, Manling Li, Darryl Hannan, Jie Lei, Hyounghun Kim, Rotem Dror, Haoyu Wang, Michael Regan, Qi Zeng, Qing Lyu, Charles Yu, Carl Edwards, Xiaomeng Jin, Yizhu Jiao, Ghazaleh Kazeminejad, Zhenhailong Wang, Chris Callison-Burch, Mohit Bansal, Carl Vondrick, Jiawei Han, Dan Roth, Shih-Fu Chang, Martha Palmer, and Heng Ji. 2022. RESIN-11: Schema-guided Event Prediction for 11 Newsworthy Scenarios. In *Proceedings of the 2022 Conference of the North American Chapter of the Association for Computational Linguistics: Human Language Technologies: System Demonstrations*, pages 54–63, Hybrid: Seattle, Washington + Online. Association for Computational Linguistics.

Daniel Gildea and Martha Palmer. 2002. The necessity of parsing for predicate argument recognition. In *Proceedings of the 40th Annual Meeting on Association for Computational Linguistics*, ACL '02, page 239–246, USA. Association for Computational Linguistics.

Paul Kingsbury and Martha Palmer. 2002. From TreeBank to PropBank. In *Proceedings of the Third International Conference on Language Resources and Evaluation (LREC'02)*, Las Palmas, Canary Islands - Spain. European Language Resources Association (ELRA).

Sha Li, Heng Ji, and Jiawei Han. 2021. Document-level event argument extraction by conditional generation. In *Proceedings of the 2021 Conference of the North*

American Chapter of the Association for Computational Linguistics: Human Language Technologies, pages 894–908, Online. Association for Computational Linguistics.

Sha Li, Qiusi Zhan, Kathryn Conger, Martha Palmer, Heng Ji, and Jiawei Han. 2023. GLEN: General-purpose event detection for thousands of types. In *Proceedings of the 2023 Conference on Empirical Methods in Natural Language Processing*, pages 2823–2838, Singapore. Association for Computational Linguistics.

Kevin Meng, Arnab Sen Sharma, Alex J Andonian, Yonatan Belinkov, and David Bau. 2023. Mass-editing memory in a transformer. In *The Eleventh International Conference on Learning Representations*.

George A. Miller. 1995. Wordnet: A lexical database for english. *Commun. ACM*, 38(11):39–41.

Mahir Morshed. 2023. Using wikidata lexemes and items to generate text from abstract representations. *Semantic Web Journal p.(submitted)*.

Natasha Noy, Yuqing Gao, Anshu Jain, Anant Narayanan, Alan Patterson, and Jamie Taylor. 2019. Industry-scale knowledge graphs: Lessons and challenges. *Commun. ACM*, 62(8):36–43.

Martha Palmer, Daniel Gildea, and Paul Kingsbury. 2005. The proposition bank: An annotated corpus of semantic roles. *Comput. Linguist.*, 31(1):71–106.

Fabio Petroni, Tim Rocktäschel, Sebastian Riedel, Patrick Lewis, Anton Bakhtin, Yuxiang Wu, and Alexander Miller. 2019. Language models as knowledge bases? In *Proceedings of the 2019 Conference on Empirical Methods in Natural Language Processing and the 9th International Joint Conference on Natural Language Processing (EMNLP-IJCNLP)*, pages 2463–2473, Hong Kong, China. Association for Computational Linguistics.

Alessandro Piscopo and Elena Simperl. 2019. What we talk about when we talk about wikidata quality: A literature survey. In *Proceedings of the 15th International Symposium on Open Collaboration*, OpenSym '19, New York, NY, USA. Association for Computing Machinery.

James Pustejovsky. 1995. *The Generative Lexicon*. MIT Press.

Karin Kipper Schuler. 2005. *VerbNet: A broad-coverage, comprehensive verb lexicon*. Ph.D., University of Pennsylvania, United States – Pennsylvania. ISBN: 9780542200496.

Kartik Shenoy, Filip Ilievski, Daniel Garijo, Daniel Schwabe, and Pedro Szekely. 2022. A study of the quality of Wikidata. *Journal of Web Semantics*, 72:100679.

Elizabeth Spaulding, Kathryn Conger, Anatole Gershman, Rosario Uceda-Sosa, Susan Windisch Brown, James Pustejovsky, Peter Anick, and Martha Palmer. 2023. The DARPA Wikidata Overlay: Wikidata as an ontology for natural language processing. In *Proceedings of the 19th Joint ACL - ISO Workshop on Interoperable Semantic Annotation (ISA-19)*, pages 1–10, Nancy, France.

Ann Taylor, Mitchell Marcus, and Beatrice Santorini. 2003. The Penn Treebank: An Overview. In Anne Abeillé, editor, *Treebanks: Building and Using Parsed Corpora*, Text, Speech and Language Technology, pages 5–22. Springer Netherlands, Dordrecht.

Denny Vrandečić. 2020. Architecture for a multilingual wikipedia. Technical report, Google.

Denny Vrandečić. 2021. Building a multilingual wikipedia. *Commun. ACM*, 64(4):38–41.

Denny Vrandečić and Markus Krötzsch. 2014. Wikidata: a free collaborative knowledgebase. *Communications of the ACM*, 57(10):78–85.

Xingyao Wang, Sha Li, and Heng Ji. 2023. Code4Struct: Code generation for few-shot event structure prediction. In *Proceedings of the 61st Annual Meeting of the Association for Computational Linguistics (Volume 1: Long Papers)*, pages 3640–3663, Toronto, Canada. Association for Computational Linguistics.

Reference and discourse structure annotation of elicited chat continuations in German

Katja Jasinskaja[♠], **Yuting Li**[♠], **Fahime Same**[♡], and **David Uerlings**[♠]
[♠]Department of German Language and Literature I, Linguistics, University of Cologne
[♡]Department of Linguistics, University of Cologne
katja.jasinskaja, yuting.li, f.same, duerlin1@uni-koeln.de

Abstract

We present the construction of a German chat corpus in an experimental setting. Our primary objective is to advance the methodology of discourse continuation for dialogue. The corpus features a fine-grained, multi-layer annotation of referential expressions and coreferential chains. Additionally, we have developed a comprehensive annotation scheme for coherence relations to describe discourse structure.

1 Introduction

Elicited discourse has been used as a source of data for the study of language, communication and the human mind in a variety of settings. While the data are inevitably less 'natural' than in naturally occurring discourse, elicitation makes it possible to observe discourse phenomena under more or less controlled conditions and to test specific hypotheses that might be difficult to test in the wild. The degree of control of the context in which the discourse is produced ranges vastly from giving just a general direction of the communication (e.g. the Switchboard corpus, Godfrey and Holliman, 1993), to asking the participants to fill in gaps in a preconceived template (e.g. Blum-Kulka and Olshtain, 1984). Discourse continuation experiments clearly belong to the higher end of this spectrum: the participants are given the beginning of a story (one or a couple of sentences), and are asked to continue the story by writing one or more sentences. Over the years, this method has established itself in the study of the interpretation and the production of referring expressions (Stevenson et al., 1994), as well as the interaction between reference and coherence relations—meaningful links between sentences and clauses that represent the function of each sentence or clause in the text and ultimately make us perceive the sequence as a coherent whole (Kehler et al., 2008).

However, the method has been used almost exclusively to elicit monologue, and experimental dialogue continuation studies are few (e.g. Tolins and Fox Tree, 2014; Kehler and Rohde, 2017). Typically, dialogue is spoken, whereas discourse continuation is easier to implement as a written task. Although spoken discourse continuation elicitation studies also exist (e.g. Jescheniak, 2000), combining the spoken mode with the interactive setting of dialogue makes the task much more challenging. (For instance, in a situation with multiple speakers, how do we reliably make sure that the participant continues in the role of the right speaker?)

One of the main goals behind the creation of the present corpus was to extend and further develop the discourse continuation methodology in application to dialogue. However, we wanted to avoid the complexities of the elicitation and the analysis of spoken data, and at the same time to make the task as natural as possible for the participants. Thus, we chose chat as the dialogue form for our elicitation experiment. Since the advent of smartphones, written dialogue has become an everyday activity for a vast majority of adult population (Niedermann, 2019), so we decided to rely on people's familiarity with common instant messaging applications such as WhatsApp, Telegram, and Skype, and frame the task as chat continuation.

Furthermore, there is a constant need for the development of high-quality annotated corpora that encompass a diverse range of languages, language uses, and genres in the NLP world. Traditionally, NLP resources have relied heavily on formal written sources such as Wikipedia and newspaper articles, which, while valuable, represent only a portion of human communication inventory. This issue has led to a growing awareness of the need to include more varied forms of language, especially those that mirror everyday communication, like spoken conversations and chat messages.

Chat messages offer a blend of the immediacy and informality of spoken language with the structured format of written texts. However, they

Proceedings of The 18th Linguistic Annotation Workshop (LAW-XVIII), pages 176–187
March 22, 2024 ©2024 Association for Computational Linguistics

also bring unique challenges, such as handling the excessive use of abbreviations (Varnhagen et al., 2010), emojis (Miller et al., 2021; Dainas and Herring, 2021), non-standard grammar (Verheijen, 2017), and slang (Craig, 2003; Farina and Lyddy, 2011) that are common in chat communication. As with the spoken data, another significant challenge is ethical considerations, particularly in privacy and data protection. Chat messages often feature personal communications, necessitating strict anonymization rules and adherence to data protection laws such as General Data Protection Regulation (GDPR). The present corpus circumvents these problems by eliciting chat conversations in an experimental setting, which allows us to preserve the spontaneous and informal nature of real chats while avoiding legal and ethical concerns.

In Section 2, we present an overview of available corpora for the study of reference, coherence relations, and previous efforts in creating chat corpora. Section 3 details the data collection procedure. Section 4 sets out the motivation for our annotations and the annotation plan we pursued. In Section 5, we show the application of the annotation by presenting case studies.

2 Related work

Reference-annotated corpora differ from one another in the genre and modality of the texts they include. Some are specifically designed for studying reference, while others serve more general purposes. Another difference is in the nature of their source materials—whether these corpora are based on pre-existing texts or are compiled from data gathered in systematically designed experiments (Viethen, 2012).

OntoNotes (Weischedel et al., 2013) and GUM (Zeldes, 2017) are examples of general-purpose corpora with layered annotations, including syntax, part of speech, and coreference. OntoNotes features a range of genres, from news to phone conversations, and provides extensive annotations of coreferential chains. However, it does not specifically annotate the type (e.g., pronoun, proper name, or definite NP) of each referring expression. GUM offers broader annotation scope, including detailed reference and rhetorical structure annotations in discourse. On the other hand, GREC-2.0 and GREC People (Belz et al., 2010) are specialized for analyzing referring expressions within context, derived from Wikipedia article introductions. They provide extensive annotations on the form and grammatical role of referents, but GREC-2.0 is limited to annotations related to the main subject, and GREC-People exclusively annotates human referents.

In addition to the above corpora, which are constructed from existing resources, there exists also a range of corpora developed in experimental settings for the study of reference. These corpora, including SCARE (Stoia et al., 2008), COCONUT (Di Eugenio et al., 1998), TUNA (Gatt et al., 2008), G-TUNA (Howcroft et al., 2017), GIVE-2 (Gargett et al., 2010), and PENTOREF (Zarrieß et al., 2016), are derived from elicited language in controlled settings like virtual reality games and computer-mediated dialogues. These corpora, involving tasks like instruction-giving or furniture-buying, predominantly feature short exchanges about inanimate objects. Consequently, their annotations focus almost exclusively on inanimate entities, disregarding annotations for animate referents.

Most corpora annotated with coherence relations, such as the Penn Discourse Tree Bank (Webber et al., 2019) and the German Potsdam Commentary Corpus (Stede et al., 2015) consist of written texts, primarily newspaper articles. STAC is an example of a dialogue corpus with extensive coherence annotations, containing chats between the players in an online *Settlers* game (Asher et al., 2016), whose approach to annotation we selectively adopt in the present project.

The corpus showcased in our study combines informal (non-task-oriented) written dialogue with comprehensive annotations of both animate and inanimate referents, and coherence relations, essential for understanding natural communication.

3 Data collection

3.1 Theoretical background and hypotheses

The original research question that motivated the data collection was how the perceived communicative success or failure of an utterance influences the speaker's planning of subsequent discourse. Based on previous research on dialogue interaction (Clark and Schaefer, 1989; Clark, 1996) we assumed that the joint goal of the communication participants is to reach common ground, which includes reaching mutual understanding and agreement on a set of communicated contents. The process that leads to establishing common ground is called *grounding*, in which the addressee's role is to give feedback to the speaker on how far the grounding process has

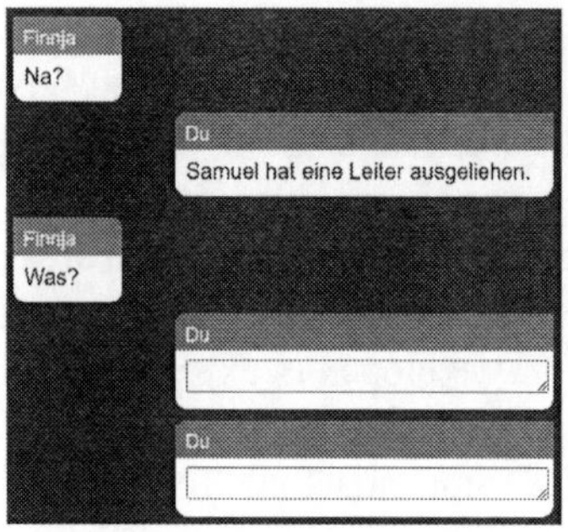

Figure 1: feedback failure

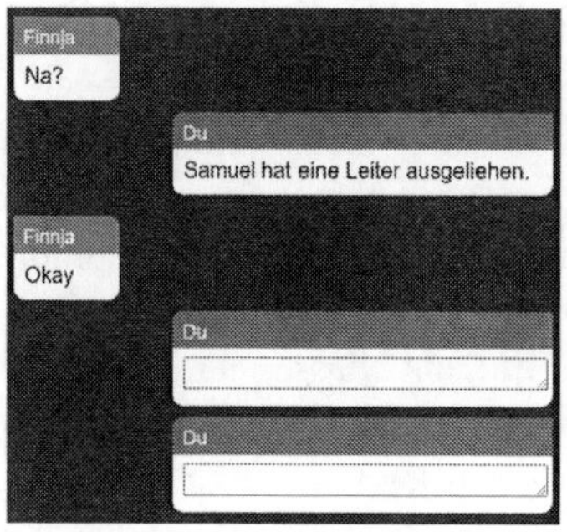

Figure 2: feedback success

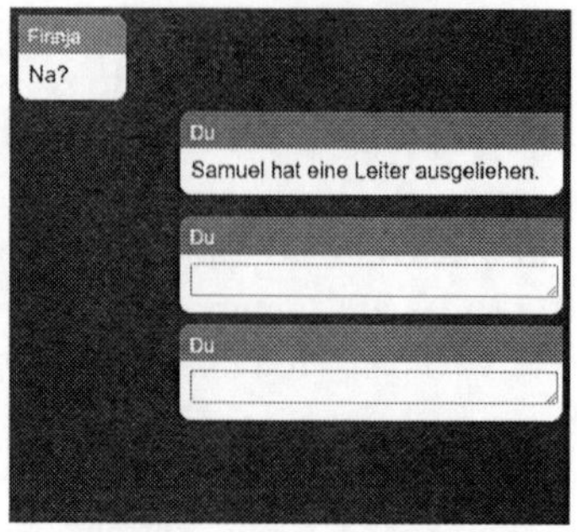

Figure 3: without feedback

succeeded. Backchannel utterances like *yeah* and *mhm*, for instance, indicate that the communication is going smoothly, whereas reactions like *pardon?* or *really?* suggest that the previous utterance was not understood or not accepted as true.

Following Zickenheiner (2020), we assume that speakers' goals are subject to a principle of *inertia*, meaning that speakers do not immediately give up their communicative goals when they encounter obstacles.[1] Therefore, after feedback signalling grounding failure, the speaker would normally still try to achieve the original goal of the utterance, by elaborating on it, explaining it, providing evidence or motivation. Therefore, *Elaboration* and *Explanation* are among the coherence relations that we expect to appear more often in this case. Since the speaker needs to dwell longer on the content of their original utterance, we also expect more references to the same individuals in such continuations.

In contrast, if communication is going smoothly, the speaker is more likely to move on to the next point on their agenda, we expect more coherence relations like *Narration*, *Parallel*, and *Contrast* after feedback indicating grounding success, as well as fewer references to the previously introduced individuals and more references to new individuals.

3.2 Design

To test the above hypothesis, we created a set of chats that included feedback utterances indicating grounding success or failure of a previous statement and asked our participants to write an appropriate continuation. We simulated an interface similar to that of WhatsApp, see figures 1–3. According to a survey conducted by the Allensbach Institute (Niedermann, 2019), 85% of German internet users over the age of 14 use WhatsApp at least occasionally, so we hoped that the presentation format would be familiar to most participants. The utterances of the "other" interlocutor (*Finnja* in figures 1–3) were presented on the left hand side of the screen, and the utterances of the interlocutor whose role the participant was supposed to take on (*Du* 'you') as well as the prompts for participants' input were presented on the right hand side. It seems that the participants quickly adopted this layout, and did not raise any concerns or complaints about it.

While WhatsApp provides users with the ability to engage in individual or group chats through a multimodal approach, including emojis, voice messages, and photos, we limited the possible inputs in this experiment to text only, and therefore did not use the actual WhatsApp platform. Participants were explicitly instructed not to use emojis, even if their input devices allowed emoji entry.

3.3 Stimuli

We created thirty chat dialogues like those in figures 1–3, cf. the English translation in (1). Each dialogue started with an *opening question* (1-a) from the other interlocutor (Finnja), followed by the main *stimulus sentence* (1-b), presented as if produced by the participant of the experiment (You). After that, the two prompts either appeared immediately as in figure 3, or after a *feedback utterance* of Finnja (1-c).

(1)
a. Finnja: So?
b. You: Samuel borrowed a ladder.
c. Finnja: What? / Okay / -
d. You: [prompt 1]
e. You: [prompt 2]

[1]This principle is a specific manifestation of a more general tendency of speakers to stick to the same subject-matter by default, whereas any changes in the course of the discourse would be signalled explicitly. The principle of Topic Continuity (Givón, 1983) or *NEW in optimality-theoretic pragmatics (Zeevat, 2010) are other manifestations of the same phenomenon.

The **opening questions** were generic conversation starters of ten kinds distributed evenly over the 30 items: *Na?* 'So?', *Hi, alles okay soweit?* 'Hi, everything okay so far?', *Hallo, wie gehts?* 'Hi, how are you?', *Alles klar bei dir?* 'Everything okay with you?', *Wie läufts so?* 'How is it going?', *Na, wie läufts bei dir?* 'So, how's it going for you?', *Hey, was gibts Neues?* 'Hey, what's new?', *Und, alles klar?* 'And, everything okay?', *Wie gehts dir?* 'How are you?', *Alles gut?* 'All good?'.

All the thirty **stimulus sentences** were set in the perfect tense and contained a human subject, identified by a unique proper name. These names were distinct from the names of interlocutors (e.g. Finnja). In addition, 16 of the stimuli included a non-human object (2-a), 8 included a non-human modifier (2-b), while the remaining 6 stimuli contained an intransitive verb (2-c) and no referring expressions except the subject. The gender of both the speakers and subjects was balanced.

(2) a. [Moritz] hat [die Küche] geputzt.
[Moritz] cleaned [the kitchen].
b. [Stephan] ist in [einen Nagel] getreten.
[Stephan] stepped on [a nail].
c. [Charlotte] ist fremdgegangen.
[Charlotte] cheated.

The last part of the items differed per condition. In the grounding failure condition, 'Finnja' reacted to the stimulus sentence with a **feedback utterance** indicating grounding failure, i.e. showing that she did not understand or failed to believe the utterance (figure 1). We used the folloing feedback utterances: a. *Wie bitte?* 'Excuse me?'; b. *Ähm?* 'Uh?'; c. *Was?* 'What?'; d. *Hm?*; and e. *Häh?* 'Huh?'.

In the grounding success condition, the feedback utterance indicated successful grounding, i.e. showed that the stimulus sentence was understood and accepted (figure 2). The utterances we used were: a. *Oh!*; b. *Krass!* 'Sick!', slang 'cool, great'; c. *Okay*; d. *Oh nein* 'Oh no'; and e. *Ohje* 'Oh dear'. It is important to note that while expressions like *Oh no* and *Oh dear* convey negative emotions, they are still categorized as feedback for successful grounding, based on the understanding that for a speaker to express these emotions, they must first comprehend and believe the pivot utterance.

In the third condition, there was no feedback utterance (figure 3). This condition was most closely comparable to the classical monologue continuation task, as e.g. in Kehler et al. (2008).

The selection of the feedback utterances was based on the results of a series of pretests. We first gathered a broad range of feedback utterances by asking participants to offer short, non-specific responses in chat sessions under time constraints. We then chose 28 feedback utterances and integrated them into diverse scenarios within a chat simulator. The task for the participants was to determine if the feedback utterances suggested that (a) the addressee understood and believed the previous utterance; (b) understood but did not believe it; or (c) neither understood nor believed the utterance. For the main study, we used the least ambiguous utterances from the sample: utterances that received an overwhelming majority of (a)-responses were used in the success condition, and utterances that received almost only (b)- and (c)-responses were used in the failure condition.

We created 30 additional filler items that contained chats with or without feedback utterances, with or without opening questions of varying specificity, and varying numbers of conversational turns.

3.4 Procedure

Participants were instructed to imagine being a participant of the chat displayed on the screen and to contribute meaningfully to the conversation. They were instructed to compose at least two sentences, using both prompts. The experimental items were distributed over three lists following the Latin Square Design. Both experimental and filler items were presented in a randomized order. The participants had no time constraints and had the opportunity to give feedback and comments at the end of the experiment.

3.5 Participants

Valid data were collected from thirty native speaker of German (14 male, 16 female, mean age = 34.90 years, age range = 18-72 years), resulting in 900 chat continuations. Participants were recruited via Prolific, and received a compensation of £5.82 (£9.97/hr) for their participation, which was higher than the minimum pay allowed on Prolific.

4 Annotation

Most of the annotations were conducted by two of the authors of the paper. Our annotation scheme was reexamined on a continuous basis, leading in some instances to changes of earlier annotation phases. The annotations were conducted with the web-based annotation software INCEpTION (Klie et al., 2018), see Appendix A for an example. We annotated referring expressions (RE) and coreference relations between them (section 4.1), identified elementary discourse segments and their types (section 4.2), as well as the coherence relations between them (section 4.3).

4.1 Referring expressions and coreference

We annotated the following types of referring expressions, using the schema of Repp et al. (2023) with minor modifications: proper names; definite NPs (*der Arzt* 'the doctor', *seine Wohnung* 'his flat'); indefinite NPs (*einen Kuchen* 'a cake', ACC, *irgendeinen Typen* 'some guy', ACC); universal quantifiers (*alle* 'all', *beide* 'both'); personal pronouns (*ich* 'I', *sie* 'she, they'); possessive pronouns (*mein* 'my', *sein* 'his'); demonstrative pronouns in the narrow sense (*dieser* 'this'); D-pronouns, the series of demonstrative pronouns *der/die/das* including their contractions with prepositions (*danach* lit. 'thereafter', *drin* lit. 'therein'); relative pronouns, zeroes and clauses.

Relative pronouns were only annotated as REs if they introduced a non-restrictive relative clause, otherwise the entire relative clause was considered part of the RE of its syntactic head. Zero REs were annotated on the finite verb of a clause if they represented the missing grammatical subject, for instance in coordinated VPs, or if they represented any missing argument of the verb in topic drop constructions resulting in main clauses with an otherwise obligatory but here unrealized constituent in the preverbal position. Clauses were annotated only if pronouns or zeroes in subsequent discourse referred back to the abstract objects (facts or events) encoded by the clause.

The following expressions were not annotated as REs: vocatives; reflexive and reciprocal pronouns (*sich* 'him-/herself', *einander* 'each other'); definite and indefinite NPs in the predicative function or non-specific (in)definites in non-veridical contexts; negative quantifiers (*nichts* 'nothing'); and nominal expressions that do not introduce a specific referent because they constitute parts of idioms (e.g. *Angst* 'fear' in *Angst haben* 'be afraid', lit. 'have fear'). Unlike Repp et al. (2023), we annotated not only animate but also inanimate referents.

We continue annotating other properties of REs, such as their syntactic function (subject, object, etc.), as well as person, number and gender.

Coreference was only annotated in the strict sense, excluding part/whole-relationships. Due to the dialogical nature of our corpus, personal pronouns such as *you* and *I* were often used coreferentially and annotated accordingly.

In our inter-annotator agreement analysis of referring expression type annotations, the annotators reached a 79.6% direct agreement rate. Cohen's Kappa was 0.734 ($P < 0.001$), showing substantial agreement among the annotators.

4.2 Discourse Segments

The chats were segmented into elementary discourse segments following the standard assumption dating back to Rhetorical Structure Theory (Mann and Thompson, 1988) that main clauses, adverbial clauses, and non-restrictive relative clauses constitute independent discourse segments. Our corpus also contains a large number of non-sentential utterances, which were annotated as independent segments if they were separated from their context by sentence punctuation (full stops, exclamation marks and question marks), line breaks (<BR>), or prompt boundaries. Only in exceptional cases, sequences stretching across prompts or line breaks were regarded as a single segment if viewing the parts as separate segments resulted in ungrammatical structures or incoherent interpretations. Main clause segments were further annotated according to their sentence type as declaratives (decl), interrogatives (int), imperatives (imp), or exclamatives (excl). Subordinate clauses and non-sentential utterances were marked as lacking sentence type (NA).

4.3 Coherence relations

For coherence relations in the traditional sense, i.e. relations holding between assertions of the same speaker, we used the reduced "consensus list" of relations from Jasinskaja and Karagjosova (2020), including: *Elaboration*, *Explanation*, *Parallel*, *Contrast*, *Correction*, *Narration*, and *Result* relations. For instance, in a sequence of discourse segments U_1 and U_2, an *Explanation* holds if U_2 reveals why or gives sufficient reason to understand that the content of U_1 is the case. Accordingly, (3-d) is an *Explanation* of (3-b). *Result* is the reverse of *Explanation*, the causal relation holds in the opposite direction where U_1 represents the cause and U_2 the effect, e.g. (3-e) is a *Result* of (3-d).[2]

[2]All German examples are followed immediately by their English translations. To save space, we refer to the "other interlocutor", e.g. Finnja in (1), uniformly as A, and to the

(3) a. A: Hallo, wie gehts?
b. B: Ariana hat ein Regal gebaut
c. A: Wie bitte?
d. B: Sie wollte mehr Platz für ihre Sachen
e. B: Und hat jetzt kurzerhand ein Regal bestellt un d zusammengevbaut

(4) a. A: Hi, how are you?
b. B: Ariana has built a shelf
c. A: Pardon?
d. B: She wanted more space for her things
e. B: And ordered and assembled a shelf without further ado

For typical dialogue relations across turns of different speakers we borrowed *QAP* (question answer pair), *Acknowledgement*, and *Clarification Request* from Asher and Lascarides (2003). Due to the controlled conditions of the experiment, the stimuli contained recurring structures which were automatically pre-annotated for all stimuli. For instance, *QAP* was generally assumed to hold between the opening question and the stimulus sentence, e.g. between (5-b) and (5-a). A *Clarification Request* is a relation between a clarification request and the utterance it is supposed to clarify, which was the assumed relation between the feedback utterance in the failure condition and the stimulus sentence, e.g. (3-c)–(3-b). Feedback utterances signalling grounding success were generally treated as *Acknowledgements* of the stimulus sentence, e.g. (7-c) is an *Acknowledgement* of (7-b) in section 5.

(5) a. A: Hi, alles okay soweit?
b. B: Elisa hat drei Spiele verloren
c. A: Wie bitte?
d. B: Wir haben heute Mensch ärger Dich nicht gespielt
e. und Elisa hat drei Mal verloren.
f. B: Was war bei Dir heute los?

(6) a. A: Hi, everything okay so far?
b. B: Elisa lost three games
c. A: Pardon?
d. B: We played ludo today
e. and Elisa lost three times.
f. B: What was going on for you today?

interlocutor represented by the participant (You) as B. The beginning of the text produced in each prompt is designated by another 'B:'. Discourse segments are labeled with Latin letters 'a.', 'b.', etc.

Questions were annotated in the same way as a felicitous reply would be in their place. For instance, in example (5), the expected answers to the questions (5-f) and (5-a) are both comments on the general state of affairs in the life of the respective addressee, which is why the relation between (5-a) and (5-f) was annotated as *Parallel*—a relation that holds between propositions that are similar in some relevant respects, e.g. concern the general well-being of a person in both (5-a) and (5-f), but distinct along some dimension, e.g. *whose* well-being is under discussion.

In addition to elementary discourse segments, we also annotated complex segments in cases where the first elementary segment in a sequence did not relate in any meaningful way to the previous context, creating a sense of local incoherence, but where the sequence as a whole could be attached by a coherence relation. For instance, (5-d) on its own is neither an *Explanation*, nor an *Elaboration*, nor a *Result*, etc., of (5-b), but the complex segment (5-d)–(5-e) is more plausibly an *Elaboration* of (5-b)—a relation that holds between descriptions of the same state of affairs, possibly but not necessarily at different levels of abstraction or detail.

Finally, following Asher and Lascarides (2003) and Asher et al. (2016), we allow for non-tree graphs in our discourse structures. For instance, (3-d) is an *Explanation* of (3-b), while (3-e) is a *Result* of (3-d), but at the same time an *Elaboration* of (3-b), resulting in a circular graph. The annotation of coherence relations is still ongoing; therefore, the quality measurement, including the inter-annotator agreement for that level, will be conducted afterwards.

5 Studies

In the following, we show examples of analyses that can be performed using our corpus. Section 5.1 presents a number of quantitative characteristics of the corpus, whereas section 5.2 illustrates some observations based on the qualitative analysis of the elicited chats.

5.1 Referring expressions, referential chains, and discourse segments

The corpus contains a total of 3114 REs in the utterances produced by the participants in both prompts (i.e. excluding the REs in the stimuli). As shown in table 1, the largest group that constitutes nearly a half of all REs are personal pronouns

(1451, 46.6%), followed by definite and indefinite NPs (555, 17.8% and 372, 11.9% respectively), the fourth largest group being zero referents (266, 8.5%). The number of proper names in the elicited utterances is relatively low (79, 2.5%) compared to the number of proper names in the stimuli (900).

RE Type	N	RE Type	N
Pronouns:		Proper name	79
Personal	1451	Definite NP	555
D-pronoun	170	Indefinite NP	372
Demonstrative	35	Universal Q	27
Possessive	103	clause	51
Relative	5	zero	266
total			3114

Table 1: Number of referring expressions (RE) by type

There are altogether 2541 referential chains that start or continue in the elicited part of the chats, ranging between 1 and 6 mentions in length, table 2. Trivial chains of length 1, i.e. referents mentioned only once in the chat, make up about a half of all chains (1314, 51.71%). (This number excludes referents mentioned only in the stimuli.) There is also a substantial number of chains of length 2 (884, 34.79%) and 3 (277, 10.9%), suggesting that participants kept re-mentioning the same individuals within the limited space of the chat continuations.

Ref chain lengh	N	%
1	1314	51.71%
2	884	34.79%
3	277	10.90%
4	54	2.13%
5	11	0.43%
6	1	0.04%
total	2541	100.00%

Table 2: Length of the elicited referential chains

Unsurprisingly, pronouns and zeroes mostly refer to previously introduced, "old" referents, whereas the majority of clauses, definite and indefinite NPs and universal quantifiers constitute the first mention of their referents in the chain. Proper names are distributed evenly between first and non-first mentions, cf. table 3. The relatively high number of personal pronouns referring to new referents (31,9%) is not unexpected considering that most of the pronominal (as well as zero) first mentions are due to deictic 1st and 2nd person reference.

The counts for discourse segments in the elicited utterances are shown in table 4. Participants entered up to 5 discourse segments in both prompts.

RE Type	new		old	
	N	%	N	%
Relative pro	0	0.0	5	100.0
Demonstr. pro	3	8.6	32	91.4
D-pronoun	15	8.8	155	91.2
Possessive pro	16	15.5	87	84.5
zero	51	19.2	215	80.8
Personal pro	463	31.9	988	68.1
Proper name	38	48.1	41	51.9
clause	43	84.3	8	15.7
Definite NP	486	87.6	69	12.4
Indefinite NP	327	87.9	45	12.1
Universal Q.	24	88.9	3	11.1
total	1466	47.1	1648	52.9

Table 3: Types of expressions referring to new (mentioned for the first time) vs. old (previously mentioned) referents

Giving the participants two prompts rather than one obviously made them produce at least two discourse segments in almost all trials, as we had intended. There is a decrease in the number of discourse segments from the grounding failure condition, over the grounding success condition, down to the condition without feedback, suggesting that the participants felt the need to say more after a perceived grounding failure than in both other cases.

N of segments	failure	success	without
1	3	6	4
2	171	194	221
3	93	74	54
4	18	14	5
5	2	1	2

Table 4: Number of elicited discourse segments in both prompts per condition

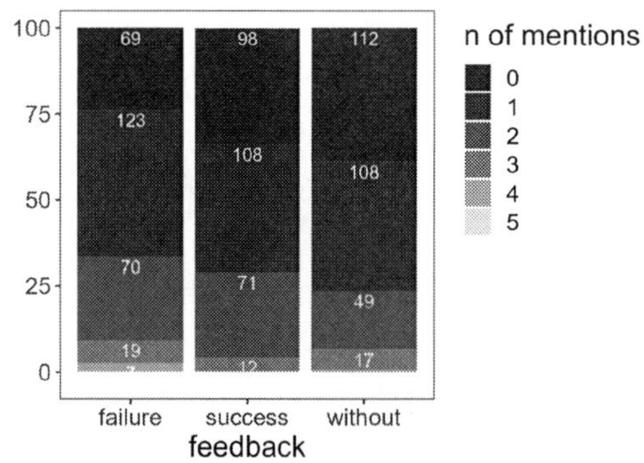

Figure 4: Number of elicited mentions of REF1, the subject of the stimulus sentence, per condition

A similar decrease across the conditions can be observed in the number of mentions of REF1, the referent of the human subject of the stimulus sentence, cf. figure 4. The lower number of REF1 mentions in the success condition than in the failure condition corroborates our hypothesis that after perceived grounding success speakers will tend to move on to the next issues on their agenda and talk less about previously introduced referents. At first glance, the surprising part in both counts (table 4 and figure 4) is that the 'without feedback' condition shows the lowest numbers of both discourse segments and references to REF1, contrary to the expectation based on e.g. Clark (1996) that the absence of feedback is interpreted as evidence of grounding failure and should therefore pattern with the failure condition. However, considering the results of Tolins and Fox Tree (2014) for a similar study on conversational narrative, who found that after 'continuers', i.e. feedback utterances that signal addressees' attention and invite the speaker to continue, the participants were less likely to elaborate on the previous utterances, it is possible that the absence of feedback was interpreted by our participants as a silent continuer, rather than a signal of trouble, which suggests that the generalizations based on spoken dialogue cannot be transferred one-to-one to written instant messaging dialogue, the latter still awaiting deeper investigation.

5.2 Relations between speech acts

The on-going annotation of the elicited chats with coherence relations has presented interesting challenges that led to new findings. The very notion of coherence relation (Mann and Thompson, 1988; Kehler, 2002; Lascarides and Asher, 1993) as well as most existing annotation schemes were developed with monologue in mind. That is, relation definitions were fine-tuned to describe sequences of almost exclusively assertions presented by the same speaker or writer, and although various adaptations of these taxonomies to dialogue have been proposed (Asher and Lascarides, 2003; Taboada, 2004), we have encountered multiple cases in our data which do not seem to fit easily into any common classifications. These do not only include relations between utterances of different speakers, but also relations that involve non-assertive speech acts, as well as metatalk utterances.

The dialogue in (7), for instance, contains an expressive speech act in (7-d). The participants could not send pictures as part of their responses, but the following sequence (7-e)–(7-f) is something one would typically say to accompany a picture. The intention of speaker B is clear: the picture is supposed to show A how sweet Diana's cat is. It would be presented as evidence to elicit not or not only a certain belief in A, but also an emotion which B wants to share with A. The utterance in (7-e) is essentially a pointing gesture, intended to draw attention to the picture, whereas (7-f) is a promise to send the picture, and it is implied that the promised action is performed immediately.

(7) a. A: Alles klar bei dir?
b. B: Diana hat eine Katze adoptiert
c. A: Okay
d. B: Die ist so süß!
e. B: Hier
f. ich schick dir mal ein Foto.

(8) a. A: Everything okay with you?
b. B: Diana adopted a cat.
c. A: Okay
d. B: She is so sweet!
e. B: Here
f. I'll send you a photo.

While it is clear that the (7-e)–(7-f) sequence together with the implied picture are supposed to make (7-d) more evident, they do not fit any standard definition of an *Evidence* relation. The RST *Evidence* is supposed to make its pivot more believable to the reader, and SDRT *Evidence* makes it more probable. While belief and probability might contribute to the intended effect of (7-d), the ultimate purpose of the sequence is to make the expressive emotionally more relatable, as the main point of expressives, unlike assertions, is not belief or truth. Second, neither (7-e) nor (7-f) actually provide any evidence. Comprehending (7-e) alone does not make (7-d) more believable, and a proposition to be assigned probability is lacking entirely. Similarly, (7-f) only promises evidence.

To analyse such cases, Jasinskaja and Zickenheiner (in prep.) introduce the notion of *support relations*, which hold between a speech act that fails or is not trusted to achieve its goal and another speech act that helps achieve that goal. The standard *Evidence* relation is an instance of this broad category, but the notion is not only applicable to assertions, and covers a number of interesting cases in our data that do not lend themselves easily to more traditional analyses.

In (9), the relation between the opening question and the rest of the item presents a different puzzle. The experimental items were constructed in such a way that the stimulus sentence (9-b) could be interpreted as the answer or part of the answer to the opening question (9-a) and were pre-annotated as *QAP* (question-answer pair). However, this participant obviously chose a different interpretation. Even though the opening question in (9) remains unanswered, the utterances (9-b)–(9-d) clearly have a function with respect to it: (9-b) and (9-c) explain why B cannot answer right now, and (9-d) promises to resume interaction (and presumably answer the question) in a minute.

(9) a. A: Wie läufts so?
   b. B: Jonas ist aufgewacht
   c. B: Muss schnell zu ihm.
   d. B: Melde mich gleich.

(10) a. A: How is it going?
   b. B: Jonas woke up
   c. B: Need to go quickly to him.
   d. B: I'll get back to you in a minute.

It seems that the relationship between these utterances is easier to understand if we look at questions in the spirit of classical speech act theory (Searle, 1969) as requests for answers. The sequence (9-b)–(9-c) constitutes an indirect rejection of that request, cf. request–rejection as an adjacency pair relation in Clark and Schaefer (1989). And (9-d) is a promise, another type of appropriate response to a request. In addition (9-d) can be viewed as a way to mitigate the "pain" of the rejection. In this function, (9-d) stands in a support relation to (9-b)–(9-c), making the rejection more acceptable to A. These examples show how the data in our corpus can be used to address issues of dialogue structure and speech act connectivity that have received less attention within approaches to discourse structure based on coherence relations.

6 Discussion and conclusion

To summarize, we have created a corpus of German chats elicited in an experimental setting, which can be used to study the choice of Referring Expressions (REs) and coherence relations in naturalistic language use. We find the creation of this corpus and the extensive annotations we have conducted valuable for the following reasons: (1) the data has an informal dialogic nature in a simulated interactive setting, that represents an adaptation of the established discourse continuation task to dialogue; (2) since it is an experiment, there is data available from multiple participants for the same scenarios, enabling the study of individual variation, as well as quantitative generalizations over comparable structures; (3) in addition to the annotation of coreference, the corpus presents an extensive annotation of referring expression forms; (4) the data contains an annotation of coherence relations to give a better picture of referring in naturalistic settings; (5) the data has been collected for the German language, however, the experimental setting is easily expansible to other languages, which makes cross-linguistic comparisons possible. The raw and annotated data, along with the annotation guidelines, are publicly available and can be accessed on our GitHub repository: `https://github.com/Yli671/GermanChatCorpus`

Acknowledgements

The research for this paper has been funded by the Deutsche Forschungsgemeinschaft (DFG, German Research Foundation) – Project-ID 281511265 – SFB 1252 "Prominence in Language" in the project C06 at the University of Cologne, Department of German Language und Literature I, Linguistics.

References

Nicholas Asher, Julie Hunter, Mathieu Morey, Farah Benamara, and Stergos Afantenos. 2016. Discourse structure and dialogue acts in multiparty dialogue: the STAC corpus. In *10th International Conference on Language Resources and Evaluation (LREC 2016)*, pages 2721–2727.

Nicholas Asher and Alex Lascarides. 2003. *Logics of Conversation*. Studies in Natural Language Processing. Cambridge University Press.

Anja Belz, Eric Kow, Jette Viethen, and Albert Gatt. 2010. Generating referring expressions in context: The GREC task evaluation challenges. In *Empirical Methods in Natural Language Generation: Data-oriented Methods and Empirical Evaluation*, volume 5790 of *Lecture Notes in Computer Science*, pages 294–327. Springer.

Shoshana Blum-Kulka and Elite Olshtain. 1984. Requests and apologies: A cross-cultural study of speech act realization patterns (CCSARP). *Applied linguistics*, 5(3):196–213.

Herb H. Clark and Edward F. Schaefer. 1989. Contributing to discourse. *Cognitive science*, 13(2):259–294.

Herbert H. Clark. 1996. *Using Language*. Cambridge University Press.

David Craig. 2003. Instant messaging: The language of youth literacy. *The Boothe Prize Essays*, 1:116–133.

Ashley R Dainas and Susan C Herring. 2021. Interpreting emoji pragmatics. *Approaches to internet pragmatics: Theory and practice*, pages 107–144.

Barbara Di Eugenio, Pamela W. Jordan, Johanna D. Moore, and Richmond H. Thomason. 1998. An empirical investigation of proposals in collaborative dialogues. In *COLING 1998 Volume 1: The 17th International Conference on Computational Linguistics*.

Francesca Farina and Fiona Lyddy. 2011. The language of text messaging: "Linguistic ruin" or resource? *Irish Psychologist*, 37(6):145–149.

Andrew Gargett, Konstantina Garoufi, Alexander Koller, and Kristina Striegnitz. 2010. The GIVE-2 corpus of giving instructions in virtual environments. In *Proceedings of the Seventh International Conference on Language Resources and Evaluation (LREC'10)*, Valletta, Malta. European Language Resources Association (ELRA).

Albert Gatt, Anja Belz, and Eric Kow. 2008. The TUNA challenge 2008: overview and evaluation results. In *Proceedings of the Fifth International Natural Language Generation Conference on - INLG '08*, page 198, Salt Fork, Ohio. Association for Computational Linguistics.

Talmy Givón. 1983. Topic continuity in spoken English. In Talmy Givón, editor, *Topic Continuity in Discourse*, pages 347–363. John Benjamins, Amsterdam.

John J Godfrey and Edward Holliman. 1993. Switchboard-1 release 2 ldc97s62.

David Howcroft, Jorrig Vogels, and Vera Demberg. 2017. G-TUNA: a corpus of referring expressions in German, including duration information. In *Proceedings of the 10th International Conference on Natural Language Generation*, pages 149–153, Santiago de Compostela, Spain. Association for Computational Linguistics.

Katja Jasinskaja and Elena Karagjosova. 2020. Rhetorical relations. In Daniel Gutzmann, Lisa Matthewson, Cécile Meier, Hotze Rullmann, and Thomas Ede Zimmermann, editors, *The Companion to Semantics*. Wiley, Oxford.

Katja Jasinskaja and Frank Zickenheiner. in prep. Speech acts that support other speech acts. Manuscript.

Jörg D Jescheniak. 2000. The cataphoric use of spoken stress in narratives. *Psychological Research*, 63(1):14–21.

Andrew Kehler. 2002. *Coherence, Reference, and the Theory of Grammar*. CSLI Publications.

Andrew Kehler, Laura Kertz, Hannah Rohde, and Jeffrey L. Elman. 2008. Coherence and Coreference Revisited. *Journal of Semantics*, 25(1):1–44.

Andrew Kehler and Hannah Rohde. 2017. Evaluating an expectation-driven question-under-discussion model of discourse interpretation. *Discourse Processes*, 54(3):219–238.

Jan-Christoph Klie, Michael Bugert, Beto Boullosa, Richard Eckart de Castilho, and Iryna Gurevych. 2018. The inception platform: Machine-assisted and knowledge-oriented interactive annotation. In *Proceedings of the 27th International Conference on Computational Linguistics: System Demonstrations*, pages 5–9. Association for Computational Linguistics. Event Title: The 27th International Conference on Computational Linguistics (COLING 2018).

Alex Lascarides and Nicholas Asher. 1993. Temporal interpretation, discourse relations and commonsense entailment. *Linguistics and Philosophy*, 16:437–493.

William C. Mann and Sandra Thompson. 1988. Rhetorical Structure Theory: Toward a functional theory of text organization. *Text*, 8(3):243–281.

Hannah Miller, Jacob Thebault-Spieker, Shuo Chang, Isaac Johnson, Loren Terveen, and Brent Hecht. 2021. "Blissfully Happy" or "Ready to Fight": Varying interpretations of emoji. *Proceedings of the International AAAI Conference on Web and Social Media*, 10(1):259–268.

Anne Niedermann. 2019. Freiwillige und informierte Einwilligung in die Nutzungsbedingungen von Online-Diensten? Accessed: 2023-12-10.

Magdalena Repp, Petra B Schumacher, and Fahime Same. 2023. Multi-layered annotation of conversation-like narratives in German. In *Proceedings of the 17th Linguistic Annotation Workshop (LAW-XVII)*, pages 61–72.

John Rogers Searle. 1969. *Speech acts: An essay in the philosophy of language*. Cambridge university press.

Manfred Stede, Sara Mamprin, Andreas Peldszus, Andre Herzog, David Kaupat, Christian Chiarcos, and Saskia Warzecha. 2015. *Handbuch Textannotation*. Potsdamer Kommentarkorpus 2.0.

Rosemary J. Stevenson, Rosalind A. Crawley, and David Kleinman. 1994. Thematic roles, focus and the representation of events. *Language and Cognitive Processes*, 9(4):519–548.

Laura Stoia, Darla Magdalene Shockley, Donna K. Byron, and Eric Fosler-Lussier. 2008. SCARE: a situated corpus with annotated referring expressions. In *Proceedings of the Sixth International Conference on Language Resources and Evaluation (LREC'08)*, Marrakech, Morocco. European Language Resources Association (ELRA).

María Teresa Taboada. 2004. *Building coherence and cohesion: Task-oriented dialogue in English and Spanish*. John Benjamins.

Jackson Tolins and Jean E Fox Tree. 2014. Addressee backchannels steer narrative development. *Journal of Pragmatics*, 70:152–164.

Connie K Varnhagen, G Peggy McFall, Nicole Pugh, Lisa Routledge, Heather Sumida-MacDonald, and Trudy E Kwong. 2010. Lol: New language and spelling in instant messaging. *Reading and writing*, 23:719–733.

Lieke Verheijen. 2017. Whatsapp with social media slang? Youth language use in Dutch written computer-mediated communication.

Henriette Anna Elisabeth Viethen. 2012. The generation of natural descriptions: Corpus-based investigations of referring expressions in visual domains.

Bonnie Webber, Rashmi Prasad, Alan Lee, and Aravind Joshi. 2019. The Penn discourse treebank 3.0 annotation manual.

Ralph Weischedel, Martha Palmer, Mitchell Marcus, Eduard Hovy, Sameer Pradhan, Lance Ramshaw, Nianwen Xue, Ann Taylor, Jeff Kaufman, Michelle Franchini, et al. 2013. Ontonotes release 5.0 ldc2013t19. *Linguistic Data Consortium, Philadelphia, PA*, 23.

Sina Zarrieß, Julian Hough, Casey Kennington, Ramesh Manuvinakurike, David DeVault, Raquel Fernández, and David Schlangen. 2016. PentoRef: A corpus of spoken references in task-oriented dialogues. In *Proceedings of the Tenth International Conference on Language Resources and Evaluation (LREC'16)*, pages 125–131, Portorož, Slovenia. European Language Resources Association (ELRA).

Henk Zeevat. 2010. Optimal interpretation for rhetorical relations. In Anton Benz, Peter Kühnlein, and Candy Sidner, editors, *Constraints in Discourse 2*, pages 35–59. John Benjamins, Amsterdam.

Amir Zeldes. 2017. The GUM corpus: Creating multilayer resources in the classroom. *Language Resources and Evaluation*, 51(3):581–612.

Frank Zickenheiner. 2020. *Goals in Discourse: From Actions to Rhetorical Relations*. Ph.D. thesis, Universtiy of Cologne, Germany.

A An Example from INCEpTION

Figure 5 shows the multi-layer annotations in INCEpTION, including coreference annotations and coherence relations for one of the items. The English translation of the item is:

(11) a. A: And, everything okay?
  b. B: Elena has tried bungee jumping.
  c. A: Uh?
  d. B: Yes
  e. That was also my reaction.
  f. B: I would never have thought she would do it.

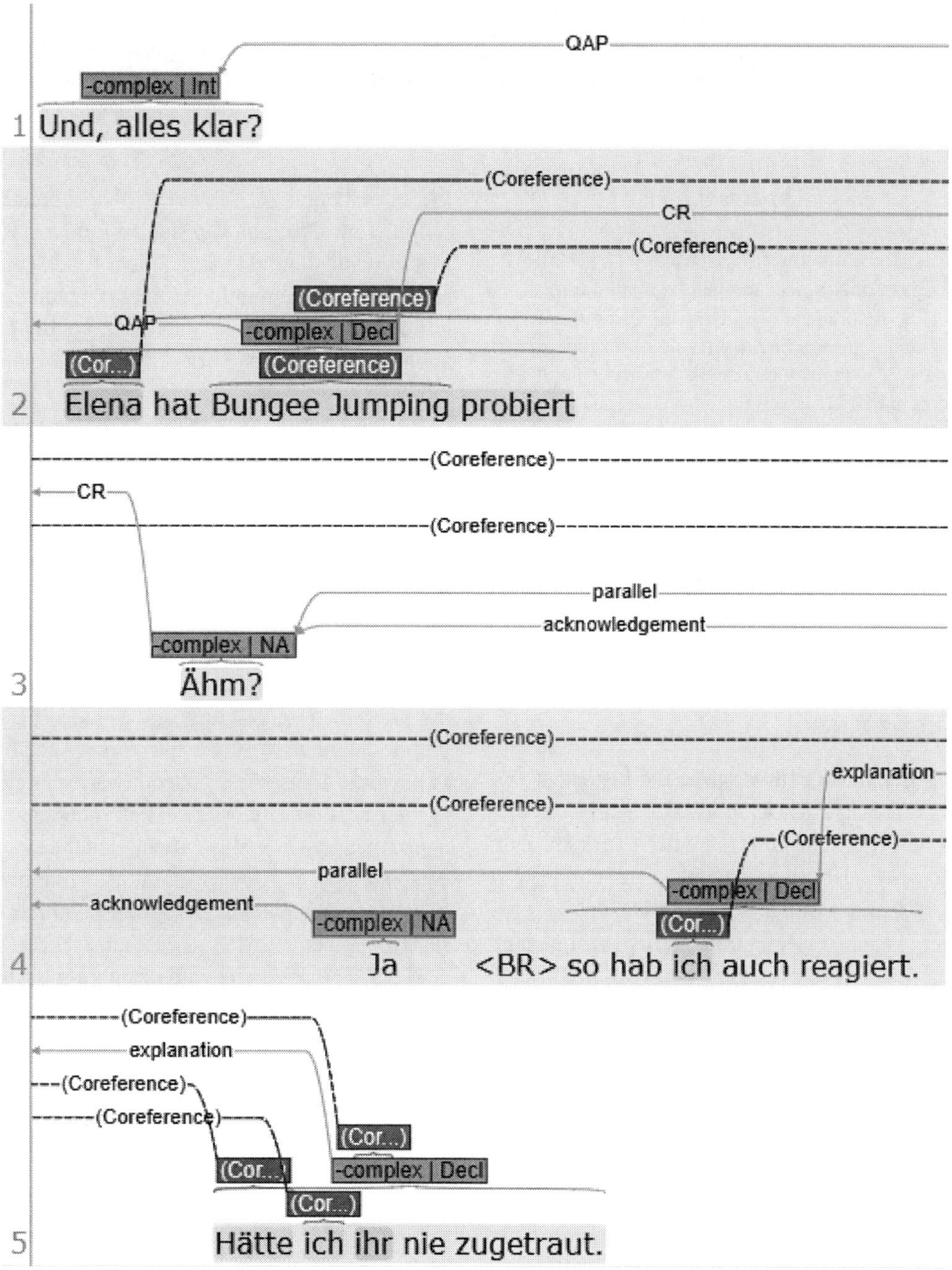

Figure 5: An example from the INCEpTION annotation window

Dependency Annotation of Ottoman Turkish with Multilingual BERT

Şaziye Betül Özateş*, **Tarık Emre Tıraş***, **Efe Eren Genç***,
Esma F. Bilgin Taşdemir‡
*Boğaziçi University, ‡Medeniyet University, Turkey
saziye.ozates@bogazici.edu.tr, {tarik.tiras,efe.genc}@std.bogazici.edu.tr,
esmabilgin.tasdemir@medeniyet.edu.tr

Abstract

This study introduces a pretrained large language model-based annotation methodology for the first dependency treebank in Ottoman Turkish. Our experimental results show that, iteratively, i) pseudo-annotating data using a multilingual BERT-based parsing model, ii) manually correcting the pseudo-annotations, and iii) fine-tuning the parsing model with the corrected annotations, we speed up and simplify the challenging dependency annotation process. The resulting treebank, that will be a part of the Universal Dependencies (UD) project, will facilitate automated analysis of Ottoman Turkish documents, unlocking the linguistic richness embedded in this historical heritage.

1 Introduction

The Ottoman Turkish is one of the historical versions of Turkish. It was in use for nearly six centuries before it evolved into modern Turkish. During that period, it went through many changes in terms of lexicon and, to some extent, syntax.

There is an increasing trend in digitization campaigns that aim to preserve historical documents and facilitate user access to these resources. Numerous institutions publicly share images of their historical documents written in Ottoman Turkish. As these historical materials become more accessible in digital form, a crucial need for automated processing and retrieval of their content arises. However, unlike modern languages with well-established linguistic resources and corpora, Ottoman Turkish has quite a limited availability of annotated data, dictionaries, and linguistic references. That scarcity of resources hinders the development and training of robust NLP models for the Ottoman Turkish.

A possible solution for the problem of resource scarcity can be leveraging Turkish resources based on the fact that they are actually two versions of the same language. However, the linguistic evolution from Ottoman Turkish to modern Turkish involves substantial changes over time. This transition impacts semantic nuances, vocabulary, and grammatical structures, making it challenging to apply contemporary Turkish NLP techniques directly to historical texts.

It is a common approach to prepare the necessary resources manually in the case of low-resource languages. However, manual tagging and annotation are both time-consuming and expensive. In the case of dependency annotation, there is also a need for experts specialized in the task at hand.

To simplify and speed up the manual annotation process for our objective of constructing an Ottoman Turkish dependency treebank, we propose to use pretrained Large Language Models (LLMs) as pseudo-annotators. LLMs have proven themselves as powerful tools widely used in various fields due to their adaptability. They excel in understanding natural language, making them valuable across diverse areas, from downstream tasks like machine translation (Yang et al., 2020) and sentiment analysis (Hoang et al., 2019) to data annotation (Tejani et al., 2022). We experiment with a multilingual BERT-based parsing model for dependency annotation in our treebank. Our proposed methodology suggests generating pseudo-annotations using the parsing model, then correcting them manually and fine-tuning the model with the corrections, and then using the updated model to pseudo-annotate new data in a repeated cycle.

In this study, we present our LLM-enhanced syntactic annotation methodology for the first Ottoman Turkish dependency treebank, which will be a part of the Universal Dependencies (UD) project (Nivre et al., 2016). We investigate the impact of enhancing the accuracy of pseudo-annotations by fine-tuning the parsing model with labeled Ottoman Turkish data. We show that utilizing a multilingual BERT-based parsing model in dependency anno-

Proceedings of The 18th Linguistic Annotation Workshop (LAW-XVIII), pages 188–196
March 22, 2024 ©2024 Association for Computational Linguistics

tation leads to better pseudo-annotations, which eases the manual annotation of the Ottoman Turkish treebank job for human annotators. With the creation of this treebank, we aim at facilitating the automatic analysis and understanding of Ottoman Turkish documents, thereby facilitating a more comprehensive exploration of this linguistically rich heritage.

2 Background and Related work

We present some background on the Ottoman Turkish and discuss its differences from modern Turkish in this section. The section includes a summary of the related works from the literature as well.

2.1 The Ottoman Turkish

Ottoman Turkish is the historical form of the Turkish language used in the Ottoman Empire from the late 13th to the early 20th century. It has a writing system based on an extended version of the Arabic script where five additional characters are used to represent some Turkish sounds. Ottoman Turkish has a significant number of loanwords borrowed from Arabic and Persian. Furthermore, it contains some complex grammatical forms borrowed from these two languages, like long noun phrases with multiple words and particular word ordering. Finally, the number of words in a sentence can get quite large, especially in the texts written in the early periods of the Ottoman Empire.

The Arabic alphabet-based writing system was replaced with a Latin alphabet-based one in 1928. Also, the language reforms in the early 20th century led to significant modifications in the vocabulary, where many of the loanwords of Arabic and Persian origin were replaced with words borrowed from European languages or newly coined words. These language reforms have led to a substantial divergence between modern and Ottoman Turkish.

A comparison of modern Turkish and Ottoman Turkish in terms of the percentage of loanwords can be helpful in understanding the differences between the two versions. The well-known Ottoman dictionary "A Turkish and English Lexicon" by James W. Redhouse (Redhouse, 1884) contains 79,491 words, of which 57% are Arabic-origin and 12% are Persian-origin. In contrast, a study by (Moore and Uni, 2015) reports that approximately 25% of the selected 3,270 most frequently used Turkish words are Arabic-origin, and the percentage of Persian loanwords is only 6% in the selected vocabulary. On the other hand, of the 104.481 words in the standard Turkish Dictionary by TDK (Turkish Language Institution), 6,463 (~6%) are Arabic-origin and 1,374 (~1%) are Persian-origin (TDK, 2005).

2.2 Related Work

The Universal Dependencies (UD) Project[1] is a collaborative effort that aims to develop cross-linguistically consistent treebank annotation for many languages. The project provides a standardized framework for annotating the grammatical structure of sentences, encompassing parts of speech, syntactic dependencies, and other linguistic features. Most of the treebanks in UD are dedicated to annotating modern languages. Efforts to include historical languages in the project have been limited. Ancient Greek is one of the lucky historical languages having three UD treebanks (Bamman and Crane, 2011). Ancient Hebrew (Swanson and Tyers, 2022), Classical Chinese (Lee and Kong, 2012), and Coptic (Zeldes and Abrams, 2018) treebanks are some other notable UD treebanks that contain annotated sentences from historical languages. Using trained models as pseudo-annotators is a common practice in data annotation (Haunss et al., 2020; Benato et al., 2021; He et al., 2022). In the context of dependency annotation, there are some studies that utilize automatic parsers to parse raw data as an initial step in order to provide human annotators with a starting point in the manual annotation process (e.g., the Belarusian HSE UD Treebank[2]). However, to the best of our knowledge, these studies use machine assistance as a one-time process only; none of them adopted an iterative approach as we do.

3 OTA-BOUN: A UD Treebank for Ottoman Turkish

As an initial endeavor towards enriching Ottoman Turkish Natural Language Processing (NLP) resources and enhancing the effectiveness of existing NLP tools on Ottoman Turkish texts, we have initiated the creation of the Ottoman Turkish UD Treebank. In Section 3.1, we provide information about the source and language of the treebank. Section 3.2 details our annotation process, and Section 3.3 states the challenges encountered in annotating Ottoman Turkish sentences, accompanied by

[1] https://universaldependencies.org/introduction.html

[2] https://github.com/UniversalDependencies/UD_Belarusian-HSE

illustrative examples, and clarifies the approaches undertaken to overcome these challenges.

3.1 Data

The creation of an Ottoman Turkish dependency treebank is an ongoing project. The first version of the treebank[3] is planned to contain 500 syntactically annotated Ottoman Turkish sentences. The annotated sentences exist in two writing styles in the treebank; 1) written with the Latin-based Turkish alphabet, and 2) written with the Perso-Arabic alphabet. (See Figure 3 for CoNLL-U representation[4] of treebank items.)

The sentences are sampled from seven texts by four different writers. All of the texts are from literature published between 1900 and 1928. There are two articles, excerpts from two history texts, two stories, and one excerpt from a novel. Our ultimate goal is to include annotations for a total of 2,000 sentences, sourced from various origins, in the final version.

Figure 1 shows two example sentences from the dataset in Ottoman and modern Turkish.In the figure, some of the words that have been replaced by modern versions can be seen in red boxes. A group of defunct words can be replaced by a single word (ex. *ihraç ediliyor –> çıkarılıyor (is being extracted)*) and vice versa (ex. *muvafakatiyle –> uygun bulması ile (with the approval of)*). A noun phrase form that is mostly obsolete is replaced with its modern counterpart where the word order changes (ex. *mebde-i kelam –> konuşma başlangıç(ı) (the beginning of the speech)*). Here, the words are also replaced with synonyms in the modern version.

In addition to changes in vocabulary, the syntactical features of an Ottoman Turkish sentence can be different from those of the modern version. Figure 2 shows the dependency trees of two versions of a sentence: the original one and its translation to modern Turkish. The difference in grammatical structure of both sentences is visible through their dependency trees. To give a concrete example, the way the subject of the sentence (*Damat İbrahim Paşa*), which is a person, is connected to the verb is different in the original sentence (via an *oblique* relation through one of its parent nodes) and in its translation (directly via *nominal subject* relation).

Another example of their differences is in the way they indicate that *Muşkara*, a place name, is the subject's birthplace. This is done indirectly in the original sentence by connecting them at the *root* word. The connection is more straightforward in its translation to modern Turkish, which is done directly using a clausal modifier.Due to such differences in the grammar and vocabulary of Ottoman and modern Turkish, the annotation process is not straightforward.

3.2 The Annotation Scheme

For the annotation of the Ottoman Turkish treebank, we used a team of two annotators who are linguists and have comprehensive knowledge of Turkish grammar and general linguistics, as well as grammatical theories. Assisting the team of annotators in the process of manual annotation are two senior computer scientists with extensive expertise both in NLP and in Ottoman Turkish.

In the annotation process, we employ double annotation for a randomly chosen set of 50 sentences. We measure Cohen's kappa between the annotated dependency labels as 0.85 for determining the inter-annotator agreement. The unlabelled and labeled attachment scores between the annotations are found to be 82.20% and 76.91%, respectively. The rest of the annotation is held separately. After each annotator finishes their respective portions, the annotated sentences are examined, and any disagreement is resolved within the linguist team.

In most cases, we adhered to the conventions of Universal Dependencies but referred to the Suggested UD Guidelines for Turkish[5] when necessary. At the current step, we do the manual annotation on the syntactic level. Following the UD scheme, the annotated data is stored in CoNLL-U format. Figure 3 depicts this format on an annotated sentence from our treebank. As mentioned, we preserve the original Arabic script version of the data, providing the text value both in Latin and Arabic letters. The tokens of the sentence in Latin script are found in the second column, while their Arabic counterparts are provided in the last column.

3.3 Challenges in the Syntactic Annotation

Deformation of Turkish Morphosyntax In the process of annotating Ottoman Turkish, a significant challenge encountered was that certain structures influenced by Arabic and Persian do not require Turkish inflectional suffixes, which distin-

[3]The treebank will be released with the next scheduled release of UD (v2.14).

[4]https://universaldependencies.org/format.html

[5]https://github.com/boun-tabi/UD_docs/blob/main/_tr/dep/Turkish_deprel_guidelines.pdf

1-

a) Koyu mavi gözleri mütefekkirane, mahzunane bir halde, kırık ciheti eski bir paçavra ile örtülmüş olan pencereye matuf idi.

b) Koyu mavi gözleri düşünürcesine, kederli bir halde, kırık tarafı eski bir paçavra ile örtülmüş olan pencereye çevriliydi.

(her) dark blue eyes as if thinking sadly in a way broken side of old a rag with covered that is to the window turned

c) *Her dark blue eyes were turned sadly, as if thinking, towards the window, the broken side of which was covered with an old rag*

2-

a) Nihayet, mebde-i kelâm kabul ettiğimiz tarihten dört gün evvel, İtilâf Devletleri'nin muvâfakatiyle Yunan ordusu da İzmir'e ihraç ediliyor.

b) Nihayet, konuşmamıza başlangıç olarak aldığımız tarihten dört gün önce, İtilâf Devletleri'nin uygun bulması ile Yunan ordusu da İzmir'e çıkartılıyor.

Finally, to our conversation start that we take as from the date four days before of the Allied Powers with the approval Greek army too to Izmir is landed

c) *Finally, four days before the date we take as the date of starting to our conversation, the Greek army was landed in Izmir with the approval of the Allied Powers.*

Figure 1: Two Ottoman Turkish sentences (in Latin script), their modernized versions and English translations.

guishes them from modern Turkish syntax and morphology. For example, *münasebet tabian* in Example 1 means *subject to relationship*. The word *tabian* is a verbal adverb derived from the Arabic word *tabi (subject to)* and the Arabic adverbial suffix *-An*. In modern Turkish, the phrase can be expressed as follows: *münasebete tabi olarak (by being subject to a relationship)*. As seen, the noun *münasebet* is inflected with a dative case *-A*. In Ottoman Turkish, however, a dative case is not needed in some instances, making a difference from modern Turkish. The excessive exposure to Arabic led some suffixes to disappear without a narrowing in meaning, consequently causing difficulties in the annotation process.

(1) *güneş-in* *sema* *üzerin-de-ki*
sun-GEN.3SG sky above-LOC-ADJ
seyr-i *ile* *münasebet* *tabian*
journey-POSS.3SG COM relationship subject_to
'with respect to the trajectory of the sun in the sky'

The application of Turkish suffixes to structures in Arabic and Persian poses difficulties for both the parser and our team. For instance, in the phrase *Harb-i Umumi'de (in the world war)* in Example 2, although *harb* is the head, the locative suffix is attached to the dependent, diverging from standard modern Turkish rules and leading to incorrect automatic annotations.

(2) *Memleket-i* *Harb-i* *Umumî-ye* *sevk*
country-ACC war-EZ general-DAT dispatch
ed-en-ler
make-REL-PL
'Those who sent the country to the World War'

Foreign Compounds Another challenge was identifying compound verbs formed with foreign words not commonly used in modern Turkish, such as *mehcur bırakmak (to leave abandoned)*. The high frequency of uncommon phrasal verbs poses a challenge to the annotation process.

Abundance of Foreign Words It was additionally observed that the aforesaid cultural interactions influenced the lexicon of Ottoman Turkish. The influence led to confusion about determining the part-of-speech of certain words with two meanings without showing any structural difference. They make sense within the context in which they are used, making them challenging to annotate just by looking at their syntactic and morphological structures. In *sû-i muamelat (unpleasant behavior)* given in Example 3, *sû* is an adjective. However, in *sû-i tefehhüm (misunderstanding)*, it acts as an adverb. At first glance, these phrases appear to have no difference, both syntactically and morphologically. This similarity poses a challenge, as it demands substantial lexical knowledge of Arabic.

(3) *yap-ıl-an* *su-i* *muâmel-ât-ta*
do-PASS-REL bad-EZ treatment-PL-LOC
millet-in *medhaldar*
nation-GEN.3SG responsible
bul-un-ma-dığ-ın-ı
find-PASS-NEG-NMLZ-POSS.3SG-ACC
'that the nation is not responsible for the mistreatment done'

There are foreign words in Ottoman Turkish that preserve morphological features gained in their original language. The challenge arises from the fact that the derivational morphemes remain productive, making it difficult to determine their syntactic relations. The primary reason for this challenge is the necessity of understanding the nature of the language from which the words originate. Consider the phrase *i'tâ-yı ma'lûmat (giving information)* in Example 4. The verbal noun *i'tâ*, derived from *aṭā (grant)*, requires knowledge of Arabic grammar to identify it as a verbal noun.

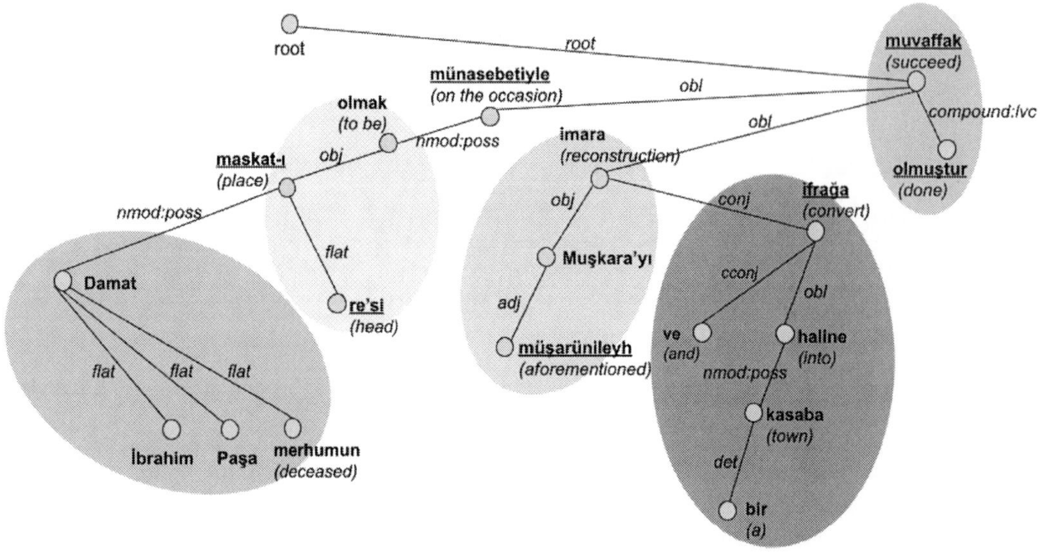

Damat İbrahim Paşa merhumun maskat-ı re'si olmak münasebetiyle müşarünileyh Muşkara'yı imara ve bir kasaba haline ifrağa muvaffak olmuştur.

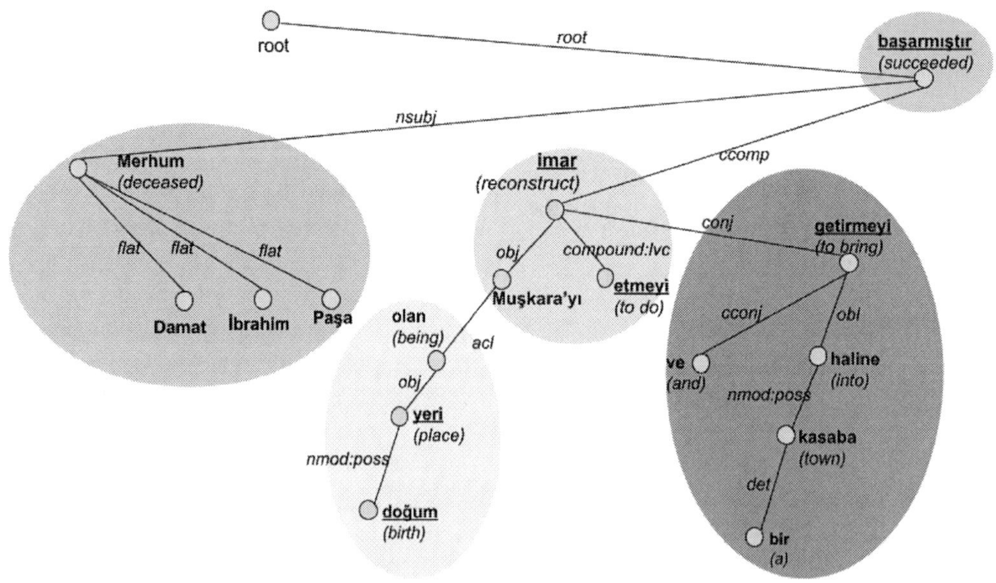

Merhum Damat İbrahim Paşa doğum yeri olan Muşkara'yı imar etmeyi ve bir kasaba haline getirmeyi başarmıştır.

Figure 2: Dependency tree representations of an Ottoman Turkish sentence (above) and its rephrased version using the modern Turkish (below). The highlighted portions enclosed in colored circles indicate corresponding segments in the sentences. English translations of words are provided in italics within parentheses. Words of a sentence that do not exist in the other sentence are underlined in the figure. **English translation of the sentence:** "The late Damat İbrahim Paşa succeeded in developing Muşkara, his birthplace, and turning it into a town."

Such examples are prevalent in Ottoman Turkish, posing difficulties in annotation.

(4) *Hedef-i siyasi-ler-i hakkında* *itâ-yı malum-ât eyle-mek*
goal-EZ political-PL-POSS.3 about give.NMLZ-EZ known-PL make-NMLZ

'to give information about their political goals'

```
# sent_id = nutuk_51

# text_latin = Binâenaleyh cemiyet, aynı esbâb ve vesâitle mücehhez olarak hukuk-ı milliye ve tarihiyeyi müdafaaya
               çalışıyor.
# text_arabic = بناء علیه جمعیت , عینی اسباب و وسائطله مجهز اولەرق حقوق ملیه و تاریخیەیی مدافعەیه
               چالیشیور .
1   Binâenaleyh Binâenaleyh ADV   _     _                                  15  advmod        _  بناء علیه
2   cemiyet     cemiyet     NOUN  _     Case=Nom|Number=Sing|Person=3      15  nsubj         _  جمعیت|SpaceAfter=No
3   ,           ,           PUNCT Comma _                                  15  punct         _  ,
4   aynı        aynı        ADJ   Adj   _                                  5   amod          _  عینی
5   esbâb       esbâb       NOUN  _     Case=Nom|Number=Sing|Person=3      8   obl           _  اسباب
6   ve          ve          CCONJ _     _                                  7   cc            _  و
7   vesâitle    vesâit      NOUN  _     Case=Ins|Number=Sing|Person=3      5   conj          _  وسائطله
8   mücehhez    mücehhez    NOUN  _     Case=Nom|Number=Sing|Person=3      14  advcl         _  مجهز
9   olarak      ol          VERB  Conv  Polarity=Pos|VerbForm=Conv         8   compound:lvc  _  اولەرق
10  hukuk-ı     hukuk-ı     NOUN  _     Case=Nom|Number=Sing|Person=3      14  obj           _  حقوق
11  milliye     milli       NOUN  _     Case=Dat|Number=Sing|Person=3      10  amod          _  ملیه
12  ve          ve          CCONJ _     _                                  13  cc            _  و
13  tarihiyeyi  tarihiye    NOUN  _     Case=Acc|Number=Sing|Person=3      11  conj          _  تاریخیەیی
14  müdafaaya   müdafaa     NOUN  _     Case=Dat|Number=Sing|Person=3      15  ccomp         _  مدافعەیه
15  çalışıyor   çalış       VERB  _     Aspect=Imp|Number=Sing|Person=3    0   root          _  چالیشیور|SpaceAfter=No
                                        |Polarity=Pos|Tense=Pres
16  .           .           PUNCT Stop  _                                  15  punct         _  .
```

Figure 3: CoNLL-U Representation of an example sentence from our Ottoman BOUN UD Treebank.

Annotation of Regular Structures Another issue is annotating phrases borrowed from foreign languages. According to UD, names with a regular syntactic structure should be annotated with regular syntactic relations rather than being annotated as *flat*. It is also noted that foreign language expressions should be annotated as *flat*. Despite these guidelines, due to their significant effects, we aimed to preserve frequently used grammar structures obtained from foreign languages as much as possible. For instance, in *Harb-i Umumi (World War)*, *harb* is a noun meaning *war* and *umumi* is an adjective meaning *universal*. This phrase could have been created in Turkish grammar as *Umumi Harp*. Although the structure is foreign, we annotated *Harb-i Umumi* and similar phrases as regular structures.

4 Iterative Annotation with Multilingual BERT

Because dependency annotation is both cost- and time-intensive, and given the challenges outlined in the previous section, we recently contemplated whether we could ease our manual annotation phase by leveraging state-of-the-art Large Language Models (LLMs). To test this idea, we conducted an experiment where we utilized the multilingual BERT model[6] (Devlin et al., 2019). The experiment is set up as follows:

- Initially, we fine-tuned a multilingual BERT-based parsing model (Grünewald et al., 2021) using the Turkish BOUN UD Treebank (Türk et al., 2022) containing only modern Turkish sentences.
- The fine-tuned model pseudo-annotated a subset of 50 sentences from the Ottoman Turkish corpus. This pseudo-annotated 50 sentences will be referred to as 'First-Batch-Pseudo-Annotated'.
- Subsequently, our human annotators reviewed and corrected the 'First-Batch-Pseudo-Annotated', the result of which is 'First-Batch-Gold'.
- We then further fine-tuned our parsing model with 'First-Batch-Gold'.
- Using this updated model, we pseudo-annotated another set of 50 sentences, denoted as the 'Second-Batch-Pseudo-Annotated'.
- Finally, our human annotators corrected 'Second-Batch-Pseudo-Annotated', resulting in the 'Second-Batch-Gold'.

Figure 4 depicts this iterative annotation scheme for two iterations.

Thus, in this initial phase of annotation, we have 100 manually annotated Ottoman Turkish sentences in two iterative batches of 50 sentences each. We should note that, because of the difficulty in finding parallel Ottoman Turkish and modern Turkish data, the sentences in these two batches originated from different sources and different genres. This has led to variations in the annotation complexity of the two batches due to the diversity in their origins.

With the data obtained in this manner, we have the opportunity to address our research question: Has fine-tuning the multilingual BERT model with Ottoman Turkish data facilitated the manual annotation and correction phase? To answer this question,

[6]https://huggingface.co/bert-base-multilingual-cased

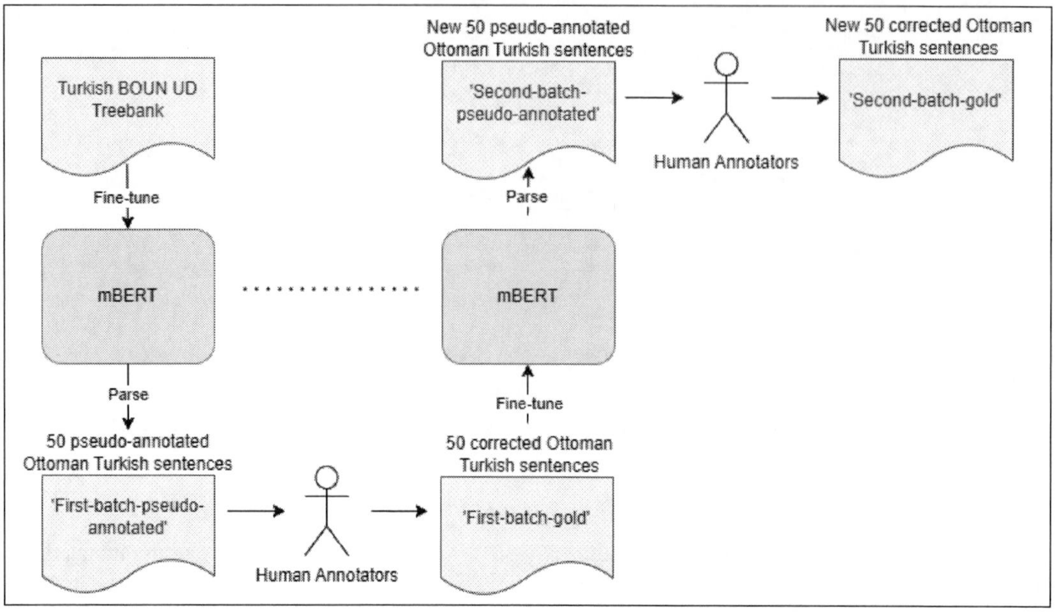

Figure 4: The experimental setup using the iterative annotation scheme.

	First Batch	Second Batch
Size (# of sentences)	50	50
Ave. word count	17.84	**20.45**
UAS	81.64	**82.58**
LAS	**77.65**	76.19

Table 1: Comparison of the two batches in terms of unlabelled and labelled attachment scores.

we did the experiment using the two batches of annotated Ottoman Turkish sentences.

4.1 Evaluation

In the experiment performed, we hypothesize that the difference in the annotations between 'Second-Batch-Pseudo-Annotated' and 'Second-Batch-Gold' should be less than the difference between 'First-Batch-Pseudo-Annotated' and 'First-Batch-Gold.' In other words, there should be fewer erroneous dependency relations to correct for human annotators in the second batch compared to the first batch.

To test this hypothesis, we measure the unlabeled and labeled attachment scores (UAS and LAS, respectively) between 'First-Batch-Pseudo-Annotated' and 'First-Batch-Gold' and between 'Second-Batch-Pseudo-Annotated' and 'Second-Batch-Gold'. Table 1 depicts the UAS and LAS F-1 scores of these measurements.

In Table 1, we observe that further fine-tuning the BERT-based model with Ottoman gold-annotated data increases the success of the model in accurately predicting dependency arcs. However, there is a performance drop in correctly identifying the types of dependency relations.

4.2 Quantitative Analysis

To understand the performance drop in dependency type prediction of the updated parsing model, which was fine-tuned with Ottoman Turkish data, we compute confusion matrices for the first and second batches separately in Figure 5.

We observe that in the second batch there are many more *nmod:poss* relations compared to the first batch. When we investigate the data, we see that a significant number of *nmod:poss* relations in the second batch consist of Persian grammatical structures, which pose several challenges to annotation (see Section 3.3). Such structures are almost not present in the first batch. To be precise, in the second batch, approximately 20% of the noun phrases are constructed using Persian grammar, whereas this figure is around 3% in the first batch. The number of light-verb compounds is also higher in the second batch.

In addition to this, when we take into account the average word count in a sentence given in Table 1, which is also higher in the second batch, we can conclude that annotating the second batch is a more challenging task for both the parsing model and human annotators. This might explain the slight per-

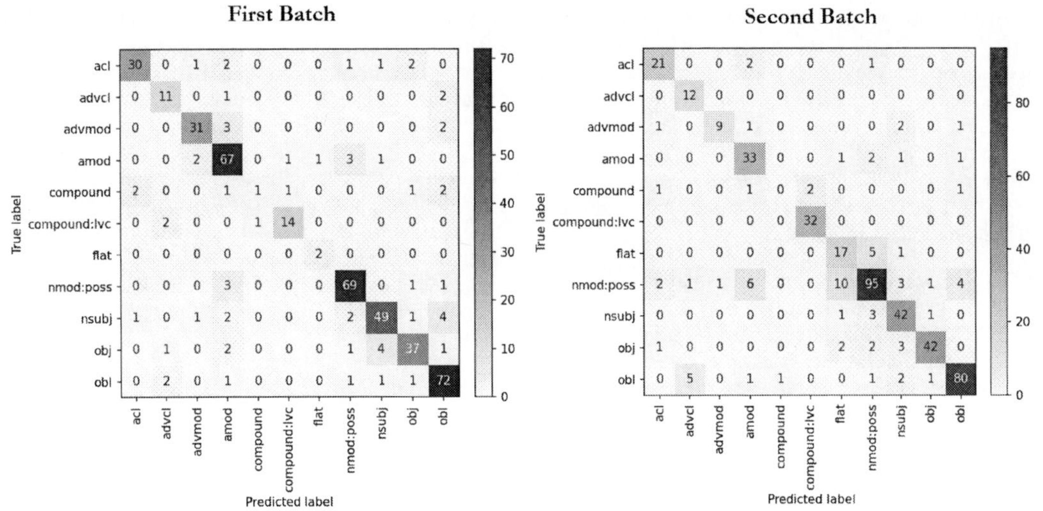

Figure 5: Confusion matrices of gold and predicted dependency types on the first batch and the second batch. The x-axis in each plot shows the dependency types in the pseudo-annotations of the corresponding batch. The y-axis shows the dependency types in the gold annotations.

formance drop in the LAS of the model when predicting the dependency types of the second batch.

Another factor that could affect the performance of the parsing model is the size of the fine-tuning data. The first batch is pseudo-annotated with the parser that is fine-tuned using BOUN, which has 7,803 annotated modern Turkish sentences in its training set. The second batch is pseudo-annotated after this parser is further fine-tuned with only 50 annotated Ottoman Turkish sentences. Such a small amount of data may not be sufficient for effectively fine-tuning the model. We anticipate that as we annotate new batches using this iterative annotation method, the performance of the parser will improve progressively.

Based on the results of the first and second batch runs, we can say that our iterative approach helps understand the difficulties of annotating Ottoman texts layer by layer. The first batch of fine-tuning process reveals mostly lexical issues. The results of the second batch of fine-tuning point to the complex grammatical issues that can be quite prevalent in certain types of texts.

4.3 Conclusion

Generation of a treebank for Ottoman Turkish is a difficult process that requires expertise in more than one language. The defunct grammatical forms and obsolete vocabulary make manual annotation a challenging task. We present an iterative approach utilizing a pretrained large language model, multilingual BERT, for annotating the first Ottoman Turkish dependency treebank. Our empirical findings suggest that performing the manual data annotation iteratively in a human-in-the-loop fashion improves and eases the process of dependency annotation. We anticipate that, when completed, the resulting treebank will enhance the NLP of Ottoman Turkish texts and enable a more profound exploration of Ottoman Turkish linguistic and cultural nuances.

References

David Bamman and Gregory Crane. 2011. The ancient Greek and Latin dependency treebanks. In *Language Technology for Cultural Heritage: Selected Papers from the LaTeCH Workshop Series*, pages 79–98. Springer.

Bárbara C Benato, Alexandru C Telea, and Alexandre X Falcão. 2021. Iterative pseudo-labeling with deep feature annotation and confidence-based sampling. In *2021 34th SIBGRAPI Conference on Graphics, Patterns and Images (SIBGRAPI)*, pages 192–198. IEEE.

Jacob Devlin, Ming-Wei Chang, Kenton Lee, and Kristina Toutanova. 2019. BERT: Pre-training of deep bidirectional transformers for language understanding. In *Proceedings of the 2019 Conference of the North American Chapter of the Association for Computational Linguistics: Human Language Technologies, Volume 1 (Long and Short Papers)*, pages 4171–4186, Minneapolis, Minnesota. Association for Computational Linguistics.

Stefan Grünewald, Annemarie Friedrich, and Jonas Kuhn. 2021. Applying Occam's razor to transformer-based dependency parsing: What works, what doesn't, and what is really necessary. In *Proceedings of the 17th International Conference on Parsing Technologies and the IWPT 2021 Shared Task on Parsing into Enhanced Universal Dependencies (IWPT 2021)*, pages 131–144, Online. Association for Computational Linguistics.

Sebastian Haunss, Jonas Kuhn, Sebastian Padó, Andre Blessing, Nico Blokker, Erenay Dayanık, and Gabriella Lapesa. 2020. Integrating manual and automatic annotation for the creation of discourse network data sets. *Politics and Governance*, 8(2):326–339.

Xuanli He, Islam Nassar, Jamie Kiros, Gholamreza Haffari, and Mohammad Norouzi. 2022. Generate, annotate, and learn: NLP with synthetic text. *Transactions of the Association for Computational Linguistics*, 10:826–842.

Mickel Hoang, Oskar Alija Bihorac, and Jacobo Rouces. 2019. Aspect-based sentiment analysis using BERT. In *Proceedings of the 22nd Nordic Conference on Computational Linguistics*, pages 187–196.

John SY Lee and Yin Hei Kong. 2012. A dependency treebank of classical Chinese poems. In *Proceedings of the 2012 Conference of the North American Chapter of the Association for Computational Linguistics: Human Language Technologies*, pages 191–199.

Daniele Moore and Kazuhito Uni. 2015. L'emprunt linguistique comme pont d'apprentissage. quelques réflexions à partir de l'étude des emprunts au français, à l'arabe et au persan dans les langues turques [language loan as a bridge for learning: Reflections from a study on French, Arabic and Persian loanwords in Turkic languages]. *Revue japonaise de didactique du français*, 10:197–213.

Joakim Nivre, Marie-Catherine De Marneffe, Filip Ginter, Yoav Goldberg, Jan Hajic, Christopher D Manning, Ryan McDonald, Slav Petrov, Sampo Pyysalo, Natalia Silveira, et al. 2016. Universal dependencies v1: A multilingual treebank collection. In *Proceedings of the Tenth International Conference on Language Resources and Evaluation (LREC'16)*, pages 1659–1666.

J.W. Redhouse. 1884. *A Turkish and English Lexicon: Shewing in English the Significations of the Turkish Terms*. Number 1. böl. in A Turkish and English Lexicon: Shewing in English the Significations of the Turkish Terms. American mission.

Daniel Swanson and Francis Tyers. 2022. A universal dependencies treebank of ancient Hebrew. In *Proceedings of the Thirteenth Language Resources and Evaluation Conference (LREC'22)*, pages 2353–2361.

TDK. 2005. *Türkçe sözlük*. Number 1. c. in Sözlük Bilim ve Uygulama Kolu yayınları. Atatürk Kültür, Dil ve Tarih Yüksek Kurumu, Türk Dil Kurumu.

Ali S Tejani, Yee S Ng, Yin Xi, Julia R Fielding, Travis G Browning, and Jesse C Rayan. 2022. Performance of multiple pretrained BERT models to automate and accelerate data annotation for large datasets. *Radiology: Artificial Intelligence*, 4(4):e220007.

Utku Türk, Furkan Atmaca, Şaziye Betül Özateş, Gözde Berk, Seyyit Talha Bedir, Abdullatif Köksal, Balkız Öztürk Başaran, Tunga Güngör, and Arzucan Özgür. 2022. Resources for Turkish dependency parsing: Introducing the BOUN treebank and the BoAT annotation tool. *Language Resources and Evaluation*, pages 1–49.

Jiacheng Yang, Mingxuan Wang, Hao Zhou, Chengqi Zhao, Weinan Zhang, Yong Yu, and Lei Li. 2020. Towards making the most of BERT in neural machine translation. In *Proceedings of the AAAI Conference on Artificial Intelligence*, volume 34, pages 9378–9385.

Amir Zeldes and Mitchell Abrams. 2018. The Coptic universal dependency treebank. In *Proceedings of the second workshop on universal dependencies (UDW 2018)*, pages 192–201.

DONKII: Characterizing and Detecting Errors in Instruction-Tuning Datasets

Leon Weber-Genzel[▲,🤖] and **Robert Litschko**[▲,🤖] and **Ekaterina Artemova**[▲,*] and **Barbara Plank**[▲,🤖,⊘]

[▲] MaiNLP, Center for Information and Language Processing, LMU Munich, Germany
[🤖] Munich Center for Machine Learning (MCML), Munich, Germany
[⊘] Department of Computer Science, IT University of Copenhagen, Denmark
{leonweber, robert.litschko, b.plank}@lmu.de

Abstract

Instruction tuning has become an integral part of training pipelines for Large Language Models (LLMs) and has been shown to yield strong performance gains. In an orthogonal line of research, Annotation Error Detection (AED) has emerged as a tool for detecting quality problems in gold standard labels. So far, however, the application of AED methods has been limited to classification tasks. It is an open question how well AED methods generalize to language generation settings, which are becoming more widespread via LLMs. In this paper, we present a first and novel benchmark for AED on instruction tuning data: DONKII. It comprises three instruction-tuning datasets enriched with error annotations by experts and semi-automatic methods. We also provide a novel taxonomy of error types for instruction-tuning data. We find that all three datasets contain clear errors, which sometimes propagate directly into instruction-tuned LLMs. We propose four AED baselines for the generative setting and evaluate them extensively on the newly introduced dataset. Our results show that the choice of the right AED method and model size is indeed crucial and derive practical recommendations for how to use AED methods to clean instruction-tuning data.

1 Introduction

Recent successes in instruction tuning (InstT) have shown that Large Language Models (LLMs) can generalize to a wide range of tasks in the zero-shot setting (Wei et al., 2022; Sanh et al., 2022; Ouyang et al., 2022). InstT achieves this by training an LLM on *instruction-output* pairs, where the instruction describes the task and the output contains the expected solution to the task. After fine-tuning on the InstT dataset and an optional reinforcement learning phase (Ouyang et al., 2022), LLMs are able to generalize to instructions not seen during fine-tuning. In an orthogonal line of inquiry, researchers have studied Annotation Error Detection (AED), which allows to detect erroneous annotations in labelled datasets. These low quality instances are then corrected or removed in a semi-automated process (Vlachos, 2006; Klie et al., 2022; Weber and Plank, 2023). However, how to best apply AED for natural language generation has so far not been studied. In this work, we combine both strands of research and ask whether AED methods can help to detect errors in InstT datasets and thus help to improve model quality by improving data quality.

Applying AED methods to InstT datasets presents a number of challenges. (1) The systematic development and comparison of AED methods requires datasets with annotations indicating which instances contain annotation errors. Such datatsets are not yet available for InstT. (2) To our knowledge, researchers have applied AED methods only in the discriminative setting (Klie et al., 2022) and it is not immediately clear how existing methods can be adapted to generative problems. (3) It is not obvious what even constitutes an error in InstT.

In this work, we address these three challenges; see also Figure 1 for an illustration of our contributions:[1] (1) We present Donkii, the first instruction tuning benchmark to enable the evaluation of AED methods. Donkii contains error annotations on top of three existing InstT datasets derived from manual error annotation efforts. We also introduce a hierarchy of error types for InstT datasets; see Figure 2. (2) We derive four AED baselines for generative problems based on recent work on training dynamics for AED (Swayamdipta et al., 2020; Pleiss et al., 2020). (3) We use Donkii to evaluate the proposed AED baselines and study the effects of model size, different types of errors, and different types of InstT data. The results show that there

*Now at Toloka.AI

[1] Data and code are available at https://github.com/mainlp/donkii.

Proceedings of The 18th Linguistic Annotation Workshop (LAW-XVIII), pages 197–215
March 22, 2024

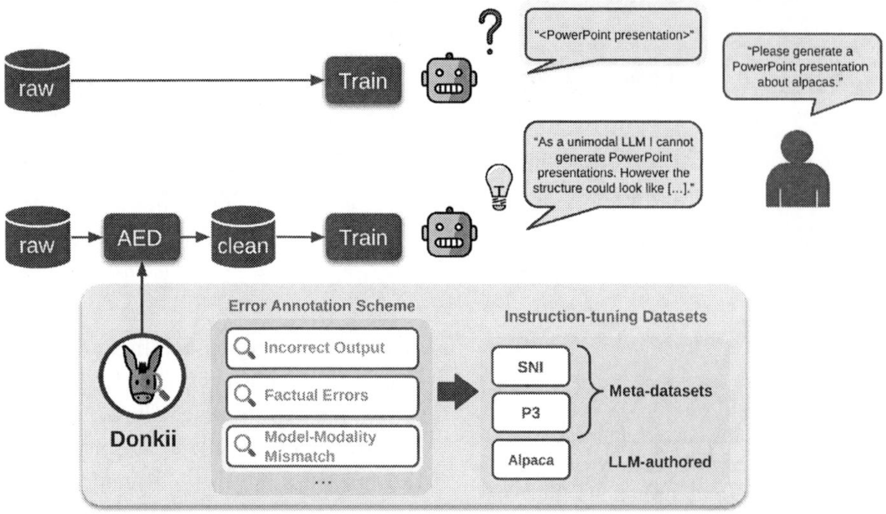

Figure 1: The Donkii dataset helps to design AED methods that can clean InstT datasets.

is a clear best-performing AED method for InstT data among the four evaluated.

2 Background

2.1 Instruction Tuning

Instruction tuning (InstT) is an emerging paradigm that leverages natural language instructions to fine-tune language models, thereby improving zero-shot performance on unseen tasks (Sanh et al., 2022; Ouyang et al., 2022; Wei et al., 2022; Wang et al., 2022b, *inter alia*). In InstT, an LLM is fine-tuned to produce a desired output given an instruction text. In some datasets, the instruction is further divided into a definition or prompt component, which defines the task and an optional input component (Wang et al., 2022b; Taori et al., 2023). In this work, we distinguish *three types of InstT datasets* based on their provenance: meta-datasets, human-authored datasets and LLM-authored datasets.

The first InstT datasets were **meta-datasets**, which convert existing NLP datasets into InstT data with human-authored prompt templates (Khashabi et al., 2020; Ye et al., 2021; Mishra et al., 2022; Sanh et al., 2022; Wei et al., 2022). Researchers typically construct them by writing one or more prompt templates for an existing NLP dataset. This template is then used to transform each instance of the existing dataset into an InstT instance. Here, we call the combination of an existing dataset and a prompt template a task. For **human-authored** InstT datasets on the other hand, the dataset creators ask human annotators to author InstT instances (Ouyang et al., 2022) or mine InstT instances from existing human-authored resources such as forums and wikis (Zhou et al., 2023). **LLM-authored** datasets instead are generated by LLMs. This is typically achieved by prompting the LLM with a few examples of what InstT instances look like and instructing the model to generate new ones (Wang et al., 2022a; Honovich et al., 2023; Taori et al., 2023) or by providing elaborate rules about what properties InstT instances should have (Bai et al., 2022; Sun et al., 2023).

Finally, dataset creators have proposed mixtures of these approaches, e.g. by manually correcting LLM-authored instances (Ruebsamen and Contributors, 2023) or by combining instances generated by different approaches (Zhou et al., 2023). Some of these works highlight the importance of high quality data (Zhou et al., 2023; Ruebsamen and Contributors, 2023), but to the best of our knowledge, our study is the first to systematically evaluate AED techniques.

2.2 Annotation Error Detection

AED for Natural Language Processing (NLP) datasets has a long tradition, which has recently been comprehensively reviewed Klie et al. (2022). Existing AED methods can be divided into six different categories (Klie et al., 2022): *variation-based* methods exploit the observation that instances with similar surface forms tend to have the same label (Dickinson and Meurers, 2003; Larson et al., 2020). *Model-based* methods use a cross-validation scheme to generate predictions for the whole dataset and then use these predictions to flag errors, e.g. by highlighting instances where the predicted label is different from the one assigned (Amiri et al., 2018; Yaghoub-Zadeh-Fard et al., 2019). *Training-dynamics-based* approaches compute statistics on quantities collected during training (Swayamdipta et al., 2020; Pleiss et al., 2020; Siddiqui et al., 2022). *Vector-space-proximity-based* methods assume that instances that are close in a suitable vector space should have the same label (Larson et al., 2019; Grivas et al., 2020). *Ensemble-based* methods use statistics of the predictions of ensemble members to find errors (Alt et al., 2020; Varshney et al., 2022) and rule-based approaches rely on manually defined rules to spot erroneous instances (Květoň and Oliva, 2002). In this work, we focus on training dynamics because they performed well in a recent evaluation (Klie et al., 2022), can be relatively easily adapted to generative settings and have a low computational overhead. We leave the evaluation of other types of methods to future work.

An orthogonal classification of AED methods is into flaggers and scorers (Klie et al., 2022). Flaggers model AED as a binary classification task (error vs non-error) and scorers assign an error score to each instance that reflects the likelihood that the instance contains an annotation error. In this work, we focus on scorers, because the ranking induced by them allows more fine-grained decisions about which instances to inspect (Weber and Plank, 2023) and they can be converted to flaggers by choosing an appropriate threshold (Swayamdipta et al., 2020).

3 Proposed AED baselines for text generation datasets

We present four AED baselines for text generation datasets. For this, we adapt methods based on training dynamics that were previously used for AED in classification problems (Swayamdipta et al., 2020; Pleiss et al., 2020). We chose these methods because they performed well in earlier work (Klie et al., 2022; Weber and Plank, 2023) and because their adaptation to generative settings is relatively straight-forward. All four methods assign an error score to an instance, with a higher score ideally reflecting a higher probability of an incorrect annotation. All scores use the probabilities $p_{e,l}$ that the model assigned to the token l of the instance's output sequence at epoch e during training. We propose the following measures: (1) **Perplexity**, which is the epoch-averaged perplexity of the instance based on $p_{e,l}$:

$$\text{PPL} = \frac{1}{E}\sum_{e=1}^{E} \text{ppl}_e, \quad (1)$$

where E is the number of epochs and ppl_e the perplexity at epoch e. (2) The (negative) **average probability**, determined by averaging $p_{e,l}$:

$$P_\mu = -\frac{1}{E}\sum_{e=1}^{E}\frac{1}{L}\sum_{l=1}^{L} p_{e,l}, \quad (2)$$

where L is the number of tokens in the output sequence.

(3) The (negative) **minimum probability**, derived from the minimum of $p_{e,l}$:

$$P_{\min} = -\frac{1}{E}\sum_{e=1}^{E}\min_{l=1}^{L} p_{e,l}. \quad (3)$$

(4) The (negative) **Area-under-the-Margin score** (AUM) (Pleiss et al., 2020), which we adapt to the generative setting by calculating it for each token in the output sequence and averaging the resulting scores:

$$\text{AUM} = \frac{1}{E}\sum_{e=1}^{E}\frac{1}{L}\sum_{l=1}^{L}\max_{y'_l \neq y_l} p_e(y'_l|x_l) - p_{e,l}, \quad (4)$$

where y_l is the token at position l and $\max_{y'_l \neq y_l} p_e(y'_l|x_l)$ is the maximum probability assigned by the model at epoch e for position l excluding the assigned token. In addition, we consider a variant of each score that uses only the last epoch; see §5.2 for the results of this ablation.

4 Datasets and Error Types

We describe Donkii's three different data sources that we have enriched with annotations of erroneous instances: P3-Donkii, SNI-Donkii, and ADC-Donkii.[2] Each is based on an existing InstT dataset and on manual inspection of the errors in that dataset: P3-Donkii is derived from the meta-dataset Public Pool of Prompts (Sanh et al., 2022), SNI-Donkii from the meta-dataset Super-Natural Instructions (Wang et al., 2022b),

[2]See Appendix A for our data statement.

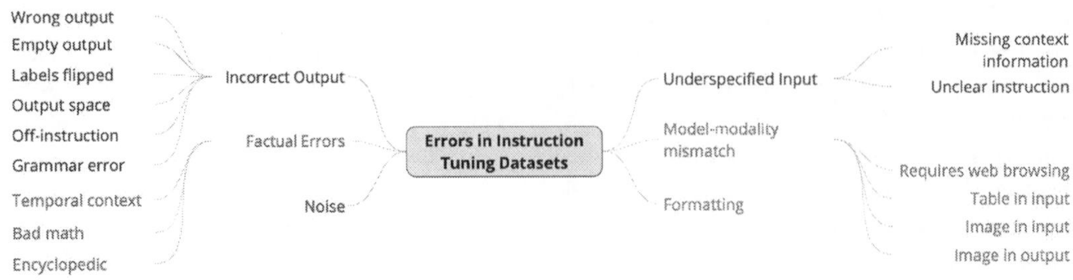

Figure 2: The DONKII taxonomy of six error categories, four of which are further divided into more specific subcategories.

and ADC-Donkii from the LLM-authored dataset Alpaca (Taori et al., 2023) and its partially corrected version AlpacaDatasetCleaned (Ruebsamen and Contributors, 2023). We enrich each of these datasets with labels indicating which instances contain errors, using different mixtures of expert annotation and programmatic analysis of the source data. For each dataset, we construct three different sets of instances: $\mathcal{X}^*$ which contains no errors, $\mathcal{X}_{\text{err}}$, for which we know that it contains errors, and $\mathcal{X}_{\text{unk}}$, for which we do not know if it contains errors. We evaluate AED methods by their ability of discriminating $\mathcal{X}^*$ from $\mathcal{X}_{\text{err}}$. We exclude $\mathcal{X}_{\text{unk}}$ from evaluation, as we do not exhaustively annotate the datasets with errors due to their sheer size and resource availability; see §5.1 for details.

4.1 P3-Donkii

Public Pool of Prompts (P3) (Sanh et al., 2022) is a meta-dataset for InstT which was created by asking researchers and open-source contributors to transform existing datasets by writing prompts using the InstT templating engine *promptsource* (Bach et al., 2022). We construct the P3-Donkii dataset by introducing different types of synthetic errors into the P3 data. We use this synthetic setup for P3 so that we have full control over the the number and types of errors in the dataset.[3] To find realistic error classes, we first detect existing errors in the P3 data. We use PPL to assign error scores to tasks in P3, employing both mean and median aggregation (see §5.2 for details on this).[4] We then manually inspect the top 20 highest scoring tasks by looking at their highest scoring instances. In our manual inspection, we found the following types of problems:

Empty output: The output is an empty string where it should not be.

Incorrect output: The output contains severe orthographic or factual errors.

Missing context information: The prompt is truncated during preprocessing. This can make crucial information unavailable, e.g. missing context in extractive QA.

We then correct the errors that we found in the 20 tasks in P3. We rebuild the empty output data from scratch using *promptsource* and verify that the output strings are not empty. We remove tasks that contain a high number of low quality outputs. We discard instances that do not fit within the set maximum length, so that there is no missing information.

Finally, we reintroduce the detected errors in a controlled manner by modelling them synthetically. For each type of error, we randomly sample five tasks and perturb their instances:

Empty output: We replace the output in all instances for the task with an empty string.

Low quality output: For each instance of the task, with a probability of 0.5, we replace the gold-standard output with output generated by prompting Llama-7b (Touvron et al., 2023).

Missing information: For each instance of the task, with a probability of 0.5, we truncate the gold-standard prompt to half of its original length.

Flipped output: For each instance, with a probability of 0.5, we replace the output with the output of another instance. This is a widely used perturbation used in AED research (Klie et al., 2022), which we adapted to InstT datasets.

We collect all perturbed instances in $\mathcal{X}_{\text{error}}$ (the set of instances the AED methods should detect)

[3]An alternative approach would have been a full manual annotation of P3 which was out of reach because of the large size of the dataset.

[4]In principle, this semi-automatic process of finding error categories with PPL could bias our evaluation results. However, our purely manual analysis of SNI shows similar error categories, so we are confident that the introduced bias is minimal.

and those of the same original[5] unperturbed task in $\mathcal{X}^*$ (the set of instances which should not be detected by the AED methods). The instances of unperturbed tasks constitute $\mathcal{X}_{\text{unk}}$.

4.2 SNI-Donkii

We construct SNI-Donkii by mining errors that arose during the creation of the Super-natural instructions (SNI) (Wang et al., 2022b) dataset and have been corrected for the current version of SNI. SNI[6] is a meta-dataset for InstT, created by a large number of researchers by transforming existing datasets into InstT tasks. It contains a total of 1,616 tasks covering a wide range of NLP tasks such as question answering, text classification, sentiment analysis, textual entailment, and summarization. The project implemented quality control through peer review conducted via GitHub[7] and a crowd-sourced evaluation.

We create SNI-Donkii by comparing the version of each task before the final round of peer review (the first version uploaded to GitHub) and after peer review (the version on GitHub at the time of writing). From the 1,613 tasks that we were able to download without error, we collect all 455 tasks $t \in \mathcal{T}$ where the output of at least one instance changed. For 17 of these tasks, all expert annotators (two co-authors and one NLP MSc student) agreed[8] that at least 90% of the changed instances contain an error. See Table 2 for an example of the annotation task and Table 3 for examples of found errors. For the annotation guidelines see Appendix B.

From this annotation, we construct SNI-Donkii as follows: For all tasks without errors, we add 64 instances of the latest version – or less if the task contains fewer than 64 instances – of it to $\mathcal{X}_{\text{unk}}$. For the erroneous tasks, we add 64 changed instances from the oldest version to $\mathcal{X}_{\text{err}}$ and 64 from the newest version to $\mathcal{X}^*$.[9] When we had fewer than 64 updated instances, we put them all into $\mathcal{X}_{\text{err}}$. In this case, we filled up $\mathcal{X}_{\text{unk}}$ with extra instances from the oldest version to keep the number of instances for each task about the same. Table 1 gives the statistics of the resulting dataset.

4.3 ADC-Donkii

Alpaca (Taori et al., 2023) is an LLM-authored dataset constructed by following the self-instruct recipe proposed by Wang et al. (2022a). The creators of Alpaca repeatedly prompted text-davinci-003[10] with in-context examples of InstT instances sampled from a pool of human and LLM-authored instances and asked the LLM to provide a new instance. This yielded a dataset of 52,000 different InstT instances. In a separate effort called Alpaca-DataCleaned (ADC) (Ruebsamen and Contributors, 2023), members of the open source community corrected errors in the Alpaca data using a mixture of manual and rule-based annotation.[11] To construct ADC-Donkii, we collect 300 instances from Alpaca that do not occur in ADC and pair each of them with the instance with the closest BM25 score from ADC. Using these pairs, three of this study's authors manually annotate whether one of the two instances is clearly preferable because the other contains at least one error. The annotation guidelines can be found in Appendix C. As with SNI, we do not disclose which instances are from Alpaca and which are from ADC to avoid introducing unnecessary bias. If, after a roundtable discussion, all three annotators agree that one of the two instances is preferable, we add it to $\mathcal{X}^*$ and the other to $\mathcal{X}_{\text{err}}$. We add all other instances from Alpaca and ADC to $\mathcal{X}_{\text{unk}}$. Table 1 shows the statistics for the resulting dataset.

4.4 Error categories

During annotation, we identified six main categories of errors, each with several subcategories. Note, that these error categories are not exhaustive and are observed in the annotated sample, rather than encompassing all possible categories of errors. A more detailed and nuanced analysis of possible errors in instruction tuning data is the subject of future work. The proposed hierarchy is shown in Figure 2; a sample from Donkii errors is shown in Table 3. More examples for each category can be

[5]Note, that for all tasks during our initial exploration of the dataset, we use the corrected error-free version of the task.

[6]`https://github.com/allenai/natural-instructions`

[7]`https://github.com/allenai/natural-instructions/commits/master`

[8]We opted for a roundtable discussion rather than majority voting because we found that annotating errors in InstT datasets is a difficult task. Even though we relied exclusively on expert annotators, they sometimes missed crucial details about instances and revised their annotations during the discussion. A disadvantage of this discussion-based setup is that we cannot reliably estimate inter-annotator agreement.

[9]We chose 64 instances because Wang et al. (2022b) find that performance plateaus with more instances per task.

[10]`https://platform.openai.com/docs/models`

[11]`https://github.com/gururise/AlpacaDataCleaned/issues/31`

	Source data	$\|\mathcal{X}_{\text{unk}}\|$	$\|\mathcal{X}^*\|$	$\|\mathcal{X}_{\text{err}}\|$	$\|\mathcal{T}\|$	$\|\mathcal{T}_{\text{err}}\|$	$\bar{L}_{\text{inp}}$	$\bar{L}_{\text{out}}$	Err	Prov
P3	Sanh et al. (2022)	399,472	12,237	12,237	417	20	118	9	Syn.	Meta
SNI	Wang et al. (2022b)	101,783	1,088	585	1,613	17	165	6	Nat.	Meta
ADC	Taori et al. (2023) (Ruebsamen and Contributors, 2023)	48,425	173	146	-	-	15	44	Nat	LLM

Table 1: Statistics for the three Donkii datasets. $|\mathcal{T}|$ denotes the total number of tasks, and $|\mathcal{T}_{\text{err}}|$ the number of tasks with at least one instance with an error. Note, that ADC does not provide a grouping of instances into tasks. $\bar{L}_{\text{inp}}/\bar{L}_{\text{out}}$ denotes the average input/output length in white-space-delimited tokens. 'Err' is the type of error (synthetic or naturally ocurring) and 'Prov' the provenance (meta-dataset vs LLM-authored). 'Lic' is the license under which the authors published their data.

Instruction 1: Name two deserts in the Sahara.
Input 1:
Output 1: The two deserts in the Sahara are the Great Western Erg and the Great Eastern Erg.

Instruction 2: Recognize the following bird's species.
Input 2: <Image of a bird>
Output 2: Western Great Egret (Ardea alba maxima).

Label: 1 is better than 2
Error category: Image in input

Table 2: Example for the pair-wise annotation task that we used to flag errors in SNI-Donkii and ADC-Donkii.

found in the Appendix D. The error categories are the following:

Incorrect output: Problems are observed in the output. This may include providing inaccurate or incorrect output, such as providing a three-letter abbreviation when a two-letter abbreviation was requested. Other problems in this category include not providing any output at all, reversing the label in binary classification tasks, and providing output that is in the wrong output space, such as answering a/b/c/d in a multiple choice question when the options are listed as 1/2/3/4. In addition, the output may be an off-instruction response that is related to the instruction but does not follow it, for example, responding with a code example that can calculate an average instead of directly outputting the average of the given numbers as requested. Finally, the output may contain ungrammatical text.

Factual knowledge and mathematics: This category covers outputs that may be time-dependent, contain factual errors, or contain incorrect arithmetic.

Noise: Instances in which the instruction, input, or output contains some form of noise. This noise can range from `NoInput` stubs to duplicating the instruction in the output.

Underspecified input: Instances in which the instruction and input do not provide sufficient information to complete the task. For example, a task may ask to find the average of a set of numbers without giving the actual numbers. This category also includes cases where the instruction is unclear and cannot be completed correctly due to a lack of specification. For example, a task may require classifying data points into multiple categories without explicitly describing the semantics of the categories or providing the data points. We argue that these instances are errors because the LLM should ask the user for the necessary input rather than assuming (i.e. 'hallucinating') input.

Model-modality mismatch: Instances that require additional modalities are placed in this category, to reflect that the examined InstT datasets are used for text-only LLMs. Unsupported modalities may include tables, images (as in Table 2), and the use of additional tools to browse and retrieve information from the web.

Formatting: Instances with corrupted formatting, such as missing white spaces and the use of punctuation instead of white spaces.

In general, the identified errors are very similar to known errors made by models for open-ended text generation (Dou et al., 2022; Ge et al., 2022), with less emphasis on issues of syntax and word choice.

5 How well does AED do in Instruction Tuning data?

In this section, we provide baseline results for error detection in InstT datasets. To do this, we evaluate the baselines introduced in §3 using the Donkii datasets proposed in §4.

Error	Source	Instruction	Input	Output (shortened)
Requires web browsing	Alpaca	Summarize the New York Times article about the rise of AI.	`www.nytimes.com/2020/06/16/opinion/ai-growth.html`	The New York Times article titled "The Rise of Artificial Intelligence" looks at the growing impact of AI on the world today. <...>
Bad math	Alpaca	Calculate the mean of the numbers 3, 4, 6, 10, 11		The mean of the numbers 3, 4, 6, 10, 11 is 6.4. This is calculated by adding the numbers together and then dividing by the number of values (5). (3 + 4 + 6 + 10 + 11 = 34; 34 / 5 = 6.4).
Unclear instruction	Alpaca	Sort the following 10 fruits into three categories.	Bananas, Apples, Pineapples, Plums, Cherries, Peaches, Grapes, Watermelons, Mangoes, Oranges	Category 1: Bananas, Apples, Pineapples, Plums, Cherries;
Formatting	SNI	[...]	story: I went down to the tidepool to watch the tide roll out. [...] selected sentence: I went down to the tidepool to watch the tide roll out.	I decide togotothe tidepool >Causes/Enables> I gotothe tidepool
Labels flipped	SNI	You are given two sentences (Sentence1 and Sentence2). Answer "Yes" if these sentences are a paraphrase of one another, otherwise answer "No".	Sentence1: The broader Standard & Poor 's 500 Index .SP> gained 3 points , or 0.39 percent , at 924 ., Sentence2: The technology-laced Nasdaq Composite Index .IXIC rose 6 points , or 0.41 percent , to 1,498 .	Yes

Table 3: Examples of some error categories of the Donkii taxonomy.

		small				base				large				xl			
	rand	PPL	P_μ	P_{min}	AUM	PPL	P_μ	P_{min}	AUM	PPL	P_μ	P_{min}	AUM	PPL	P_μ	P_{min}	AUM
P3	50.0	$73.6_{4.4}$	$\mathbf{84.3}_{1.0}$	$51.3_{0.8}$	$52.7_{0.7}$	$76.1_{0.6}$	$81.7_{0.3}$	$51.2_{0.0}$	$53.6_{0.1}$	$70.7_{3.5}$	$77.4_{0.4}$	$49.4_{0.6}$	$52.2_{0.2}$	$61.3_{0.0}$	$66.0_{0.0}$	$58.6_{0.0}$	$46.0_{0.0}$
SNI	34.9	$30.7_{0.2}$	$30.3_{0.2}$	$27.9_{0.1}$	$28.7_{0.1}$	$31.8_{0.4}$	$42.4_{0.9}$	$30.2_{0.3}$	$29.8_{0.1}$	$33.4_{1.0}$	$\mathbf{48.1}_{1.7}$	$34.5_{0.9}$	$34.1_{0.6}$	$33.0_{0.7}$	$38.9_{0.2}$	$32.2_{0.2}$	$31.6_{0.4}$
ADC	45.1	$54.5_{0.3}$	$\mathbf{55.4}_{0.3}$	$50.3_{0.5}$	$47.9_{0.7}$	$53.7_{0.21}$	$51.9_{0.5}$	$50.8_{0.7}$	$51.4_{0.7}$	$52.2_{0.4}$	$48.9_{0.2}$	$47.5_{0.5}$	$47.2_{1.2}$	$53.1_{0.0}$	$53.1_{0.0}$	$51.3_{0.0}$	$47.3_{0.0}$
AVG	43.3	52.9	56.7	43.2	43.1	53.9	**58.7**	44.1	44.9	52.1	58.1	43.8	44.5	49.1	52.7	47.4	41.6

Table 4: Results of four different AED methods applied to the Donkii datasets. All scores are Average Precision in percent. The larger number is the mean across three seeds and the smaller number the standard deviation. The best result per dataset is in bold. Rand is the random baseline.

5.1 Evaluation protocol

We follow the evaluation protocol for scoring-based AED methods for classification tasks of Klie et al. (2022) and Chong et al. (2022) – with one modification. We follow the protocol by treating the problem as a ranking task, where an AED model assigns an error score to each instance x_i. However, unlike Klie et al. (2022) and Chong et al. (2022), we have three sets of instances instead of two: $\mathcal{X}^*$, which contains few to no errors, $\mathcal{X}_{\text{err}}$ which contains many errors, and $\mathcal{X}_{\text{unk}}$ for which we do not know the proportion of errors. We judge the quality of the ranking by how well it distinguishes between $\mathcal{X}^*$ and $\mathcal{X}_{\text{err}}$ and ignore $\mathcal{X}_{\text{unk}}$ during evaluation. Note that while we use only $\mathcal{X}^*$ and $\mathcal{X}_{\text{err}}$ for evaluation, we train on $x_i \in \mathcal{X}^* \cup \mathcal{X}_{\text{err}} \cup \mathcal{X}_{\text{unk}}$. We use average precision (AP), i.e. the area under the precision-recall curve, implemented with scikit-learn (Pedregosa et al., 2011) to score the rankings and use $\frac{|\mathcal{X}_{\text{err}}|}{|\mathcal{X}^*|+|\mathcal{X}_{\text{err}}|}$ as an estimator for the random baseline (Bestgen, 2015).

We conduct all experiments with four models of different sizes from the T5 family[12] (Raffel et al., 2020) in the version that Lester et al. (2021) continually fine-tuned as language models. We chose T5 because it has worked well in previous InstT work (Sanh et al., 2022; Wei et al., 2022; Wang et al., 2022b). See Appendix E for the hyperparameters. We repeat all experiments with three different seeds and report the mean and standard deviation of the results.

[12] `https://huggingface.co/google/t5-base-lm-adapt`

5.2 Results

The results can be found in Table 4. On average, P_μ (average probability) performs the best across all model sizes, with PPL coming in second. AUM is tied for the third place with P_{min}, each outperforming the other for two of the four model sizes. This ranking is relatively stable for each individual dataset and the best configuration always uses P_μ. We conclude from this that P_μ clearly emerges as the best performing baseline for AED in our natural language generation setup. This shows the striking benefits in term of simplicity and effectiveness of our proposed P_μ metric. The improvement over the random baseline is relatively large at over 34 percentage points (pp) for P3-Donkii but more modest for SNI-Donkii and ADC-Donkii at 13.2 pp and 10.3 pp respectively. This is probably due to the fact that synthetically introduced errors are generally easier to detect than naturally occurring ones (Klie et al., 2022).

For **model size**, small is the best for P3 and ADC, while large is the best for SNI. On average, base and large perform best, while small also performs surprisingly well. Therefore, for a new InstT dataset, we recommend starting with a base-sized model for efficiency reasons.

P3	out (9777)	inp (2460)	-	-	-
rand	50.0	50.0	-	-	-
P_μ	$89.4_{0.9}$	$68.0_{0.1}$	-	-	-
ADC	out (13)	inp (13)	noi (77)	fac (14)	mul (29)
rand	37.0	48.0	48.4	29.8	50.9
P_μ	$62.6_{0.8}$	$72.2_{0.2}$	$49.8_{0.4}$	$55.7_{0.8}$	$61.5_{0.5}$
SNI	out	form (64)	noi (2)	-	mul (3)
rand	38.2	50.0	3.0	-	2.3
P_μ	$51.7_{1.7}$	$51.9_{0.9}$	$30.6_{8.6}$		$14.9_{3.9}$

Table 5: Results per error category. All scores are AP (higher is better) in percent of P_μ using the best performing model size for the dataset. The category names are abbreviated: out: incorrect output, inp: underspecified input, noi: noise, fac: factual error, mul: multi-modality, form: formatting. The number in brackets gives the number of instances per category.

We analyse the performance of the different scorers per annotated **error category**. For each dataset, we use P_μ with the respective best performing model size. The results can be found in Table 5. Interestingly, the results differ strongly across error categories and dataset. P_μ outperforms the random baseline for all but two categories, which are noisy instances in ADC-Donkii and formatting errors in SNI-Donkii. Surprisingly, other configurations, which on average perform worse than P_μ, are able to beat the random baseline for these error types with the respectively best scorers outperforming random by 18.1/13.7 pp for noise/formatting.

On instance vs task-level and epoch aggregation Our annotation of SNI and P3 showed that errors in meta-datasets often affect a large proportion of all instances for a given task.[13] We wondered whether we could exploit this property by **aggregating error scores across all instances for a given task** and thus perform AED on tasks rather than instances. For this, we conducted additional experiments using SNI-Donkii, where we computed two scores for each task by taking the mean and median across all instances for the given task. We then follow the same ranking-based evaluation protocol as for individual instances. Here, we observe a slightly different ordering of methods, with PPL achieving the highest score. On average, the aggregation by median yielded higher scores than aggregation by mean. The absolute AP is much higher than for single instance error detection at 69.3% (vs 48.1%), suggesting that task aggregation may be useful for detecting systematic errors in meta-datasets.

We also examine the effect of **aggregating scores over all epochs**. For this, we ablate the epoch aggregation by using the final logits directly to compute the AED scores. For each dataset, we compute the difference between the best performing size-score combination with and without epoch aggregation. We find that the scores drop by 1.3/3.9/1.2 percentage points AP for P3/SNI/ADC respectively *without* aggregation over epochs. This further supports the observation that averaging AED scores over epochs generally improves performance (Swayamdipta et al., 2020; Pleiss et al., 2020; Weber and Plank, 2023).

[13]This observation motivated our annotation efforts for P3 and SNI.

6 Conclusion

This work presents the first study on annotation error detection for generation tasks, in particular, instruction tuning data. Despite the popularity of InsT, there are no evaluation datasets for AED with marked errors. Therefore, we present Donkii, a suite of three existing InstT datasets enriched with novel error annotations and an error taxonomy derived from manual annotation efforts. We propose four different AED methods for generative models and systematically evaluate them on the Donkii datasets. We find that there is a clear best performing method for single instances with P_μ and for task-level AED with PPL. In any case, the choice of model size is critical for optimal AED performance. In Appendix F we report on preliminary experiments in which we investigated how annotation errors impact downstream performance. For future work, we plan to apply AED methods to more structured generative meta-datasets such as Huguet Cabot and Navigli (2021) or Fries et al. (2022).

Limitations

Identified errors in InsT datasets. We acknowledge that the error categories we have identified are not exhaustive. This is because the current errors have been annotated based on manual examination of medium-sized samples. We also acknowledge that our error category does not cover issues related to toxicity, hallucinations, and safety, as we believe that these issues are so important that they require specialized treatment in more focused work (Gehman et al., 2020; Sap et al., 2022; Raunak et al., 2021; Dziri et al., 2022; Greshake et al., 2023, *inter alia*).

Small sample size for individual categories We invested significant manual effort in annotation, but strongly favoured precision over quantity, with three expert annotators first labeling each sample individually and then discussing the results. As a result, the number of errors found per category is moderate to small (see Table 5). We believe that an even larger annotation effort would be required in the future to ensure that all findings on error categories are robust.

Ethics & Broader Impact

Instruction-tuned LLMs have been widely adopted by non-expert users (OpenAI, 2023). We believe that this makes fine-grained control over the model outputs and thus, by extension, over the content of the InstT dataset an ethical imperative. One facet of this is errors in the data, and so we believe that using AED methods to analyse InstT datasets can potentially have a positive impact on LLM users. However, the demographics of all annotators are fairly uniform, and yet in some cases there was substantial disagreement on what constitutes an error. Therefore, we believe that a broader discussion involving more stakeholders is needed to get a diverse perspective on what is the desired behaviour of LLMs and thus what constitutes an error in InstT datasets.

Acknowledgments

We thank Shijia Zhou for helping with the annotation of SNI-Donkii. Many thanks to the members of MaiNLP for their comments earlier drafts of on the paper. This research is in parts supported by European Research Council (ERC) grant agreement No. 101043235.

References

Christoph Alt, Aleksandra Gabryszak, and Leonhard Hennig. 2020. TACRED Revisited: A Thorough Evaluation of the TACRED Relation Extraction Task. In *Proceedings of the 58th Annual Meeting of the Association for Computational Linguistics*, pages 1558–1569, Online. Association for Computational Linguistics.

Hadi Amiri, Timothy Miller, and Guergana Savova. 2018. Spotting Spurious Data with Neural Networks. In *Proceedings of the 2018 Conference of the North American Chapter of the Association for Computational Linguistics: Human Language Technologies, Volume 1 (Long Papers)*, pages 2006–2016, New Orleans, Louisiana. Association for Computational Linguistics.

Stephen Bach, Victor Sanh, Zheng Xin Yong, Albert Webson, Colin Raffel, Nihal V. Nayak, Abheesht Sharma, Taewoon Kim, M Saiful Bari, Thibault Fevry, Zaid Alyafeai, Manan Dey, Andrea Santilli, Zhiqing Sun, Srulik Ben-david, Canwen Xu, Gunjan Chhablani, Han Wang, Jason Fries, Maged Alshaibani, Shanya Sharma, Urmish Thakker, Khalid Almubarak, Xiangru Tang, Dragomir Radev, Mike Tian-jian Jiang, and Alexander Rush. 2022. PromptSource: An integrated development environment and repository for natural language prompts. In *Proceedings of the 60th Annual Meeting of the Association for Computational Linguistics: System Demonstrations*, pages 93–104, Dublin, Ireland. Association for Computational Linguistics.

Yuntao Bai, Saurav Kadavath, Sandipan Kundu, Amanda Askell, Jackson Kernion, Andy Jones, Anna Chen, Anna Goldie, Azalia Mirhoseini, Cameron McKinnon, Carol Chen, Catherine Olsson, Christopher Olah, Danny Hernandez, Dawn Drain, Deep Ganguli, Dustin Li, Eli Tran-Johnson, Ethan Perez, Jamie Kerr, Jared Mueller, Jeffrey Ladish, Joshua Landau, Kamal Ndousse, Kamile Lukosiute, Liane Lovitt, Michael Sellitto, Nelson Elhage, Nicholas Schiefer, Noemí Mercado, Nova DasSarma, Robert Lasenby, Robin Larson, Sam Ringer, Scott Johnston, Shauna Kravec, Sheer El Showk, Stanislav Fort, Tamera Lanham, Timothy Telleen-Lawton, Tom Conerly, Tom Henighan, Tristan Hume, Samuel R. Bowman, Zac Hatfield-Dodds, Ben Mann, Dario Amodei, Nicholas Joseph, Sam McCandlish, Tom Brown, and Jared Kaplan. 2022. Constitutional AI: harmlessness from AI feedback. *CoRR*, abs/2212.08073.

Emily M. Bender and Batya Friedman. 2018. Data statements for natural language processing: Toward mitigating system bias and enabling better science. *Transactions of the Association for Computational Linguistics*, 6:587–604.

Yves Bestgen. 2015. Exact expected average precision of the random baseline for system evaluation. *Prague Bull. Math. Linguistics*, 103:131–138.

Derek Chong, Jenny Hong, and Christopher Manning. 2022. Detecting label errors by using pre-trained language models. In *Proceedings of the 2022 Conference on Empirical Methods in Natural Language Processing*, pages 9074–9091, Abu Dhabi, United Arab Emirates. Association for Computational Linguistics.

Markus Dickinson and W. Detmar Meurers. 2003. Detecting Errors in Part-of-Speech Annotation. In *10th Conference of the European Chapter of the Association for Computational Linguistics*, Budapest, Hungary. Association for Computational Linguistics.

Yao Dou, Maxwell Forbes, Rik Koncel-Kedziorski, Noah A. Smith, and Yejin Choi. 2022. Is GPT-3 text indistinguishable from human text? scarecrow: A framework for scrutinizing machine text. In *Proceedings of the 60th Annual Meeting of the Association for Computational Linguistics (Volume 1: Long Papers)*, pages 7250–7274, Dublin, Ireland. Association for Computational Linguistics.

Nouha Dziri, Sivan Milton, Mo Yu, Osmar Zaiane, and Siva Reddy. 2022. On the origin of hallucinations in conversational models: Is it the datasets or the models? In *Proceedings of the 2022 Conference of the North American Chapter of the Association for Computational Linguistics: Human Language Technologies*, pages 5271–5285, Seattle, United States. Association for Computational Linguistics.

Jason Alan Fries, Leon Weber, Natasha Seelam, Gabriel Altay, Debajyoti Datta, Samuele Garda, Myungsun Kang, Ruisi Su, Wojciech Kusa, Samuel Cahyawijaya, Fabio Barth, Simon Ott, Matthias Samwald, Stephen Bach, Stella Biderman, Mario Sänger, Bo Wang, Alison Callahan, Daniel León Periñán, Théo Gigant, Patrick Haller, Jenny Chim, Jose David Posada, John Michael Giorgi, Karthik Rangasai Sivaraman, Marc Pàmies, Marianna Nezhurina, Robert Martin, Michael Cullan, Moritz Freidank, Nathan Dahlberg, Shubhanshu Mishra, Shamik Bose, Nicholas Michio Broad, Yanis Labrak, Shlok S. Deshmukh, Sid Kiblawi, Ayush Singh, Minh Chien Vu, Trishala Neeraj, Jonas Golde, Albert Villanova del Moral, and Benjamin Beilharz. 2022. BigBio: A Framework for Data-Centric Biomedical Natural Language Processing. In *Thirty-Sixth Conference on Neural Information Processing Systems Datasets and Benchmarks Track*, New Orleans, Louisiana, USA.

Huibin Ge, Xiaohu Zhao, Chuang Liu, Yulong Zeng, Qun Liu, and Deyi Xiong. 2022. TGEA 2.0: A Large-Scale Diagnostically Annotated Dataset with Benchmark Tasks for Text Generation of Pretrained Language Models. *Advances in Neural Information Processing Systems*, 35:31612–31626.

Samuel Gehman, Suchin Gururangan, Maarten Sap, Yejin Choi, and Noah A. Smith. 2020. RealToxicityPrompts: Evaluating neural toxic degeneration in language models. In *Findings of the Association for Computational Linguistics: EMNLP 2020*, pages 3356–3369, Online. Association for Computational Linguistics.

Kai Greshake, Sahar Abdelnabi, Shailesh Mishra, Christoph Endres, Thorsten Holz, and Mario Fritz. 2023. Not what you've signed up for: Compromising Real-World LLM-Integrated Applications with Indirect Prompt Injection.

Andreas Grivas, Beatrice Alex, Claire Grover, Richard Tobin, and William Whiteley. 2020. Not a cute stroke: Analysis of Rule- and Neural Network-based Information Extraction Systems for Brain Radiology Reports. In *Proceedings of the 11th International Workshop on Health Text Mining and Information Analysis*, pages 24–37, Online. Association for Computational Linguistics.

Or Honovich, Thomas Scialom, Omer Levy, and Timo Schick. 2023. Unnatural instructions: Tuning language models with (almost) no human labor. In *Proceedings of the 61st Annual Meeting of the Association for Computational Linguistics (Volume 1: Long Papers)*, pages 14409–14428, Toronto, Canada. Association for Computational Linguistics.

Pere-Lluís Huguet Cabot and Roberto Navigli. 2021. REBEL: Relation extraction by end-to-end language generation. In *Findings of the Association for Computational Linguistics: EMNLP 2021*, pages 2370–2381, Punta Cana, Dominican Republic. Association for Computational Linguistics.

Daniel Khashabi, Sewon Min, Tushar Khot, Ashish Sabharwal, Oyvind Tafjord, Peter Clark, and Hannaneh Hajishirzi. 2020. UNIFIEDQA: Crossing format boundaries with a single QA system. In *Findings of the Association for Computational Linguistics: EMNLP 2020*, pages 1896–1907, Online. Association for Computational Linguistics.

Jan-Christoph Klie, Bonnie Webber, and Iryna Gurevych. 2022. Annotation Error Detection: Analyzing the Past and Present for a More Coherent Future. *Computational Linguistics*, pages 1–42.

Pavel Květoň and Karel Oliva. 2002. (Semi-)Automatic Detection of Errors in PoS-Tagged Corpora. In *COLING 2002: The 19th International Conference on Computational Linguistics*.

Stefan Larson, Adrian Cheung, Anish Mahendran, Kevin Leach, and Jonathan K. Kummerfeld. 2020. Inconsistencies in Crowdsourced Slot-Filling Annotations: A Typology and Identification Methods. In *Proceedings of the 28th International Conference on Computational Linguistics*, pages 5035–5046, Barcelona, Spain (Online). International Committee on Computational Linguistics.

Stefan Larson, Anish Mahendran, Andrew Lee, Jonathan K. Kummerfeld, Parker Hill, Michael A. Laurenzano, Johann Hauswald, Lingjia Tang, and Jason Mars. 2019. Outlier Detection for Improved Data Quality and Diversity in Dialog Systems. In *Proceedings of the 2019 Conference of the North American Chapter of the Association for Computational Linguistics: Human Language Technologies, Volume 1 (Long and Short Papers)*, pages 517–527, Minneapolis, Minnesota. Association for Computational Linguistics.

Brian Lester, Rami Al-Rfou, and Noah Constant. 2021. The power of scale for parameter-efficient prompt tuning. In *Proceedings of the 2021 Conference on Empirical Methods in Natural Language Processing*, pages 3045–3059, Online and Punta Cana, Dominican Republic. Association for Computational Linguistics.

Swaroop Mishra, Daniel Khashabi, Chitta Baral, and Hannaneh Hajishirzi. 2022. Cross-task generalization via natural language crowdsourcing instructions. In *Proceedings of the 60th Annual Meeting of the Association for Computational Linguistics (Volume 1: Long Papers)*, pages 3470–3487, Dublin, Ireland. Association for Computational Linguistics.

OpenAI. 2023. GPT-4 technical report. *CoRR*, abs/2303.08774.

Long Ouyang, Jeffrey Wu, Xu Jiang, Diogo Almeida, Carroll L. Wainwright, Pamela Mishkin, Chong Zhang, Sandhini Agarwal, Katarina Slama, Alex Ray, John Schulman, Jacob Hilton, Fraser Kelton, Luke Miller, Maddie Simens, Amanda Askell, Peter Welinder, Paul F. Christiano, Jan Leike, and Ryan Lowe. 2022. Training language models to follow instructions with human feedback. In *NeurIPS*.

F. Pedregosa, G. Varoquaux, A. Gramfort, V. Michel, B. Thirion, O. Grisel, M. Blondel, P. Prettenhofer, R. Weiss, V. Dubourg, J. Vanderplas, A. Passos, D. Cournapeau, M. Brucher, M. Perrot, and E. Duchesnay. 2011. Scikit-learn: Machine learning in Python. *Journal of Machine Learning Research*, 12:2825–2830.

Geoff Pleiss, Tianyi Zhang, Ethan Elenberg, and Kilian Q Weinberger. 2020. Identifying Mislabeled Data using the Area Under the Margin Ranking. In *Advances in Neural Information Processing Systems*, volume 33, pages 17044–17056. Curran Associates, Inc.

Colin Raffel, Noam Shazeer, Adam Roberts, Katherine Lee, Sharan Narang, Michael Matena, Yanqi Zhou, Wei Li, and Peter J. Liu. 2020. Exploring the limits of transfer learning with a unified text-to-text transformer. *J. Mach. Learn. Res.*, 21:140:1–140:67.

Vikas Raunak, Arul Menezes, and Marcin Junczys-Dowmunt. 2021. The curious case of hallucinations in neural machine translation. In *Proceedings of the 2021 Conference of the North American Chapter of the Association for Computational Linguistics: Human Language Technologies*, pages 1172–1183, Online. Association for Computational Linguistics.

Gene Ruebsamen and Contributors. 2023. Alpacadatacleaned. `https://github.com/gururise/AlpacaDataCleaned`.

Victor Sanh, Albert Webson, Colin Raffel, Stephen H. Bach, Lintang Sutawika, Zaid Alyafeai, Antoine Chaffin, Arnaud Stiegler, Arun Raja, Manan Dey, M Saiful Bari, Canwen Xu, Urmish Thakker, Shanya Sharma Sharma, Eliza Szczechla, Taewoon Kim, Gunjan Chhablani, Nihal V. Nayak, Debajyoti Datta, Jonathan Chang, Mike Tian-Jian Jiang, Han Wang, Matteo Manica, Sheng Shen, Zheng Xin Yong, Harshit Pandey, Rachel Bawden, Thomas Wang, Trishala Neeraj, Jos Rozen, Abheesht Sharma, Andrea Santilli, Thibault Févry, Jason Alan Fries, Ryan Teehan, Teven Le Scao, Stella Biderman, Leo Gao, Thomas Wolf, and Alexander M. Rush. 2022. Multitask prompted training enables zero-shot task generalization. In *The Tenth International Conference on Learning Representations, ICLR 2022, Virtual Event, April 25-29, 2022*. OpenReview.net.

Maarten Sap, Swabha Swayamdipta, Laura Vianna, Xuhui Zhou, Yejin Choi, and Noah A. Smith. 2022. Annotators with attitudes: How annotator beliefs and identities bias toxic language detection. In *Proceedings of the 2022 Conference of the North American Chapter of the Association for Computational Linguistics: Human Language Technologies*, pages 5884–5906, Seattle, United States. Association for Computational Linguistics.

Shoaib Ahmed Siddiqui, Nitarshan Rajkumar, Tegan Maharaj, David Krueger, and Sara Hooker. 2022. Metadata Archaeology: Unearthing Data Subsets by Leveraging Training Dynamics.

Zhiqing Sun, Yikang Shen, Qinhong Zhou, Hongxin Zhang, Zhenfang Chen, David D. Cox, Yiming Yang, and Chuang Gan. 2023. Principle-driven self-alignment of language models from scratch with minimal human supervision. *CoRR*, abs/2305.03047.

Swabha Swayamdipta, Roy Schwartz, Nicholas Lourie, Yizhong Wang, Hannaneh Hajishirzi, Noah A. Smith, and Yejin Choi. 2020. Dataset Cartography: Mapping and Diagnosing Datasets with Training Dynamics. In *Proceedings of the 2020 Conference on Empirical Methods in Natural Language Processing (EMNLP)*, pages 9275–9293, Online. Association for Computational Linguistics.

Rohan Taori, Ishaan Gulrajani, Tianyi Zhang, Yann Dubois, Xuechen Li, Carlos Guestrin, Percy Liang, and Tatsunori B. Hashimoto. 2023. Stanford alpaca: An instruction-following llama model. `https://github.com/tatsu-lab/stanford_alpaca`.

Hugo Touvron, Thibaut Lavril, Gautier Izacard, Xavier Martinet, Marie-Anne Lachaux, Timothée Lacroix, Baptiste Rozière, Naman Goyal, Eric Hambro, Faisal Azhar, Aurélien Rodriguez, Armand Joulin, Edouard Grave, and Guillaume Lample. 2023. Llama: Open and efficient foundation language models. *CoRR*, abs/2302.13971.

Neeraj Varshney, Swaroop Mishra, and Chitta Baral. 2022. ILDAE: Instance-Level Difficulty Analysis of Evaluation Data. In *Proceedings of the 60th Annual Meeting of the Association for Computational Linguistics (Volume 1: Long Papers)*, pages 3412–3425, Dublin, Ireland. Association for Computational Linguistics.

Andreas Vlachos. 2006. Active Annotation. In *Proceedings of the Workshop on Adaptive Text Extraction and Mining (ATEM 2006)*.

Yizhong Wang, Yeganeh Kordi, Swaroop Mishra, Alisa Liu, Noah A. Smith, Daniel Khashabi, and Hannaneh Hajishirzi. 2022a. Self-Instruct: Aligning Language Model with Self Generated Instructions.

Yizhong Wang, Swaroop Mishra, Pegah Alipoormolabashi, Yeganeh Kordi, Amirreza Mirzaei, Atharva Naik, Arjun Ashok, Arut Selvan Dhanasekaran, Anjana Arunkumar, David Stap, Eshaan Pathak, Giannis Karamanolakis, Haizhi Lai, Ishan Purohit, Ishani Mondal, Jacob Anderson, Kirby Kuznia, Krima Doshi, Kuntal Kumar Pal, Maitreya Patel, Mehrad Moradshahi, Mihir Parmar, Mirali Purohit, Neeraj Varshney, Phani Rohitha Kaza, Pulkit Verma, Ravsehaj Singh Puri, Rushang Karia, Savan Doshi, Shailaja Keyur Sampat, Siddhartha Mishra, Sujan Reddy A, Sumanta Patro, Tanay Dixit, and Xudong Shen. 2022b. Super-NaturalInstructions: Generalization via declarative instructions on 1600+ NLP tasks. In *Proceedings of the 2022 Conference on Empirical Methods in Natural Language Processing*, pages 5085–5109, Abu Dhabi, United Arab Emirates. Association for Computational Linguistics.

Leon Weber and Barbara Plank. 2023. ActiveAED: A human in the loop improves annotation error detection. In *Findings of the Association for Computational Linguistics: ACL 2023*, pages 8834–8845, Toronto, Canada. Association for Computational Linguistics.

Jason Wei, Maarten Bosma, Vincent Zhao, Kelvin Guu, Adams Wei Yu, Brian Lester, Nan Du, Andrew M. Dai, and Quoc V. Le. 2022. Finetuned Language Models are Zero-Shot Learners. In *International Conference on Learning Representations*.

Mohammad-Ali Yaghoub-Zadeh-Fard, Boualem Benatallah, Moshe Chai Barukh, and Shayan Zamanirad. 2019. A Study of Incorrect Paraphrases in Crowdsourced User Utterances. In *Proceedings of the 2019 Conference of the North American Chapter of the Association for Computational Linguistics: Human Language Technologies, Volume 1 (Long and Short Papers)*, pages 295–306, Minneapolis, Minnesota. Association for Computational Linguistics.

Qinyuan Ye, Bill Yuchen Lin, and Xiang Ren. 2021. CrossFit: A few-shot learning challenge for cross-task generalization in NLP. In *Proceedings of the 2021 Conference on Empirical Methods in Natural Language Processing*, pages 7163–7189, Online and Punta Cana, Dominican Republic. Association for Computational Linguistics.

Chunting Zhou, Pengfei Liu, Puxin Xu, Srini Iyer, Jiao Sun, Yuning Mao, Xuezhe Ma, Avia Efrat, Ping Yu, Lili Yu, Susan Zhang, Gargi Ghosh, Mike Lewis, Luke Zettlemoyer, and Omer Levy. 2023. LIMA: less is more for alignment. *CoRR*, abs/2305.11206.

A Donkii Data Statement

Following (Bender and Friedman, 2018), the following outlines the data statement for Donkii:

- A. CURATION RATIONALE Enrichment of existing instruction-tuning datasets with annotations for erroneous instances
- B. LANGUAGE VARIETY English with the exact variant(s) unkown because of the large number of different sources of data
- C. SPEAKER DEMOGRAPHIC Unknown because of the large number of different data sources
- D. ANNOTATOR DEMOGRAPHIC Three post-doctoral researchers and one Master's student (age: 25-40), gender: male and female. Native language: Russian, German. Socioeconomic status: higher-education student and university researchers.
- E. SPEECH SITUATION Unknown because of the large number of different data sources
- F. TEXT CHARACTERISTICS Unknown because of the large number of different data sources
- PROVENANCE APPENDIX
  - Alpaca (Taori et al., 2023), CC By NC 4.0, `https://github.com/tatsu-lab/stanford_alpaca`
  - AlpacaDataCleaned (Ruebsamen and Contributors, 2023), Apache 2.0, `https://github.com/gururise/AlpacaDataCleaned`
  - Public Pool of Prompts (Sanh et al., 2022), Apache 2.0, `https://huggingface.co/datasets/bigscience/P3`
  - Super-Natural Instructions (Wang et al., 2022b), Apache 2.0, `https://github.com/allenai/natural-instructions`

B SNI Annotation Guidelines

For this annotation effort, we assume a pair-wise annotation setting. You are shown two tasks and the instances that differ between them. You should judge whether one of the two tasks contains fewer errors than the other one. Each task has the following fields:

- **Definition**: The instruction to the language model. E.g. 'solve the following equation for x'
- **Instances**: Each with the following fields:
- **Input**: The input complementing the instruction. E.g. 'equation: x + 2 = 5'. Output: The gold-standard output expected from the model

There are four possible labels:

1. A is better than B
2. B is better than A
3. A and B are the same
4. I don't know

Additionally, there is a field for short free-form comments where you can (but don't have to) note a reason for your annotation.

We assume that the dataset is used to train a current text-only vanilla LLM like GPT3 or Llama. That is, it does not have access to tools and cannot process multi-modal input.

The following rules apply for differences between tasks A and B. We assume that the difference mentioned in the rule is the only difference between both (ceteris paribus). If more than one rule applies, we leave the choice to the best judgment of the annotator. The goal is to make only relative judgments for the given pair without considering the "absolute quality" of the instances. Even when both contain very little or many errors, if B clearly contains more significant errors than A, this should be annotated as "A is better than B".

Rules:

- If B contains more errors than A, but those are only few and thus don't affect the majority of the instances differing between A and B, then A and B are equal. As a guideline: If more not more than 90% contain the error, then they probably should be equal.
- Be lenient in your annotations. If you are unsure whether something is an error, then better go for A and B are equal.
- **Factual correctness**: If the output of A can be interpreted as factually correct, but the one in B cannot, then A is better than B. Example:
  - Instruction: Tell me the title of the most popular song released in 2020 so far.
  - Output A: The most popular song released in 2020 so far is "Blinding Lights" by The Weeknd.
  - Output B: The most popular song released in 2020 so far is "The Box" by Roddy Rich.
  - Explanation: A is better than B, because, while the answer to A is ambiguous (there are multiple measures of popularity), "The Box" was released in 2019 and thus is clearly wrong.
- **Noise**: If B contains noise (e.g. technical artifacts) but A does not, then A is better than B. Example:
  - Instruction: Suggest the best strategy for a five-second TV commercial.
  - Input A:
  - Input B: "NoInput"
  - Explanation: A is better than B, because "NoInput" is clearly a technical artifact (even despite A being empty - i.e. no output better than noise).
- **Only output**: Judge A and B based on the output field not instruction or input. Justification: It is not clear whether low-quality input with high-quality output improves or diminishes instruction tuning performance. Example:
  - Instruction A: Convert the following number in hexadecimal format.
  - Input A: 18
  - Instruction B: Convert the number 18 to hexadecimal
  - Input B:
  - Explanation B: A and B are equal, even though one could prefer A over B because input and instruction are cleanly separated.
- **Unclear instruction**: If it is impossible to guess user intent based on the instruction in B, but it is possible to guess it in A, then A is better than B. Example:

- Instruction A: Find the average value of the following list of numbers
- Instruction B: Process the following data and output the results
- Input: List: [3, 7, 2, 5]
- Explanation: A is better than B because for B it is not clear at all how the model should process the data.

- **Tool usage**: If B requires tool usage (e.g. access to a search engine) but A doesn't, then A is better than B. Justification: We assume that the dataset is used to instruction-tune a vanilla LM without access to tools. Example:
  - Instruction A: Provide a brief overview about the following topic.
  - Input A: Volcanology
  - Instruction B: Take a Wikipedia article and rewrite it in your own words.
  - Input B: https://en.wikipedia.org/wiki/Volcanology
  - Explanation: A is better than B because B requires access to a web browser.

- **Multi-modal input**: If B contains multi-modal input (e.g. an image file) but A doesn't, then A is better than B. Justification: We assume that the dataset is used to instruction-tune a vanilla text-only LM. Example:
  - Instruction: Critique the given painting.
  - Input A: The painting is an abstract composition of vibrant yellow, blue, and pink hues that appear in an haphazard, yet balanced form and serve as an evocation of life, joy, and emotion.
  - Input B: [Painting attached]
  - Explanation: A is better than B because B contains multimodal input.

- **Temporal knowledge**: If B contains temporal knowledge but A doesn't, then A is better than B. Justification: We want the instruction-tuned model to handle temporal knowledge gracefully. Example:
  - Instruction A: What is the name of the 46th president of the United States?
  - Instruction B: What is the name of the current president of the United States?
  - Explanation: A is better than B because the answer to B will change over time while the answer to A is static.

- **Formatting**: If A and B differ only in formatting, then A and B are equal Example:
  - Output A: - Astonished - Amazed - Shocked - Stunned - Speechless - Bewildered"
  - Output B: Astonished, amazed, shocked, stunned, speechless, bewildered. Explanation: A is equal to B because the output only differs in formatting

C ADC Annotation Guidelines

For this annotation effort, we assume a pair-wise annotation setting. You are shown two instances and have to judge which of both would you preferably include in an instruction-tuning dataset. Each instance has two to three fields:

- **Instruction**: The instruction to the language model. E.g. 'solve the following equation for x'

- **Input** (optional): The input complementing the instruction. E.g. 'equation: x + 2 = 5'. Instructions can be self-contained, thus Input is optional.

- **Output**: The gold-standard output expected from the model

There are four possible labels:

1. A is better than B

2. B is better than A

3. A and B are the same

4. I don't know

Additionally, there is a field for short free-form comments where you can (but don't have to) note a reason for your annotation.

We assume that the dataset is used to train a current text-only vanilla LLM like GPT3 or Llama. That is, it does not have access to tools and cannot process multi-modal input.

The following rules apply for differences between instances A and B. We assume that the difference mentioned in the rule is the only difference between both (ceteris paribus). If more than one rule applies, we leave the choice to the best judgment of the annotator. The goal is to make only relative judgments for the given pair without considering the "absolute quality" of the instances. Even when both are very high or low quality, if B is clearly worse than A, this should be annotated as "A is better than B".

Rules:

- **Factual correctness**: If the output of A can be interpreted as factually correct, but the one in B cannot, then A is better than B. Example:
  - Instruction: Tell me the title of the most popular song released in 2020 so far.
  - Output A: The most popular song released in 2020 so far is "Blinding Lights" by The Weeknd.
  - Output B: The most popular song released in 2020 so far is "The Box" by Roddy Rich.
  - Explanation: A is better than B, because, while the answer to A is ambiguous (there are multiple measures of popularity), "The Box" was released in 2019 and thus is clearly wrong.
- **Noise**: If B contains noise (e.g. technical artifacts) but A does not, then A is better than B. Example:
  - Instruction: Suggest the best strategy for a five-second TV commercial.
  - Input A:
  - Input B: "NoInput"
  - Explanation: A is better than B, because "NoInput" is clearly a technical artifact (even despite A being empty - i.e. no output better than noise).
- **Only output**: Judge A and B based on the output field not instruction or input. Justification: It is not clear whether low-quality input with high-quality output improves or diminishes instruction tuning performance. Example:
  - Instruction A: Convert the following number in hexadecimal format.
  - Input A: 18
  - Instruction B: Convert the number 18 to hexadecimal
  - Input B:
  - Explanation B: A and B are equal, even though one could prefer A over B because input and instruction are cleanly separated.
- **Unclear instruction**: If it is impossible to guess user intent based on the instruction in B, but it is possible to guess it in A, then A is better than B. Example:
  - Instruction A: Find the average value of the following list of numbers
  - Instruction B: Process the following data and output the results
  - Input: List: [3, 7, 2, 5]
  - Explanation: A is better than B because for B it is not clear at all how the model should process the data.
- **Tool usage**: If B requires tool usage (e.g. access to a search engine) but A doesn't, then A is better than B. Justification: We assume that the dataset is used to instruction-tune a vanilla LM without access to tools. Example:
  - Instruction A: Provide a brief overview about the following topic.
  - Input A: Volcanology
  - Instruction B: Take a Wikipedia article and rewrite it in your own words.
  - Input B: https://en.wikipedia.org/wiki/Volcanology
  - Explanation: A is better than B because B requires access to a web browser.
- **Multi-modal input**: If B contains multimodal input (e.g. an image file) but A doesn't, then A is better than B. Justification: We assume that the dataset is used to instruction-tune a vanilla text-only LM. Example:
  - Instruction: Critique the given painting.
  - Input A: The painting is an abstract composition of vibrant yellow, blue, and pink hues that appear in an haphazard, yet balanced form and serve as an evocation of life, joy, and emotion.
  - Input B: [Painting attached]
  - Explanation: A is better than B because B contains multimodal input.
- **Temporal knowledge**: If B contains temporal knowledge but A doesn't, then A is better

than B. Justification: We want the instruction-tuned model to handle temporal knowledge gracefully. Example:

- Instruction A: What is the name of the 46th president of the United States?
- Instruction B: What is the name of the current president of the United States?
- Explanation: A is better than B because the answer to B will change over time while the answer to A is static.

- **Formatting**: If A and B differ only in formatting, then A and B are equal Example:
  - Output A: - Astonished - Amazed - Shocked - Stunned - Speechless - Bewildered"
  - Output B: Astonished, amazed, shocked, stunned, speechless, bewildered. Explanation: A is equal to B because the output only differs in formatting

- **Global properties**: If A and B differ only with respect to the full dataset, e.g. because A increases grammatical diversity in the input but B doesn't, then A and B are equal Example:
  - Instruction A: The average of 10 numbers is 85. If the numbers 70 and 76 are removed from the set of numbers, what is the average of the remaining numbers?
  - Instruction B: Find the average of 85, 44 and 102.
  - Explanation: A and B are equal, even though more complex problems as A are much less frequent in the whole dataset than problems of the type B.

- **Subjectivity**: If the annotator feels that their preference for one instance is strongly subjective, then A and B are equal.

- **Leniency**: Be lenient in your annotations. If you are unsure whether something is an error, then better go for A and B are equal. If both outputs can be interpreted as correct, then A and B are equal

D Examples of errors

Error	Source	Instruction	Input	Output (shortened)
			Incorrect output	
Wrong output	SNI	Given a sentence and an entity, the task is to select the authors sentiment towards the enity. Sentiments can be Positive, Neutral and Negative. <...>	What is the sentiment of the following document towards the entity Hayley Smith ? Hayley Smith was diagnosed with chronic depression in her early twenties: "I'd been bottling up quite a bit through most of my teens. Then it hit me a like a brick wall " she said.	Neutral
Empty output	Alpaca	Create a flow chart to explain the working of a web browser.		
Labels flipped	SNI	In this task you will be given a passage and a yes/no question based on the passage. You should answer the question using the information from the passage.	Superfecundation is the fertilization of two or more ova from the same cycle by sperm from separate acts of sexual intercourse, which can lead to twin babies from two separate biological fathers. [...] question: can a woman produce twins of different fathers?	No
Output space	SNI	You are given a science question (easy-level) and four answer options (associated with "A", "B", "C", "D"). Your task is to find the correct answer based on scientific facts, knowledge and reasoning.	Which group of organisms can show significant trait changes in the shortest period of time? (A) bacteria (B) birds (C) fish (D) reptiles	1
Off-instruction	Alpaca	Given three numbers (x, y, z), find the greatest common factor.	2, 4, 2008	The greatest common factor of 2, 4, and 8 is 2.
Grammar error	SNI	In this task, you are given a question and an answer, you would be asked to create the sentence based on the Question-Answer provided. It should be contained within the Question-Answer provided.	Question: What is the most common type of cancer in adult males? Answer: prostate	Prostate is the most common type of cancer in adult males.
			Factual Errors	
Temporal context	Alpaca	What is the average annual salary for a customer service developer?		The average annual salary for a customer service developer is usually around $74,508.
Bad math	Alpaca	Calculate the average of the following three numbers: 10, 12, 15.		The average of 10, 12, and 15 is 12.67.
Encyclopedic	Alpaca	What is the average air pressure of a human's lungs?		The average air pressure in a human's lungs is between four and seven centimeters of water (4–7 cm H2O).
			Noise	
Noise	Alpaca	Write an essay about the benefits of public transportation.	No input required.	Public transportation is an invaluable resource for communities and cities around the world. <...>
			Underspecified Input	
Missing context information	Alpaca	Write a tweet summarizing this article about an animal rescue in Thailand.	The article	Amazing news! An animal rescue in Thailand has successfully freed 63 bears from animal trafficking. The rescued bears will now receive the proper care and attention they need.
Unclear instruction	Alpaca	Sort the following 10 fruits into three categories.	Bananas, Apples, Pineapples, Plums, Cherries, Peaches, Grapes, Watermelons, Mangoes, Oranges	Category 1: Bananas, Apples, Pineapples, Plums, Cherries; Category 2: Peaches, Grapes, Watermelons; Category 3: Mangoes, Oranges
			Model-modality mismatch	
Requires web browsing	Alpaca	Provide a summarization of the article.	`https://en.wikipedia.org/wiki/Artificial_intelligence`	Artificial Intelligence, commonly known as AI, refers to the simulation of human intelligence processes by machines, especially computer systems. <...>
Table in input	Alpaca		Dataset of 500 people with the variable "income".	The mean income is $50,000.
Image in input	Alpaca	How would you use this photo in a marketing campaign?	<image included in email>	The photo can be used to create a compelling marketing campaign that draws attention to the product or service. <...>
Image in output	Alpaca	Make a word cloud on the given topic.	Artificial Intelligence	<Word Cloud Output>
			Formatting	
Formatting	SNI	In this task, you will be given a short story. One sentence from the story is chosen. Consider the events that happen before that sentence, or are likely to have happened before it. Does any of them directly cause it, or simply make it possible? You should write your answer in the form " A >causes/enables> B". Try to use phrases and sentences from the story to compose your answer when possible.	story: I went down to the tidepool to watch the tide roll out. I sat on the dock and waited, while listening to my mp3 player. Once the tide was out, I saw Something shiny in the muddy bottoms. I went down and found that it was a gold ring! Today was my lucky day! selected sentence: I went down to the tidepool to watch the tide roll out.	I decide togotothe tidepool >Causes/Enables> I gotothe tidepool

Table 6: Examples of errors.

E Hyperparameters

We experiment with four sizes, namely small (60 million parameters), base (220 million), large (770 million), and 3B (3 billion) using NVIDIA A100 cards. We train each of the models for 10 epochs as a seq2seq LM using a batch size of 60 and a learning rate of $1e-3$. Note, that we train separate models for each of the three datasets and leave the exploration of possible synergies across datasets for future work. We set the maximum source length to 512/768/768 for P3-Donkii/SNI-Donkii/APC-Donkii and the output length to 256.

F Preliminary experiments on the impact of errors on downstream performance

We conduct a preliminary experiment on how errors in InstT datasets affect downstream performance in a case study. For this, we use the training and evaluation setup of Tk-Instruct (Wang et al., 2022b), which is the main model trained on SNI using the code provided by the authors.[14] To investigate the effect of errors, we contrast two models: Tk-Instruct$_{err}$ and Tk-Instruct*. Both models are based on the three billion parameter version of T5. For Tk-Instruct$_{err}$, we use all 17 tasks that we found to be erroneous in SNI-Donkii. To these, we add a sample of an additional 100 tasks from the original Tk-Instruct training data. This results in a training data set of $6,985$ instances across 117 tasks and an error rate of approximately 8%. For Tk-Instruct* we replace all erroneous instances with corrected instances from the same task. We adapt the training pipeline to our limited computational budget: We train and evaluate the model in a strict zero-shot setting without providing few-shot examples to reduce the input length of the instances. Second, we use only at most 64 instances per task, because Wang et al. (2022b) find that increasing this number does not improve performance. We train the model for 30 epochs with a batch size of 1024. We use the same held-out task mixture for evaluation as Wang et al. (2022b) but remove all tasks that are in our training data. To evaluate the impact of errors on instruction tuning, we follow Wang et al. (2022b) and use RougeL for evaluation. Surprisingly, we find that the difference between the two models is small. Tk-Instruct* achieves an overall RougeL score of 35.9%, while Tk-Instruct$_{err}$ achieves 35.7%. Moreover, Tk-Instruct$_{err}$ even generates the correct answer for instances where it observed incorrect answers during training. Both observations suggest that instruction-tuned models may be robust to small numbers of errors in their training data. However, when we prompt the published version of T0[15], the model trained on P3, with a prompt template for which during training it erroneously always observed empty strings as output[16], we find that it will always respond with an empty string. This motivates further research into when and how errors in InstT datasets propagate into models.

[14]https://github.com/yizhongw/Tk-Instruct

[15]https://huggingface.co/bigscience/T0_3B

[16]"Question 1: [...]? Question 2: [...]? Do these questions convey the same meaning? Yes or no?"

EEVEE: An Easy Annotation Tool for Natural Language Processing

Axel Sorensen[1] **Siyao Peng**[2,3] **Barbara Plank**[1,2,3] **Rob van der Goot**[1]
[1] Department of Computer Science, IT University of Copenhagen, Denmark
[2] Munich Center for Machine Learning (MCML), Munich, Germany
[3] MaiNLP, Center for Information and Language Processing, LMU Munich, Germany
axelsorensen.dev@gmail.com {siyaopeng,bplank}@cis.lmu.de
robv@itu.dk

Abstract

Annotation tools are the starting point for creating Natural Language Processing (NLP) datasets. There is a wide variety of tools available; setting up these tools is however a hindrance. We propose EEVEE, an annotation tool focused on simplicity, efficiency, and ease of use. It can run directly in the browser (no setup required) and uses tab-separated files (as opposed to character offsets or task-specific formats) for annotation. It allows for annotation of multiple tasks on a single dataset and supports four task-types: sequence labeling, span labeling, text classification and seq2seq.[1]

1 Introduction

Annotated datasets are of paramount importance to the Natural Language Processing (NLP) community. Their use is at the core of research, e.g. for training models, evaluating models, and analyzing trends. One of the first considerations when creating an annotated dataset is which annotation tool to choose. There is a variety of (open-source) tools readily available with extensive feature-sets. We were motivated by the following observed difficulties with existing tools when designing EEVEE:

- Most existing tools use tool-specific data formats, often with the main annotation happening on the character level. For token-based tasks, the annotator thus has to make a (tediously) precise selection of the token boundaries. Furthermore, many NLP tools expect token-level inputs (for example, for POS tagging, parsing, NER, and relation extraction). To obtain annotations on the token level, an often cumbersome conversion is necessary.

- Existing tools often require an installation which is especially problematic on constrained (organization) computers, where there might be no administrator access.

- Although many of the advanced features (like active learning) can lead to faster annotation over time, they require some setup time and more time for the annotators to get used to the tool. Time is costly in annotation; in many cases, annotators only annotate a small amount of data. Furthermore, most strategies to increase the speed of annotation (for example active learning) could lead to an additional bias signal for the annotator (Section 7).

- For many tasks, there are task-specific tools; for example for UD there is list of available annotation tools.[2] Instead, we focus on a generalizable and flexible tool. EEVEE supports a total of four task types: sequence labeling, span labeling, text classification, and sequence to sequence (Section 4).

Based on these observations, we propose EEVEE: a simple, free, and flexible annotation tool built around tab-separated files. It is written in Javascript and runs directly in the browser. It can also be saved as a desktop application and run offline. The intuitive interface allows novice users to import a dataset and set up multiple annotation tasks quickly. The graphical user interface has two main pages: the setup page (Section 2) and the annotation page (Section 3). It supports tab-separated files and raw text input (Section 4.1). We perform a case study on NER annotation with the System Usability Scale from usability engineering (Section 6). Finally, we compare EEVEE to other toolkits (Section 7).

[1]Code, README and tutorials of EEVEE are available on https://github.com/AxelSorensenDev/Eevee, demo video at https://www.youtube.com/watch?v=HsOsfckvnQo and the tool itself on https://axelsorensendev.github.io/Eevee/

[2]https://universaldependencies.org/tools.html#annotation-tools

Proceedings of The 18th Linguistic Annotation Workshop (LAW-XVIII), pages 216–221
March 22, 2024 ©2024 Association for Computational Linguistics

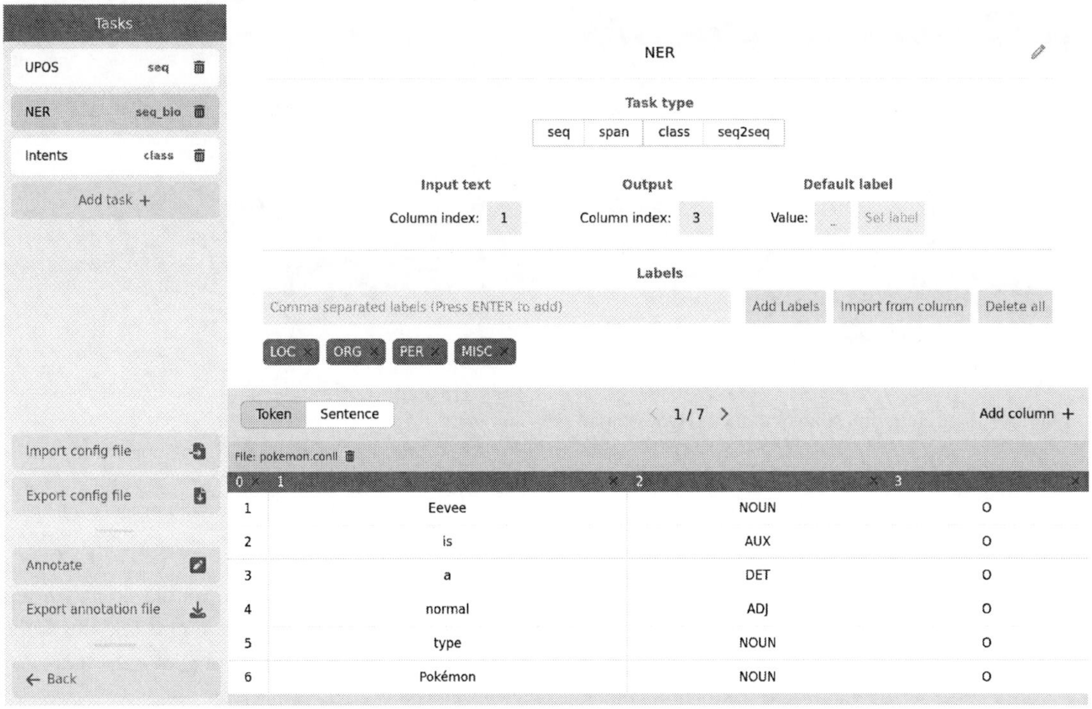

Figure 1: A screenshot of the setup page of EEVEE with multiple tasks. The user currently configures the NER task.

2 Setup page

Figure 1 illustrates the setup page where the user can define the annotation environment. Tasks can be configured in the task field (Figure 1, top right), allowing the user to specify the input column (for the input text) and output column (for the target task), as well as adding the desired labels. Labels can also be imported automatically from the annotated file (if it already contains annotations), and a default label can be set for empty annotations. For utterance-level tasks (i.e. classification), the annotation is stored in a comment above the text, in the form "# intent = inform" (see also Figure 4). To facilitate reproducibility and improve the ease of setup, the tool allows the import and export of all settings to configuration files that users can create for predefined tasks (more details in Section 4.1).

Once a dataset has been imported, the tabular data field (Figure 1, bottom right) offers a simple overview of the raw data belonging to each utterance. The user can add new columns or remove existing ones to achieve the desired result. This makes EEVEE an easy-to-use tool for extending or editing tab-separated data as well (see Section 4.1). Once the data and tasks are ready, the user simply clicks "Annotate" (Figure 1, bottom left) to continue to the "Annotation page" (see Section 3).

Figure 2: Annotation example with the keyboard setting.

3 Annotation page

Figure 2 illustrates an example of a NER task in the annotation interface. The user is presented with a clean, minimal annotation environment. The annotation process has been designed with efficiency in mind, enabling the user to navigate the interface also through keyboard shortcuts.

The navigation bar (Figure 2, bottom right) enables navigation between utterances and, similar to Prodigy (Montani and Honnibal, 2018), setting the status of a given task for a given utterance. The status can be set to four values: completed, wrong, unsure, and cleared (i.e. none). This overall sta-

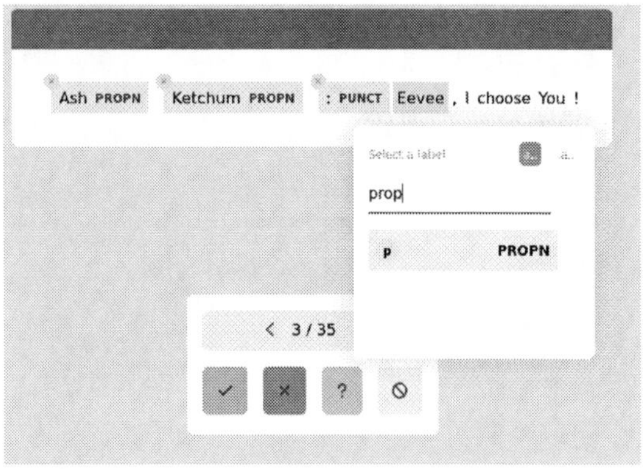

Figure 3: Searching for labels with a navigation bar.

tus is reflected in the progress bar (Figure 2, top right), allowing the user to spot missing and unsure annotations easily. The progress bar is also useful when continuing annotation on a previously saved annotation file.

EEVEE provides two different annotation modes for label-based tasks: the keyboard mode and the search mode. With the keyboard mode (Figure 2), the user can use the number keys to select labels and click/select the part of the input where the label should apply (for utterance-level tasks, simply pressing the number key is sufficient). In search mode, a small pop-up appears after selecting a word or span (see Figure 3), allowing the user to find the desired label quickly. If there are more than ten labels, EEVEE defaults to search mode. Finally, the annotation file can be exported (Figure 2, bottom left). The current datetime can be appended to distinguish between different export versions.

4 Tasks

In this section, we will describe the annotation data format used by EEVEE (for import and export, importing text files is also supported), and we will discuss all the supported task types as well as the configuration files for the setups.

4.1 Data Format

There are many different data formats used in NLP, which are often task-specific. EEVEE is based on the well-established tab-separated files ubiquitously used in the NLP field. These are also sometimes called conll-like files, based on the formats used in the CoNLL shared tasks (Tjong Kim Sang and De Meulder, 2003; Buchholz and Marsi, 2006). This format (example in Figure 4) uses empty lines to separate utterances or sentences and puts one token per line. Annotations and input tokens are separated by a tab character. Comments and utterance-level information are included above the texts and are prefixed with a # character.

```
# sent_id = gameboy-1
# intent = inform
1       What      PRON     O
2       ?         PUNCT    O
3       Eevee     PROPN    B-MISC
4       is        AUX      O
5       evolving           VERB     O
6       !         PUNCT    O

# sent_id = gary-1
# intent = goodbye
1       Smell     VERB     O
2       ya        PRON     O
3       later     ADV      O
4       !         PUNCT    O
```

Figure 4: Example of annotated tab-separated file with SEQ (POS in column 3), SPAN (NER in column 4), and CLASS (intent classification in the comments) tasks.

4.2 SEQ task-type

In sequence labeling tasks (SEQ), we annotate a single label per token, such as POS tagging or token-level language identification.

4.3 SPAN task-type

SPAN-labeling tasks are where spans are annotated as sequences of tokens (e.g. NER). Most other tools supporting this task type (e.g. Stenetorp et al., 2012; Nakayama et al., 2018) have character-level annotations, although spans normally operate on token-borders. An advantage of EEVEE is that it automatically selects the entire token if part of the token is selected, making annotation easier and faster as the annotators do not have to drag the mouse to the exact character of the token boundary. The user can simply select a label (either by clicking or pressing the corresponding number key) and then click the desired token (i.e. any character within the token) or select a span of tokens.

4.4 CLASS task-type

EEVEE also supports CLASSification tasks on the utterance level. Labels are included as a comment above the text (e.g. intents in Figure 4). The format is `# [UNIQUE NAME] = [LABEL]`, following typical meta-data format as used in conll-like formats. Usage is similar to the previous two labeling tasks, except that the user does not need to select a part of the utterance. Keyboard-only anno-

```
[{"title":"NER",
  "type":
   {"name":"seq_bio",
    "isWordLevel":true},
  "output_index":"4",
  "input_index":"1",
  "labels":["LOC","MISC","ORG","PER"],
  "id":0}]
```

Figure 5: An example of the configuration file format. The configuration file is a json file consisting of an array of tasks. Each task has a title, a type, input and output indices, and finally its corresponding labels.

tation is thus straightforward: the user can simply press a number key to select desired class labels and use the arrow keys to navigate the data.

4.5 SEQ2SEQ task-type

The SEQ2SEQ task type allows for text to text tasks (e.g. translation, question answering, summarization). This is currently the only task type without a list of provided labels; the user can directly type the target text in a text field. The annotations are utterance level and thus also saved in the comments.

4.6 Config Files

Because EEVEE runs entirely in the browser, it will not internally save the setup for the current annotation task. Therefore, it supports configuration files. These configuration files are in json format, and can thus easily be inspected by administrators, and are easy (i.e. small) to be distributed. An example of the configuration file format for named entity recognition (NER) is given in Figure 5.

5 Compatability with other services

A recent development is the Huggingface datasets library (Lhoest et al., 2021), which has indexed 62K+ datasets in two years. This library does not share the text directly but through a Python API. We provide a convenient Python script that automatically downloads data from the datasets library and converts it to the tab-separated format of EEVEE.

One of the toolkits that operates on tab-separated formats is MaChAmp (van der Goot et al., 2021), which is focused on multi-task learning. MaChAmp supports all the tasks that are included in EEVEE. For convenience, we provide a conversion script that takes EEVEE files as input and outputs a MaChAmp configuration file and the corresponding training command.

6 System Usability Study

6.1 Procedure

To assess the usability of EEVEE, we conduct a case study with two annotators on two tasks, named entity annotation (span labeling), and German dialect identification (classification). Before annotating with EEVEE, annotators spent four months labeling named entities (NE) directly on tab-separated text files in a text editor using BIO encoding and dialect identification (DID) labels as utterance-level metadata. In this case study, we ask both annotators to conduct the same NE and DID annotation tasks on a set of new documents, similar to previous ones but using the newly introduced EEVEE.

During EEVEE training, we present a 12-minute tutorial video explaining the setup and annotation pages to the annotators and provide them with tab-separated unannotated files and the json configuration files. Two annotators separately annotate the same eight documents, four from Wikipedia (*wiki*) and four from Twitter (X, *tweet*), summing up to 14.2K tokens and 16 working hours per person.[3]

6.2 Results

The System Usability Scale (SUS) was introduced as a quick and reliable tool to measure the usability of user interfaces (Brooke, 1995). It consists of a 10-item questionnaire with 5 responses ranging from 'Strongly Agree' to 'Strongly Disagree'. SUS has become an industry standard and can be validly used with small sample sizes. Therefore, we evaluate the usability of EEVEE using SUS.

The responses given by both annotators (P1 and P2) are shown in Figure 6. The ratings of the annotators result in total SUS scores of 75.0 and 87.5, both above the average of 68.0 (Brooke, 2013). The standard method for interpreting these scores is to look at which percentile they fall compared to other systems. As we are not aware of SUS being used for annotation tools, we can only compare to more general figures, where our average of 81.25 ranks at the top 10% and indicates a good (close to excellent) usability (Bangor et al., 2009). We also qualitatively survey annotators' experience and opinions after two weeks of annotation. Both annotators appraise that the tool is easy to learn and use and found it pleasant to work almost exclusively with the keyboard in a lightweight interface. Both annotators responded that they would use EEVEE for

[3]Annotators are hired student assistants and paid according to national compensation tables.

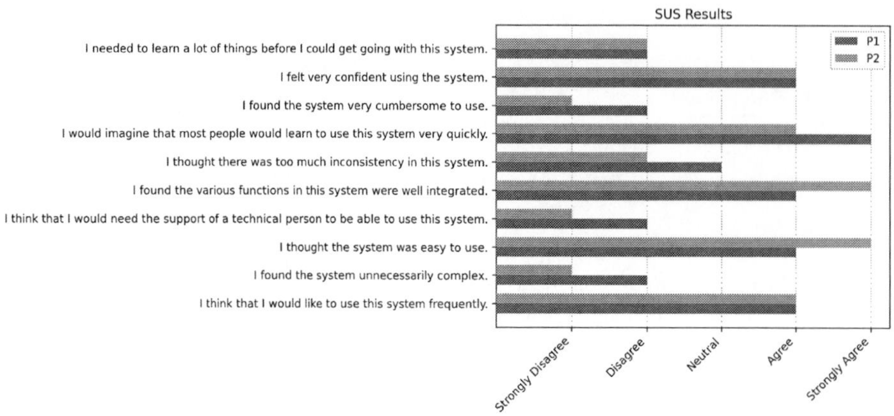

Figure 6: The results from the System Usability Scale Questionaire. The x-axis shows their agreement with a given statement, while the y-axis shows each item.

	Brat Stenetorp et al. (2012)	Potato Pei et al. (2022)	Doccano Nakayama et al. (2018)	Prodigy Montani and Honnibal (2018)	EEVEE
Open Source	✓	✓	✓	✗	✓
Character level	✓	✓	✓	✓	✗
Token level*	✗	✗	✗	✓	✓
Utterance level	✗	✓	✓	✓	✓
Data-format	standoff	json	json	json/csv	conll
Runs on	local	local	local	cloud	browser
Active learning	✗	✓	✗	✓	✗
User management	✗	✓	✓	✓	✗

Table 1: We only list the annotation export data files in this table, most tools (including EEVEE) also support importing .txt files. * Note that character level annotations are commonly used for token/span level tasks. But as noted in Section 4.3, this requires more efforts for annotation and conversion of data formats.

their next annotation jobs.

Since annotators typically spend many hours in an annotation environment, it is important that an annotation tool is built with user experience in mind. We encourage existing and future tools to consider usability studies such as SUS.

7 Comparison to other annotation toolkits

We compare EEVEE to other available toolkits in Table 1. While Eevee does not have the most functionality, it does clearly allow for a simple setup for token-level tasks. Also, EEVEE provides keyboard shortcuts for annotation speed.

Other techniques for improving annotation speed need more tuning and setup and could lead to biases. For example, active learning could lead to model bias (Berzak et al., 2016) and coloring relevant words for a task (Pei et al., 2022) could lead to biases towards these indicators. We leave the user management up to the organizer of the annotation efforts and prioritize the simplicity in tool setup. Furthermore, since EEVEE does not need installation, it does not store or send any data to the network, which is beneficial for data privacy.

8 Conclusion

We introduce EEVEE, an annotation toolkit focused on easy setup and usability. It runs directly in the browser and allows for annotation of multiple tasks. In addition, it provides convenience scripts for usage with other libraries. EEVEE's main distinguishing features, in contrast to other toolkits, are the simplicity of its setup and use, as well as annotation directly on the token level (tab-separated files). To evaluate the tool, we conducted a case study using the System Usability Scale, resulting in high usability scores. We also qualitatively surveyed the annotators' experience and noted that they would prefer to use the tool again for annotation.

Acknowledgements

We would like to thank Huangyan Shan and Marie Kolm for their invaluable feedback on EEVEE and Mike Zhang for giving feedback on earlier drafts of this paper. Huangyan Shan, Marie Kolm, Siyao Peng and Barbara Plank are supported by ERC Consolidator Grant DIALECT 101043235.

Limitations

We acknowledge that EEVEE assumes gold token detection (and annotates on the token level for SEQ and SPAN). For languages/datasets where tokenization is challenging, this would require a first pass of tokenization annotation before importing the data into EEVEE. Furthermore, the input is constrained to text in Unicode font, which is unavailable for some languages.

References

Aaron Bangor, Philip Kortum, and James Miller. 2009. Determining what individual SUS scores mean: Adding an adjective rating scale. *Journal of usability studies*, 4(3):114–123.

Yevgeni Berzak, Yan Huang, Andrei Barbu, Anna Korhonen, and Boris Katz. 2016. Anchoring and agreement in syntactic annotations. In *Proceedings of the 2016 Conference on Empirical Methods in Natural Language Processing*, pages 2215–2224, Austin, Texas. Association for Computational Linguistics.

John Brooke. 1995. SUS: A quick and dirty usability scale. *Usability Evaluation in Industry*, 189.

John Brooke. 2013. SUS: a retrospective. *Journal of Usability Studies*, 8:29–40.

Sabine Buchholz and Erwin Marsi. 2006. CoNLL-X shared task on multilingual dependency parsing. In *Proceedings of the Tenth Conference on Computational Natural Language Learning (CoNLL-X)*, pages 149–164, New York City. Association for Computational Linguistics.

Quentin Lhoest, Albert Villanova del Moral, Yacine Jernite, Abhishek Thakur, Patrick von Platen, Suraj Patil, Julien Chaumond, Mariama Drame, Julien Plu, Lewis Tunstall, Joe Davison, Mario Šaško, Gunjan Chhablani, Bhavitvya Malik, Simon Brandeis, Teven Le Scao, Victor Sanh, Canwen Xu, Nicolas Patry, Angelina McMillan-Major, Philipp Schmid, Sylvain Gugger, Clément Delangue, Théo Matussière, Lysandre Debut, Stas Bekman, Pierric Cistac, Thibault Goehringer, Victor Mustar, François Lagunas, Alexander Rush, and Thomas Wolf. 2021. Datasets: A community library for natural language processing. In *Proceedings of the 2021 Conference on Empirical Methods in Natural Language Processing: System Demonstrations*, pages 175–184, Online and Punta Cana, Dominican Republic. Association for Computational Linguistics.

Ines Montani and Matthew Honnibal. 2018. Prodigy: A new annotation tool for radically efficient machine teaching.

Hiroki Nakayama, Takahiro Kubo, Junya Kamura, Yasufumi Taniguchi, and Xu Liang. 2018. doccano: Text annotation tool for human. Software available from https://github.com/doccano/doccano.

Jiaxin Pei, Aparna Ananthasubramaniam, Xingyao Wang, Naitian Zhou, Apostolos Dedeloudis, Jackson Sargent, and David Jurgens. 2022. POTATO: The portable text annotation tool. In *Proceedings of the 2022 Conference on Empirical Methods in Natural Language Processing: System Demonstrations*, pages 327–337, Abu Dhabi, UAE. Association for Computational Linguistics.

Pontus Stenetorp, Sampo Pyysalo, Goran Topić, Tomoko Ohta, Sophia Ananiadou, and Jun'ichi Tsujii. 2012. brat: a web-based tool for NLP-assisted text annotation. In *Proceedings of the Demonstrations at the 13th Conference of the European Chapter of the Association for Computational Linguistics*, pages 102–107, Avignon, France. Association for Computational Linguistics.

Erik F. Tjong Kim Sang and Fien De Meulder. 2003. Introduction to the CoNLL-2003 shared task: Language-independent named entity recognition. In *Proceedings of the Seventh Conference on Natural Language Learning at HLT-NAACL 2003*, pages 142–147.

Rob van der Goot, Ahmet Üstün, Alan Ramponi, Ibrahim Sharaf, and Barbara Plank. 2021. Massive choice, ample tasks (MaChAmp): A toolkit for multi-task learning in NLP. In *Proceedings of the 16th Conference of the European Chapter of the Association for Computational Linguistics: System Demonstrations*, pages 176–197, Online. Association for Computational Linguistics.

Author Index

Association for Computational Linguistics
209 N. Eighth Street
Stroudsburg, Pennsylvania 18360

CURRAN ASSOCIATES INC.
proceedings.com

ISBN 978-1-7138-9454-4